D1162455

IDEAS IN CONTEXT

BETWEEN LITERATURE AND SCIENCE:
THE RISE OF SOCIOLOGY

IDEAS IN CONTEXT

Edited by Richard Rorty, J. B. Schneewind, Quentin Skinner,
and Wolf Lepenies

The books in this series will discuss the emergence of intellectual traditions
and of related new disciplines. The procedures, aims, and vocabularies that
were generated will be set in the context of the alternatives available within
the contemporary frameworks of ideas and institutions. Through detailed
studies of the evolution of such traditions, and their modification by different audiences, it is hoped that a new picture will form of the development
of ideas in their concrete contexts. By this means, artificial distinctions
among the history of philosophy, of the various sciences, of society and
politics, and of literature may be seen to dissolve.

This series is published with the support of the Exxon Education Foundation.

This book is published as part of the joint publishing agreement established
in 1977 between the Fondation de la Maison des Sciences de l'Homme and
the Press Syndicate of the University of Cambridge. Titles published under
this arrangement may appear in any European language or, in the case of
volumes of collected essays, in several languages.
New books will appear either as individual titles or in one of the series
which the Maison des Sciences de l'Homme and the Cambridge University
Press have jointly agreed to publish. All books published jointly by the
Maison des Sciences de l'Homme and the Cambridge University Press will
be distributed by the Press throughout the world.

Cet ouvrage est publié dans le cadre de l'accord de co-édition passé en 1977
entre la Fondation de la Maison des Sciences de l'Homme et le Press Syndicate de l'Université de Cambridge. Toutes les langues européennes sont
admises pour les titres couverts par cet accord, et les ouvrages collectifs
peuvent paraitre en plusieurs langues.
Les ouvrages paraissent soit isolément, soit dans l'une des séries que la
Maison des Sciences de l'Homme et Cambridge University Press ont con-
venu de publier ensemble. La distribution dans le monde entier des titres
ainsi publiés conjointement par les deux établissements est assurée par
Cambridge University Press.

BETWEEN LITERATURE AND SCIENCE: THE RISE OF SOCIOLOGY

WOLF LEPENIES

TRANSLATED BY R. J. HOLLINGDALE

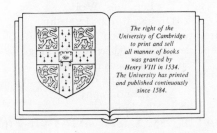

The right of the
University of Cambridge
to print and sell
all manner of books
was granted by
Henry VIII in 1534.
The University has printed
and published continuously
since 1584.

CAMBRIDGE UNIVERSITY PRESS

CAMBRIDGE

NEW YORK   NEW ROCHELLE   MELBOURNE   SYDNEY

EDITIONS DE LA MAISON DES SCIENCES DE l'HOMME

PARIS

PN
51
L3813
1988

Published by the Press Syndicate of the University of Cambridge
The Pitt Building, Trumpington Street, Cambridge CB2 1RP
32 East 57th Street, New York, NY 10022, USA
10 Stamford Road, Oakleigh, Melbourne 3166, Australia
and Editions de la Maison des Sciences de l'Homme
54 Boulevard Raspail, 75270 Paris Cedex 06

Originally published in German as *Die Drei Kulturen*
by Carl Hanser Verlag 1985
and © Carl Hanser Verlag München Wien
First published in English by Editions de la Maison des Sciences
de l'Homme and Cambridge University Press 1988 as *Between
Literature and Science: The Rise of Sociology*
English translation © Maison des Sciences de l'Homme and
Cambridge University Press 1988

Printed in Great Britain by
The Bath Press, Avon

British Library cataloguing in publication data

Lepenies, Wolf
Between literature and science: the
rise of sociology.–(Ideas in context).
1. Sociology
I. Title II. Series III. Die Drei
Kulturen. *English*
301 HM51

Library of Congress cataloguing in publication data

Lepenies, Wolf
[Drei Kulturen. English]
Between literature and science: the rise of sociology/Wolf
Lepenies: translated by R.J. Hollingdale.
p.   cm.–(Ideas in context)
Translation of: Die drei Kulturen.
Bibliography.
Includes index
ISBN 0-521-32852-7. ISBN 0-521-33010-7 (pbk.)
1. Literature and society. 2. Sociology. I. Title. II. Series.
PN51.L3913 1988
809'.93355–dc19   88-25663 CIP

ISBN 0 521 32852 7   hard covers
ISBN 0 521 33810 7   paperback
ISBN 2 7351 0228 9   hard covers (France only)
ISBN 2 7351 0230 0   paperback (France only)

BO

For Annette – and Julia, Philipp, Robert

CONTENTS

ACKNOWLEDGEMENTS

I wrote parts of this book with the aid of a subvention from the Fritz Thyssen Stiftung (Köln) while I was with the School of Social Science of the Institute for Advanced Study at Princeton, N. J., and the Maison des Sciences de l'Homme in Paris. I finished it at the Wissenschaftskolleg zu Berlin.

INTRODUCTION

In this book I describe the contention between two groups of intellectuals: on one hand the men of letters, i.e. the writers and critics, on the other the social scientists, above all the sociologists. From the middle of the nineteenth century onwards literature and sociology contested with one another the claim to offer the key orientation for modern civilization and to constitute the guide to living appropriate to industrial society. This contention played a significant role in the public life firstly of France and England, then also of Germany: its consequences are still visible today.

This competing discloses a dilemma which determined not only how sociology originated but also how it then went on to develop: it has oscillated between a scientific orientation which has led it to ape the natural sciences and a hermeneutic attitude which has shifted the discipline towards the realm of literature. The contention between a literary intelligentsia and an intelligentsia devoted to the social sciences was thus an aspect of a complex process in the course of which scientific modes of procedure became differentiated from literary modes; and this divorce was accentuated ideologically through the confrontation of cold rationality and the culture of the feelings – one of those antitheses which marked the conflict between the Enlightenment and the counter-Enlightenment.

The sciences of the eighteenth century were rich in creation-myths. From Linnaeus, who was only too glad to hear himself compared with Adam, and Montesquieu, who described the *Esprit des lois* as '*prolem sine matre creatam*', to Buffon, Winckelmann and Lavoisier, there runs through every discipline a long succession of men who asserted they had created entirely on their own account something novel that would stand the test of time. Breach with continuity and the founding of new continuities belong intimately together in this epoch of the evolution of science: most scientific investigators saw themselves as giants standing on the shoulders of dwarfs rather than the

1

reverse. Excessive ambition, in many cases a foolhardy exaggeration of the goals to be achieved, and a need for a continual commentary on one's own activities were not eccentricities but an everyday matter in the realm of science.

The day of the amateur was over and the contours of clearly circumscribed domains of research, each bent on self-sufficiency, were gradually growing visible, even if one can hardly speak yet of professionalism or specialization. The scientist had long since ceased to be a mere virtuoso whose objectives included the provision of amusement; yet the conviction still reigned that science was a calling and confession rather than a professional occupation. Many regarded the process of discovery as a purely individual, indeed a solitary act: the world around him was as a rule only a disturbance to the individual in his acquisition of knowledge. Societies devoted to science increased in number, but faith in a knowledge-promoting 'scientific community' was as yet feebly developed: within many disciplines cults founded on friendships, or even upon enmities, constituted the emotional equivalent of communities instrumental to the advancement of science.

At the end of the eighteenth century a sharp division between the modes of production of literary and of scientific works was not yet possible. The career of Buffon offers an example of how a differentiation between them occurred and then accelerated. In the eighteenth century Buffon's *Histoire Naturelle* was a best-seller: when the first volumes appeared in 1749 they were sold out within a few weeks; further printings followed in the same year, and in the end there were no fewer than 250 popular editions of the *Histoire Naturelle* in France.

Buffon was a *grand seigneur* of science and as such typical of the eighteenth century: an entrepreneur who knew well how to capitalize on his scientific abilities; a master of language, even if only of his own; at once a man of the world and a local hero who had no need to travel abroad – the age's lines of communication converged upon him as though as a matter of course.

It was as a stylist that Buffon gained his reputation: not everyone liked what he said but almost everyone was impressed by the way in which he said it. This too was how posterity remembered him: Flaubert noted in his *Dictionnaire des idées reçues* what the cultivated person was expected to say when Buffon was mentioned: '*Mettait des manchettes pour écrire.*'

To see in this nothing but a foible of an age long past would be a mistake, for Buffon's attitude was more than the whim of an eccentric: the Count represented not a unique case but a type; he embodied a role which the society of his time did not merely recognize but valued and rewarded very highly.

When, after prolonged pressure from Louis XV, Buffon was in 1753 elected to the Académie Française, he spoke on the subject of style. The fact surprised no one: it was considered quite natural that a scientist should also regard himself as an author, as someone, that is, who paid heed not only to what he said but also to the way in which he said it, and who wished not only to instruct his public but also to entertain them as he did so. Buffon's address was accounted one of the finest ever delivered before the Académie – even Baudelaire was impressed by it.

Towards the end of the century, however, that which had formerly procured celebrity for Buffon had fatal consequences for him: he was the last scholar whose reputation was founded on his talent for presentation and the first to lose his reputation because he had devoted himself too much to authorship and too little to research. During Buffon's lifetime the concept of the novel underwent a decisive re-evaluation: if his writings had at first been read and commended precisely on account of their entertainment value they were now denounced as '*romans scientifiques*', suitable for women and laymen but of no interest to the professional scientist. The formula that put an end to Buffon's career and inhibited the reception of his works was: '*Stilo primus, doctrina ultimus*'; the development therewith inaugurated, and its seeming irreversibility, can be demonstrated by reversing this formula. '*Doctrina primus, stilo ultimus*' would never be offered as a reproach to a scientist today.

The course of Buffon's career and the changes in the way his *Histoire Naturelle* was received enable us to see how the sciences gradually became alienated from literature and traditional values that could be described as literary were excluded from the canon of accepted knowledge. This process did not proceed in a straight, undeviating line, but was characterized rather by the difference in the pace at which it took place in the different disciplines: it did not encompass every discipline, and those it did encompass it affected with a differing degree of intensity. National characteristics played an instructive role. The Germans never abandoned the suspicion that the French had never seriously intended to expel literature from the sciences: whereas, according to Taine, in the French academies the men of letters long continued to treat the natural scientists as their servants – though these servants were none the less Lavoisier, Lagrange and Laplace – the Brandenburg Sozietät der

Wissenschaften first of all classified every Frenchman, whether he was a dramatist or a physicist, as a man of letters.

How rich in tension the relationship between literature and the sciences none the less remained is made clear by the phenomenon of 'storage', by which is meant the fact, of significance for the history of science, that theoretical programmes at first rejected have frequently not simply disappeared or been forgotten but, having passed a winter in concealment, have returned and re-entered the stream of scientific discussion. These places of concealment may lie within the original discipline itself or in neighbouring disciplines, and one then speaks of intra- or inter-disciplinary storage; they may, however, also lie outside the frontiers of science altogether, and of this the subsequent history of Buffon's *Histoire Naturelle* offers a striking example.

Just a hundred years after the appearance of the *Histoire Naturelle*, Balzac in 1842 composed the preface to his *Comédie Humaine*: in it he appealed, among many others, to a poet who had also been a natural scientist, namely Goethe; he also appealed, and very emphatically, to a natural scientist who had in the end been rejected by his guild as being a man of letters, namely Buffon.

Balzac wanted to do for society what Buffon had done for zoology: he wanted to analyse the social species of which French society consisted and to write the true history of morals which the historians, fixated as they were on the glories of the battles and state occasions they described, usually forgot to write. The reader of Buffon can recognize elements of the *Histoire Naturelle* in Balzac's novels down to the smallest details; and when one considers the extent to which Balzac influenced Proust it becomes clear that, *via* the *Comédie Humaine*, Buffon also found his way to Combray and the Faubourg Saint-Germain.

But what we have to do with here is more than a story of survival. We cannot confine ourselves to tracing the migration of theories and traditions out of the natural sciences into literature, for during the first third of the nineteenth century the social sciences came into being and by demonstrating their disciplinary self-sufficiency sought to gain a place in the academies and universities.

Balzac was an inheritor but he was also a creator. His work is tied to the old natural history, but at the same time it is in competition with a new discipline: sociology. Balzac himself formulated this claim, for he at first intended to call his work, not the *Comédie Humaine*, but *Etudes Sociales*; and when he described himself as a '*docteur ès sciences sociales*' there lay in this designation a little self-irony and a great deal of self-awareness: for what sociologist of the mid-nineteenth century could compete with the analytical insight of this novelist and his '*science sociale*' – not to speak of competing with his art of description? Marx, who compared himself to the hero of the *Chef d'oeuvre inconnu*, and Engels posed this rhetorical question when they maintained that they had learned more from Balzac than they had from all the professional economists and historians put together – from '*Guizot e tutti quanti*', as they maliciously called them.

As a critic and colleague, Henry James described the mediating role Balzac assumes between natural history and sociology: from the simple accumulation and assembling of the facts of society – 'social botanizing',[1] as James calls it – Balzac passes over to the construction of a social system, and the *Comédie Humaine* finally comes to constitute an exact counterpart to that which Comte, the founder of the discipline, strove to achieve with his sociology. No one had a clearer perception of this than Hippolyte Taine, whom they called 'Balzac's son' and who ranged Balzac beside Shakespeare and Saint-Simon and described his work as 'the greatest storehouse of documents on human nature that we possess'.[2] It was through Balzac that Taine detected and developed a specific view of what the social sciences could and could not do: '*Nous aurons dépassé, d'ici à un demi-siècle, la période descriptive; en biologie, elle a duré jusqu'à Bichat et Cuvier; en sociologie, nous y sommes encore; tâchons de nous y tenir, avec application et intelligence, sans ambitions excessives, sans conclusions précipitées, sans théories hasardées et préconçues, pour entrer bientôt dans la période des classifications naturelles et définitives . . .*'[3] Written in 1890, more than thirty years after Comte's death, this is an astonishing document: it recalls Buffon's dictum that natural history should be regarded as being above all '*description exacte*'; and when Taine says, in his *History of English Literature*, that our first task is to discover informative documents and then know how to interpret them, this advocacy of the modest task of description rather than a premature systematization is as much in line with the attitude of the sociological monographs of the nineteenth century as it is with that adopted by the natural history of the eighteenth. So it was that in 1902 – the year in which

[1] Where no source is given for a quotation its source is the same as the preceding reference. Henry James, 'Honoré de Balzac' [1875], in *Literary Criticism (French Writers, Other European Writers, The Prefaces to the New York Edition)* (New York: The Library of America, 1984), p. 37.
[2] Hippolyte Taine, *Balzac: A Critical Study*, translated, with an appreciation of Taine, by Lorenzo O'Rourke (New York: Haskell House, 1973), p. 240.
[3] H. Taine to A. Delaire, 19 April 1890; quoted from Carlo Mongardini, *Storia e sociologia nell' opera di H. Taine* (Milano: Giuffrè, 1965), p. 251.

Emile Durkheim arrived in Paris – Paul Bourget could speak of the *'enseignement sociologique'*[4] of the *Comédie Humaine* as being a crowning feature of Balzac's work.

As soon as sociology had advanced its claim to be a self-sufficient discipline it saw itself confronted not only by the ill will of the established disciplines but also by competition on the part of literature; one reason for this last was that, in the climate of belief in science that characterized the nineteenth century, some branches of literature claimed a status equal to many scientific disciplines so far as the advancement of knowledge was concerned.

His great ambitions notwithstanding, Balzac's attitude towards science had something playful about it. With Flaubert all is serious. The *'impassibilité'* he demands of the writer is the transference to literature of a maxim of scientific research: literature must become more scientific if it wants to survive. As Baudelaire demanded in 1852: *'Le temps n'est pas loin où l'on comprendra que toute littérature qui se refuse à marcher fraternellement entre la science et la philosophie est une littérature homicide et suicide.'*[5] When Flaubert, who boasted of his solitary situation in isolation from society – *'Bédouin, tant qu'il vous plaira; Citoyen, jamais'*[6] – wrote to George Sand in 1871 that if France were to awaken it must abandon inspiration in favour of science, give up every kind of metaphysics and begin to practise criticism, i.e. investigate things themselves, he therewith formulated a programme which would – even in its choice of words – have delighted an Emile Durkheim. At once a critic of the sciences and a believer in science, Flaubert was self-confident in both what he revered and what he despised: a Claude Bernard seemed to him more sacrosanct than Pius IX, but he could not take seriously the pretensions of an Auguste Comte and called for a modern Aristophanes to excite general mockery of this theory-manufacturer's fantasies. Flaubert undoubtedly regarded his work as a finer kind of social science – he felt superior to the sociologists because he believed that as an author he could elude the constraints of society: *'Qui êtes-vous donc, ô société, pour me forcer à quoi que ce soit?'*[7]

[4] Paul Bourget, *La Politique de Balzac* (1902); Bourget, *Sociologie et Littérature*, Etudes et Portraits, No. 3 (Paris: Plon, 1906), p. 46.

[5] Charles Baudelaire, 'L'Ecole païenne' [1852], in *Oeuvres complètes*, texte établi, présenté et annoté par Claude Pichois (Paris: Bibliothèque de la Pléiade, 1976), Vol. 2, p. 49.

[6] Gustave Flaubert to Louise Colet, 23 January 1854; Flaubert, *Correspondance II (July 1851–December 1858)*, édition établie, présentée et annotée par Jean Bruneau (Paris: Bibliothèque de la Pléiade, 1980), p. 515.

[7] Flaubert to Mademoiselle Leroyer de Chantepie, 18 May 1857; Flaubert, *Correspondance II*, p. 719.

Flaubert's claim to be able to see through society and at the same time elude its ties and duties contains a great deal of presumption. In Zola this attitude is, where possible, enhanced. His theory of the experimental novel – which had, to be sure, little connection with his practice as a writer – became the foundation of the claim to scientificality advanced by a certain type of literature which understood itself as a finer kind of sociology: when Zola spoke of the '*sociologie pratique*'[8] that characterized his novels he implied that in the last resort it was he who practised true sociology.

Sociology was thus faced with growing and dangerous rivals, and the social sciences were well aware of this competition, which threatened their disciplinary identity at its core: for, unlike the historical disciplines – whose idiographic orientation furnishes them, especially in Germany, with a methodological counterweight to the nomothetic claims of the exact sciences – the social sciences, above all in France and England, fortified their struggle for an academic reputation by imitating the natural sciences. The proximity of and competition from literature served to intensify this strategy.

Thus there was soon set in train an inner-disciplinary process of purification: disciplines such as sociology, which at first lacked recognition within the system of knowledge and had to acquire it, sought to do so by distancing themselves from the early literary forms of their own discipline, whose purpose was rather to describe and classify than to analyse and reduce to a system. From this process there arose a competition between a literary intelligentsia composed of authors and critics and a social-scientific intelligentsia. The problem of sociology is that, although it may imitate the natural sciences, it can never become a true natural science of society: but if it abandons its scientific orientation it draws perilously close to literature.

Sociology's precarious situation as a kind of 'third culture' between the natural sciences on the one hand and literature and the humanities on the other was exacerbated by the fact that the intellectual traditions of the Enlightenment and the counter-Enlightenment struggled with one another over its destiny.

From the founding of the French and English academies in the seventeenth century onwards, the natural sciences had achieved the high prestige they enjoyed and the possibility of acquiring state subvention not least through the absence of passion or self-interest that

---

[8] Emile Zola, 'Le Roman expérimental' [1880], in *Oeuvres critiques I: Notices et notes de Henri Mitterand* (Paris: Cercle du livre précieux, 1968), p. 1188.

supposedly characterized them. Initially the social sciences followed this pattern; it was no accident that Condorcet, who embodied as no one else did the Enlightenment's faith in science, should have been the decisive champion of a social mathematics. Once the correct employment of the faculty of reason had been mastered there were no grounds for thinking that morality, politics and political science would not pursue a course of development as sound and purposeful as those disciplines making hectic progress in the investigation of nature. It was not least because they were academic latecomers that the social sciences exhibited in the nineteenth century a degree of optimism as to the possibilities of knowledge which was exceeded by no other discipline: that nature had set no limits to what we might hope for, and that human reason would eventually lead mankind to Elysium, are among its original dogmas.

Already by the end of the eighteenth century, however – and not least as a consequence of a general sobering up engendered by the abuses fostered by the French Revolution – the practice of the social sciences in imitating the natural sciences was coming to seem more and more problematical: the insight grew that the aim of the 'moral sciences' was to reduce to the formulae of science domains of life which were in principle other than natural objects. The natural sciences had achieved their successes through experimentation – all too soon it was to become apparent that in the realm of society experiment could not simply be substituted for experience. It also became increasingly questionable whether the sciences of man ought to be pursued in a dispassionate and disinterested manner, whether the heart ought to be sacrificed to the head and religion to reason. It was the champions of the Enlightenment themselves who first formulated, not a distrust of reason in principle, but a recognition of the harmful effect of its over-estimation, as, for example, did Lessing in the lines:

> Die grübelnde Vernunft dringt sich in alles ein,
> Und will, wo sie nicht herrscht, doch nicht entbehret sein ...
> Gebieterisch schreibt sie vor, was unsern Sinnen tauge,
> Macht sich zum Ohr des Ohrs, und wird des Auges Auge.

(Brooding reason forces its way into everything,/ and where it does not rule it nonetheless demands to be indispensable . . ./It imperiously decrees the worth of our senses,/ makes of itself the ear of our ear and becomes the eye of our eye.)[9]

However widely they might differ in other respects, the cham-

---

[9] Gotthold Ephraim Lessing, *An den Herrn Marpurg über die Regeln der Wissenschaften zum Vergnügen*, Lessing, *Werke*, Band 1 (München: Hanser, 1970), p. 163.

pions of the counter-Enlightenment were united in their critique of the over-estimation of reason, and in their determination to protect society from abstract political and social experiments of which the criminal experiment of the French Revolution was the prime example. None of these thinkers who espoused the counter-Enlightenment stood closer to sociology than did Count Louis de Bonald, whom Robert Spaemann was right to regard as one of the founding fathers of the discipline, which he called a '*discipline du fait*' [10] that anticipated positivism. De Bonald, who was accounted a scholastic and was anything but a *bel esprit*, at the beginning of the nineteenth century set down in a number of brief and exceedingly clear-sighted sketches the dilemma facing the social sciences as they oscillated back and forth between an orientation towards science and an inclination for literature.

De Bonald saw in the widening divorce between science and literature a sign of modernity and thus a symptom of decadence. Even in an age as recent as that of Louis XIV no distinction had been made between *sciences* and *lettres*, and the dictionary of the Académie Française was consistent when under the rubric *science* it referred the reader to *littérature* and defined *lettres* in the plural as '*toute sorte de science et de doctrine*'. [11] De Bonald mourned for an age in which the sciences were related to literature as content is to form: to him Massillon was a representative of a theological, Montesquieu of a political, Bossuet of a historical and La Bruyère of a moral *literature* – they spoke on behalf of disciplines the outcome of whose researches could in no way be separated from the form in which it was presented. Buffon's *Histoire Naturelle* demonstrated the extent to which even the natural sciences could be at one with literature.

The divorce between literature and the sciences was the responsibility not least of a new class produced by the Enlightenment: if there had in the early phase been scholars who lacked feeling for form, '*savants sans littérature*', [12] among modern intellectuals an over-estimation of form concealed a lack of content: they were '*littérateurs sans véritable science*'. Under the dominating influence of these men of letters, who were devoid of all knowledge, the natural sciences, with mathematics at their head, had come to represent the leading disciplines of the modern age; the '*sciences exactes*' were now accounted the '*hautes sciences*'. This change in prestige among the scientific disciplines was producing harmful effects not least in the world of edu-

[10] Paul Bourget, 'Le Réalisme de Bonald' [1904], in *Sociologie et Littérature*, p. 43.
[11] Louis de Bonald, 'Des Sciences, des lettres et des arts' [1807], in *Oeuvres, Mélanges littéraires, politiques et philosophiques* (Paris: Librairie d'Adrien Le Clerc, 1852), p. 294.   [12] *Ibid.*, p. 296.

cation. Literary decadence and scientific decadence were only two sides of the same coin: as the tragedy of the Ancien Régime became the bourgeois drama, so the title of honour '*hautes sciences*' passed from the '*sciences morales*' to the '*sciences physiques*'.

It was precisely their exactitude, however, that precluded the natural sciences from being placed at the head of the scientific disciplines: it was precisely because, as Pascal and Leibniz had shown, they could also be pursued by machines that these sciences were of the second rank as compared with theology or ethics, jurisprudence, politics or history, which required the use of language and would therefore always remain human.

In de Bonald's eyes the superiority of the moral sciences to the natural sciences was manifest: the anthropocentricism of the latter if nothing else, their unavoidable reliance on the concepts of 'character', 'family', 'intention', 'affect', demonstrated their inability to survive without borrowing from the sciences of man. The ideology of progress propagated by the natural sciences was a chimera: fundamentally they followed the identical principles they had followed since primeval times and as a rule their learned men proffered nothing but elucidations of popular practices which worked just as well without them. From reading the *Journal de Physique* de Bonald gained the impression that the age of great discoveries was past in the natural sciences; they were now dominated by '*le petit esprit*' [13] and were engaged less in discovering than in improving on what was already known and further refining what was already perfect. Whatever airs the mathematicians might give themselves, mankind would still build houses and spin wool even if there were no such thing as geometry.

It was not the self-overestimation of the natural sciences that constituted for de Bonald the decisive problem: of greater consequence was the possibility that the state would appropriate this self-overestimation and derive from it the fundamental principles of its educational policy. That in the mechanical sciences, where machines were gradually replacing man, there should appear more and more men who resembled machines was a regrettable fact but one whose consequences could be lived with; what was incomparably more detrimental was that modern society's ideas of truth and utility, exactitude and solidity, were associated almost exclusively with the natural sciences. It was not only the social sciences that suffered harm: the core of society itself was affected by it.

The natural sciences required for their legitimation the belief in

---

[13] de Bonald, 'Des Progrès ou de la décadence des lettres' [1810], in *Oeuvres*, p. 446.

progress: if this belief was unmasked as superstition the claim to predominance advanced by the exact disciplines would be undermined.
With the moral sciences it was different: *non nova, sed nove*[14] was their
imperishable motto, and all they were concerned with was the discovery of new, contemporary forms for the old and timeless truths.
This function was all the more vital in that, in an age in which as a
consequence of the Enlightenment the authority of the revealed
religions was being increasingly called into question, the moral
orientation of mankind had to be provided by the moral sciences.
Christianity in scientific form, the moral sciences had for their
objective the preservation of society through moral direction of the
individual and stabilization of the legitimate political regime: for
this reason too the moral sciences – the '*sciences morales*'[15] – were in a
narrower sense both the sciences of society – the '*sciences de la société*' –
and for society.

What was required was the undoing of the new hierarchy of the
disciplines created by the Enlightenment: the natural sciences were
only ancillary to the first of all sciences, the *science de la société*. Studies
in the natural sciences might assist the reputation of a scholar – they
would do nothing to advance the fame of a nation. If modern society
were to abandon the natural sciences no noticeable disorder would
ensue; if the propagation of the principles of Christian morality with
the aid of the social sciences were to cease, however, society would
be plunged into moral and political chaos.

Count Louis de Bonald was no unprejudiced observer of the contentions arising between literature and the sciences in the wake of
the Enlightenment: he was a partisan of the Ancien Régime, a stead-
fast royalist and a member of the Catholic Church. But as the royalist
and Catholic Balzac, who frequently cited de Bonald, was capable of
describing the society of his time with an uncompromising realism
that evoked the admiration of Marx and Engels, so de Bonald, the
ideologist of the Restoration, could just as clearly foresee the future
destiny of the social sciences as, carried along by the Enlightenment's enthusiasm for science, they began to imitate the natural
sciences:

*Les sciences morales, qui ont longtemps régné sur les sciences et sur les lettres, quoique
amies de la paix, ne peuvent rien pour la maintenir, depuis que la philosophie a envahi ou
ravagé leurs plus beaux domaines, le politique et la théologie, et qu'elle fait journellement
des courses même sur la morale. Repoussées par les sciences exactes, dédaignées par les
lettres frivoles, elles sont hors d'état de faire respecter leur médiation ou leur neutralité, et*

---

[14] de Bonald, 'Des Sciences', p. 316.
[15] de Bonald, 'Sur la Guerre des sciences et des lettres' in *Oeuvres*, p. 387.

subiront la loi du vainqueur. Mais comme elles ont tout à craindre des sciences, dures et orgueilleuses, leurs voeux secrets seront pour les lettres, plus humaines et plus généreuses, et qui n'ont pas perdu tout souvenir de leur ancienne et étroite alliance avec les sciences morales.

De Bonald wrote in an age which he saw threatened by the domination of the '*petit esprit*' and the loss of those serious and manly virtues that had characterized the Ancien Régime. In the spirit of the Ancien Régime he generally took refuge in military metaphors to describe the fluctuations of the spiritual contentions in which he himself took part. The intellectual debates scholars conducted with one another in earlier times were like contentions between regular soldiers commanded by generals of equal competence: discipline and chivalry reigned; victory brought honour but defeat was in no way dishonourable. An aspect of the Age of Enlightenment was that this honourable war between combatants of equal rank had ceased to exist: ill-armed scribblers fought guerrilla engagements with one another in *feuilletons* and pamphlets, and in this '*petite guerre contre tout ce qui est bon et juste*' [16] reason was obliged to accommodate itself to forms of warfare essentially alien to it.

We must bear this context in mind if we are to understand the meaning of the title de Bonald gave to his little treatise on the future destiny of the social sciences caught between literature on one side and the natural sciences on the other: '*Sur la guerre des sciences et des lettres*'. To de Bonald, what was reflected in the disunion of the social sciences was the contention between the Ancien Régime and the modern age, Restoration and Revolution, Enlightenment and counter-Enlightenment. It is of this battleground that my book is a report.

In his *Lectures on Aesthetics* Hegel described the novel as the art-form which recovers the 'order and prose of reality'. [17] The novel, the modern bourgeois épopée, 'presupposes a reality already ordered as *prose . . .* One of the most common and, to the novel, appropriate conflicts is therefore that between the poetry of the heart and the prose of everyday circumstances and the accidents of the external world that oppose it . . .' Hegel's description makes it clear why from the moment of its inception sociology became both a competitor and a counterpart of literature. On the one hand, when sociology desired

[16] de Bonald, 'Avertissement', in *Oeuvres*, p. 2.
[17] Georg Wilhelm Friedrich Hegel, *Vorlesungen über die Asthetik I–III (1818–1829)*, *Werkausgabe*, ed. Eva Moldenhauer and Karl Markus Michel, Band 15 (Frankfurt am Main: Suhrkamp, 1970), pp. 392–3.

to be sociography it came into conflict above all with the realistic novel over the claim to offer an adequate reproduction of the 'prose of everyday circumstances'; when, on the other, it claimed to be social theory it incurred the suspicion of degenerating into a 'closet science',[18] that is of belonging to that group of disciplines which, according to Nietzsche's malicious definition, are unable to demonstrate 'that any kind of grand cultural goal lies within their horizon': this arid closet science was then contrasted with literature in its capacity to express the 'poetry of the heart'.

In this competition over the claim to be the rule of life appropriate to industrial society sociology cannot, however, simply be equated with rationality and literature with feeling. Occasionally there are coalitions: Dickens, for instance, acted as an advocate of the culture of feeling when in *Hard Times* he scourged the dehumanizing effects of the utilitarianism of a James Mill; Flaubert, on the other hand, coldly determined to dissect the modern world like an anatomist, censured the exaggerated poetizing that marked the nineteenth century, and felt entitled to make merry over the speculations of an Auguste Comte not least because he took the *métier* of literature seriously and pursued it with scientific pretensions.

In essence, however, the battle lines are drawn as follows: sociology is a discipline characterized by cold rationality, which seeks to comprehend the structures and laws of motion of modern industrial society by means of measurement and computation and in doing so only serves to alienate man more effectively from himself and from the world around him; on the opposite side there stands a literature whose intuition can see farther than the analyses of the sociologists and whose ability to address the heart of man is to be preferred to the products of a discipline that misunderstands itself as a natural science of society. This is the argument advanced by English poetry and literary criticism from Matthew Arnold to T. S. Eliot, and by the French literary intelligentsia from Charles Péguy onwards. Germany constitutes a special case: here, on the one hand, the social sciences, taking up and developing impulses from the philosophy of life, have neither formed a sharply defined discipline, as is the case in France, nor become a recognized constituent of social 'common sense', as they have in England; on the other, the antithesis of literature and poetry has been maintained in all its

---

[18] Friedrich Nietzsche to Paul Deussen, October 1868; Nietzsche. *Briefe. September 1864–April 1869*, Briefwechsel, Kritische Gesamtausgabe, ed. Giorgio Colli and Mazzino Montinari, Erste Abteilung, Band 2 (Berlin and New York: de Gruyter, 1975), p. 329.

severity only in Germany, where it has been exacerbated through an asociality of poetical production in principle, that even sees its chief task as being the 'refutation of the social' (Hugo von Hofmannsthal). [19]

The conflict between cold reason and the culture of feeling, typical of the competition between the social sciences and literature, is not confined to the realm of scientific and literary publications: it also sets its stamp on the lives, private and public, of the writers and scholars we are to consider. And this is consistent with the fact that in this contention, which I see as a kind of 'secret history' of the modern social sciences, so significant a role is played by women: Clotilde de Vaux, Harriet Taylor, Beatrice Webb.

The assault on sociology by literature and the men of letters – in many instances an assault inspired by the spirit of the counter-Enlightenment – has always been successful wherever sociological thinking, overpowered and transported by the desire to imitate the natural sciences, has claimed the ability wholly to replace metaphysics and religion and become a substitute for faith and the heart. The expulsion of the feelings from the social sciences and other disciplines has taken place in the name of an arrogant rationality which desires to be not only the means to knowledge but at the same time a philosophy of life and a substitute religion. In attempting this, however, rationality attempts too much and promises more than it can perform; and when the self-doubt thus engendered does not suffice for self-healing the feelings do not merely regain their rights– they are enhanced to a cult of irrationality such as finds expression in the totalitarian ideologies.

In the long run, therefore, there occurs a build-up of the longing for real objects of belief which appeal to the feeling and not only to the mind; and when the way back to such objects is barred new ones are sought and calamitous alternatives found, as the French literary men of the political right found proto-Fascism and such English socialists as Sidney and Beatrice Webb found Soviet Communism during its most degenerate period. In this regard, an attempt to turn the sociological intelligentsia towards literature, or the playing off of poetry and social science against one another, is the first sign of a drift into a totalitarian ideology: it is instructive that the official disbandment of German sociology in National Socialist Germany is associated with the name of Hans Freyer, the author of the *Revolution*

[19] Hugo von Hofmannsthal, 'Das Schrifttum als geistiger Raum der Nation' [1927], in *Natur und Erkenntnis: Essays* (Berlin and Darmstadt: Deutsche Buch-Gemeinschaft, 1957), p. 173.

of the Right, who has been called the Expressionist among German sociologists, and that Helmut Schelsky, who at the end of his life styled himself an anti-sociologist, united his apostasy from his discipline with a despairing appeal to Heinrich Böll to overcome the traditional German schism and bring Germany's literary and sociological intelligentsia together again.

PART I

FRANCE

1

The transformations of Auguste Comte:
science and literature in early positivism

The style of the scientist

Not even his friends regarded Auguste Comte as a great writer. Even
that they concealed insights of an unheard-of intrepidity did nothing
to ameliorate the ponderous tone of his treatises. When the correspondence between Comte and John Stuart Mill was published, a
critic commented: 'One of them almost always writes excellent
French, and I do not have to tell you it is Mill; the other employs an
idiom for which there are no words in any language, and I do not
have to tell you it is Comte.'[1]

Every demand that he should change his manner of writing was,
however, disregarded by Comte; and when in 1824 his long-standing
friend Valat once again complained of his style the founder of
positivism reacted with one of the many declarations of principle
which had marked his life and work from the beginning.

According to Comte, questions of style were of little importance
in the sciences, if only because no two authors had ever been able to
agree on what good style was. He complacently asserted that it was
precisely literary men and those readers who judged him as a writer
rather than as a scholar who made a point of lauding his style. The
way in which a scientist expressed himself ought not to be determined by artificial rules but must accord with the subjects under discussion – and that was the case with him, because he modelled
himself, not on rhetoricians, but on such scientists as Berthollet,
Bichat and Cuvier. To be compared to them was the highest form of
praise. He employed no artifice but allowed himself to be guided
solely by his thoughts – he could do no other than follow his inspiration. Later on, perhaps, when he had turned to more concrete
problems, he might write in a livelier and more variegated and

---

[1] Emile Faguet, 'Auguste Comte et Stuart Mill' [1899], in *Propos Littéraires*, Deuxième
Série (Paris: Société française d'imprimerie et de librairie, 1904), p. 153.

ornate manner. Comte appealed to Count Buffon: '*Le style est l'homme même*' meant that a man and his style were both unalterable.

Thirty years later Comte set down the rules of style he intended to adhere to thereafter. No sentence should be longer than two lines of manuscript – which, given his cramped handwriting, amounted to five lines of print. No paragraph should contain more than seven sentences; any hiatus had to be strictly avoided. The same word should not occur twice either in the same sentence or in successive sentences – excepting only single-syllable auxiliary verbs. Apart from its introduction and conclusion, every treatise of Comte's would in future comprise seven chapters. Each chapter would be in three parts, each part in seven sections, and each section would consist of a leading paragraph of seven sentences and three further paragraphs each of five sentences. Rules of this kind would, he maintained, bestow on his prose a strictness of form previously possessed only by poetry.

John Stuart Mill, who had once extolled the author of the *Cours de philosophie positive* as an extraordinarily lucid and methodical writer, concluded his book on Comte and positivism with an enumeration of these rules of composition; he saw in them a clear sign of the 'melancholy decline of a great mind'.[2] They also signalled the termination of a development in the course of which the founder of sociology had amended his attitude towards literature and devoted greater and greater attention to the problems involved in the presentation of his grandiose projects.

Fear of intellectual infection

Before he had published anything at all Comte was already certain he would make a success. Although for the whole of his life he was to acquire no better position than that of an 'ambulatory professor'[3] – an external examiner for the Ecole Polytechnique– he none the less prophesied for his still uncompleted doctrine a pervasive power comparable only to the irresistible diffusion of Christianity. He saw himself, not merely as having continued the work of Descartes, but as having completed and perfected it; and when he once received a letter from Germany addressed only to '*M. Auguste Comte, auteur du*

---

[2] John Stuart Mill, Auguste Comte and Positivism (1865; Ann Arbor: The University of Michigan Press, 1961), p. 199.

[3] Comte to Valat, 25 December 1824; August Comte, *Correspondance générale et confessions*, textes établis et presentés par Paulo E. de Berrêdo Carneiro et Pierre Arnaud (Paris: Mouton, 1973), Vol. 1, p. 151.

système de politique positive, à Paris[4] he was flattered by the fact but could not refrain from remarking enviously that on one occasion the address 'Europe' had sufficed to direct a letter to Newton. His first publications had hardly appeared before he was describing his own books as classics.

Modesty was not Comte's strong suit. When he proposed to Guizot the institution of a chair of the history of science at the Collège de France he recommended himself as the only suitable candidate for it and appended a scheme for financing it: he should be paid from the funds expended on the chair of political economy, which was to be abolished – it was a vague and irrational discipline which his own teachings had long since rendered superfluous. When the final volume of the *Cours de philosophie positive* appeared in 1842, Comte resolved henceforth to abandon polemics: so far as he was concerned the time for discussion was over. In 1854 he demanded that the Vendôme column should be torn down to make way for a monument to himself, the founder of the occidental republic.

But a conspiracy in his favour on the part of the *Zeitgeist* such as Comte had even in his youth set all his hopes on was in reality out of the question. Since his every attempt at finding for himself a secure position came to grief, the *Zeitgeist* seemed, rather, to have been conspiring against him. Without abandoning his pretensions, or wavering in his own self-assessment, Comte soon became aware how difficult it was to lead a speculative and theoretical existence in an age in which science was increasingly becoming an industry. French scholarship was still something admirable, but the scholars of France were degenerating more and more into opportunists. However remote from reality Comte's opinions might be, he was not wholly unjustified in asserting that he could recognize better than anyone else the strong and the weak among the academics: it was precisely his experience of the business of science which ensured that some remnant of a reality-principle was still active even in his boldest flights of fancy. He defined the '*faits sociologiques*'[5] – not without an ironical glance at himself – exactly as Emile Durkheim was later to define them: they were the things one had to come to terms with.

All Comte's writings are marked with the headlong self-overestimation of their author. His analyses were calm and confident, his judgements direct and decisive, his predictions rash and

---

[4] Comte to Valat, 16 November 1825; *Correspondance*, Vol. 1, p. 168.
[5] Comte to John Stuart Mill, 16 May 1843; *Correspondance* (Paris: Mouton, 1976), Vol. 2, p. 153.

foolhardy. In the middle of the nineteenth century he wanted to persuade his adherents that in Europe the danger of war had receded for ever. Thirty years later the Russians had the costly Crimean War behind them, the Austrians had been beaten by the Germans and Italians, and Sedan had set the seal on the defeat of France in its contention with Prussia. It was prognostications of this kind that incited such scientists as Pasteur to deride the sociology of Comte, the would-be founder of a science of society.

But if Comte constantly overestimated his abilities he often had good excuse for doing so. The lectures on the positive philosophy which he delivered at his house in the rue Monsieur-le-Prince were attended by such world-famous scholars as Alexander von Humboldt, Blainville and Poinsot. Although he was no more than an outsider in the French world of science he was again and again the recipient of manifestations of sympathy from great contemporaries; glad though he was to receive them, they none the less seemed never to surprise him. When John Stuart Mill moved Comte's English admirers to subscribe to a pension to secure his livelihood, Comte was grateful yet considered that in the last resort he self-evidently had a right to such assistance: the only thing that puzzled him was that it had been so long delayed, and when in the end it was discontinued he regarded this as an error which must in the long run reflect discredit on his former patrons rather than on him. That his teachings were found attractive by many scholars whose reputation even his enemies could not call into question strengthened Comte in his self-confidence. As his prospects of a normal career grew fainter he came to feel that in maintaining his outsider status he was fulfilling a mission.

Auguste Comte had that about him which, while it does not render the fanatic very lovable, does make him worthy of respect: he did not spare himself, and in this he adhered to those principles of whose correctness he sought to convince others. No one had exceeded Comte in the resoluteness with which the radicalism of a method has been imposed upon the workings of everyday life; his native language, indeed, already presents an attempt to make life and work sustain one another: *expérience* means both experiment and experience, and the concept of '*expérience sociologique*'[6] which Comte derived from it determined his conduct like a rule of a religious order. His urge to systematization was a reflection of the way in which he moulded his own life, his expectations of others were a reflection of the high

---

[6] Comte to John Stuart Mill, 29 June 1843; *Correspondance*, Vol. 2, p. 171.

demands he made of himself. The asceticism he also practised was a modern kind of asceticism, in as much as it was decidedly directed towards productivity: though Nietzsche may have been right to call the older Comte a Catholic visionary, John Stuart Mill none the less had good reason to call attention to the Calvinist traits in Comte's life and work.

The compulsive nature of many of Comte's actions is unmistakable, and this too is why his language frequently descends into the grotesque. When he reports to Mill that he has indulged in a couple of days of 'horizontal meditation',[7] instead of saying simply that he has had to stay in bed, he recalls the excesses of Buffon which d'Alembert and others derided. And yet it is moving and impressive when Comte gives up coffee, then tobacco, and finally wine as well; when he scrupulously weighs out his daily food on a pair of scales down to a margin of five grammes; when after every lecture he has given he goes through systematic breathing exercises, and as a corrective to his sedentary mode of life takes long walks all over Paris, which, since he never ceases to ponder on his projects, becomes for him one huge workroom.

'Hygiene' and 'diet' determined not only Comte's everyday life – they were in perhaps even greater measure the *leit-motifs* of his life as a scholar. From 1838 onwards he ceased to read newspapers and magazines, and only occasionally did he continue to glance at the fortnightly bulletin of the Académie des Sciences. This was part of the *'hygiène cérébrale'*[8] through which he intended to concentrate exclusively on the completion of his own work. His fear of intellectual infection was deep-seated, so that interruptions of his spiritual diet were rare and were precisely noted – such as his reading of Vico, of the writings of John Stuart Mill and of that article in the *National* which Emile Littré devoted to the work of Comte and which finally transformed a system into a school and a doctrine into a movement.

Apart from this, music, painting and poetry provided the only variety. The sociologist Comte avoided society, but he regularly attended the Italian opera once or twice a week, and his favourite poets were Dante, Petrarch, Tasso and Ariosto, because the expressive melody of their poetry approached closest to music. He counted his love of art as the surest sign that he was continuing to develop; if he ever ceased to enjoy music his intellectual progress would also come to a halt.

[7] Comte to John Stuart Mill, 21 October 1844; *Correspondance*, Vol. 2, p. 288.
[8] Comte to John Stuart Mill, 20 November 1841; *Correspondance*, Vol. 2, p. 20.

Comte was no utopian. He made a distinction between the dreamer and the theoretician whose conviction it is that ideas have first to be reformed by dint of patient and assiduous labour before institutions can be reformed. Convinced of the lucidity of his teachings, he always appeared astonished when they failed to strike everyone as revelations. He laid part of the blame on the state of the colloquial language of his time, which the sociologist could not avoid using: permeated as this language was with the flowery rhetoric of the age of theology and metaphysics, it was almost impossible to formulate in it the principles of a positive philosophy or positivist policies. The coining of new worlds was no answer: Montesquieu had been the last with sufficient self-confidence to clothe new insights in new words. and Rivarol had in fact spoken against the coining of neologisms and against the odious tendency to bestow new meanings upon familiar words: it was 'like moving the furniture around in the room of a blind man'.[9]

It was not least the literary pedanticism that dominated his age that dissuaded Comte from constructing a new language. But even without that he was always convinced of his power to communicate: the intimate harmony between true positivists required no secret language, and even when his differences with John Stuart Mill grew more serious nothing could shake his belief that a few hours of public discussion would produce – in his favour, of course – a unanimity of opinion.

Comte hated those *littérateurs* who won over their hearers and readers by the employment of rhetorical tricks – such *littérateurs* as Victor Cousin, who was as successful as a speaker as he was shallow as a philosopher. Later on, when it was still necessary to distinguish the science of sociology from its literary predecessors, this verdict was to be echoed by Emile Durkheim. Comte's friends were well aware of his attitude in this matter, not least of them Gustave d'Eichthal, who was responsible for acquainting Comte with German philosophy. In 1824 he sent him a number of lengthy extracts from Herder's *Ideen*, comparing the author with Buffon in his ability to combine elevated thoughts with warmth of presentation. 'But you should not let this deceive you,' d'Eichthal added: Herder had successfully sought to unite the sciences of nature, life and society, and his theological-sounding language was to be thought of rather as a mask. In reality he was *'excessivement positif'*.[10] When d'Eichthal reported on Hegel he

[9] Louis Dimier, *Les Maîtres de la contre-révolution au dix-neuvième siècle*, nouvelle édition revue et corrigée (Paris: Nouvelle Librairie Nationale, 1917), p. 83.
[10] Gustave d'Eichthal to Comte, 18 June 1824; *Correspondance*, Vol. 1, p. 386.

did not omit to refer to his favourable judgment on the first part of the *Cours*: Comte's reflections were, he said, very similar to many of the ideas of Hegel, who was a sworn enemy of the poet–philosophers to be found in such numbers in Germany.

Comte measured out his reading like a trusted medicine. He read the same few authors again and again: for him to extend his reading experience required an exceptional stimulus. When he learned that positive philosophy was arousing interest in Germany he wanted in his own way to demonstrate his gratitude: in order to get to know the Germanic way of thinking at its source he promised to read Goethe in the original. This sounds less like a pleasure than an act of duty, especially as he added heroically that in so doing he would be content to employ the assistance of a little dictionary. Shortly afterwards he informed John Stuart Mill that he no longer thought learning German so very pressing a matter; for the dissemination of his works beyond the Rhine he could in any case rely on translations. Thus he never read Goethe properly, and Schiller, whom he likewise knew only in translation, remained for him an incompetent imitator of Shakespeare.

The books that Comte did read, however, helped greatly to sustain him. They accompanied him through the crises that preceded every new creative phase. He suggested to Mill that he ought to combat his melancholia with a choice selection of '*impressions esthétiques*',[11] without realizing that in 1826 – the year in which Comte himself had experienced the worst of his disorders – Mill had in fact overcome a threatened mental breakdown by turning to poetry, or that thereafter he had called on Coleridge and above all Wordsworth to guard him against the ill-consequences of his overdriven utilitarianism. As before, however, music, painting and literature remained for Comte only a means to an end: they created the cheerful preconditions for intellectual productivity without being a part of it. Art was an indispensable agent for enhancing the capacity for knowledge but was itself incapable of knowledge, valuable as a means but possessing no value in itself.

Comte's 'Education Sentimentale'

Auguste Comte was not a natural ascetic. He harboured needs of the heart that required satisfaction, and he was frequently involved in piquant episodes or perpetrated those little *sottises*, as he called them,

[11] Comte to John Stuart Mill, 16 July 1843; *Correspondance*, Vol. 2, p. 176.

that cost five francs. Among the prostitutes of the Palais Royal he discovered Caroline Massin, whom against the embittered opposition of his parents he subsequently married – the biggest mistake he ever made, as he later confessed. This relationship cast a shadow over his entire life, even after he had, in 1842, finally separated from Caroline. In this same year he completed the *Cours de philosophie positive*; in 1844 he lost his position as examiner at the Ecole Polytechnique. It was at this time that Littré began his series of articles in the *National*. Repeatedly brought to a halt by nervous crises, Comte took in hand his next great work, the *Système de politique positive*.

The concentration he brought to bear on his work grew, if possible, even greater as, after the breakdown of his marriage, he sought in it a satisfaction of his emotional needs too. In September 1842 he wrote to John Stuart Mill, who always took a great interest in his personal misfortunes, that in future the only pleasant private relationships he would have would come from contacts in the scientific world; he recalled the '*intimes convergences philosophiques*'[12] which, their differences over the women's rights question notwithstanding, had always existed between them, and suggested to Mill that when he next visited Paris he should stay with him so that they might enjoy the pleasures of living together as brothers.

As it turned out they were never to see one another. Mill's union with Harriet Taylor served to cool even more a friendship-by-letter that was already burdened by differing standpoints on the question of female emancipation. In the 'great biological–sociological discussion'[13] he and Mill conducted, Comte even drew on the findings of comparative anatomy to demonstrate that exceptions to the natural superiority of the male sex were to be found only in the lowest reaches of the animal kingdom among the invertebrates. A characteristic of women that proved their inferiority was their incapacity for abstract thought, the way in which their reasoning was disrupted by the intervention of the passions: that was why they were unsuited both to directing a firm and to leading an army; offices of government should be strictly prohibited them. Women had never produced anything of consequence in painting, music or poetry: they were by nature, and thus for all time, the inferiors of men.

Neither as a fact nor as a principle was Comte willing to recognize female emancipation. Acts of militancy by women could lead to nothing but a renewed, and by this time definitive, confirmation of

[12] Comte to John Stuart Mill, 30 September 1842; *Correspondance*, Vol. 2, p. 93.
[13] Comte to John Stuart Mill, 14 November 1843; *Correspondance*, Vol. 2, p. 206.

their inferiority. That an emancipation of women had not taken place was especially clear in the case of literature: the number of female writers had constantly increased, to be sure, but could even one of them endure comparison with Madame de Sévigné, Madame de Lafayette, Madame de Motteville, or any of the other great *femmes de lettres* of the seventeenth century? Comte appeared not to notice how dangerous this argument was for his own position: women, it seemed, were not at all the inferiors of men by nature but only as an outcome of certain historical forces. When Sarah Austin remonstrated with him on this account, Comte admitted merely that women might be of consequence for the reception and dissemination of ideas originating in great men. That she had come to the aid of Descartes lent even Christina of Sweden a certain significance.

Comte saw in the growing horde of *littératrices* only another proof of the lamentable state of spiritual anarchy in which contemporary society found itself. That a female author who decked herself out with the name of a man could become famous – Comte was thinking of George Sand – was a scandal. Whatever else might be held against his own wife, Comte contentedly affirmed, at least Caroline had not taken to scribbling . . .

Then, however, the April of 1845 arrived, and there began what true positivists call to this day the Incomparable Year. By the time it had ended Comte's position with respect to art and literature had been as thoroughly transformed as had his attitude towards women: what had been a scientific thesis became a religion, and the needs of the heart were suddenly no longer a purely private affair; art was now accorded the importance it deserved, and Comte, the self-proclaimed high priest of humanity, came to desire nothing more than to be a poet uniting in himself the virtues of Dante and Petrarch so as to celebrate her who was for him Beatrice and Laura in one. It was in this fissure in Comte's biography that there originated that division in positivism which from the middle of the nineteenth century onwards not only had a lasting influence on the history of the social sciences but also produced far-reaching political effects, and not only in France but in England as well.

In this transformation of positivism from a scientific thesis into a religion a novel played an important role. On 30 April 1845 Comte lent Clotilde de Vaux a copy of Henry Fielding's *Tom Jones*. He sent her a French translation and told her she need not read it in haste as he himself possessed the original English version of this 'admirable masterpiece'.[14] Clotilde thanked him the following day; she hoped that she and Comte would soon be able to talk over Fielding's book together. These two letters are the first of the *correspondance sacrée*.

Clotilde was the sister of Maximilien Marie, who was one of Comte's pupils. In September 1835 she had married a certain Amédée de Vaux, who after four years had fled both her and a host of gambling debts and had vanished without trace; since then Clotilde had lived a withdrawn life in the circle of her family, which was where Comte met her for the first time in October 1844.

Soon after the first exchange of letters Clotilde visited Comte in the rue Monsieur-le-Prince in the company of her brother; he then visited her at her parents' home. Not without intellectual ambition, she hoped to gain instruction and inspiration from a philosopher who, though he belonged to no university, had none the less acquired a reputation that extended far beyond Paris and France. So far as he was concerned it was a *coup de foudre*: Comte was instantly convinced – and in this he was right – that his love for Clotilde would liberate him from his personal miseries and bestow a new impetus on his work. It seemed that the needs of his heart could now for the first time be satisfied in a worthy way. He wrote two or three letters to Clotilde without receiving an answer; he explained why he felt drawn towards her, he indicated what he hoped for from her. At length she replied, but it was not the reply he had been waiting for: in a tone of friendly but solemn resolution she asked Comte to keep his feelings under control and, while assuring him of her respect and affection, denied that she could love him. Comte understood but refused to give up, and their long, moving, distressing correspondence was thereafter on his side an uninterrupted effort to transform Clotilde's respect for him into love; on her side it was an unyielding and successful resistance to this desire.

Comte was in love, but his love-letters are treatises; he speaks from the depths of his heart, yet the impression one receives is that everything he says has been carefully thought out beforehand. Clotilde was not in love, but her letters produce an effect of spontaneity; they are full of warmth, even when she is repulsing him. Sound common sense is always on her side, and so is sound use of language: she quite simply writes better than Comte. She did so, in fact, before she knew him: one of Clotilde's descendants, Charles de Rouvre, goes so far as to compare her early letters with those of Madame de Sévigné. Some of her expressions do indeed possess the

[14] Comte to Clotilde de Vaux, 30 April 1845; *Correspondance* (Paris: Mouton, 1977), Vol. 3, p. 3.

lucidity of those moral maxims in which French literature is so rich; Romain Rolland quoted her in his correspondence with Thomas Mann.

The transformation accomplished in Comte's way of thinking was profound. It consists in a rehabilitation of feeling – to which the maxim of Vauvenargues that all great thoughts come from the heart may serve as a motto – in a revision of the role Comte had hitherto assigned to women, and not least in an enhancement of the value of literature.

On 2 June Catholics celebrate the feast of St Clotilde. Comte, the critic of the age of theology, employed the opportunity to compose for Clotilde de Vaux an essay on the *commémoration sociale*, one of the many little theoretical *billets* he went on to write for the purpose of making her more closely acquainted with the teachings of positivism. He stressed that at the heart of positivism philosophy, poetry and politics ought to stand on an equal footing: philosophy regulated human life; poetry beautified it and ennobled our existence through the idealization of feeling; politics, finally, a species of social engineering whose centre was morality, co-ordinated our public actions with our private ones. Positivism thus united thought, feeling and action – with the goal of perfecting the outer and the inner existence of man. In this process the social influence of women would increase and finally come to play a commanding role. The chaste reverence for women that had characterized the knighthood of the Middle Ages had been admirable – even if its influence had been considerably curtailed by the dominant theology of the age: the point now was to discover for this Catholic spirituality a new field of activity.

Clotilde replied three days later, though without referring to the ideas Comte had written to her about. In the schoolmasterly tone he had adopted she had detected the unrelinquished desire to make her wholly his, and she therefore entreated him not to pay any further calls on her for the time being. She confessed that for two years she had been in love with another man. As she was still married and believed in the indissolubility of marriage she had no hope of ever winning this man for herself: she must now find peace for her emotions, and the same applied to Comte. She was, moreover, engaged upon a weighty work which she trusted would restore to her her peace of soul.

Clotilde became a writer; in the epistolary novel *Lucie* she depicted her own fate. *Lucie* appeared on 20 June 1845 in the literary section of the *National*, whose editor, Armand Marrast, was among the most influential Parisian journalist of his day. Comte had once commended Marrast for his critique of Cousin's spiritualism; and he must also have been well disposed towards his paper, since it was in the *National* that Littré had introduced the teachings of positivism to a wider public. The publication of *Lucie* none the less came as a shock to him – not least because he suspected that it was not only as a contributor that Marrast had sought to secure Clotilde. The latter had now become one of those *littératrices* his contempt for whom he had never attempted to conceal, but, long accustomed to submitting to the *faits sociologiques*, Comte had by now also learned to live with a *fait accompli*.

He read the '*charmante nouvelle*'[15] for the first time on 23 June and wrote at once to Clotilde thanking her for the 'delicious tears' he had shed while reading it: so carried away had he been he had even failed to notice the printing errors which, like the proud new author she was, she had taken care to point out to him. In *Lucie* Comte believed he encountered again the rudiments of his own teaching; he considered Walter Scott just about good enough for one of his works to be compared with Clotilde's first production. Clotilde wrote back to him, telling him of the '*petits bonheurs*'[16] the novel had brought her; as a consequence Comte at once read it again – for this, after all, provided a welcome opportunity of writing to her once more.

Comte took an inventory of his past life and drew up detailed plans for the future. Through his relationship with Clotilde he had come to the turning-point of his personal and scholarly development. Henceforth his teaching would accord feeling and intellect equal status. Initially he had had to emphasize the rationality of his ideas; now, when the issue was their application, appropriate room could be made for the emotions. In this sense the work he was now taking in hand, his *Système de politique positive*, would be more harmoniously balanced than anything he had written before. He again warmed towards Catholicism – evidence for which is not least his reading of Augustine – and the systematic positivists seemed to him more and more to be the sole legitimate successors of the great men of the Middle Ages.

In the meantime a career had opened up for Clotilde: Armand Marrast had offered her regular employment with the *National*. Twice a week the literary section was to be devoted to educational

[15] Comte to Clotilde de Vaux, 23 June 1845; *Correspondance*, Vol. 3, p. 40.
[16] Clotilde de Vaux to Comte, 23 June 1845; *Correspondance*, Vol. 3, p. 41.

and feminist questions, and Clotilde was to take on the reviewing of women's novels. She was, as she wrote to Comte, happy with the idea; in accomplishing this task she counted on the support of his friendship and his knowledge.

Before Comte could reply his organism reacted, as it so often did: his old insomnia returned and he fell into a condition of profound melancholia. Then he wrote to Clotilde one of his long, tormenting letters in which the complex exposition of philosophical questions served only to conceal his fear of expressing his real desires. Comte warned Clotilde against accepting Marrast's offer: however seductive it might seem, the literary *métier* could in no way promote her moral or intellectual development. Journalism, that concentration on criticizing the work of others which paralysed all one's own creativity, would be bound to end in spiritual ruin; Clotilde ought to write on subjects of real importance, not submit herself to the frivolous exigencies of the daily press.

Clotilde did not become a journalist: working regularly for the *National* would in any case have been difficult for her on account of her continually declining health. When Comte and Clotilde acted as godparents to Maximilien Marie's son Comte seized the opportunity of laying bare, in a philosophical letter on the subject of baptism, the extent of his attachment to her: as godparents they had entered into a spiritual marriage, and now he felt he was indissolubly united with her. For some time yet the difference in tone between the letters they exchanged was painfully evident to him: he idolized her, she on the other hand was sparing with those phrases and compliments whose aphoristic brevity even today makes her letters worth reading. But the obstinacy of her '*très cher philosophe*'[17] did not fail to affect her, and on 5 September 1845 to Comte's delight she for the first time signed a letter with her forename alone, and concluded with the sentence: '*Adieu*, take care of yourself and allow us to put aside passionate feelings. I entrust to you the remainder of my life.'[18]

Such a statement was of course in no way calculated to bridle Comte's emotions, and there now commenced a lengthy phase in which he continued to woo her and she gave him to understand that her still extant marriage and her unfulfilled attachment to another man would for ever set bounds to their relationship. The Clotilde cult which Comte evolved even while she was still alive was a systematic compensation for an unfulfilled passion; and the more

[17] Clotilde de Vaux to Comte, 1 September 1845; *Correspondance*, Vol. 3, p. 101.
[18] Clotilde de Vaux to Comte, 5 September 1845; *Correspondance*, Vol. 3, p. 108.

ascetic his life became the more sensual grew his doctrines, so that often they grazed the borders of the steamily erotic and many times, indeed, overstepped them.

At the same time Clotilde, her attachment to Comte still largely intellectual, undertook a systematic study of the teachings of positivism, perhaps with the assistance of Littré; she could have had no suspicion that the letters she exchanged with Comte almost daily were already effecting a decisive modification in the positivist doctrine that would in the end lead to a breach between such 'scientific' positivists as Littré and the founder of positivism. Comte was engaged in founding a religion, and in this conversion literature played a decisive role.

Comte turned his asceticism into productivity. The harmony which, thanks to Clotilde, he had won between his public and his private life convinced him he would be able to complete his new work, planned in five volumes, the 'tremendous opus'[19] of the *Politique positive*. So sure of himself did he feel, that– a rare thing indeed with him– traces of self-deprecation began to appear in his letters. Looking back on his correspondence with Clotilde he recognized that he had hitherto comported himself more like Don Quixote than Don Juan; on the other hand, however, he felt he could justify himself: if Don Quixote had not dreamed of his Dulcinea he would have remained only a commonplace blockhead.

He intended to assist and support Clotilde in her literary career not least so as to help her to attain to a similar harmony between public and private existence. An opportunity to do so soon presented itself: Clotilde sent him the first part of her new novel, *Willelmine*, which Comte read with close attention – describing himself as a benevolent critic of it. Further parts of the novel, into which Clotilde sought to work her new-won philosophical insights – though not without experiencing some surprise at the reluctance of her pen to follow her thoughts– offered Comte another occasion for warning her against the intellectually harmful consequences of the literary life. He advised her in matters of style, he accepted that the novel was a medium through which he and Clotilde could exchange ideas and feelings whose outward expression life had denied them, but what he could not bring himself to do was to sustain her in her desire to obtain public recognition as an authoress. He wanted to further her 'justified personal emancipation'[20] but also to continue

[19] Comte to Clotilde de Vaux, 26 August 1845; *Correspondance*, Vol. 3, p. 97.
[20] Comte to Clotilde de Vaux, 16 November 1845; *Correspondance*, Vol. 3, p. 196.

to control it, and he thus suggested to her she might in future become a contributor to the *Revue positive*, which Littré was at just that time preparing to launch.

For this position she was in Comte's eyes all the more qualified in that she had instinctively understood that the positivism of the future would embody a unity of thought, feeling and action; and she had, moreover, demonstrated in which sphere of human life woman could make her particular contribution to the progress of society: with that lucidity which Molière, a positivist *avant la lettre*, had admired in women, she had in her novel delineated a heart's conversion to positivism.

The rank Comte accorded his relationship with Clotilde rose even higher: Mademoiselle de Lespinasse and d'Alembert, Voltaire and Madame du Châtelet were the couples with whom he now compared it. When Clotilde sent him a little poem, *Les Pensées d'une fleur*, which reads exactly as its title leads one to suppose it would and of which a critic had said it challenged comparison with the worst poems of Chateaubriand, he expressed his admiration for its poetical and philosophical sensibility – though he also prudently criticized one line – and at once deposited the manuscript among the treasures of his little private library. After he had read the 'ravishing canzone'[21] a third time he had become convinced it would have aroused the jealousy of Petrarch – especially since nothing comparable existed in the French language at all.

It was not only his relationship with Clotilde that revealed how greatly Comte's attitude towards women had altered. When George Sand, whom he had in earlier years slaughtered as the very worst of all *littératrices*, put herself out to try to gain admittance to one of his lectures, he asked Laffitte if at the soonest opportunity he would reserve an especially good seat for the 'celebrated lady';[22] he regretted the brusqueness with which he had previously treated her, for if positivism was to be further disseminated it could not do without women.

Clotilde, growing ever weaker from a progressive consumption, summoned all her strength to bring out her new novel, 'my child',[23] as she called it. In the end it amounted to a race with her illness: 'Whenever I pick up this accursed pen I am seized with an attack of fever,'[24] she wrote on 2 March 1846, and added: 'In the midst of my

[21] Comte to Clotilde de Vaux, 4 December 1845; *Correspondance*, Vol. 3, p. 216.
[22] Comte to Pierre Laffitte, 26 January 1846; *Correspondance*, Vol. 3, p. 303.
[23] Clotilde de Vaux to Comte, 24 February 1846; *Correspondance*, Vol. 3, p. 332.
[24] Clotilde de Vaux to Comte, 2 March 1846; *Correspondance*, Vol. 3, p. 342.

pens and my books I seem to myself like Tantalus.' Comte begged her to take better care of herself and to think less about her work; on the other hand he wanted her to complete the task she had undertaken, which he regarded as being of such significance. He averred that it was only through her that he had become a complete philosopher, since before he had known her he had lacked that grand passion through which alone one could truly get to know the emotional side of human life. Now, when he had come to understand that feeling is as important as intellect, if indeed not of even greater consequence, he was able to confess to Clotilde that fundamentally it was she who had completed and perfected the doctrine of positivism. But, although she was already mortally ill, he still stood in fear of her literary career, and again and again he begged her to emancipate herself and to do so with his and only with his help. 'Dare, Clotilde, dare once and for all, with my help to be wholly yourself!'[25]

Clotilde lived only a few doors from her parents. On 2 April 1846 her family sent for a priest to administer the last sacraments: for, her emancipation from theology notwithstanding, she preserved, as Comte did, a profound respect for the rites of the Catholic faith. The day was her thirty-first birthday. In front of witnesses she bequeathed to Comte the letters he had written to her and the unfinished manuscript of *Willelmine*. Comte and the members of the Marie family crowded around Clotilde, disputing with one another their right to be present at the death bed: though in agony, Clotilde had several times to try to calm down the ever renewed quarrelling. Beside himself with grief, Comte wanted to prevent anyone from being admitted to her; and when he even sought to give orders to the doctor treating her it was only by the use of force that the latter was able to bring Clotilde's father to his daughter's bedside. On 5 April, the day Clotilde died, the room was in a state of complete pandemonium. As she lay in a coma the struggle to attend at her bed resumed more vigorously than ever: it ended with Comte and his maidservant, Sophie, who had long tended Clotilde, bolting themselves in her room and, despite all attempts by her family to force an entry, opening the door again only when Clotilde was already dead.

Enchanting and improving mankind

Comte's affair with Clotilde de Vaux represents a bizarre episode in the history of the social sciences. Neatly bundled and scrupulously

---

[25] Comte to Clotilde de Vaux, 11 March 1846; *Correspondance*, Vol. 3, p. 356.

numbered, their letters to one another are today preserved in Comte's house, 10, Rue Monsieur-le-Prince: one cannot see them without being moved, but one has occasionally to shake one's head when one reads them – those of Comte especially, for the *esprit de système* never deserted him even as a lover. In the end every commonplace event that occurred in his incomparable year with Clotilde took on a religious significance.

The religion of humanity and the rites with which Clotilde was and is venerated have now but few adherents. The paintings, mostly by Brazilian artists, depicting episodes from the incomparable year are rarely of that pure naivety that silences criticism: frequently, indeed, they overstep the borders of *Kitsch*. The same applies to the monument to Comte and Clotilde that stands in the Place de la Sorbonne in Paris. While Comte's apartments, beautifully preserved and lovingly tended, are today not only a place of remembrance but also a centre of research, very few know Clotilde's house in the rue Payenne close to the Musée Carnavalet: those who turn into this street are usually looking for the Square George-Cain, with its little enchanted garden, and ignore the Temple of Humanity on the left. Moreover, as we know today from documents in the local land-registry office, the positivists of Brazil and Liverpool purchased and renovated the wrong house: 5, rue Payenne, Clotilde lived in the building next to the present temple, 7, rue Payenne: it has long since been demolished.

And yet to relapse into irony would, as Raymond Aron wrote fifty years ago, be the greatest error a biographer of Auguste Comte could commit. Comte was a self-willed but not a comical figure, and Clotilde, though a mediocre writer at best, was a psychologist of everyday life of an unequalled sensibility. Comte's love affair, which remained as ascetic as the romances of his beloved troubadours, brought about a decisive change in the positivist doctrine: later it led Comte's successors to divide into two separate strands, which at the end of the nineteenth century were involved in a bitter conflict with one another.

Two weeks after Clotilde's death Comte resumed work on his *Système*. The time of private passions was now past: henceforth he would, 'in noble melancholy',[26] concentrate wholly on completing his work. For many long years he had had to compensate for his domestic troubles – his failed marriage to Caroline Massin, his delay in separating from her, his increasing estrangement from his parents

[26] Comte to Lenoir, 22 April 1846; *Correspondance*, Vol. 3, p. 374.

– with his work: it was only his year with Clotilde that had shown him
that public and private life were not necessarily antithetical, that
each could permeate and enhance the other. Clotilde, whose literary
career had ended so abruptly, had been destined to become his
'worthy colleague':[27] in them science and poetry would have
become one.

Since the end of the Middle Ages the mind had in Europe exercised
an extraordinarily productive hegemony; now the heart was to
receive its due – a correction to which Comte intended to devote the
second half of his career. Here, too, he would let himself be led by
Clotilde, who had felt what positivism meant without having had to
study it.

Among those who had castigated Comte's style was his English
translator, G. H. Lewes, who was working on a biography of Goethe:
his sentences were as a rule too long and contained too much verbal
repetition, many of the adverbs and epithets he employed were
superfluous, too many *rappels* and *anticipations* succeeded one
another. As though alarmed at his own temerity in criticizing Comte,
Lewes hastened to add that, being a writer, he was prejudiced in the
matter, and that he had no intention whatever of asserting the
priority of a pleasing style over the importance of truly great ideas.
He was certainly not suggesting that Comte should squander his
time in polishing sentences: the '*labor lineae*'[28] was the task, not of the
scientist, but of the man of letters, and he would be prepared and
happy to relieve Comte of it. His style was in any case very easy to
improve; up to now its relatively trifling defects had done nothing to
impair the persuasive power of the ideas of positivism.

Twenty years previously Comte had reacted angrily to a similar,
though perhaps not quite so flattering, letter from Valat: this time
he expressed his gratitude for the well-meant advice and promised to
follow it whenever the character of his work permitted. He realized
he needed a literary critique and what advantages he would gain from
it: in future he would make an effort to write better.

Such readers and counsellors as Lewes now became more and
more important to Comte, who was enraptured to learn that Lewes
saw in Goethe a precursor of positivism, just as he himself had seen
one in Molière. Again he expressed a wish to learn German: once
more he intended to do so with the aid of a '*beau Goethe*'[29] and a little

---

[27] Comte to John Stuart Mill, 6 May 1846; *Correspondance* (Paris: Mouton, 1981),
Vol. 4, p. 6.
[28] G. H. Lewes to Comte, 20 February 1847; *Correspondance*, Vol. 4, p. 241.
[29] Comte to G. H. Lewes, 2 April 1847; *Correspondance*, Vol. 4, p. 112.

dictionary – this time, however, not so as to settle his intellectual debt to German philosophy but in order to perfect his knowledge of Western art and literature. The *Bibliothèque positiviste au dix-neuvième siècle*, whose 150 volumes include thirty belonging to the realm of *belles-lettres*, is as eloquent a witness to the growing significance accorded to literature as is Comte's detailed advice to Jacquemin, a literate workman who had asked the master for guidance for his book-hungry sister. The *Bibliothèque* was, to be sure, also a kind of positive index which indicated what the true positivist ought to read: as the social significance of literature increased, so too did the need for a critique. The rules of cerebral hygiene were still in force.

The reading of the great works of literature passed by the positivist censor was now no longer limited to the objective of relieving the philosopher of the toil of scientific productivity: the true poets furnished rather an uncommonly weighty '*condensation philosophique*';[30] provided one was in possession of a sociological theory, as Comte was, the fundamental nature of an epoch could best be inferred from its literary masterpieces.

Scientific and artistic careers were equally valid, and such men as Lewes had to be admired for knowing how to unite the two. John Stuart Mill, on the other hand, declined more and more in Comte's estimation: at bottom he had remained a metaphysician who, though attracted by the intellectual values of positivism, had never recognized its true social significance. With him positivism had in fact become as arid as its enemies said it was. Mill had plundered Comte in order to embellish his *logic*, just as Cousin had once read Hegel so as to rejuvenate himself. The English in general sought to confine positivism to its intellectual content: they wished to know nothing of its affective side. Mill became for Comte a half-hearted and thus unreliable and dangerous adherent.

Among the ablest defenders of Comte in England was his subsequent translator J. H. Bridges. If his assertion was correct that what Comte had wanted to say in his *Synthèse subjective* was nothing other than what Wordsworth had said in his *Ode on Immortality* or Shelley in his *Prometheus Unbound*, then Mill's critique of Comte was in fact dishonest, for Wordsworth and Shelley were among the poets to whose works Mill had devoted himself after his physical crisis of 1826, and since this time Mill too had never ceased to advocate a union of feeling and understanding.

---

[30] Report by Pierre Laffitte of a conversation with Comte; *Correspondance*, Vol. 4, p. 221.

The completed *Système de politique positive, ou traité de sociologie, instituant la religion de l'humanité* is, as its title alone reveals, a kind of memorial to Clotilde. The quotation from Alfred de Vigny which Comte reproduces in the foreword – 'What is a great life? An idea of youth which in maturity becomes actuality' – lends to the course of his life and to his intellectual development a consistency which neither possessed. Comte explained the fact that, while in the *Cours* the mind rules, in the *Système* the heart is dominant, by saying that his initial objective had been to prove the intellectual superiority of positivism over all systems of theology, while what he had subsequently to do was to demonstrate the moral excellence of the only true religion. But whether one sees in Comte's later writings the natural completion of positivism, which is what he himself and his faithful adherents proclaimed them to be, or deplores them, as the positivist dissidents do, as a defection from the great and true conceptions with which he began – all of this was far less the planned outcome of theoretical reflections than the unforeseen consequence of a profound life-crisis.

When he published the first volume of the *Système* in 1851, Comte apologized for having devoted insufficient attention to perfecting the work's literary form. The reason, he said, was lack of time: to have gone through the book and revised it again would have demanded another six years' labour. He thus guarded himself against renewed reproaches on the part of the literary men; not the least of the reasons he incorporated some of his early writings into the *Système* was to demonstrate to his critics that he could write well if only he had sufficient time. More important, however, than the question whether his later works are or are not better written than many of his earlier ones is the fact that Comte now accepted that the question of style was not without its significance: he admitted that philosophical ideas could gain greatly in persuasiveness if one bestowed upon them, if not an elegant, at least an appropriate form of linguistic expression. He undertook to revise his book again from the point of view of its style provided his retirement gave him the opportunity.

The greatest acquisition that positivism perfected would offer to everyone, a 'holy harmony between private and public life'[31], Comte himself had been permitted to enjoy already. Three admirable women had brought this about: his mother, Rosalie Boyer; his maid-servant, Sophie Bliot, the 'significant proletarian';[32] and finally

---

[31] Comte, *Système de politique positive, ou traité de sociologie, instituant la religion de l'humanité* (Paris: L. Matthias, 1851), Vol. 1, p. 10. [32] *Ibid.*, p. 12.

Clotilde de Vaux. With their help his aesthetic inclinations had been able to develop without coming into conflict with his scientific mission. The aesthetics of positivism, which Comte was to exhibit for the first time in the *Système*, were connected with his new attitude towards the feminist question; if, therefore, he had incorporated in his book Clotilde's *Lucie*, her canzone and his letter on the *commémoration sociale*, this was not merely an act of piety: his intention was to offer a demonstration of that union of aesthetic and scientific interests that was henceforth to characterize positivism. Only positivism was capable of furnishing a universally valid theory of the fine arts; the poetic ideal would hereafter assume the role of mediator between the philosophical idea and the political act, and would thereby open up to modern art and literature undreamed-of possibilities.

Comte campaigned tirelessly to prevent this new philosophy, which accorded so great a significance to art and literature, from being confused with its science-dominated preamble. Hitherto scientists – and Comte did not exclude himself – had been justly reproached for the aridity that characterized their writings, an aridity that was connected with the unhealthy specialization that had characterized former ages; now the epoch of synthesis had dawned, an age of solidarity between philosophers, women and the proletariat, who would demonstrate in their temples, salons and clubs the unity of the positivist doctrine. This social solidarity was the most important precondition of a new impetus for and elevation of art.

Women in whom physical, intellectual and moral beauty had together become incarnate would be the guardians of art. Yet Comte cautioned against burdening the arts with expectations they could not fulfil. It was not least the unhappy role played in the French Revolution by politicizing men of letters that determined Comte in future to keep the poets at a distance from politics: philosophers were incapable of action but at best suited to offering political counsel; neither activity was the business of poets. When artists presumed to the office of regulators of society they gambled away the only true vocation of art, 'to enchant and improve mankind'.[33] Science analysed reality, art beautified it: it brought the theoretician's highly abstract reflections closer to reality, it encouraged the practical man occasionally to leave reality behind and become speculative. It was only the positivists who had come to recognize

[33] *Ibid.*, p. 280.

the extent to which the poets anticipated the discoveries of science. Cervantes had, in his admirable *Don Quixote*, sketched out the true nature of insanity long before any biologist had done so: with profound insight he had described how our emotions influence our perceptions. It was the moral task of art, and above all of literature, to mediate between affect and rationality.

Within the positivist sociocracy the utopianists, whom Comte had hitherto been inclined to condemn as apostates, would also be entrusted with a weighty task. A new genre would come into being: sociologically inspired poetry in whose mirror the nations of the West would see a reflection of their future. The task of the high priest of humanity would be to unite in himself systematic reason, poetical enthusiasm, womanly sympathy and proletarian energy; if he should live as long as Fontenelle or Voltaire his later work would be dedicated wholly to poetry and art. A positivist had in general to devote a part of every day to poetry and to read at least one canto of Dante.

Comte, who recognized no contemporary peers but was always on the lookout for predecessors, identified the poets in whose works the realization of the positivist ideal had already announced itself: those 'thirteen truly great poets'[34] whose long line extended from Homer to Walter Scott. But it was significant that he saw the truly exemplary union of the scientific and the artistic spirit anticipated in that scholar whose later reputation was so greatly injured by precisely this combination: Buffon. The great Buffon embodied for Comte the indivisibility of every true theoretical culture; his work was immortal. Buffon was the first and greatest representative of the modern age, a scientist who had come as close to positivism as it was possible to come in an age without sociology.

Auguste Comte and the political right in France

Among the opponents who mocked at the later Comte was Friedrich Nietzsche, who, repelled by the 'eternal-womanly' (*Ewig-Weibliche*) of his writings that only Frenchmen and Wagnerians could endure, read him with repugnance. Viewing him from his own self-willed perspective, Nietzsche saw in Comte, who had none the less been an enemy of the *philosophes*, a continuation of the eighteenth century, that is to say 'domination of *la tête* by the *coeur*, sensualism in epis-

---

[34] Comte, *Catéchisme positiviste* (1852), chronologie, introduction et notes par Pierre Arnaud (Paris: Garnier-Flammarion, 1966), p. 169.

temology, altruistic ecstaticism'.[35] Comte, who had allowed himself to be lauded as the founder of altruism, had with his formula *vivre pour autrui* outchristianed Christianity; he was nothing but a Jesuit 'who wanted to lead his Frenchmen to Rome via the *détour* of science'.[36] In the end he became 'priestly and poetic',[37] a gardener and fruit-grower who now desired to enjoy the produce of his own earlier labours only in easily palatable form – the most frightful of all examples of the fate that threatened the philosopher in his old age:

And so it happens that the aged thinker appears to elevate himself above the work of his life, though in reality he ruins it through infusing it with enthusiasms, sweetness, spices, poetic mists and mystic lights. This is what happened in the end to Plato, this is what happened in the end to that great honest Frenchman beside whom, as embracer and conqueror of the strict sciences, the Germans and English of this century can place no rival, Auguste Comte.[38]

As the anti-sociologist Nietzsche argued, so did those who had learned scientific positivism from Comte himself and now regarded it as their duty to defend the earlier, scientific Comte against the later, religio-literary Comte. Many republicans were positivists; Gambetta and Jules Ferry were strongly influenced by Comte. The Comte of the republicans, however, was as a rule the earlier, scientific Comte, and the aberrations of his old age showed that positivism was by no means a finished doctrine: according to Littré sociology was something that still had to be created. The Société de Sociologie, founded in 1872, honoured Darwin and Wundt, but its model was above all Spencer, a kind of Comte who had stayed true to himself, a sociologist who had preserved his discipline from contamination by religions of humanity and other obscuranticisms. Emile Durkheim, too, allied himself with the earlier Comte, and even if he did reproach him with exaggerated intellectuality he was at no time in danger of adhering to the later Comte.

By way of compensation, Comte discovered disciples in a political grouping which at the turn of the century stood in fanatical opposition to the sociology of Durkheim and to its influence in the New

[35] Friedrich Nietzsche, *Nachgelassene Fragmente* [1887], *Sämtliche Werke: Kritische Studienausgabe in 15 Bänden*, ed. Giorgio Colli and Mazzino Montinari (München: Deutscher Taschenbuch Verlag, 1980), Vol. 12, p. 441.

[36] Nietzsche, *Götzendämmerung* [1889], *Kritische Studienausgabe*, Vol. 6, p. 113.

[37] Nietzsche, *Reinschrift zur Morgenröthe* [1881], *Kritische Studienausgabe*, Vol. 14, p. 226.

[38] Nietzsche, *Morgenröthe* [1881], *Kritische Studienausgabe*, Vol. 3, p. 311.

Sorbonne. In 1905, Henri Vaugeois and Charles Maurras founded the Institut de l'Action Française. What the universities of the Third Republic had suppressed was here to be propagated: Catholicism, the positive polity of Auguste Comte and the doctrines of a Fustel de Coulanges. The first director of the institute was Louis Dimier, who had taught rhetoric and classical languages at the Institut Catholique, and among its sympathizers was Monseigneur de Cabrières, a bishop and afterwards cardinal from Comte's home town of Montpellier.

A chair of positive philosophy was established at the institute and named after Auguste Comte: its first occupant was Count Léon de Montesquiou-Fezensac, an early adherent of the Action Française who was to become a tireless propagator of Comte. Montesquiou was not only impressed by positive philosophy and polity; he revered Comte the man with a religious fervour, and the little notebook in which he had inscribed extracts he had made from Comte's later work he called his '*livre de prières*'.[39] He admired Clotilde de Vaux no less than he did Comte. But he was among the most impressive speakers of the Action Française, and his reverence for Comte did not blind him to the fact that Comte's style had deterred a larger public from reading him: he therefore exerted himself, in lectures and publications, to make Comte's ideas comprehensible to the average reader. In 1910 he was elected to the committee that administered Comte's posthumous papers.

To the political right in France Comte's teaching became an *idée directrice*. It was more than merely a matter of political theory: the later, Catholic, literary Comte was accorded an admiration amounting to reverence.

To the Action Française and its sympathizers Comte was one of those social scientists whose work could be seen as a solitary protest against the French Revolution and its consequences. He was among the heroes of the counter-revolution, a sworn enemy of the literary men who believed that, with the *Contrat Social* in their heads, they were able to pursue a politics of theoretical precepts in opposition to a politics of practical experience. On the other hand, Comte's significance lay precisely in his desire to unite in his work the enthusiasm of poetry and the severity of reason. It was true that, in contrast to the misled Romantics, he demanded of poetry only that it should enchant; he denied it the right to be the leading-string of

[39] M. Coudekerque-Lambrecht, *Léon de Montesquiou: Sa vie politique* (Paris: L'Action Française, Nouvelle Librairie Nationale, 1925), p. 174.

society. One could, indeed must, follow him along this path if one was to abolish the confusion produced in the heads of the younger generation by the cold sociology of Durkheim and its prophets. In the period just before the outbreak of the First World War the aesthetic maxims of positivism were to serve as a guide to French artists and writers in an age of intellectual anarchy.

Nietzsche can hardly have had Clotilde de Vaux in mind when he spoke of the 'literature-woman'[40] faced with the alternative *aut liberi aut libri* – yet she does indeed make one think of the authoress of *Lucie* and *Willelmine*. At first sight it would seem that Comte's relationship to Clotilde de Vaux must endanger his standing with the political right: feminism and far-reaching proposals for the emancipation of women were not exactly a feature of Action Française ideology, and in these circles the *femme de lettres* was regarded as the 'ugliest monstrosity the earth is capable of producing'.[41] When Mme de Noailles ventured to seek a place in the Académie Française, Vaugeois, consumed with rage, called her a 'paragon of ugliness and absurdity'.[42] One could value the feminine traits in poetry, but one must never forget that for their full unfolding they required male knowledge and male wisdom. Woman should above all provide inspiration and leave initiative and action to man; exceptions to this rule were those *Grandes Dames de France* whose most prominent representative had been Jeanne d'Arc. In opposition to the detestable *femme de lettres* there stood the *femme d'esprit*, who wrote in the classical style and exerted charm as an authoress who had still remained a woman. Mme de Staël and George Sand were *femmes de lettres*, Mme de Sévigné and Mme de Lafayette were *femmes d'esprit*: Clotilde de Vaux counted among the latter. It was not to be forgotten, moreover, that the love between Comte and Clotilde had been no romantic passion: moderation, not excess, had characterized the philosopher's relationship with his muse. It was a classical love that recalled not Musset but Corneille.

Their admiration for Auguste Comte was what, all the differences between them notwithstanding, united Maurice Barrès and Charles Maurras. Barrès considered the intelligence a surface phenomenon: in spite of all his rationalization man remained at bottom an affective being. Precisely this had been the teaching of the later Comte. Like

---

[40] Nietzsche, *Nachgelassene Fragmente* [1887 to 1889], *Kritische Studienausgabe*, Vol. 13, p. 29.
[41] Colette Capitan Peter, *Charles Maurras et l'idéologie d'Action Française: Etude sociologique d'une pensée de droite* (Paris: Editions du Seuil, 1972), p. 120.   [42] *Ibid.*, p. 121.

him, Barrès followed a leading idea of Thomas à Kempis: to feel as intensely as possible while analysing as minutely as possible. Barrès counted Comte among his gods because the latter had turned against parliamentarianism, a system of intrigue and corruption in which tyranny was everywhere and responsibility nowhere; and Comte was also Barrès' chief witness for the contention that if French nationalism was to be kept alive and strong it must be through an alliance between the Catholics and the positivists.

In the case of Charles Maurras, admiration for Comte assumed – the many doubts he harboured notwithstanding – hymnic qualities. Himself from Provence, Maurras loved in Comte one of the characteristics of the Provençal: a profound sense of the seriousness of life. The same applied to the idea of regionalism, an idea propagated by Maurras and Barrès, who was from Lorraine, employing as authorities not only Comte but also such Catholic sociologists as Le Play and the Marquis de la Tour du Pin. Maurras has described in his memoirs the contention which he, a devoted admirer of Mistral, was involved in at the Société des Félibres in Paris, where he had to defend Comte's federalist ideas against the attacks of Pierre Laffitte, whom he had mistakenly believed to be a true positivist. He had to listen horrified as Laffitte laid bare Comte's supposed errors: 'The ceiling did not fall, nor did the chandeliers go out.'[43] Excluded from the society, Maurras finally founded his own Ecole Parisienne du Félibrige.

The work of the later Comte became for Maurras the touchstone by which a mind declared its quality. An Edmond de Goncourt, who had mocked at it, was no longer to be taken seriously. In the Bibliothèque Nationale there was a copy of the *Système de politique positive* in which Taine had on an early page scribbled a revealing note: he was, it said, simply incapable of continuing the wearying reading. Whether he had done this out of laziness or from ill will, Taine had in either case paid with his subsequent intellectual decline for his unwillingness to understand one of the few philosophers who still philosophized with his whole heart and soul and whose talent had enabled him to produce that which as a rule only a poet could achieve: a gay science.

Without being obliged to share Taine's opinion, the present-day reader none the less finds it hard to discover in Comte's *Système* the beauty and gaiety that Maurras believed he had found there. Maurras

---

[43] Charles Maurras, *Au Signe de Flore: Souvenirs de vie politique* (Paris: Les Oeuvres Représentatives, 1931), p. 35.

created out of Comte a stylized hero: in his death mask he beheld the lineaments of both Napoleon and Baudelaire. Without being involved in the cabals of the rival positivist groups, unable to boast of any profound religiousness in himself, Maurras wrote of Comte as a disciple writes of his master.

Comte's Latin blood protected him against the anarchic aberrations of political liberalism and against that Protestantism in which continual self-examination never led to a definitive verdict. In Comte the nostalgia of the Catholic alienated from his faith became productive: if one had lost God, one longed all the more to discover order in one's thoughts, in life and in society. Everyone needed a dogma, but a dogma that he could love: so that positivism, a word possessing so frightful a sound to so many, was for the initiated an expression of 'gentleness, tenderness, constancy and incomparable certainties'.[44] Following the path indicated by de Maistre and de Bonald, Comte became the theoretician of practice who repudiated theory for the sake of theory as a sign of academic degeneration. Transported by exalted truths, he had inscribed sentences that could be set beside those of a Virgil or a Corneille.

Such were the dithyrambs Maurras penned on Comte. They are the more impressive when we remember what a good hater and terrifying polemicist this man was. But even if Maurras found his attachment to Comte useful to him politically, it was none the less genuine; and whether or not his account is faithful historically, he certainly depicted Comte as Comte himself had wanted to be remembered:

When quietly at work at night, the mind, overcome by weariness, is sometimes plunged into perplexity and confusion. The pen falls from the hand and the flow of ideas ceases. One rises, one shakes off the stiffness caused by immobility; but neither a walk nor bodily refreshment can restore to the mind its lost assurance; it now needs a support that is likewise of the nature of mind and can move it with images worthy of it. This is not the moment to seek refuge with the poets or to open any kind of learned book; pure science would at that moment seem too cold, poetry would engender only a tremendous emptiness. I count the men of my generation fortunate who, without being positivists in the narrower sense, are in such a situation able to call to mind the moral and logical writings of Auguste Comte.[45]

Like a bond the doctrines of the later Comte held them together: Maurras, Barrès, Dimier and Lasserre, and Charles Péguy too, who

[44] Maurras, *Romantisme et révolution* (Paris: Nouvelle Librairie Nationale, 1922), p. 93.   [45] *Ibid.*, p. 91.

liked to quote Clotilde de Vaux. In their struggle against Durkheim and the sociology of the New Sorbonne, these royalists and republicans, socialists and reactionaries, atheists and Catholics persisted in the assertion that there existed a legitimate sociology serving the national interests of France: the sociology of their Comte. Living in an age in which, for good or ill, their political ideology compelled them to become sociologists, these men of letters directed all their affections to Comte, the sociologist who had of his own free will become a poet.

To view Auguste Comte's house in the rue Monsieur-le-Prince is not an easy task. In the concierge's window on the ground floor there hangs a notice informing the visitor that if he wishes to proceed further he must obtain the written permission of the president of the Positivist Society, who is as a rule a Brazilian academic currently residing in his own country. By the time this written permission arrives one is on the point of leaving Paris. If one is lucky, however, and has been able to get into the house, one is taken aback at how completely the spirit of Comte continues to dwell there. That serious life, in which fame was always attended by suffering, is palpably present. The egoism of Comte is painfully evident. In his will he decreed that his house was to be kept exactly as he had left it: his desk, the visitor is assured, still stands where it stood when Comte used it, namely against a wall; upon this wall, occupying the entire width of the table, there hangs a mirror. When he sat and wrote Auguste Comte was always looking at himself.

◁ ══════════════════════════════ ═══ ▷

2

Agathon and others: literature and sociology in France at the turn of the century

The attack on the New Sorbonne

The French Third Republic began with the suppression of the Commune. It was an epoch in which – as one of its greatest fanatics, Charles Maurras, put it – the French did not like themselves, the age of the Panama scandal and the Dreyfus affair, the age in which sociology made itself at home at the Sorbonne.

Three monuments reveal to us even today the extent of the transformation that took place there at the turn of the century: within the university the statues of Victor Hugo and Louis Pasteur dominate the entry court, while outside it the Place de la Sorbonne contains that of Auguste Comte. With the aid of donations it was erected there in 1902, the year in which Emile Durkheim, who had already been professor of the social sciences at Bordeaux, came to the Sorbonne. Literature and the sciences were firmly installed within the university; sociology on the other hand had to fight its way in from outside.

To the enemies of Durkheim, however, it was not the ancient venerable Sorbonne which had admitted sociology – it was merely the 'Nouvelle Sorbonne', a university which the republicans had radically altered, into which this pseudo-science had penetrated. Under a massive literacy campaign directed by Jules Ferry attendance at elementary school had become obligatory in the Third Republic, elementary instruction in state institutions free. The anticlericalism that was official policy had also set its stamp on the reform of the universities: science was to replace religion, moral philosophy was to replace metaphysics. As faithful pupils of Comte the republicans seemed to be doing everything they could to make his law of the three stages of human evolution correspond to reality. In this endeavour sociology played a decisive role; and those who attacked it were not least those who also attacked the Republic.

This campaign attained a high point in a series of articles which, appearing under the pseudonym 'Agathon' in the *Opinion* from the summer of 1910, in March the following year was published as a brochure by the Mercure de France with the title *L'Esprit de la Nouvelle Sorbonne*. It was one of the many rearguard battles fought in the wake of the Dreyfus affair – though it was by now four years since Alfred Dreyfus had been not merely rehabilitated but made a member of the Legion of Honour. The old war-fronts had not changed in principle: at the most they had been straightened out. The subjects of contention were still the same. In Agathon's pamphlets a certain group of the literary intelligentsia directed their attack against the *parti intellectuel*, against the New Sorbonne, and against sociology, that *nouveau riche* discipline which, through nepotism and by promising to serve the republicans as a fountain of ideology, had not only gained surreptitious entry into the university but had become a decidedly fashionable department of study: as one of its critics complained, you could no longer visit a charitable institution or a night-shelter without becoming involved in a discussion of sociology.

The reform of the university was undertaken on ideological as well as practical grounds. The natural sciences – the modern Humaniora – were henceforth to take over the task of education more completely than had hitherto been usual in France, and to promote the democratization not only of the university but of society as a whole: in this programme the enemies of the Republic saw an attack on the classical culture of France, whose intellectual capital, accumulated over long ages, was in danger of being frittered away by the reform-obsessed republicans. If every discipline had to adopt the methods of science, or at least imitate them, history threatened to degenerate into philological exegesis, philosophy into sociology. If a student proposed to his professor that he should study Spinoza, the professor would insist that the work he did must be free of all interpretation:

Under the influence of M. Durkheim sociology is content to assemble facts, to accumulate patient observations, among which the customs of savages occupy pride of place. Morality, now called more learnedly the science of custom, is now no more than a branch of historical sociology.[1]

The arts, the study of which once shaped the taste and intelligence of anyone who wanted to cultivate himself into an *honnête homme*, had fallen under the dictatorship of a historical method that was debasing

[1] Agathon, *L'Esprit de la Nouvelle Sorbonne* (Paris: Mercure de France, 1911), p. 27.

it to the collecting of documents. The task of the study of literature was suddenly no longer the interpretation of great works of literature as time-defying aids to life and thus also as interpreters of the present: it had to confine itself to understanding these works in their historical context. Renan had to share responsibility for this relativism: he had declared that everyone had to admire Pascal's *Pensées* and the sermons of Bossuet, but only as masterpieces of the seventeenth century; if they appeared today they would be unworthy of attention. And Renan prophesied that in future the study of literary history would increasingly replace the reading of works of literature themselves; was it an accident that the great critic Lanson conformed to this prophecy in the very lecture on 'Literary History and Sociology' that he delivered at Emile Durkheim's invitation at the Ecole des Hautes Etudes Sociales in the year 1904?

We critics resemble Monsieur Jourdain: we produce prose, i.e. sociology, without realizing it... We must do in literature what has already taken place in the science of history, namely replace systematic philosophy with an inductive sociology... Let us produce an objective, good sociology founded on observation, for if we do not produce a good sociology of our own free will we shall be compelled to produce a bad one.[2]

Agathon did not want to be misunderstood: he was not advocating a return to that kind of literary study which had characterized the Sorbonne at the beginning of the nineteenth century and which had been nothing more than empty rhetoric and criticism at second or even third hand. A century later, however, this disorderly discipline had already been sufficiently enfeebled, and a reform was devoid of all proportion if it forgot that the primary purpose of works of art was to bring us into touch with art, not with grammar or lexicology.

Nothing characterized the scientific excess of the New Sorbonne more than its obsession with questions of method: it was the reformer's favourite catchword. The beginner in every field of study had first to take in hand methodological treatises which in their aridity and the ponderous pedanticism of their style were a match for any German textbook. The most curious example of this was once again furnished by Emile Durkheim: through his *Règles de la méthode sociologique*, which was full of metaphysics, philosophers were introduced to a sociology founded on the axiom, as astonishing as it

---

[2] Gustave Lanson, 'L'Histoire littéraire et la sociologie', *Revue de Métaphysique et de Morale* 12 (1904), pp. 626, 629.

was scandalous, that the 'facts of society' were something quite different from and wholly independent of the individuals that composed it. And Durkheim was not the least of those who had propelled the university into a scientific superstitiousness for whose attention no detail was too small. In earlier days there had been in the Sorbonne a room in which students could read classic authors whose works were obligatory reading. This room was originally called an *étude*: 'Today, however, so modest a name is no longer adequate to describe such estimable work as goes on in such a room. Nowadays it is called a *Laboratoire de philologie française*.'[3]

In these laboratories there ruled the cult of the card-index and the filing-cabinet. The students were so much in the grip of the passion for bibliography that in the end they no longer read Molière or Racine, or even Rousseau, but only critical catalogues of their sources and editions and of commentaries on them: the Sorbonne was coming more and more to resemble a restaurant in which the only thing to eat was the menu. Literature had become purely an exercise for improving the memory, no longer having anything whatever to do with educating the taste. Of science there was nothing left but a form of atrophy: the techniques of scientific labour. Why, Agathon asked, was it not realized that an historical work can be no better than the person who writes it? How had it come to be forgotten that science needs, not only stone-breakers and piece-workers, but above all original minds?

Whenever it was possible to do so Agathon seized on the utterances of Emile Durkheim, to justify, indeed to intensify, the trenchancy of his polemics; and the scientific ideal championed by Durkheim was in fact bound to alienate the enemies of the New Sorbonne. For sociology was a discipline whose progress depended less on cultivated individuals than on the cultivation of capable research groups; in this endeavour division of labour and co-operative undertakings were vital, as was the question of classification— a question of paramount importance to any discipline at the beginning of its development. It might even be that its classification of the facts of society was the only thing that would remain of sociology; the main task, however, was to strengthen the team at the expense of the individual:

Of all the services we can perform, the most important is that of showing there exist in sociology workers who are more concerned to come closer to

[3] Agathon, pp. 35–6.

one another so as to co-operate than to segregate themselves from one another so as to make themselves original.[4]

How completely Durkheim was here in accord with the republican *Zeitgeist* was demonstrated by an address given by Alfred Croiset, the dean of the faculty of philosophy, at the opening of the semester– an address that scandalized Agathon and his allies. For the dean saw the task of the university as no longer lying exclusively in the training of gifted men and amiable dilettantes: '*La France a besoin aussi de travailleurs.*'[5] It was only logical that university professors should compare themselves with brick-layers and wish to have nothing to do with art or literature.

Under the burden of useless erudition, however, which mediocre students were only too glad to saddle themselves with, Latin agility and clear-sightedness was perishing, as was the ability to think logically. Heads were gradually growing heavy, like German heads, and, as Maurice Barrès complained, the tired French brain was more and more losing its finesse. The sociological worker was to replace the original literary genius: this was the real scandal of the New Sorbonne.

To the defender of a classical education the very titles of Durkheim's books and the subjects he treated in them constituted a provocation: he wrote of the sociological normality of deviant behaviour, started from the position that all religions were in principle equal, and – impudently appealing to Descartes for support – emphasized again and again the significance of the correct employment of method. While the adherents of the Old Sorbonne bewailed the downfall of the creative individual in modern industrial society, Durkheim soberly maintained that original talent and a wholly personal sensibility had also been rare in earlier times. On the other hand, he saw precisely in division of labour a chance of rescue for the individual, for 'individual natures, while specializing, become more complex, and by that are in part freed from collective action and hereditary influences which can only enforce themselves upon simple, general things'.[6]

In the spirit of Durkheim, the adherents of the New Sorbonne opposed to the venerable ideal of general education their courses of specialized study whose objective was not to educate whole human

---

[4] Emile Durkheim to Célestin Bouglé, 13 August 1901; 'Textes inédits ou inconnus d'Emile Durkheim, réunis par Philippe Besnard', *Revue française de sociologie* 17 (1976), p. 178. [5] Agathon, p. 152.
[6] Durkheim, *On the Division of Labor in Society*, trans. George Simpson (New York: MacMillan, 1933), p. 404.

beings but merely to drill technicians. These latter had no need of a command of their mother tongue such as literature would inculcate: for the practice of their craft a command of a precise terminology was quite sufficient. The more instruction was directed to preparing for a trade, the more did the vocabulary of the factory penetrate into the university; not only was the study of the languages of antiquity being forced into the background, but French itself was increasingly losing its standing:

In the Sorbonne they now speak German, English, Russian, Hungarian and the dialects of Wallachia and Manchuria – to say nothing of the jargon only sociologists understand; on the other hand, apart from a few exceptions no one any longer writes good French.[7]

So completely had the sociologists and their jargon permeated the university that even the dean of a faculty of philosophy could make the soothing assertion that, while French composition had admittedly declined in elegance of late, it had by way of compensation gained in precision and directness.

This assertion was unheard-of; it could not be true. It went without saying that it was not only an author's style that betrayed something of his character; the truth-content of what he said did so too. To make a distinction between elegance and precision was profoundly un-French, so that the director of the Ecole des Sciences Politiques, Anatole Leroy-Beaulieu, was more to be trusted when he said that an inquiry had established that the French his students wrote was declining in both elegance and precision. Those who knew Buffon and Rivarol had foreseen such a development. The French language was bound to experience a crisis as the Third Republic led France into an epoch of decadence: national decline and the decay of language went hand in hand.

Agathon recalled Ernest Renan's malicious observation that it would be seen as barbarous to deprive the simple university worker of the innocent delight *paperasser* affords. In the age of democratization a scholar could acquire a reputation very cheaply: all he had to do was to rummage in documents, draw up dossiers, arrange index-cards and conscientiously produce bibliographies of bibliographies. Though he was partly to blame for the decadence of the sciences under the rule of the republicans, Renan had none the less never gone so far as to deny the importance for historiography and the moral sciences of their mode of presentation: it was time,

[7] Agathon, p. 282.

Agathon declared, to reassert in the university the claims of the art of writing, which was after all nothing other than the art of thinking made visible, and to defend a general and philosophical culture against the cult of specialization. A respect for good breeding, and not command of a jargon comprehended only by initiates, was the mark of a truly democratic disposition. Voltaire's *Lettres philosophiques* still spoke to every educated person, their aim was to persuade and instruct; Lanson's edition of them, on the other hand, was accessible only to a handful of specialists, Voltaire's educative intentions having thereby been thwarted. Thus a philosophy which pretended 'to be democratic has become aristocratic through what it has produced'.[8]

Naturally, in the university too it was necessary to work – to work on style. Such work embodied a high social virtue, for only well-written works could reach the larger public. To forget this was particularly absurd in an age in which even the Germans were beginning to feel the detrimental consequences of specialization and Theodor Wolff was, in the *Berliner Tageblatt*, bewailing the decline of the essay in German science. The Germans could, if they wanted to, retain that ponderousness of expression to which their nature corresponded – the prestige of the French mind demanded they insist on the importance of the question of style and cling to the advantage of their traditional literary culture.

The republican politicians who were reforming the Sorbonne were well aware that, if the object was to transform students into educated adherents of democracy, the training up of specialists was not enough: the republic needed a doctrine. One discipline above all seemed in a position to furnish this doctrine: the sociology of Emile Durkheim. In the Ministry of Education, so Agathon reported, Durkheim exercised considerable influence; at the New Sorbonne he had long been a kind of prefect of studies, a regent and sole ruler beneath whose rod the faculty of philosophy did as it was told. Nor did Durkheim confine his ambitions to sociology: he also taught pedagogy, and his course in this subject was the only one at the Sorbonne at which attendance was obligatory for all teaching-students. Durkheim concentrated first and foremost on the history of pedagogy, so as to repudiate once and for all the traditional maxims and methods of education. He knew what the new regime had need of: 'Let us set to work and in three years we shall have a morality.'[9]

The Third Republic was a republic of professors and teachers, and, since Durkheim's sociology was preached in the teachers' seminars as though it were a theology, the Republic was threatening to become a republic of sociologists as well. It was thus not without good reason that Albert Thibaudet had compared it to the Czech republic of Tomas Masaryk, who was a sociologist and whose book *Suicide as a Social Mass Phenomenon* Durkheim had quoted.

In earlier times philosophy had dominated the university; now the individual disciplines had taken its place. At the summit stood sociology: it was impossible to examine this discipline too closely, for it was the key-science of the New Sorbonne and therewith of the Third Republic. A mystique of the collective and the environment was gaining ground which banished man from the humanities and the masterpiece from literature. Lanson was nothing more than an accomplice of Durkheim's who despised the heart and the feelings as lower segments of ourselves and revered in the world only that which was 'as vague, monstrous, tyrannical, incomprehensible and cruel as the god of the Jews, the social being . . .'[10]

Agathon found enthusiastic supporters. Among them was Charles Maurras, who had published a series of articles under the same pseudonym in Larousse's *Revue encyclopédique*. Barrès was more restrained in his praise: he was disturbed at the arrogance of an attack on the New Sorbonne which ignored the shortcomings of the old university. Georges Sorel felt that Agathon's campaign was imprudent: it would strengthen the determination of the Sorbonne to adhere to its course rather than otherwise. The writer's naivety was revealed in the astonishment he evinced at the behaviour of the professors: Agathon had not understood that an oligarchy of the educated must necessarily arise in a republic, and that scholars then had no more fervent desire than to play the clowns in the circus of human rights.

The Sorbonne rose in uproar: its highest dignitaries replied to the polemic, open letters were exchanged, the Chamber and the Senate had to discuss Agathon's charges. Since the author was extremely well-informed, and could even report on what went on at sittings of the university's council, he must belong to the inner circle of the Sorbonne. A campaign on the largest scale seemed to be in preparation, in which the bourgeoisie was going to attempt to regain some of the political territory it had lost in the education system.

In truth, however, the authors – for two writers were involved – were hardly older than most of those whom they attacked. Alfred de

---

[10] *Ibid.*, p. 112.

Tarde had been a lawyer before he had settled down in Arcachon to write a novel. Henri Massis, a writer by profession, had made his debut with a study of Zola's working methods. When the two met for the first time in the spring of 1910 Tarde congratulated Massis on an article he had just published in the *Paris-Journal* under the title 'Let us defend ourselves against German culture!' Although he did not know the Sorbonne as well as Massis, Tarde agreed with the younger man: his critique of Durkheim's sociology and its dangerous influence on the policies of the university seemed to him of great significance. It was a problem with which he was already familiar through the works of his father.

A rival of Durkheim: Gabriel Tarde as novelist

At the turn of the century Gabriel Tarde contested with René Worms and Emile Durkheim the domination of French sociology. Born at Sarlat, in Périgord, in 1843, he was still a magistrate in his home town when he wrote the book that was to become his principal work of sociology: *Les Lois de l'imitation* (1890) – a key to fit every lock, as Taine remarked in his ambiguous commendation of it. In 1894 Tarde became the head of the department of legal statistics at the Ministry of Justice in Paris; six years later he was appointed to the chair of modern philosophy at the Collège de France.

Tarde's sociology was fundamentally social psychology: to him society was dominated almost exclusively by processes of invention and imitation. Tarde was anti-determinist and convinced that every society was divided into a small, creative elite and a broad mass confined to imitation. A chronology of his life discloses a glittering career, yet he did not succeed in acquiring imitators or pupils to keep his teaching alive. The chair at the Collège de France was more prestigious than a position at the Sorbonne, yet its influence on the public education system was none the less slight. Despite his success with the higher bourgeoisie, in the salons, and with the Catholics, Tarde soon fell under the shadow of Durkheim, who had long since assembled a team around him and concentrated it in the journal *Année sociologique*. Tarde's attempt to have the *chaire de philosophie moderne* of the Collège de France reconsecrated into a chair of *psychologie sociologique* came to nothing. He died in 1904.

In the series *'Les Grands Philosophes français et étrangers'* the sons of Gabriel Tarde, his 'natural and favourite pupils',[11] published a selec-

---

[11] Gabriel Tarde, *Introduction et pages choisies par ses fils*, préface de H. Bergson (Paris: Louis-Michaud, n.d.), p. 25.

tion of their father's writings. The foreword to it was written by
Henri Bergson, who had at Tarde's death succeeded to his chair at
the Collège de France; Bergson spoke of Tarde's seductive and surprising *aperçus*, of his willingness to be drawn through all the domains
of knowledge, and of the ease with which he was able to move from
one problem to another, usually employing analogy as his guide.
The author of the *Essai sur les données immédiates de la conscience* meant
this commendation seriously, and yet precisely what he says in his
foreword makes clear why, in an era of specialization, Tarde could
create no enduring system and acquire no firm circle of pupils within
the environment of the New Sorbonne. Even more revealing in this
regard is the long, reverent introduction with which Tarde's sons
preface their selection.

Gabriel Tarde, they say, united in himself to a degree previously
unknown even in France the intellectual power of the philosopher
and the sensibility of a poet: traces of his first poetic attempts, which
excited the admiration of Maurice Barrès, can still be discovered in
his later social philosophy. All his life he retained the appearance of a
poet whose thinking is characterized by spontaneity, imagination,
and an inexhaustible gift for improvisation. In all he did and wrote
he sought to preserve an indispensable measure of artistic freedom.
Possessing a self-confident, serenely original talent that sought to
elude influence from without, Tarde was of a rebellious nature and a
proud autodidact who remained unaffected by the grand philosophical
systems of his age, whether they originated with Comte or with
Spencer. Scientists often reproached him with being a mere man of
letters, but it was precisely his literary inclinations that preserved
Tarde from the illusions of dogmaticism into which the sciences
were lapsing at the turn of the century:

Tarde's method . . . is perhaps rather literary than scientific: he narrates an
idea rather than explaining it, and he narrates it in the way in which it came
to him. Instead of waiting until his ideas are fully mature and can thus be
expressed in a logical fashion, he so to speak puts on to paper the working
out of his ideas.[12]

Tarde's weakness as a dogmaticist constitutes his charm: with him,
who refused to follow a '*méthode sociale d'écrire*',[13] one could recover
from the pedantry of everyday science.

In their selection Tarde's sons also included a number of his
unpublished juvenile poems. In 1879 he had published a volume of

[12] *Ibid.*, p. 37.   [13] *Ibid.*, p. 38.

stories and poems, though he quickly withdrew it again; in the same year he wrote a utopian novel, *Fragment d'histoire future*. Tarde took his time about publishing this novel: only after three books which he accounted serious work had been published did the *Fragment* appear – in 1876, in a sociological journal run by a rival. René Worms, the editor of the *Revue internationale de sociologie*, declared that the *Revue* was really more interested in questions pertaining to the past and the present, yet it did not want to let pass the opportunity of placing before the professional public these remarkable visions of the future on the part of an important sociologist. Tarde himself apologized for publishing his 'sociological fantasy'[14] in a professional journal: he ventured to do so only because the leading idea of his utopian novel, which he had encountered in the diary of the Goncourt brothers, originated with Marcelin Berthelot, who was a scientist.

Tarde's novel begins in an age in which world peace has finally dawned after a 150-year war. In a society of the twenty-second century that has abolished sickness Greek has become the universal language. Greek literature has been rediscovered at the expense of the rest of the European classics: Homer, Sappho and Sophocles occupy the seats of Shakespeare, Goethe and Victor Hugo. Literature is flourishing and poetry stands at the summit of all human activities. There are few workers, and they spend only three hours a day in giant *phalanstères*. Science is progressing comfortably and occupies, as though with self-evident right, the place in the heads of men formerly possessed by the catechism.

This idyll, already threatened from within by the power of habit, is destroyed by an '*apoplexie solaire*,' an ever-increasing cooling down of the sun which delivers all mankind over to death by freezing. A saviour for the few survivors appears in Miltiades, '*slave croisé de Breton*,'[15] who preaches a neo-troglodytism as a way out and on whose advice a small remnant of mankind finally lives on under the earth. Their dependence on nature now ceases, since hereafter the sun no longer interrupts the rhythm of social life. Those who have been saved see the disaster that overtook them as a piece of good fortune, as it has made possible a long-term sociological experiment: an experiment to discover what will become of this social being, man, when, freed from the bonds of nature, he is delivered over wholly to himself.

[14] Tarde, 'Fragment d'histoire future', *Revue Internationale de Sociologie* 4 (1896), p. 654.
[15] Tarde, *Fragment d'histoire future*, présentation de Raymond Trousson (Paris and Geneva: Slatkine Reprints, 1980), p. 37.

Like every utopia, Gabriel Tarde's *Fragment* is less a presentiment of the future than a faithful reflection of the age in which it was written. This is especially so in the divided role played by sociology in the subterranean society. By comparison with that modern form of sophistry, economics, sociology appears as advanced as chemistry does by comparison with alchemy: in the end society is held together, not only by an exchange of services, as the economists have wanted to make us believe, but by a system of imitations. Men mimic one another and, however paradoxical it may seem, in this way develop their individuality. The urban civilization of earlier ages, dominated as it was by producers and consumers, employers and employees, presented only an imperfect picture of the pure social relationships such as now evolve under the earth. Pre-forms of this society, though only primitive ones, can be found in certain eighteenth-century salons, in painters' studios and in the houses of great actors. Suddenly Herbert Spencer appears as the sociologist of the future, for his law of segregation also applies under the earth: in the twenty-second century there evolve cities of musicians and sculptors, of mathematicians, naturalists and psychologists; only the philosophers find it impossible to live together permanently, for to them belong the sociologists, the most unsociable of all the tribes.

In Tarde's '*humanité toute humaine*',[16] in which mankind has finally found the way to itself, all sociology orientated towards collectivism loses its right to exist: after the abolition of social constraints the only sociology that holds good is a sociology of the ego, a discipline which concentrates on sociableness in its pure forms, the key science of an epoch in which at any given time 'a minimum of utility-orientated work'[17] is combined with 'a maximum of aesthetic work'. Under the earth Durkheim's sociology has disappeared, Tarde's social psychology has survived. Written before he himself had appeared in public as a sociologist, Tarde's utopia anticipates the dispute between the sociologists of the Third Republic and the contention between the sociological ideal of education and the literary ideal that permeated the reorganization of the Sorbonne and of the entire French education system at the turn of the century.

The adherents of Durkheim received Tarde's utopia in differing ways. Noteworthy was the reaction of Célestin Bouglé, who spoke of the work of a brilliant sociologist who had begun by writing poems and was now amusing himself by 'competing with a Morris or a

---

[16] *Ibid.*, p. 75.   [17] *Ibid.*, p. 80.

Wells'.[18] This was well-observed, for it was only years later that H. G. Wells – that early promoter of sociological thinking and equally early critic of the discipline of sociology – was to write a foreword to the English edition of the *Fragment* in which he welcomed not least Tarde's aversion to the profession of sociologist. Bouglé, however, who commended Tarde's anti-determinism and anti-naturalism, none the less foresaw the dangers that lay in his pathos of sociability and in the mysticism of a pure socialization. The men of letters might perhaps praise this anti-Rousseau who preached distancing from nature, but the scientists would undoubtedly criticize him. On the other hand, Tarde's prose had been stigmatized as 'extraordinarily inflated and tortuous':[19] even Auguste Comte, who certainly did not write well, always wrote better than this. Such criticism turned his own guns on an author who wanted to be sociologist and poet in one.

Tarde's sons accorded the contention between Durkheim and their father a kind of universal significance. In this they certainly went too far; but they were right about one thing: the conflict between Durkheim and Tarde was not only a contention between two schools of sociology, it was also a dispute between two temperaments in the course of which Tarde repudiated Durkheim as a scholastic and Durkheim repudiated Tarde as a mere man of letters. These were, in fact, the two contrary positions that were of the essence of the struggle for the New Sorbonne – a struggle exacerbated by the pamphlets of the mysterious Agathon. It is therefore not very surprising to find that one of the names concealed behind this pseudonym is that of Alfred Tarde, a son of Gabriel.

When sociology was still young and sure of itself

In his *History of the French Revolution*, Michelet connected the end of the Terror, which he always characterized as anti-natural, with a dramatic change in the political vocabulary: after 1795, 'life' replaced 'nature' and became the key concept of a new age. Paul Bourget observed a similar verbal shift before the First World War, and again it was '*la vie*' whose ever more frequent employment did away with the catchword that had ruled since the middle of the cen-

---

[18] Célestin Bouglé, 'La Société sous la terre (une utopie de G. Tarde)', *Revue Bleue* 3 (1905), p. 333.

[19] Lucien Herr, review of Tarde's *Les Lois de l'imitation* (*Revue d'Histoire et de Littérature*, 1891), in *Choix d'écrits. II. Philosophie, Histoire, Philologie* (Paris: Rieder, 1932), pp. 71–2.

tury: '*la science*'. In the contest between Durkheim and Bergson, whom most of the enemies of the New Sorbonne chose for their hero, words too struggled for domination. The turn of the century was a time in which science was subjected to much criticism: the impression was more and more gaining ground that the speed of scientific and technological progress was curtailing the powers of the imagination and reducing men to a state of disorientation. People talked of the bankruptcy of science and quoted with approval Victor Hugo's remark that every scholar reminded one a little of a corpse.

In the second half of the nineteenth century the influence of Hippolyte Taine and Ernest Renan in France was comparable only with that exercised in the eighteenth by Voltaire and Rousseau. No one could ignore their work: one had either to follow them or try to wrest oneself free of them. The faith in science which gradually faded at the *fin de siècle* had been preached not least by Taine and Renan. Did Taine not say in his book on La Fontaine that man could be regarded as a kind of higher animal which spins philosophy and poetry out of itself as a silkworm spins its cocoon? Did Renan not maintain that the man instructed in science was of decisively greater worth than the credulous being of earlier ages governed by instinct? And yet, measured against the excrescences of scientific positivism neither Taine nor Renan could be condemned. Taine's pretentious scientificality was unbearable; he comported himself like a 'Procrustes in a frock-coat',[20] his unquenchable thirst for moralizing made him more and more resemble a pastor; but he could at least write, and his deep-rooted aesthetic sensibility frequently prevailed over his superficial scientific optimism. And Renan never forgot that at the beginning of his career he had once said that others would call his philosophy literature and that the novel was the best medium for getting a subtle psychology accepted and for depicting a character.

Taine had been presumptuous enough to call himself an anatomical historian who intended to describe his subject as calmly and minutely as a naturalist describing an insect. When the historians of the New Sorbonne subsequently pilloried him for his inexactitudes, Taine found his defenders: that the author of the *Origines de la France contemporaine* had occasionally been unfaithful to his own principles and had ventured on a descriptive freedom which, though unjustifi-

---

[20] Léon Daudet, *Devant la Douleur: Souvenirs des milieux littéraires, politiques, artistiques et médicaux de 1880 à 1905* (Paris: Nouvelle Librairie Nationale, 1915), p. 195.

able as historical truth, could be justified as poetic truth, rendered him sympathetic to the enemies of the New Sorbonne.

People said that France had lost both her eyes when Renan died in 1892 and Taine in 1893. As 'masters of the counter-revolution'[21] both were received into the pantheon of the political right: in retrospect it must have seemed to them of great symbolic significance that in 1883 the aged Renan had bestowed the prizes of the Lycée Louis-le-Grand not only on Paul Claudel but also on Léon Daudet, who was later to become a leading light of the Action Française.

It was precisely because many of its members and sympathizers regarded the intellect as only a surface phenomenon and man as primarily an affective being that the Action Française devoted the attention it did to the politics of science. In 1905 the Institut de l'Action Française was founded: it was a kind of royalist Sorbonne in which the values of France's traditional literary culture were to be fostered. Louis Dimier, the institute's first director, intended even his lectures on Buffon, which he delivered from January to April 1918, as a contribution to the counter-revolution. Dimier wanted to restore the reputation of Buffon, who to him embodied, together with Descartes and Bossuet, the French spirit in its perfection. Nothing had harmed Buffon more than the attention he had devoted to questions of style; with the rise of Charles Darwin he had been forgotten. Now, however – this, at least, was Dimier's opinion – Darwinism was increasingly on the decline, and the academic disciplines of the day were being harmed by the neglectful way in which they treated questions of presentation. The coterie of enlighteners who had laughed at Buffon were a coarse-minded collection: they had failed to see that Buffon had been not only a great writer but also an exact observer and a qualified scientist. Happily, the fame of Jean-Henri Fabre, the entomologist from Sérignan whose talent for observation Darwin himself had held in the highest esteem, had during the previous decade spread all over Europe. The very title of Fabre's *Souvenirs entomologiques* recalled the profoundly French tradition of a science tending towards biography and literary form; it had contributed to the revival of that descriptive natural history once so brilliantly embodied in the unjustly reviled and forgotten Buffon.

Buffon had by no means been a literary man shy of empirical

---

[21] Louis Dimier, *Les Maîtres de la contre-révolution au dix-neuvième siècle*, nouvelle édition revue et corrigée (Paris: Nouvelle Librairie Nationale, 1917).

observation, as his enemies and those who envied him said he was: on the contrary, he had discovered the only appropriate method of drawing a picture of a natural world whose omnipotent power spoke to the heart and whose aliveness eluded all constricting systems. Buffon had depicted the hierarchies of nature as the productions of a divine power which the spirit could only wonder at and before which the reason stood powerless: he could thus also serve as an ideological model. To call attention to him and rehabilitate his reputation was not enough: his work had to be carried further forward. To the Action Française science was by its nature as authoritarian and aristocratic as nature itself: the advance of the *esprit démocratique*, that pernicious outcome of the Revolution, had not only weakened France politically, French science too had suffered under it. If intelligence was still to be rescued from the barbarism that threatened it in France one had to go back a hundred years in the organization of study: that, at least, was Charles Maurras' proposal, and it referred back to an age in which sociology did not yet exist.

For at the turn of the century sociology was still a youthful discipline even in France. Comte had, it is true, already given it a name – a name which, being a combination of Greek with Latin, sounded abominable to the classically educated, and not only to them – but no one could say what the subject-matter of sociology really was or in what its particular method consisted. The few scholars already calling themselves sociologists differed markedly from one another, and there was in addition a row of rival disciplines, such as philosophy, history and psychology, whose whole interest lay in making the new discipline seem superfluous. Under these circumstances it is surprising to see with what confidence Durkheim in his very first book, the treatise on division of labour (1893), claimed he was pursuing sociology as a positive and completely valid science. Nor did this exclude the fixing of practical objectives, for 'at the same time that [sociology] teaches us to respect the moral reality, it furnishes us with the means to improve it'.[22] This was an essential reason why Durkheim's doctrine prevailed over rival offers of theories – Gabriel Tarde's sociology of the individual, for example – in the French university system and with the appropriate ministerial bureaucracy: Durkheim's sociology counted not least as a moral science; it seemed to be in a position to furnish an effective secular alternative to traditional clerical education. Nothing, moreover, was

[22] Durkheim, *On the Division of Labor*, p. 36.

better calculated to repulse the dangerous pretensions of the Catholic clergy in questions of education than Durkheim's resolute assertion that all religions were equally true.

Durkheim was propagandist and researcher in one: he did not shrink from audacious theorizing, but took care to see that it possessed a basis in social reality. In France, which was still to a large extent an agricultural country, many intellectuals had failed to notice the extent to which the dynamic development of the Western industrial societies had made traditional value-conceptions seem more and more remote from reality. In a condition of anomy, discontent replaced analysis; the catchword 'decadence' excited everyone and explained nothing. It was the task of sociology patiently to bridge the gulf between social reality and the erroneous conceptions of it present in most people's heads. As this task was too big for any single individual, the recruiting and training of a staff of friends, colleagues and fellow-workers at the *Année sociologique* which Durkheim undertook with so much vigour was an obligation deriving directly from the kind of knowledge sociology was seeking. The structural changes industrialization and urbanization brought with them made it no longer permissible to formulate statements about man and society in neatly turned *aperçus* based merely on traditions or personal experience: the line of the classic moralists was now at an end, inquiries were more important than recollections, tables constituted a modern form of social aphorism. Durkheim, too, was a sceptic, but he did not lack self-confidence when it came to the efficiency of his discipline: when Bouglé, one of the early *durkheimiens*, wanted to abandon a project in discouragement, his chief wrote to him: 'Objectively there are no grounds at all for being discouraged. No, the facts of society are certainly not going to elude us. They are just as amenable to discipline as the others.'[23]

Durkheim's steadfastness in pursuing his programme provoked a reaction not least from all who mourned the passing of the old France and sighed that those who had not lived under the Ancien Régime did not know what it was to be happy: his enemies, various though they were, were none the less united in their anti-modernism, in looking longingly back to an age in which the *homme moyen* of the statisticians did not yet exist, his place being occupied merely by the *Français moyen*, a creature who felt quite at home in his motherland, and by a literary culture with at its centre that *honnête homme* who knew his place and how to address his betters. What in

---

[23] Durkheim to Bouglé, 21 November 1902; 'Textes inédits', p. 179.

many cases turned opposition to Durkheim, the republicans'
favoured sociologist, into downright enmity, and rejection of his
theories into downright hatred of them, was not least a sense of
astonishment that his sociology, though still so young, was none the
less already so sure of itself.

But this sociology did not lack allies: they were to be found above
all among the functionaries of the higher education system, who had
no interest in seeing the Sorbonne restored to being a stronghold of
rhetoric – on the contrary, they desired a further reduction in all
courses of study of the part played in them by the languages of antiquity, and a diminution of the prestige enjoyed by the cultivation
of literature in the image the universities had of themselves. Even
those professionally engaged in the study of literature no longer saw
any possibility of halting the decline of the French language. What
did it matter if no one any longer wrote well? It was part of the price
to be paid for universal progress. And the gradual disappearance of
impressionism in the sciences was also a good thing: it was in any
event endurable only in the case of such geniuses as Sainte-Beuve
and Chateaubriand, and geniuses were a nuisance rather than anything else in a university whose principal aim was the training of professional technicians. Even historians were finding the *esprit littéraire*
increasingly unattractive: Michelet had ceased to be their model;
they too wanted to emulate such natural scientists as Bichat, Laplace
and Claude Bernard. The deep-rooted inclination for general ideas
and brilliant rhetoric which characterized the French was to be
replaced by an unprejudiced love of facts and a rigorous application
to method. The degree of civilization a modern nation had attained
to had long since been measured by its productivity of knowledge
and no longer by its feeling for language: that a writer possessed a
fine style no longer permitted any conclusion as to how much truth
there was in his ideas. A fine style was like an ornament, pleasing, but
useless.

An opponent of Durkheim: Charles Péguy

Durkheim's attempt to create for sociology a secure and influential
position within the French university was only half successful. Not
long after his death in 1917, indeed, it became clear that even the
bonds that united the clan surrounding the *Année sociologique* were
somewhat fragile. It seemed as though the triumphal procession of
sociology had been no more than the personal accomplishment of a
charismatic producer of theories: the discipline was in any event a

very long way from being accepted in France as a part of everyday existence, although during his lifetime Durkheim could rightly be described, by his opponents as well as his adherents, as the *'penseur quasi-officiel'*[24] of the Sorbonne. Durkheim was represented as an intellectual tyrant and as a self-appointed guardian of truth, and the despotism of his teaching was deplored all the more in that sociology was a science which had gained admittance to the university only as an outcome of the detested democratization of France.

The most resolute, irreconcilable and fluent of the opponents of Durkheim and sociology, however, sprang up, not within the inner circle of the university, but outside it. If you leave the entry court of the Sorbonne, cross over the narrow rue de la Sorbonne, and walk a few steps to the right, you find yourself in front of the shop of Charles Péguy, a dark, confined room in which from 1901 he published the *Cahiers de la Quinzaine*, which he had founded the year before. Today it is again a bookshop, bulging with books piled high on the floor through which you have painstakingly to make your way to reach the bookshelves. There is very little on them that is topical. On the other hand, the old bookseller has the historical topography of the place in his head: he shows the visitor the place where Péguy could usually be found and where the shop's only basket-work chair stood – it was reserved for Maître Sorel, who was accustomed to sit in it and expatiate until Péguy fell out with him too.

Charles Péguy was born in Orléans in 1873, the son of a carpenter and a chair-weaver. His father died when Charles was less than a year old. He had grown up, Péguy wrote forty years afterwards, in the old France – as had every child had who had grown up in a provincial town between 1873 and 1880: it was a world 'in which you earned nothing and spent nothing, but in which everyone could live'.[25] All his life Péguy longed to be back in Orléans and his native Beauce, for he hated the modern world in which there had been more changes in thirty years than there had been from the birth of Christ to the present day. This, too, was a fact ascertainable by sound common sense without the aid of the 'arithmetic of the sociologists'.[26]

In 1893 Péguy was accepted into the Ecole Normale but asked to be excused from attendance after only a year: a pretext was offered by an eye infection. During this time he learned typography in Orléans, founded a socialist group and began writing his *Jeanne d'Arc*,

---

[24] Agathon, pp. 212–13.
[25] Charles Péguy, 'L'Argent' [1913], in *Oeuvres en prose 1909–1914*, avant-propos et notes par Marcel Péguy (Paris: Bibliothèque de la Pléiade, 1961), p. 1103.
[26] *Ibid.*, p. 1107.

a subject from which he was never again to get free. The first article
he produced was on the economist Walras; it appeared in the *Revue
Socialiste*. In 1898 – the year of Zola's *J'accuse* – Péguy, who as the
holder of a scholarship was prohibited from undertaking any work
for profit, opened a socialist bookshop under an assumed name.
Three months later he failed the *agrégation* in philosophy: all prospect of a university career faded therewith, and he remained in his
shop, which stood before the mighty walls of the Sorbonne like
David before Goliath, as a writer, publisher, typographer and tireless polemicist.

Charles Péguy became a Dreyfusard. Together with Lucien Herr,
who from being a caustic critic of Durkheim had become a champion of the new sociology, he fought battles at the Sorbonne in the
cause of Dreyfus and Zola; but when Herr talked of how he and
Péguy had together commanded the batallions of students and sympathizers, Péguy insisted on precision: when there was fighting to be
done, he said, he had given the orders, when there was nothing to do
Herr had taken over command.

Faithful to the traditional values of his childhood and his home,
Péguy was not one to cleave to modern doctrines and slogans once
he had seen through them: then he was capable of changing his viewpoint, a genius in love and hatred and a fanatic in controversy who
must have been thinking of someone else when he wrote: '*Je ne suis
pas polémiste.*'[27] He saw how the Dreyfus affair had altered his friends,
who had suddenly acquired a taste for giving orders and a pleasure in
power. He was not ashamed of the engagements he had participated
in on Dreyfus' behalf, but he was soon also turning his attack on
those opportunist Dreyfusards who saw in the everlasting affair only
a means of profit; and it also vexed him that Dreyfus himself had not
behaved more heroically. For Péguy there were two Dreyfus affairs:
his own had been a struggle for political justice and morality, that of
the rest nothing but a sordid contest for power and political
influence. So far as his business was concerned the affair had in the
end only harmed him: from now on people ceased to buy books and
read only newspapers.

When Péguy severed his ties with Herr and the adherents of
Durkheim the cause was not only the financial quarrels that arose in
connection with his activities as a publisher but not least the different ways in which they conceived what was meant by socialism.
Péguy's faith was less the socialism of Karl Marx than the socialism

---

[27] Péguy, 'Note conjointe sur M. Descartes et la philosophie cartésienne' [posth.], in
Oeuvres en prose 1909–1914, p. 1411.

of Francis of Assisi: an attitude towards life, not a doctrine; an *engagement* one lived through every day, not a programme inscribed in party statutes. And Péguy was also suspicious of a socialism whose supreme goal appeared to consist in turning as many workers as possible into bourgeois. Herr called Péguy an anarchist; yet this was no apt description of one who preferred to fight for himself alone rather than belong to the '*petit clan de la Sorbonne*'[28] around Durkheim. The vehemence of the struggle Péguy's bookshop waged with Durkheim's Sorbonne originated not least in the fact that each side justified its position morally: Péguy opposed sociology because in his eyes its claim to be a moral science was unjustified.

Though always surrounded by faithful followers, Péguy never allowed himself to be appropriated by any school or clique, not even when, like him, it was engaged in the struggle against the New Sorbonne or against that hated bourgeoisie which was responsible for all the evils of the modern world. But his solitary situation was not wholly of his own choosing: as Daniel Halévy has remarked, his as it were natural place in the political right had been appropriated by Barrès and Maurras, and a combative if hardly practising Catholic such as he found it hard to hold his own beside Paul Claudel. Péguy was, moreover, a pro-semite, and since, as he himself said, he could be a better Catholic among Jews than he could among many of his fellow Catholics, he was for a time alienated from his faith, which he returned to only in 1908.

Le style est l'homme même, and Péguy's prose was anything but agreeable: the endless repetitions, alliterations and echolalia, the childish games with punctuation-marks and typographical mannerisms, and the over-elaborate arrangement of pages especially in the *Cahiers*, were such that Proust spoke of Péguy's bombastic fustian, while others called it a psychiatric phenomenon. Maurras called it unreadable. Yet Péguy maintained that criticism of his style was only a pretext for an attack on his convictions: 'If I had demonstrated that Jeanne d'Arc was a whore, M. Langlois would consider me a great writer.'[29] The sole institution to which Péguy, 'the first among France's writing soldiers',[30] really accommodated himself was the French army; in relation to all the others he remained a militant outsider. As a born writer he had to become an adversary of the sociologists.

The influence of Taine and Renan, however, those early sociologists who were too big for a youthful discipline to lay exclusive claim to,

---

[28] Péguy, 'L'Argent', p. 1138.
[29] *Ibid.*
[30] André Suarès, *Péguy* (Paris: Emile-Paul Frères, 1915), p. 27.

was bound to affect Péguy too: even to him they were the masters in whose work the modern had found its expression. Yet both were at the same time the fountainhead of the intellectualism that had poisoned the nineteenth century, demagogues of modern science to whom the *vir scientificus* seemed greater than God. Péguy mocked at the sociological literary criticism of Hippolyte Taine, who could not write so much as a sentence about La Fontaine without digressing into a treatise on anthropological geography: one word of Pascal – who had himself, to be sure, been too much given to argufying – was mighty enough to shatter every monument Renan had erected. But there none the less existed, for history as well as for the humanities, particular methods, '*des méthodes humainement historiques*',[31] which did not have to be borrowed from the natural sciences and which Michelet already knew. The historian of earlier times who believed in God remained a man: the modern historian who had lost belief in God was himself growing ever more god-like. Ernest Renan was not venerated as a saint until he had left the bosom of the Church, and the adherents he assembled about him were like a priesthood of intellectuals.

And yet Renan had been only a half-hearted apostate: his alienation from Catholic dogma by no means meant a breach with the Catholic way of life. The old saying '*Tu es christianus in aeternum*'[32] retained its validity: an informed reading of Renan left one in no doubt as to how firm a hold the language of Catholicism had kept upon him. In the case of Taine, as in that of Renan, there appeared a contradiction between what they wrote and the way in which they wrote it: all their faith in science notwithstanding, they remained the authors of metaphysical novels. Both of them were great, not because they represented a particular party in the contentions of the moderns, but because each had embodied in a single person the decisive conflict of the epoch, 'the old contention between science and art'.[33] But their adherents were hardly in a position to maintain such an ambivalence, and they were the less so in that in the Third Republic a renunciation of Catholicism also suggested itself on grounds of political opportunism.

But what Péguy failed to understand was how an entire generation could desert Catholicism on account of its supposed metaphysical contradictions, when the immediate result was only 'to involve

[31] Péguy, 'Zangwill' [1904], in *Oeuvres en prose 1898–1908*, introduction et notes de Marcel Péguy (Paris: Bibliothèque de le Pléiade, 1959), p. 739.
[32] Péguy, 'De la situation faite au parti intellectuel dans le monde moderne' [1906], in *Oeuvres en prose 1898–1908*, p. 1038.   [33] Péguy, 'Zangwill', p. 739.

themselves in difficulties infinitely more difficult, in contradictions infinitely more contradictory, with metaphysics infinitely more uncouth – that is to say, the difficulties, impossibilities, contradictions, metaphysics of history and sociology in the modern world'.[34] The sciences of history and sociology were, even so, not in the same situation. The certitudes of history provided sociology with no certainties at all; but where history was uncertain sociology too lacked any firm basis. The discipline was rich in pretensions but poor in results, because sociologists believed one had only to be a sociologist to understand all the societies of mankind – as though all that was needed for acquiring courage was to put on a uniform. Dreadful indeed was the jargon–gibberish of the sociologists, which was gradually forcing its way into everyday speech; and they regarded as a blockhead anyone who had forborne to study their pseudoscience. Their so-called methods were their greatest piece of deception, for they had as yet eventuated in not a single demonstrable result: they were products of pure fantasy, invented by a sociological propaganda designed to persuade young students from the bourgeoisie that it was possible to make something without doing any work. Beyond all this, sociology came to grief precisely in its claim to be analysing contemporary society, for how could it succeed in doing that if what was involved was an attempt to reduce Roman law, classical culture and French social life to a system of totem and tabu? Even the seemingly enviable elegance and finesse of a Marcel Mauss could not elude Péguy's mockery. He preferred his monk's hood to the sociologists' long proletarian trousers and 'republican frills'.[35]

But if its basic assumptions were notoriously vague, its methods fictions and its analyses of the contemporary world false, why did sociology represent such a danger? Péguy's differing polemical strategies towards historians and sociologists provide the answer. When he attacked historians he named them individually; but he as good as never named a sociologist, 'because when dealing with the sociologists you would have to quote them all'.[36] Sociology as a whole was an expression of the *Zeitgeist* against which Péguy struggled. However much Durkheim might emphasize the practical goals of the new moral science, as a university discipline it was

---

[34] Péguy, 'De la situation faite à l'histoire et à la sociologie dans les temps modernes' [1906], in *Oeuvres en prose 1898–1908*, p. 1028.

[35] Péguy, 'Victor-Marie, Comte Hugo' [1910], in *Oeuvres en prose 1909–1914*, p. 669.

[36] Péguy, 'De la situation faite au parti intellectuel dans le monde moderne devant les accidents de la gloire temporelle' [1907], in *Oeuvres en prose 1898–1908*, p. 1136.

capable neither of diagnosis nor of therapy: it was merely the most striking symptom of a time that was out of joint.

Péguy, who revered the saints, his '*saints patrons*',[37] was a sworn enemy of all worldly patronage: that alone made him a temperamental foe of Durkheim, who was a virtuoso in the employment of the system of patrons, coteries and *chapelles* for the purpose of gaining the admittance of sociology into the university. As his follower and subsequent opponent Hubert Bourgin put it, Durkheim was, even as an individual, a school in himself; that he was in addition a socialist and a politician, a sociologist from moral rather than scientific motives, a priest rather than a scholar, a 'sacral figure... filled with a religious mission',[38] was what truly ignited Péguy's wrath, for he bore several of these characteristics himself. Péguy, the great solitary, saw in Durkheim above all the demagogue: what he and his companions were doing no longer had any connection with the discipline Comte had once wanted to establish. That is why he resolved to call Durkheim's sociology only *sociagogie*.

Durkheim's tyranny was unendurable: he surrounded himself with followers who confused the Sorbonne with a police station. Durkheim was a '*patron* against philosophy'[39] who had made up his mind to destroy the old French system of education. Herr and Durkheim boasted shamelessly of the success they had achieved in exorcizing humanism and classical culture from the youth of France. Fanatics for reform, they sacrificed everything to their vision of a collective consciousness that was nothing more than an expression of the philosophy of life of the bureaucratized middle class and therewith of the *cadres* upon which the Republic depended. In the battle between the Old and the New Sorbonne, in the contention between a literature-orientated humanism and scientific sociology, there was reflected a new '*Querelle des Anciens et des Modernes*':

The battle for the Sorbonne... is the battle of the saints and heroes against the modern world, against that which they call sociology, against that which they call science. And a chair will always be kept vacant at the Sorbonne for those who declare that the best thing to do with the saints is to send them to [the mental asylum at] Charenton.[40]

Durkheim's audacious assertion that he could prove sociology had as much right to exist as any other natural science seemed to Péguy

---

[37] Henri Massis, *Les Idées restent* (Lyon: Lardanchet, 1941), p. 50.
[38] Hubert Bourgin, *De Jaurès à Léon Blum: L'Ecole Normale et la politique* (Paris: Fayard, 1938), p. 218.
[39] Péguy, 'L'Argent suite' [1913], in *Oeuvres en prose 1909–1914*, p. 1187.
[40] *Ibid.*, p. 1273.

and his disciples hubris and stupidity combined. The sociologists threw overboard the equipment of a literary culture without ever being able to achieve the exactitude of the natural sciences; they pretended to see into the heart of man and his society, and deceived no one but themselves. And their imitation of the exact disciplines seemed all the more ludicrous in that genuine scientists such as Curie and Poincaré were at that time exerting themselves to hold scientific dogmatism within bounds:

The scientific faculties graciously relinquish to those of the arts the monopoly in scientific fanaticism ... For themselves they claim rather the literary qualities of finesse, moderation and taste that characterize the French spirit... The handful of mediocre historians and a group of terroristic sociologists represent only a part of the Sorbonne: that part which talks, agitates and dogmatizes, but does no work.[41]

Thus there arose a sociological metaphysics which did more harm to its adherents than any military invasion: the destruction of their inner life.

This was why Péguy and many anti-sociologists of the turn of the century set such store by Henri Bergson, who in their eyes could be compared only with Michelet, the '*historien essentiel*'[42] who had been historical researcher and philosopher of history in one. They hailed in Bergson the renaissance of a metaphysics that could preserve reason from the clutches of the sociologists: Bergson taught that reality could not be exhausted by the cold, analytical understanding, and drew from this insight consequences that applied also to scientists, whose maxim must now be: 'do not be too system-bound: say what you see'.[43]

In the archives of the Ecole Normale there can be found the assessments meted out to Durkheim and Bergson when they took their entrance examinations. The latter made an excellent impression: he seemed cultivated and of exceptional intelligence, an enrichment of the school. 'Too cold and surly'[44] was the judgment on Durkheim. It was as though Péguy and his flock wanted to seize on these early judgments – which in Durkheim's case were soon revised – and make them permanent: Bergson, who studied Latin, Greek and philosophy, and from early days insisted he had freed himself completely from the influence of German culture, carried off the victory over

---

[41] Agathon, pp. 367–8.
[42] Péguy, 'De la situation faite à l'histoire et à la sociologie', p. 1007.
[43] Péguy, 'Note sur M. Bergson et la philosophie bergsonienne' [1914], in *Oeuvres en prose 1909–1914*, p. 1317.
[44] Louis M. Greenberg, 'Bergson and Durkheim as Sons and Assimilators: The Early Years', *French Historical Studies* 9 (1976), p. 633.

Durkheim, the son of a rabbi who belonged to that northern French Jewry who concentrated on arid exegesis of the Bible and on Talmudic jurisprudence, and in whose picture of the world 'imagination, mysticism, artistic sensibility and poetry' had no place.

If you leave Péguy's shop, cross the courtyard of the Sorbonne and pass through several of its long corridors, you find yourself when you get out again in the rue St Jacques. Here, facing the Sorbonne and just as venerable and impressive, stands the Collège de France: this was where Bergson worked from 1904, and whenever Péguy and the faithful went across to hear him lecture they must have done so with the feeling they were taking a decisive step in the struggle against the New Sorbonne and its sociology.

All the more incomprehensible, therefore, were the attacks on Bergson mounted by the Action Française and the Catholic Church: these, it appeared, were too blind to see that 'everything they took from Bergson would benefit only Spencer and not St Thomas'.[45] Conflict with the church grew more intense when it placed Bergson's works on the Index. And Péguy spoke contemptuously of the 'action dite française'[46] because it attacked the only philosopher who could liberate France from the intellectual yoke of Germany.

The influence of Germany and the Germanization of the Sorbonne

What lent a decisive edge to the contention between the literary and sociological intelligentsia at the turn of the century, however, and turned a dispute between intellectuals into a bitter political struggle, was the fact that at this time, on the eve of the First World War, there came a renewed outbreak of the 'German crisis in French thought'.[47] The opponents of the New Sorbonne wagered everything on demonstrating that sociology was a profoundly German discipline and that, under the influence of Durkheim and his followers, the French university was in danger of becoming Germanized once and for all, since in it 'ideas of scientific exactitude, after the German model, were beginning to prevail over humanism',[48] as Proust's Professor Brichot complained.

---

[45] Péguy, 'Note conjointe sur M. Descartes', p. 1538.   [46] Ibid., p. 1409.
[47] Claude Digeon, La Crise allemande de la pensée française (1870–1914) (Paris: Presses Universitaires de France, 1959).
[48] Marcel Proust, 'Sodome et Gomorrhe', in A la Recherche du temps perdu (Paris: Bibliothèque de la Pléiade, 1954), Vol. 2, p. 868.

In the nineteenth century an educated Frenchman could hardly elude the influence of German music, German philosophy or German poetry. When Ernest Renan became acquainted with German literature it seemed to him as though he were setting foot in a temple: everything appeared to him pure, elevated, moral, beautiful and moving. Unlike Renan, Baudelaire can hardly have felt a desire to become a Protestant pastor in Germany – yet, because he was bored to death with a society in which everyone resembled Voltaire, or at least tried to do so, even he turned to Richard Wagner. But it was not only German erudition, art and philosophy that exerted an influence: it seemed as though the French spirit was being drawn more and more strongly to the German. Edmond Goncourt noted:

I observed a man in the library. While he was reading he held the hand of a young woman sitting beside him. I returned two hours later. The man was still reading his book and still holding the young lady's hand. They were a German couple. It was Germany.[49]

The mood of the French changed, it is true, after the war of 1870–1, yet Germany still attracted them, if for other reasons. The fervent desire to regain Alsace–Lorraine and to restore to France its former strength could best be fulfilled by learning from the enemy: the Prussian schoolmaster had been the victor at Sedan, and France had lost the war not least because German influence had not yet sufficiently permeated its institutions of higher education. Though hoping that the Prussian victory would signify the beginning of the decline of Germany, the French none the less did not cease from imitating their neighbours beyond the Rhine, for had they not once replied to their defeat at Jena by founding the University of Berlin?

In 1897, Paul Valéry, a youthful amateur who knew neither the German language nor Germany, wrote for the London *New Review* an essay later entitled '*Une conquête methodique*'; in it he asked about the reasons for the political, economic and scientific rise of Germany, which the French were observing with a mixture of admiration and mistrust. The principal one, he said, was the methodical sense the Germans had evolved: lack of discipline, the vice of the intelligentsia, had vanished from among them. In Moltke there was embodied the new ideal of the perfectly disciplined human being who was as much at home in the barracks as he was in the university. Flaubert too was impressed by those Prussian officers

[49] Edmond and Jules de Goncourt, *Idées et sensations* (Paris: Charpentier, 1904), p. 112.

who had also taken a degree and had a command of Sanscrit. The
English and the French could, it was true, discipline themselves in
the same way if need be; but for them such a thing must always
involve a sacrifice, whereas in Germany discipline was life itself. A
longing for organization and division of labour was part of the German
national character: compared with the Germans the French appeared
like a horde of savages charging a trained and organized army.

The most gifted young *agrégés* the French universities could
produce made a pilgrimage to Germany: as a senior official of the
Education Ministry in Paris put it, France needed a bath in realism,
and the country's intelligentsia went off to the German universities
in order there to pass through the hard school of factuality. In 1885
Emile Durkheim too left for Berlin and Leipzig; and it was not least
his sojourn in Germany that determined the way in which the social
sciences afterwards evolved in France.

In the detailed running of the German university Durkheim found
much to criticize: its general organization was anything but perfect,
its studies were too eclectic, the students worked almost exclusively
with a view to passing examinations, and an effective division of
work was lacking in both teaching and study. A sense of the power
and greatness of Germany was widespread, but no one seemed
interested in the everyday questions of politics and those who
happened to hold the positions of responsibility were accorded
unquestioning trust. Seen from a somewhat greater remove,
however, the German university could be only an object of admiration. It was unique in being a living institution in which the most
various parts cohered: you had only to enter a university to be overcome by the feeling that professors and students were striving after
one and the same goal, even if they seemed not always to be clear
what this goal really was. Filled with envy, the sociologist attributed
this to the sense of community that permeated the German university but was wholly lacking in France.

Durkheim was particularly impressed by such socialists of the
chair as Gustav Schmoller and by the experimental psychology of
Wilhelm Wundt: both men were seeking a scientific solution to ethical
problems, and Durkheim's goal was also precisely this. He had
recognized that, committed as it was to an uncompromising separation of church and state, the Third French Republic would need
before all else a secular morality: this morality, a kind of substitute
Catholicism, was in future to be furnished by sociology.

Emile Durkheim was by no means an uncritical admirer of the
German spirit and the German system of education: on the contrary,
he returned home convinced that the scientific sociology of the

future would be at heart a French discipline. He arrived at this prognosis not least by comparing the national characteristics of the two countries. The French were incorrigible Cartesians: they strove for clarity before all else and tended by nature to elucidate complex states of affairs with the simplest explanations they could discover; in doing so they forgot how complicated the life of society actually was. To the Germans, on the other hand, nothing seemed simple: often, indeed, they doubted that the world was explicable at all and withdrew into irrationality. French theorizing was as a rule too simplistic, German theorizing in general too intricate and muddled. The French were optimists and were never at a loss for an explanation; the Germans brooded on the dark obscurity of life and the soul and resigned themselves to never altogether understanding either of them. That, Durkheim triumphantly concluded, was why with the Germans sociology would always remain an imperfect science – while the clear-thinking French, once instructed by the Germans as to the complications of the life of society, would make of sociology the key discipline of the modern world. Thus he went on to formulate his doctrine and create a school, to spread his influence in Bordeaux and in Paris, and to conquer the New Sorbonne.

With the increase in political tension between France and Germany in the period before the First World War the young French scientist's German travels took on a different character: what had at first been a pilgrimage and a mark of distinction became first a matter of routine, then a duty, and finally a sacrifice. When they got back home Parisian scholars rejoiced at the sight of the Ile-de-France, with its poplars and elm trees, after having had to endure nothing but pines and fir trees for so long; one of them complained he had learned nothing in Germany: all he had done was ruin his stomach in the dreadful Berlin pension he had had to live in for a year. Many who had left France as republicans returned as nationalists. And as the attractiveness of Germany declined, there was an increase in attacks at home on Durkheim, who was denounced as a representative of the now hateful German spirit.

Durkheim arrived in Paris in 1902. In the same year the curricula of the French university were subjected to extensive reform; and it was not without reason that Durkheim was suspected of being the architect of that New Sorbonne from which its critics prophesied that philosophy, history, literature and the languages of antiquity would soon vanish to make way for sociology and for execrable language-teaching *à la* Berlitz.

The literary intelligentsia, which stood politically far to the right and included a number of subsequent adherents of the Action

Française, were not least among those who rejected every scientific claim advanced by Durkheim and his school. Maurice Barrès described them as pure metaphysicians, a crack-brained crowd of intellectuals who took a criminal delight in the products of their own corrupted minds. The time had come to degermanize the French elite. How could the *durkheimiens*, who devoted such an indecent amount of attention to the customs of primitive peoples, possibly claim to understand the society of France? Barbarism ruled in the Sorbonne. The success of Durkheim's sociology was alarming: how was it to be explained? The chronology of its penetration of the university furnished the answer.

Sociology had for a long time been the Cinderella of the French university system: there were as a rule no more than two or three *normaliens* interested in the new discipline. Durkheim's early publications had been critically annihilated by such socialist writers as Charles Andler and Lucien Herr, who refused to recognize as a science a discipline which consisted of a confusion of statistics, travellers' tales, second-rate handbooks and so-called observations, and which lacked any precise evaluation whatever of the sources it employed. Sociology was a discipline that could not even state the problems it was proposing to solve. Probably it was already too late to abolish this discipline, but every student should be dissuaded from studying it, and those who none the less did so should be treated with contempt.

The Dreyfus affair, however, brought about a dramatic change: the anti-sociologists – the word existed even then – and the adherents of Durkheim suddenly found themselves in the same boat. Now that they possessed a common enemy they could forget why they had once fought with one another. A similar thing happened to Emile Zola: those who had denounced him as a pornographer embraced him after he had declared for Dreyfus. All at once it seemed to the socialist intellectuals that anyone who was a zealous Dreyfusard and a loyal supporter of the *Ligue des droits de l'homme*, and was thus serving the common cause, could not possibly produce a bad book; and since, as Georges Sorel asserted, all sociologists were on the side of Dreyfus, the discipline they practised could not be such a bad one after all. What had made Durkheim and his adherents the masters of the New Sorbonne was not their intellectual capabilities, it was their political opportunism, the '*dreyfusisme des sociologues*'.[50]

---

[50] Pierre Lasserre, *La Doctrine officielle de l'université. Critique du haut enseignement de l'état. Défense et théorie des humanités classiques* (Paris: Garnier, 1913), p. 180.

Although Durkheim's sociology was, as Pierre Lasserre phrased it, nothing but bad metaphysics in search of an empirical alibi, it would by itself have posed no danger to the French spirit. The so-called French school of sociology, however, resembled above all a German philosophical system: German pantheism was threatening to over-run the Sorbonne, and whereas formerly no one had been in any doubt that the discovery of truth was something to which the French Catholic was pre-eminently suited, the Sorbonne was now suffering increasingly from the influence of Protestant and Jewish minorities. Durkheim was, moreover, not only a Germanophile, he was also the son of a rabbi and his forenames were David Emile.

With Durkheim the era of Victor Cousin seemed suddenly to have returned – that Victor Cousin who had once written to Hegel asking him to unveil the truth to him; to his own people, the French, he would then communicate as much of it as they could understand. It was plain that Durkheim and his adherents had Germanized the Sorbonne. Hippolyte Taine, who was himself partly responsible for it, had foreseen this worst of all forms of decadence: 'We have become political economists, mathematicians, metaphysicians, dilettantes, Englishmen and especially Germans, and have ceased to be writers and Frenchmen.'[51]

Durkheim's sternest critics asked whether his sociology contained anything French at all: German influence upon it was too over-whelming; the entire discipline was 'made in Germany'. But how could it be otherwise, since this discipline was in fact altogether Germanic, and its founding father not Comte but Adam Müller? The Germans instinctively understood what was meant by such expressions as *Volk* and *Volkswirtschaft*, whereas Durkheim's conception of society as a unity *sui generis* was nothing but a cabbalistic formula, an idea that could never take root in France.

Durkheim reacted to reproaches of this kind with the repeated assurance that sociology was by its nature profoundly French. During the First World War his utterances on the subject of his discipline and its place within the culture of France became ever more political: it was with total commitment that he supported the propaganda campaign against Germany, whose aggressive temperament, bel-ligerent posture and violation of all the laws of international justice he deplored; and he expressed his contempt not least for those German colleagues with whom he had once trafficked but who were now the

[51] Hippolyte Taine, 'Madame de la Fayette', in *Essais de critique et d'histoire* (Paris: Librairie Hachette, 1904), p. 259.

accomplices of German militarism and its unheard-of atrocities. According to Durkheim, the relapse of the civilized German nation into the morality of paganism began in the middle of the nineteenth century. The blindly nationalistic attitudes of such an anti-sociologist as Treitschke had led to the worst case of social pathology that could possibly be imagined: the First World War. Durkheim came to the conclusion that it would fall to the historians and sociologists to discover the causes of this sickness and the cure for it. Anticipating the defeat of Prussia, he expressed the hope that henceforth the geography of Europe would be founded on a basis of reason and morality. The victory of France should also be a victory for French sociology.

Even Durkheim's assurance that he had never worked so hard as he had on behalf of his country's war propaganda failed to appease his enemies inside France: as late as 1916 the nationalistic and anti-semitic *Libre parole* called him a Boche with a pasteboard nose and accused him of being an agent of the German war ministry. In the same year his only son, André, fell at the front. Durkheim himself died in 1917.

In the long run, however, the enemies of Durkheim and the New Sorbonne could not suppress the fact that sociology also had its origin in the Restoration or that such counter-revolutionaries as de Maistre and de Bonald must be counted among its forefathers: so that the assaults by the literary intelligentsia of the right were ultimately not assaults on sociology as a whole but only on its illegitimate variety, the sociology of Emile Durkheim and his school. This species of sociology was now confronted by that legitimate because autochthonous sociological doctrine embodied in the works of the later Comte, Le Play and such Catholic social scientists as the Marquis de la Tour du Pin.

The attempt by the ideological right to represent the *durkheimiens* as politically unreliable and to denounce their discipline as an alien one counted on the traditional xenophobia of the French academic world; but in the end it was bound to fail, because the facts too obviously contradicted these calumnies. The *durkheimiens* and their chief were every bit as patriotic as their opponents, only their patriotic enthusiasm was more far-sighted and their critique of Germany and its intellectual tradition less unbridled than was the case with the political right.

What is striking in this regard is the consistency that marks Durkheim's and Lucien Herr's judgment of Germany over the decades: few of those who made the pilgrimage to Germany departed on it as sceptically as they did, and not all returned with their scepticism intact. This appears most strikingly in the case of Herr, who had described Germany as his intellectual fatherland. Of the early *durkheimiens* Herr probably knew the country best, and Charles Andler did right to speculate that it might perhaps have been he and not Wilhelm Dilthey who would have written the account of Hegel's youth if only he had been allowed access to the philosopher's papers; but Karl Hegel, the philosopher's son, rejected his request and wrote to Herr in December 1888 that it was his duty to relinquish his father's manuscripts into the care of German scholars and not to trust them to the hands of a Frenchman and therewith to a nation 'that is so full of peril and animosity for us Germans'.[52]

Herr was a sharp-eyed observer of political life in Germany, whose lack of vitality had struck him as forcibly as it had Durkheim. At bottom he was surprised at how far, contrary to all expectations, France was ahead of the Germans:

There was once a time when a philosophical journey to Germany was a kind of voyage of discovery; with a little skill and luck you could easily bring back home with you a great writer who had never yet been published . . . When you go there today it is neither as a discoverer nor as a pilgrim; yet the trip is none the less still an interesting one. There is little new to learn there. You almost always know it all already. But you do learn to understand better what you already know.[53]

Herr the secretive, a foe not only to all rhetoric but – as his enemies asserted – to all art and poetry as well, Herr the librarian wanted above all things to be a scholar, a *savant*, which was why he was especially attracted to that scientific tendency in sociology associated with the name of Littré. But he could see that on the threshold of the twentieth century no science, not even positivist sociology, was capable of offering a solution to the pressing political and economic questions of the day entirely on its own resources: the sciences needed a dogma. Herr discovered this dogma in socialism: more precisely in scientific socialism, which he sought to distinguish from the mystical socialism of a Péguy. When Lucien Herr called Péguy an anarchist, the latter found it hard to regard this as a reproach; similarly, Herr could accept Péguy's assertion that the sociology of the Durkheim school was the same thing as socialism as a kind of wish-fulfilment. In 1889 there had appeared the *Fabian Essays*: the

[52] Charles Andler, *Vie de Lucien Herr (1864–1926)* (Paris: Rieder, 1932), p. 42.
[53] *Ibid.*, p. 38.

anti-Romantic, rational, scientific and gradualist socialism they espoused made an uncommonly strong impression on Herr; a socialism of this sort would offer a counter to the irrationalism that was more and more infiltrating the spiritual life of France.

Among the Germans, who were by nature disciplined and submissively accepted the ideas and orders of those on whom they had bestowed their trust, there could flourish only a German socialism founded on hierarchy and subordination; French socialists, on the other hand, conceived the alliance that united them as a voluntary one, an association held together not by obedience but by mutual confidence. Maurras had asserted that, of all the European forms of socialism, only the French was not nationalistic; it was the only one in which the idea of class and party predominated over that of country. But it was precisely as a socialist that Lucien Herr, the ally of Durkheim, was a French patriot.

The rise of sociology and the crisis of literature

In May 1909 a pupil at the Clermont-Ferrand high school, Armand Nény, shot himself in the classroom. The incident excited attention; and Maurice Barrès soon seized on it as affording an opportunity for raising in the Chamber the whole question of the state of the French educational system. He pointed to the increasing number of suicides among school pupils and students – e.g. in the Département Seine-et-Marne, in Var, in Bourg-en-Bresse, in Nîmes, and in Lyon – and asked the minister responsible for a statement on the physical and moral health of the French institutions of learning. Twenty-five years previously, he said, the university had been pedantic and ponderous, to be sure; but the sense of repose it exuded had given both professor and student the feeling of security and mutual solidarity they needed.

Now a part of the teaching body had deserted the foundations upon which there rested the ancient system of values of France: unlike their predecessors, these new teachers could no longer speak to their pupils of the security of the family, veneration of their ancestors, the honour of a good name or the consolations of religion, because they themselves no longer believed in these things. In France a generation of cynical teachers was raising a generation of disillusioned pupils. In earlier days schools had been honoured with the names of Rollin and Descartes; now the shameless proposal was being entertained to name a high school after Fragonard, and thus to give a licence to libertinism by order of the state. The public morality of France was in danger, and, Barrès reproached the minister, it was easy to detect who was responsible:

It is incontestable, it is a fact, that we are today confronted by a problem of morality. It is a fact that in the university your teachers and your sociologists, people in the highest places of authority, are there to preach 'a new morality'.[54]

Barrès, on the other hand, did not believe in a 'new' morality: in the matter of correct conduct every rule of behaviour that was not as old as mankind itself was an error. The needs of the soul could be satisfied only if man possessed a family, a country and a religion; religion especially was the decisive force that held societies and civilizations together. And after constant interruptions by cries of protest from the left, Barrès added triumphantly: 'Don't protest! It is not I, but one of your own, M. Durkheim, who has told you in his book on suicide: "Religion undoubtedly exercises a prophylactic influence on one in danger of committing suicide." '[55]

In this passionate-sounding but in fact well-calculated interjection of Barrès there is audible the ambivalent attitude which the literary intelligentsia of the right was constrained to adopt towards the French school of sociology: it condemned the views of Durkheim because they embodied the loss of values that was threatening to destroy the classical culture of France, but at the same time it had need of this same sociology as the source of its own political agitation. Barrès diaries show him to have been a close reader of Durkheim; and it is revealing that, when in November 1912 he encountered Jaurès in a bookshop at the Place Victor-Hugo, the first thing the latter asked him was whether he had read Durkheim's latest book, the *Formes élémentaires de la vie religieuse*.

Sociological problems play an important role in the correspondence between Maurras and Barrès; in October 1895 Barrès delivered in Marseille a lecture on '*La Commune et la région, laboratoires de sociologie*'. And although Maurras continued to regard Auguste Comte as the most important of sociologists, although Barrès counted on, and received, the aid pre-eminently of Gabriel Tarde in his pursuit of the question that lay closest to his heart, that of the decentralization of France – none the less, once they had caught the contagion of sociological thinking they were never again able to elude the influence of Durkheim, the sociologist *par excellence*. It was such *durkheimiens* as Dominique Parodi who noted, with a certain sur-

---

[54] Maurice Barrès at the sitting of the Chamber of Deputies of 21 June 1909; Barrès, *Mes Cahiers*, Vol. 7 (1908–9) (Paris: Plon, 1933), p. 219.   [55] *Ibid.*, p. 223.

prise but evident satisfaction, that the logic of the problems they had
concerned themselves with and the influence exerted upon them by
such writers as Comte and Taine had compelled the politicizing
literary men of the right to conclusions similar to those of Durkheim
– their political and ideological opponent. On the other side,
sympathizers with the literary right admired the sacrifice such
writers as Paul Bourget and Maurice Barrès made when they laid
aside important literary projects

in order to concern themselves with the common welfare. This is a thing
neither amusing nor profitable: for sociology usually leads to contentions
and brings with it small success in the bookshops. But there's no help for it!
It has to be. And future ages will perhaps be grateful to these writers for their
courageous and necessary sacrifice.[56]

It was also such authors as Bourget who searched among writers of
the past for sociologists who could serve the French as counter-
models to Durkheim and his school. First and foremost among them
was Balzac, who had designated himself *docteur ès sciences sociales* and in
the *Comédie Humaine* had depicted a panorama of French society that
was exemplary for all sociologists. Balzac could be named in the
same breath with Bossuet and de Bonald: he was a true sociologist
who showed by his example that science and democracy were by no
means necessarily conjoined, as the ideologists of the Third
Republic maintained they were.

In the literary opponents of Durkheim there was embodied that
anti-Romantic mode of thought which played so significant a role in
the ideological contentions of modern France. In their struggle
against Protestantism and the doctrines of Rousseau such literary
men as Charles Maurras quickly reached the point at which they were
obliged to abandon pure literature for direct political action; when
Maurras analysed the political ideas of Chateaubriand, Michelet and
Sainte-Beuve he composed, in his own words, a treatise on positive
politics, and thereby consciously placed himself in the tradition of
Comte. Writers such as Maurras, who set so much store by the '*petit
fait bien choisi*',[57] and Barrès, who in his youth had preached the cult of
the ego, became in their struggle against Romanticism, which they
regarded as being essentially a German movement, champions of a
sociological aesthetic. And however much they might desire to

[56] Jacques Bainville, 3 August 1906; Bainville, *Journal 1901–1918* (Paris: Plon, 1948),
p. 40.
[57] Maurras to Barrès, 4 November 1888; Maurice Barrès and Charles Maurras, 'La
République ou le Roi', in *Correspondance inédite (1888–1923)* (Paris: Plon, 1970),
p. 18.

appear like social scientists when compared with certain French Romantics, they none the less remained adherents of the counter-Enlightenment, of the later Comte and Le Play, and therewith of writers who had advocated a kind of Romantic sociology. It was in this that the dilemma confronting these reactionary literary men lay: anti-Romantic self-treatment, as Nietzsche called it, did not agree with them, so that the nostalgic disposition they evidenced continually produced, in relation precisely to such sociologists as Durkheim, a profoundly Romantic effect.

In addition to this, there was no ignoring the fact that in an epoch extending from the beginning of the realistic novel to Zola, from Flaubert to the '*petits naturalistes*',[58] literature had acquired a scientific colouring and had thus grown closer to this unloved sociology: the literary right thus called upon a scientist to stigmatize this development as being on the wrong track. Léon Daudet, who had studied medicine for seven years and had been a guest at Charcot's salon, reported that the latter had spoken well of Balzac, little of Flaubert and ill of Zola: with a copy of the *Rougon-Macquart* in his hand he was accustomed to allude to this last as an 'egregiously dirty-minded fellow'.[59]

When the political right assailed a literature they did not like two main centres of attack can be distinguished: one was to damn it as a Romanticism whose conservative orientation could not outweigh its pernicious individualism and whose symbolic representative was Victor Hugo, the 'bard of universal suffrage';[60] the other was to reject it as a Naturalism culminating in the excesses of the 'absurd Zola'.[61] But it is difficult to draw a clear picture of the literary predilections and aversions of all those who gave themselves out to be enemies of Durkheim and the New Sorbonne and defenders of the classic literary culture of France – their temperaments and party allegiances differed too widely for that. Maurras, for example, was barely acquainted with Proust, Mauriac, Gide or Claudel, while Barrès was acquainted with them all and no one did more for Marcel Proust than Léon Daudet.

Confusions were bound to occur. When Marcel Proust, who had been a supporter of Dreyfus from the first, was awarded the Prix Goncourt at the instigation of Léon Daudet, it was rumoured that

---

[58] Maurras to Barrès, 10 April 1892; *ibid.*, p. 61.
[59] Léon Daudet, *Devant la Douleur*, p. 15.
[60] Daudet, 'Victor Hugo ou la légende d'un siècle', *Les Oeuvres dans les hommes* (Paris: Nouvelle Librairie Nationale, 1922), p. 15.
[61] Daudet, *Devant la Douleur*, p. 31.

Daudet had procured the prize for him by way of thanks for Proust's support in the struggle against the Dreyfusards! Misunderstandings of this kind arose among those who believed in the pure exclusivity of political and literary attachments and could not imagine arrangements that cut across them. And it was, moreover, precisely the writers of the right who so often adopted a critical posture towards art and literature; it was not only Maurras who saw the danger of decadence looming above all in literature and warned of an enfeebling and feminizing of France through the instrumentality of art.

Nor did there exist on the right any unanimity of opinion as to how literary production should be organized. Léon Daudet wrote as late as 1938 that nothing was more vital to society – '*la société avec un petit s*'[62] – than a good, independent pen, '*solidement emmanchée*', which knew how to write and dared to call things by their right names. This sounded very like Buffon and recalled Maurras' esteem for the aristocracy of letters. Quite apart, however, from the fact that this heroization of the solitary writer was hard to reconcile with an opposition to Romantic individualism, Maurras and Daudet were both describing a mode of literary production long out of date. In their contempt for modern society they had failed to notice that literary undertakings had long since developed within it in which writers worked not so much from a sense of calling as in order to earn a living. Sainte-Beuve had foretold the appearance of this 'literary industry'[63] as early as 1839; even if one deplored the works representative of it, which were of a boldness unknown to the seventeenth and eighteenth centuries, their existence – they were a phenomenon attending the rise of the daily press and literary democracy – could not be denied.

In their critique of the *chapelles littéraires* Henri Massis and Pierre Lasserre adopted a different tone. To Massis, the values of French culture received expression above all in its literature, whereas in England there existed in this sense no literary culture at all: it was significant that in England the favoured *genre* was biography, a conversation conducted by an author with one other person. In France, on the other hand, literature was a pronouncedly social phenomenon, and behind its multiplicity of styles there lay concealed a common sense of values and a discipline accepted by everyone and the relinquishment of which was not without its perils. But this was precisely

---

[62] Daudet, *Du Roman à l'histoire: Essai* (Paris: Fernand Sorlot, 1938), p. 9.
[63] Charles-Augustin de Sainte-Beuve, 'De la littérature industrielle' [1839], in Sainte-Beuve, *Portraits contemporains*, nouvelle édition revue et corrigée (Paris: Didier, 1855), Vol. 1.

what had happened at the turn of the century; authors who counted as belonging to the political right, such as Péguy and Claudel, hated the age in which they lived so much that they had become fanatics and ended by isolating themselves:

> The most frequent result of such a spiritual condition is that the qualities in which the writer is unique become exaggerated, talent is pushed to the edge, to a place outside, the intellectual is transformed into a being existing for himself alone and his work into something incomprehensible. The contrast is even more striking in the case of those who, like Claudel or Péguy, are through their faith, through the object of their beliefs, members of a great human community.[64]

To the right a literature exclusively for men of literature seemed for political reasons a dangerous thing: they too believed that a literature that produced an effect on society depended for its existence on the existence of a corresponding *conscience collective* on the part of the authors of it. *Conscience collective* is a central concept of Durkheim's sociology: Henri Massis did not employ the term, yet it is hard not to think of Durkheim when Massis deplores the aesthetic individualism of a Paul Claudel and regrets the absence of those quiet workers among writers whose object is not a display of their own uniqueness but *'de faire oeuvre positive'*. In language Durkheim would have understood, Massis and Lasserre called for a literature of solidarity; they confirmed an axiom of the sociology they combatted when they declared that writers could not preserve their individuality in isolation but only through a sharing of their ideas. Only if French literature clung to its relevance to society could it become a 'science of man'[65] or remain the 'essential element of culture'.[66]

On the other side, opinions on the nature of literature were also expressed that those who believed in firm and immovable fronts found no less surprising. Gustave Lanson, for example, who regarded a sociology of literature as quite feasible and a sociological criticism of literature as altogether necessary, was very far from supporting any tendency to turn literature into a science. He knew why programmes of this kind had first been formulated: Romanticism had itself been a reaction to the scientification and politicization of literature by the *philosophes* of the Enlightenment; now the pendulum was swinging back, and some, at any rate, of those who had renounced Romanticism had fallen prey to a faith in science. This

---

[64] Henri Massis, 'Les Chapelles littéraires (Claudel et Péguy)', in *Jugements* (Paris: Plon, 1924), Vol. 2, p. 254.
[65] Pierre Lasserre, *Cinquante ans de pensée française* (Paris: Plon–Nourrit, 1922), p. 266.　　[66] Henri Massis, *Au long d'une vie* (Paris: Plon, 1967), p. 263.

was what made the attack on Romanticism by the political right
seem so paradoxical: they could hardly make such an attack without
putting their own values at risk.

At the same time, to leave Romanticism behind and simultaneously
to curtail the ambitions of a Zola presented no problem at all:
science generalized and quantified, and if the 'roman à intention scien-
tifique'[67] did this it was in danger of debasing itself to mere vulgar
reportage – as had in fact happened with several of the novels of
Zola. Fortunately, as Flaubert had been quick to remark, a trace of
Romanticism could be found even in the Naturalism of a Zola, for
Zola, whose ambition it was to be a Claude Bernard of literature, had
turned out to be merely its second Jules Verne, and when he
credulously quoted the words of some natural scientist he sounded
no different from Maurice Barrès conjuring up St Ignatius. To Lanson,
moreover, the science of history was as much a branch of literature
as was psychology – a discipline in which everything was uncertain
and everything possible. And could anything be more typically
French than to assert that literature had never been closer to the
sciences than in the writings of La Rochefoucauld and La
Bruyère?

And as on the one side the writers were becoming sociologists, so
on the other the sociologists around Durkheim were in no way
inclined to undervalue the capacity of literature to elucidate the real
world. Félix Alcan's publishing house in Paris – a safe retreat for
positivist sociology and home of Durkheim's productions and those
of his school – put out a comprehensive volume entitled La Société
française sous la troisième république d'après les romanciers contemporains; in
his foreword to it the author, Marius-Ary Leblond, maintained that
literature had long ago become a science: that was why in his presentation of certain social characteristics of the Third Republic he had
employed as his sources the novels of the period. This procedure
offered an invaluable advantage over the traditional methods of
science:

Here the analysis, verdict, synthesis is no longer the work of a stiff-necked
historian, a specialist shut up in his study and imprisoned in his discipline,
with all the prejudices his class, his calling and his theories impose upon him;
it is that of twenty novelists, men in the closest touch with life who have
rejoiced in and suffered from it, witnesses and participants who, whether
from naivety or from vanity, have given true and honest evidence . . .[68]

[67] Gustave Lanson, 'La Littérature et la science', Revue Bleue 50 (1892), p. 387.
[68] Marius-Ary Leblond, La Société française sous la troisième république d'après les romanciers
contemporains (Paris: Alcan, 1905), pp. vii–viii.

In view of the *déformation professionelle* that no scientist could avoid in the course of his career, the truth to reality of his depictions of the world had to be regarded with a certain scepticism: if, on the other hand, you took for your basis the works of a number of writers whose positions in life and philosophical outlooks overlapped and complemented one another you had before you a series of social frescoes which reflected and at the same time interpreted contemporary society and constituted something resembling a sociological system. Science had, it seemed, grown increasingly alienated from reality, while literature had become more and more a repository of the empirical world.

Durkheim's opponents differed from one another in their assessment of his aesthetic competence and capacities as a writer. Some, such as the renegade Bourgin, denied him all artistic taste or ability; others admitted that he had at least demonstrated he could write 'good French'.[69] But all those who criticized Durkheim, though they could hardly be said to have read him, failed to see that he was one of those sociologists who was not only familiar with works of literature but knew how to employ them for sociological ends. It was with the aid of literary examples that, in his most empirically orientated book, the treatise on suicide (1897), he developed a classification of types of suicide that has retained its fascination and influence within sociology to the present day: it was Faust and Werther, Musset's Rolla and Don Juan, Lamartine's Raphael and Chateaubriand's René upon whom he drew to distinguish between different species of suicide. Durkheim believed that literature contained a store of human types which sociology could greatly benefit by making use of, for such writers as Lamartine and Chateaubriand had already evolved a differentiation between egoistic and anomic suicide which was highly instructive sociologically. It was certainly not the case that literature furnished in these instances insights of interest only to psychologists; it might be said, rather, that many literary works were more informative than the sort of tractates psychologists usually produced. To draw conclusions of this kind, suggested to him by the way in which many of the characters in novels and dramas behaved, obviously gave Durkheim much pleasure, for, though literature could be made to serve a political end, it could also be employed to refute all those who, like his arch-competitor Gabriel Tarde, persisted in believing they could reduce sociology to psychology.

[69] Pierre Lasserre, *Les Chapelles littéraires* (Paris: Garnier, 1920), p. 199.

The severe depression in sales which affected the whole of French publishing from 1890 to the eve of the First World War left in its train a generation of disappointed aesthetes whose hopes of making a career as critic or author had come to nothing. Many attached themselves to the anti-semitic movement of Drumont, who was himself one of those frustrated literary men, or joined the Action Française; but those *hommes de lettres* who were able as before to make their profession of their predilection also experienced at the turn of the century a cultural change that decisively modified their sense of what it was to be a critic or an author. The novel element in the contentions surrounding the French university was not the sharpness of its polemics, it was the breakdown in communication between the participants. The great men of 1830 – Victor Hugo, Lamartine, Balzac and Michelet – were also continually involved in polemics, but their opponents still spoke the same language as they did; they were 'one and all cultivated in literature, and even if they disliked something they enjoyed getting to know it, reading it and rejecting it – simply because to enliven discussion gave them pleasure and seemed to them the right thing to do'.[70]

Those with whom Agathon and others contended were rarely men of letters: their opponents not only spoke a jargon of their own, they called into question the very presuppositions of the literary culture of France. Everyone, moreover, had the feeling that a tradition had come to an end: around the year 1890 that great workshop, the literature of France, was empty – it stood like a house left open to wind and weather. So wrote Daniel Halévy, and he added: 'Prose, verse, drama: they all had to be created anew, through trial and error and on their own initiative.'[71] This new beginning was made all the more difficult in that it would have to take place at a time when it seemed that public celebrity no longer accrued to poets but only to scientists and to the sociologists and philosophers who aped them: it was of great symbolic significance that in Guillaume Apollinaire's *Poète assassiné* (1916) an agro-chemist from Leipzig should call for a pogrom of poets.

To say that sociology has exerted a marked influence on the development of French literature since the turn of the century would be to go too far. But the rise of this discipline and the role it played as the key discipline in the republican university certainly contributed to an alteration in the cultural climate that also had an

[70] Daniel Halévy, *Péguy et les Cahiers de la Quinzaine* (Paris: Grasset, 1941), p. 215.
[71] *Ibid.*, p. 214.

effect on literature: Marcel Proust spoke of having sought to present in the *Recherche* a sociology of Combray and the Faubourg Saint-Germain; Romain Rolland described in his *Jean-Christophe à Paris* how the intellectuals of France were assembling beneath the banner of sociology; and Jules Romains characterized the mode of thought exhibited in his unanimism as 'meta-sociology', called Durkheim the Descartes of unanimism, and described the novelist as a particular kind of social scientist – which promptly inspired the *durkheimiens* to classify him as the 'poet of sociology'.[72]

On the other side, Lucien Herr's attack on the nationalism of Maurice Barrès inaugurated a campaign in which the right of something as poor in experience as this kind of literature to possess a voice at all in questions of public policy was increasingly contested:

If only you could set aside that which is mere literary excitation you would discover at the bottom of your national patriotism, not old France, which possessed a head and not merely a soul, but conquering, arrogant, brutal, Napoleonic France – that is to say, the chauvinist, flag-wagging patriotism of the big cities and a passionate thirst for fame in war; once again, that is, a barbaric tumultuousness, hatred and a pride in brute force.

All this is literature: it is neither truth nor life.[73]

In the twentieth century no book has influenced the debate on the role of the intellectual more than Julien Benda's *La Trahison des clercs* (1927). Maurras and Barrès appear in it as prototypes of those intellectuals who abandon the defence of eternal values for the pursuit of practical goals. The disastrous inclination of the *clercs* for political action, however, and their scientific ambition, were also the outcome of their confrontation with sociology, that discipline which derived its right to exist from the assertion that the problems of society could be not only represented in literary form and resolved politically but also analysed scientifically. On the other side the upper hand had been seized by the *littérateurs*, in whose work the emotions predominated, form was more important than content, and the desire to please often excluded respect for truth – a new preciosity blind to the social problems of France.

The literary men of the right were thus hostile towards sociology and, because they increasingly feared the competition of the *durkheimiens* in the public discussion of questions central to the nation, denounced them as collaborators of the Germans in science

---

[72] Célestin Bouglé, *Bilan de la sociologie française contemporaine* (Paris: Alcan, 1935), p. 17.

[73] Lucien Herr, 'Lettre à Maurice Barrès', *La Revue Blanche* 15 (1898); Herr, *Choix d'écrits. I. Politique* (Paris: Rieder, 1932), pp. 44–5.

and politics. Through the tempo of historical evolution treasured doctrines soon became waste paper. To call upon the values of old France sounded only like an exercise in nostalgia, and it was because those who did so knew their cause was hopeless that they pursued it with such unheard-of belligerency. While agitated men of letters inscribed and orated themselves into the world of political action, an almost contemplative tone reigned among the sociologists: because nothing could shake them in their conviction that their conceptions exhibited a higher degree of reality, Durkheim and Lucien Herr always produced a more tranquil impression than Maurras and Barrès, Péguy and Massis. Sometimes they may have gone wrong, as they did concerning the coming of the First World War; but to foresee the long-term changes that were to overtake French society they needed only to observe the reality around them, while conservative men of letters had to conjure up a vanished world, or effect a radical change in the society of the present, if they were again to feel at home in it.

This contention was not simply a confrontation between sociologists and men of letters. The borders between the two groups fluctuated: there were writers among the adherents of Durkheim and the right laid claim to sociologists of its own, above all to Auguste Comte, the darling of Maurras. But there was none the less such a thing as a literary and a sociological philosophy of life: in France at the turn of the century 'literature' and 'sociology' became current catchwords with which familiar fronts allowed themselves to be renamed. As Péguy clearly saw, what lay concealed behind the literary men's attacks on the sociology of Emile Durkheim was fundamentally the struggle of the old France against the way in which modern industrial society was tending to evolve.

PART II

ENGLAND

◁ ══════════════════════════════════════ ▷

3

Facts and culture of the feelings:
John Stuart Mill

In May 1820 a young Englishman left for France on his 'Grand Tour'. He had just attained his fourteenth year. During his travels he kept a journal and sent what he had written to his father back in England, so as to keep him regularly informed of what he was doing; as, for example, in the following entry, written in Toulouse:

July 7. Rose at 5¾; till 7, read five chapters of Voltaire; till 7½, 46 lines of Virgil; till 8, commenced Lucian's Jupiter Confutatus. Went then to M. Larrieu's to tell him not to come this morning... found him already set out; returned home; and till nine o'clock took my lesson of Principes de Musique. Till half after nine, continued Lucian; breakfasted; finished Jupiter Confutatus at 10¼. A short time after, M. Daubuisson the astronomer whom I have told you of, came in, which obliged me to dress, but I was not called into the drawing room. Till 11½, read Thomson, made Chemical Tables; from 11¾ to a quarter after twelve read seven propositions of Legendre ... Till 1½ wrote exercises, and various miscellanies: till 2¼, read another portion of the treatise on the Use of Adverbs in the Gram[maire] des Grammaires; till 3¼, read again Thomson. Wrote my Livre Geographique etc. – miscellanies till 5 o'clock; when, by Mr G's advice, I took something to eat ... at after five went to receive a music lesson ... Went immediately after dinner to M. Larrieu's, and took my dancing lesson; returned home and drank tea ... with my Latin, Greek, Mathematics, etc. You see I shall not lead an idle life here.[1]

This young Englishman, who read Lucian and Voltaire before breakfast and often took up a tragedy of Corneille's after dinner, was John Stuart Mill. His father, James Mill, had settled in London in 1802, after having long sought in vain a clerical living in Scotland. Compelled to support a family, which grew to include nine children, by journalism and writing, he began in 1806 a history of India which he intended to complete in three years but which in the end required

[1] *John Mill's Boyhood Visit to France. Being a Journal and Notebook Written by John Stuart Mill in France, 1820–21*, ed. with an introduction by Anna Jean Mill (Toronto: University of Toronto Press, 1960), pp. 36–7.

ten. His *History of India* became a standard work; and, although it was not sparing in its criticism of the East India Company, James Mill acquired in 1819 a post at India House and pursued the steady and secure career of a senior official there. In 1808 he had become acquainted with Jeremy Bentham, the founder of utilitarianism, whose pupil and colleague he remained for the rest of his life, without, however, ceasing to preserve the integrity of his own individual views. James Mill played an important role in the founding of London University; more even than Bentham – whose works, whether consciously or unconsciously, always exhibited traces of waywardness and who remained all his life an oddity and eccentric – he appeared to spectator and friend alike an embodiment of the philosophy of utility: a cold and sober accountant whose every step, in his own existence and in the existence of those he was able to influence, was scrupulously calculated. Bentham was called the spiritual father of Mill, James Mill the spiritual father of Ricardo, and thus also of the science of political economy.

Filled with an imperturbable faith in the revelatory power of facts, constantly on guard against words, which as a rule opened the way to misinterpretations, a foe to all mysticism and sentimentality, James Mill counted as a man without feeling to whom the beauties of art and nature were a closed book. Utilitarian principles and not least the example of Jeremy Bentham, who had learned Greek and Latin at his father's knee and had been called a philosopher when he was only five years old, permeated the methods of education practised by the elder Mill. John Stuart Mill wrote later that he never played cricket and had never been a real boy – he was one of the many children without childhood for whom Rousseau and his *Emile* had failed in their effect.

In his autobiography John Stuart Mill called his own education unusual but hardly worthy of imitation: his father had demanded of him, not merely the greatest effort of which he was capable, but also achievements of which he was altogether incapable. He learned Greek at the age of three, Latin at the age of eight; Pope's translation of the *Iliad* – the first English poetry he attempted – he read twenty to thirty times. Even before breakfast his father employed the walk they regularly took together to examine his son on his lessons. The latter had to instruct in Latin first his sister and then his other brothers and sisters – the part of James Mill's experiment in education which John detested the most. Although James Mill failed to share the general admiration of Shakespeare, and largely neglected the English poetry of his own time, his son had none the less also to write poems: for there were ideas that could be expressed better in verse, and an element of the public had a taste for poetry. Even the practice of reading aloud had a calculated motive behind it: it facilitated the acquisition and exercise of certain rules of modulation of the voice.

Writing his autobiography John Stuart Mill distanced himself from his father's methods of education, but he was too much under the influence of the utilitarian way of thinking to repress the remark that as a child they had enabled him to elude the corrupting influence of other boys and the danger of being infected by vulgar ideas and vulgar expressions of feeling; his father's experimental methods had, by his reckoning, given him a twenty-five-year educational advantage over his contemporaries.

During his youthful sojourn in France John Stuart Mill learned to appreciate the free and unconstrained atmosphere of life on the Continent, the pleasing deportment of a society in which, by contrast to England, everyone did not regard everyone else as either an enemy or a bore. Later he wrote to Comte that the winter of 1820–1 which he spent in Montpellier had been the happiest months of his life. After his return from France Mill founded a debating club which he called the Utilitarian Society: he took the name from John Galt's novel *Annals of the Parish* (1821), in which a parson warns his congregation against abandoning the gospel and becoming 'utilitarians'. The society ceased to exist in 1826, but it was from just that time that its name became a familiar concept. In 1823 John Stuart Mill had also found a position with the East India Company. His material future seemed assured, his spiritual orientation clear: imitating the French *philosophes* of the eighteenth century, he would advocate the radicalism formulated by Bentham and James Mill.

But in October 1826 John Stuart Mill awoke as though from a dream – and the account he gives in his *Autobiography* of this turning-point in his life makes it incomprehensible that Carlyle should have judged the book one of the least interesting he had ever read: he called it the confessions of a steam-engine. From when he had first read Bentham, Mill had also wanted to be a world-betterer; but when he first asked himself seriously what all his knowledge and all his accomplishments meant to him, the answer was devastating:

In this frame of mind it occurred to me to put the question directly to myself: 'Suppose that all your objects in life were realized; that all the changes in institutions and opinions which you are looking forward to, could be completely effected at this very instant: would this be a great joy and happiness to you?' And an irrepressible self-consciousness distinctly answered, 'No!' At this my heart sank within me: the whole foundation on which my life was constructed fell down . . . I seemed to have nothing left to live for.[2]

Mill was struck by this crisis in the year Auguste Comte experienced the worst of his mental disturbances: but whereas Comte's evaluation of the affective side of life and the role literature could play in the cultivation of the affects altered only nineteen years later, when it altered dramatically on his becoming acquainted with Clotilde de Vaux, Mill discovered an immediate remedy for his crisis in poetry and in a reassessment of the culture of feeling. At the same time he began the painful process of liberating himself from the model example represented by his father.

To his son James Mill united the qualities of the Stoic, the Epicurean and the Cynic of antiquity: he was a Stoic in all that pertained to his personal behaviour; his morality was Epicurean, in as much as he evaluated actions entirely according to whether they were conducive to pleasure or to pain; he counted as a Cynic because pleasure seemed to mean nothing to him – he was not unsusceptible to it, but the price which contemporary society exacted for it seemed to him on the whole too high.

As John Stuart Mill wrote in 1835, the fame of England rested on its docks, its canals and its railways. The English intellect was distinguished by a sound and sober common sense that abstained from every kind of extravagance; it directed itself to those tasks that could be best accomplished if they were performed with the precision of a machine, and in doing so itself became more machine-like. James Mill was ashamed of exhibiting emotions of any kind, as most Englishmen were; and since they were not exhibited they finally atrophied altogether. He was not cold or insensitive, he was merely convinced that the feelings could be left to themselves; all he was concerned with was the performance of actions that accorded with the principles of the greatest possible utility. The commanding role played by logic and analysis in his life's economy led to a neglect of the culture of feeling and therewith to an underestimation of poetical literature and the imagination.

In the winter of 1826–7, whose melancholy mood he was subsequently able to recall in every detail, John Stuart Mill could no longer unburden himself to his father: to have done so would have been to

---

[2] John Stuart Mill, *Autobiography and Literary Essays*, ed. John M. Robson and Jack Stillinger, Collected Works of John Stuart Mill, 1 (Toronto: University of Toronto Press, 1981), p. 139.

demonstrate to him that his educational regime had failed. But it was wholly in the spirit of James Mill that his son should in the end have acquired relief from a book: in the memoirs of Marmontel he read the account of the death of Marmontel's father and was reduced to tears; he came to realize that he possessed not only an intellect but feelings as well.

It is not only psychoanalytically-minded biographers who have interpreted Mill's recollection of this reading experience as the expression of a desire for the death of his own father. Mill makes no mention of another, earlier passage in the memoirs, though he had certainly read it, which shows how completely Marmontel's father had been the antithesis of James Mill:

I had a great desire to learn, but nature had denied me the gift of memory... it was as wearisome as if I had written in sand... the labour was too much for the strength I possessed at that age; my nerves were affected by it. I behaved like a sleepwalker: during the night I arose while asleep and with my eyes open recited the lessons I had learned. He will go mad, my father said to my mother, if you do not let him give up this miserable Latin; and my study of it was broken off.[3]

His reading of Marmontel and Thomas Carlyle's vehemently expounded theory of 'anti-self-consciousness' convinced John Stuart Mill of the necessity of developing new principles of an indirect conduct of life: it seemed that you could be happy only if you did not strive after happiness; it was something acquired only incidentally, and to ask yourself if you were happy was already proof you were not. The individual's philosophical duty lay in trying to establish an equilibrium between his capacities; and since his father's educational methods had led to an over-straining of Mill's intellectual capacity, he resolved that henceforth emphasis would be placed on cultivation of the feelings. In this, music played an important role; he listened to Mozart and to Weber's *Oberon*. But even this enjoyment was not without its difficulties, for Mill's tendency to calculation, strengthened as it had been by his father, remained as lively as ever: once you knew each individual piece of music the pleasure you derived from it declined; the range of possibilities of musical expression was, moreover, limited, and the likelihood of new Mozarts and Webers arising in the future was small. Such curious reflections demonstrated, not only how little Mill under-

---

[3] Jean François Marmontel, *Mémoires* [1804], édition critique établie par John Renwick (Clermont-Ferrand: Collection Ecrivains d'Auvergne, G. de Bussac, 1972), Vol. 1, p. 5 (Livre premier).

stood of music, but also that his reason was still ruling his feelings and impairing his capacity for enjoyment.

It soon became apparent to Mill how wise his decision had been to adopt the method of an indirect conduct of life. Since he felt an affinity with Byron's heroes Harold and Manfred, he had at first read Byron in the spirit of taking a dose of medicine; but the cure had been unsuccessful. The poems of Wordsworth, however, which he read in 1828 purely out of curiosity, had had an immediate salutary effect and freed him from his depression for ever. Wordsworth's rural scenes calmed him; Wordsworth's mountains recalled to him his sojourn in France and the excursions to the Pyrenees on which he had once been so happy. Wordsworth's poems acted therapeutically because the poet depicted in them, not only exterior beauty, but states of feeling, thoughts which in their enthusiasm for the beautiful were coloured by feeling. In the poems of William Wordsworth Mill discovered that 'culture of the feelings'[4] for which he had been seeking. Wordsworth had himself passed through a crisis comparable to Mill's; he was the poet of unpoetical nature, a poet–therapist for those in need of help in the enhancement of their sensibilities.

Mill wanted to share his enjoyment of Wordsworth's poetry; and on two discussion evenings at the Debating Society he publicly defended his new hero. His opponent was Roebuck, who stood as an advocate of Byron, maintaining that Byron was to be preferred to Wordsworth as a poet of human life; the latter he deprecatingly described as the poet of flowers and butterflies. Roebuck was, as Mill emphasized, not typical of the adherents of Bentham and the doctrine of utilitarianism: he was sensitive and receptive to the arts, and thus presented an admirable example of how greatly the English national character and the peculiarities of English society stood in the way of the creation of a true culture of feeling.

In 1829 Mill withdrew from the Debating Society; and the more alienated from his former friends he became, the closer he drew to his former opponents, the 'intuitionists' who allied themselves with Coleridge. At the end of 1798 Coleridge had left for Germany in the company of Wordsworth and Wordsworth's sister, Dorothy, and had stayed there until August 1799: through Coleridge, who sought to re-establish the imagination as the true foundation of poetry, Continental thought, and German literature especially, acquired ever increasing significance in England. Goethe, whose multi-

---

[4] Mill, *Autobiography*, p. 151.

fariousness everyone tried to emulate, became a leading figure; *Wilhelm Meister* was revered as the 'gospel of experience'.[5] Mill did not remain unaffected by all this: as late as April 1843 he congratulated Auguste Comte on his decision to read the German poets rather than the German thinkers. As to Goethe's rank as a poet he and Comte were of one opinion, but he strove to revise the latter's harsh verdict on Schiller: he recommended *Wallenstein*, the *Jungfrau von Orleans* and *Wilhelm Tell* to him, saying he had discovered in them the abilities of a true, if not first-rate poet. He also commended the novels of Tieck and Jean Paul, which he preferred even to Goethe's.

In the light of the hostility towards art and literature evinced by the early utilitarians, Mill's conversion to literature and his public advocacy of Wordsworth and Coleridge take on the aspect of a revolt. Bentham had been a rigorous adherent of empiricism and a fanatical champion of applied science of a kind that concerned itself with theoretical problems only when their solution promised immediate practical results. Fixated to the goal of practical utility, Bentham and James Mill stood alienated from art and literature: if poetry was of no practical utility, reading poems was on a par with playing skittles. In Bentham's eyes the only difference between prose and poetry was that in the case of poetry the lines of print did not always reach the margin of the page; to him, the arts and sciences were 'excellent substitutes for drunkenness, slander and the love of gaming'.[6] Between poetry and truth there existed the sharpest contradiction that could possibly be imagined: no matter how loudly a poet might proclaim he was striving for veracity, he could never become a philosopher but would always remain a 'dealer in fictions'.[7] If Taine maintained that in the head of an Englishman there could be discovered 'many facts but few ideas, no capacity for generalization and no feeling for the pleasures of literature; the inside of an Englishman's head looks like a simple storeroom filled with serious and verified documents',[8] the responsibility for such an image rested not least with the utilitarians.

In the *Westminster Review*, which Bentham and his friends had founded in 1824, the reviewers made short work of poetry and literature: an age which owed the progress it had made solely to the sciences, and

[5] John Sterling, 16 October 1841; Caroline Fox, *Memories of Old Friends. Being Extracts from the Journals and Letters of Caroline Fox ... from 1835 to 1871*, ed. Horace N. Pym (London: Smith, Elder and Co., 1882), p. 142.
[6] F. Parvin Sharpless, *The Literary Criticism of John Stuart Mill* (The Hague and Paris: Mouton, 1967), p. 23.   [7] *Ibid.*, p. 24.
[8] Hippolyte Taine, *Notes sur l'Angleterre* (Paris: Hachette, 1899), p. 324.

above all to those disciplines that concerned themselves with politics and justice, with the economy, business and mathematics, could only renounce the practice of literature as mere phrase-making. Literary men, *bel esprits* and bluestockings were sick, and they had to be isolated in case they infected others. And since it was just those qualities of mind which 'fit a man for the production of fine poetry' that 'tend in a great degree to incapacitate him for the strict process of logical deduction',[9] a scientific propaedeutic ought to replace instruction in dead languages and literatures in the schools. Historical novels and poems were harmless only when they treated of the very distant past; and few utilitarians were prepared to accept contemplative poetry at all.

Mill, however, seemed more and more to retreat from his original views. When the July Revolution broke out he at once journeyed to Paris, where he became acquainted with Lafayette and deluded himself he was about to begin a wholly new existence. For the *Examiner* he wrote, from January to May 1831, a series of articles entitled 'The Spirit of the Age': in his autobiography he characterized them as a mixture of poetry and German metaphysics and as being filled with a distrust of everything upon which his thought and actions had previously been founded. Thomas Carlyle read the articles on his lonely Scottish moor at Craigenputtock and hailed John Stuart Mill, the son of James Mill and Bentham's fellow-worker, as a new mystic.

In reality, however, Mill was far from transforming himself into a mystic; that it was precisely Wordsworth who came to act as a poet–therapist to him shows, indeed, that the danger of that happening had never been very great, for Wordsworth championed a form of Rousseauism in which the precise description of personal experience constituted the basis of poetry and to that extent brought poetry closer to science. William Wordsworth was no poet of fantasy but one who depicted with precision those 'regular feelings'[10] that characterized rural life. In the preface to the second edition of his *Lyrical Ballads* (1800) he sought to develop systematically the theory that underlay his poetry; and he also desired to distance himself from the fashionable craze for the sensational and exotic which found expression in turbulent novels and pathological German tragedies – an inevitable consequence of the ever greater accumulation in the

---

[9] Peregrine Bingham in the *Westminster Review* 1 (1824), p. 18, in Sharpless, *The Literary Criticism of John Stuart Mill*, p. 37.

[10] *The Poetical Works of William Wordsworth*, ed. William Knight (Edinburgh: William Paterson, 1883), Vol. 4, p. 276.

cities of masses of men seeking in this way to escape from the compulsory uniformity of their lives.

To readers such as Mill it was important that Wordsworth preferred the common differentiation of poetry and prose to what he called the philosophical distinction between poetry and science or knowledge of facts: for Wordsworth the activity of the poet was distinguished by its seriousness; poetry was not an amusement or a pastime, but a tireless search for universal truth. Fidelity to fact was harder to achieve for a biographer or a historian than it was for a poet who took his job seriously. What the poet communicated was not the specialized knowledge of a lawyer, a physician, an astronomer or a natural scientist, but knowledge that was of utility because it evoked delight and sympathy: following in the wake of the natural scientist, the poet endeavoured to bring to the findings of science an emotional reaction – in anticipation of the day when all men would be on familiar terms with science.

Wordsworth's poetic practice did not always correspond to his theories: the poet in him was often at odds with the thinker. Coleridge deplored the sober factuality of Wordsworth's ballads, yet this was the quality in them that attracted Mill: Wordsworth defined poetry with didactic seriousness as a science of the feelings – so that Mill, who, though he was trying to distance himself from it, was still captive to utilitarian thinking, could call upon him as his chief witness when he pleaded the case for according a larger significance to the culture of the feelings.

In an unpublished address he gave in 1827 or 1828, Mill described the current state of literature in England: by literature he understood, in accordance with the usage of the time, not only works of imagination or *belles-lettres* but any publication directed at the general interested reader and dealing with political, ethical or in the narrower sense literary subjects. Philosophy and the natural sciences were regarded as something distinct from this 'literature' – but the division was not nearly as sharp as that made by Bentham and James Mill when they characterized scientific activity as useful and renounced literary activity as a useless waste of time. Whether or not Mill had read Wordsworth at the time of this address, his assertion that every writer was a human being first and only then a poet, philosopher or scientist levelled the trench the utilitarians had dug between literature and science and corresponded exactly to Wordsworth's view of the matter. Curiously, Mill wrote his address on the back of the manuscript of Jeremy Bentham's essay on 'Evidence', which

Bentham had written in 1806: when he turned to literature Mill was trying to free himself from the fetters of utilitarianism without giving it up altogether.

Poetry, history, sociology

During the years 1829 to 1843 Mill concerned himself with problems of aesthetics – in essays that rang as firm and definite as statements of principles and in reviews of volumes of poetry and works of history in which he stated his position regarding the relationship between poetry and history only incidentally. Like Wordsworth he set poetry, or the expression of feelings and emotions, in opposition to factual knowledge, or science; in addition he laid stress on according poetry a status higher than that of the novel: poems were profound because they expressed the feelings of the innermost man, while novels, on the contrary, were superficial because they employed actions and events merely to draw a picture of the external world. A passion for story-telling belonged to an early stage of development, whether of the individual or of society; it was especially strong in children and in primitive peoples.

Mill conceived the process of writing poetry as a solitary act and the poem as a monologue: while the speaker addressed an audience, the poet spoke only to himself; the former one listened to, the latter one overheard. Poetry was the natural fruit of solitude and meditation. But it was necessary to distinguish between two kinds of poet: the 'poet of culture'[11] who transformed prosaic objects into poetry, as Wordsworth clothed his thoughts in feelings, and the 'poet of nature' who, like Shelley, was the embodiment of a poetical temperament. Wordsworth was a poet because he had decided to become one; Shelley was a poet because he had no other choice.

The philosopher could not become a poet, but the poet could certainly become a philosopher: he had to, indeed, when the feelings he sought to express were so weighty that only an intellect of a like capacity could sustain them. Such poet–philosophers engaged Mill's sympathies more than the pure poets did: every great poet – and Tennyson was another example – who had exerted a lasting influence on mankind was also a great thinker and possessed a philosophy, even if he did not call it that.

Of all the genres in which poetry and science were thus mingled the greatest was historiography, and of all works of historiography

[11] Mill, 'Thoughts on Poetry and its Varieties' [1833], in Mill, *Autobiography and Literary Essays*, p. 356.

the greatest was Thomas Carlyle's *French Revolution*, in which the
'laborious accuracy of a chronicler'[12] was united with the 'vivid
imagination of a poet':

This is not so much a history, as an epic poem; and notwithstanding, or even
in consequence of this, the truest of histories. It is the history of the French
Revolution, and the poetry of it, both in one; and on the whole no work of
greater genius, either historical or poetical, has been produced in this country
for many years.[13]

Although he was altogether critical of Carlyle's style, and mocked at
some of his phraseology as having been borrowed from German
poetry and metaphysics, Mill discovered in the *French Revolution* a
poetic–historical power otherwise to be found only in *Wallensteins
Lager*. Carlyle's method was that of the artist, not that of the scientist; instead of dissecting the individual elements into their constituent parts he joined them together to create greater unities. He
brought to light the poetical aspect of reality, the feelings that were
at the bottom of all actuality: 'At the deathbed of every peasant there
is enacted the fifth act of a tragedy.'[14]

What applied to Carlyle applied also to a large number of French
historiographers, though because most English people were content
to read only Balzac and Eugène Sue these French historiographers
were unknown in England. The French were equally adept at narration and argumentation, at historical research and historical depic-
tion; and since, unlike in England, poetry and politics in France were
not regarded as mere pastimes but taken with perfect seriousness,
poetry and politics there illumined one another, and French historians not only wrote history but made it as well. Thierry's *Récits des
Temps Merovingiens*, for example, possessed a charm and beauty that
made a reading of it as pleasing as if the true events it narrated had
been invented.

Every attempt to understand the past as it really was demanded the
imaginative powers of a poet; and Michelet, the 'subjective historian
of the Middle Ages',[15] was a poet even whose errors were to be preferred to the banal prose in which history was commonly written.
His sketch of Brittany had only to be versified to become a genuine
poem. Michelet was a historian–poet because he did not content

---

[12] Mill, 'Michelet's History of France' [1844]; in *Dissertations and Discussions . . . in four
volumes*, 3rd edition (London: Longmans, Green, Reader and Dyer, 1875), Vol.
2, p. 120.
[13] Mill, 'Carlyle's *French Revolution*' [1837], in *Mill's Essays on Literature and Society*, ed.
with an introduction by J. B. Schneewind (New York: Collier Books, 1965),
p. 184.   [14] *Ibid.*, p. 190.   [15] Mill, 'Michelet's History of France', p. 141.

himself with describing the spiritual life of the cultivated or the social life of the people, but took an interest in the inner life of men, in their thoughts and feelings.

How well suited the confrontation between the scientific and the poetical temperament was for an understanding of the foundations of the nineteenth century is shown by Mill's essays on Bentham (1838) and Coleridge (1840). Bentham was a progressive, Coleridge a conservative; Bentham asked 'Is this true?',[16] Coleridge asked 'What does this mean?' In the nineteenth century every Englishman was either a Benthamite or a Coleridgian.

Bentham was the great subversive, a critical spirit that always denied and called into question all that existed, one of those negative thinkers who possess no programme of their own because they are wholly occupied in exposing the absurdities of their age. Bentham's originality lay in his method, which, though it did justice to details, in the process lost sight of the whole or represented it falsely. Bentham was the first to formulate the problems of ethics and the philosophy of politics with precision, yet he lacked the imagination and poetical cultivation that would have enabled him to put himself in the place of those who thought differently from him. Thus Bentham's knowledge of human nature was limited: he embodied the 'empiricism of one who has had little experience'.[17]

In Coleridge, on the other hand, the over-reaction of the Romantic, poetic nineteenth century to the excesses of the eighteenth found expression: 'It is ontological, because that was experimental; conservative, because that was innovative; religious, because so much of that was infidel; concrete and historical because that was abstract and metaphysical; poetical, because that was matter-of-fact and prosaic.'[18]

In the essays on Bentham and Coleridge Mill united acuteness of argument with hermeneutic discoveries. In Bentham and Coleridge he found embodied not only the tendencies of the age but also ways of thinking that struggled with one another in his own mind; so that when he considered plausible Leibniz's judgment that sects are usually right in what they revere and wrong in what they damn, and drew from it the conclusion that to perfect their own doctrines Bentham and Coleridge had only to comprehend those of their opponents, he was expressing a desire to preserve in himself the best

---

[16] Mill, 'Coleridge' [1840], in *Essays on Ethics, Religion and Society*, ed. J. M. Robson, Collected Works of John Stuart Mill, 10 (Toronto: University of Toronto Press, 1969), p. 119.   [17] Mill, 'Bentham' [1838], in *Essays on Ethics*, p. 92.
[18] Mill, 'Coleridge', p. 125.

of both of them: care for detail and view of the whole, rigorousness of method and culture of the feelings, factual knowledge and poetry. Traces of this desire can still be detected in 1843 in his *System of Logic*.

In this early logic of the social sciences Mill rejects two procedures as being inappropriate for sociology: the experimental chemical procedure espoused by the followers of Bacon, and the abstract geometrical procedure which consisted in starting from some general assumption, such as the social contract, and applying it to a particular situation. Even if sociology, this 'most complex of all studies',[19] admitted of no exact prognosis, sociological knowledge could none the less assist in the description of developmental tendencies and thus help to orientate action in the right direction.

What made the composition of sociological theories and the practical application of sociological knowledge so difficult was that the facts of society with which they dealt were all interwoven with one another: if you treated any of them in isolation you ran the risk of being unable either to explain societies or to regulate them. The only procedure appropriate to sociology was the inverse-deductive or historical method:

While it is an imperative rule never to introduce any generalization from history into the social science unless sufficient grounds can be pointed out for it in human nature . . . history does, when judiciously examined, afford Empirical Laws of Society. The problem of general sociology is to ascertain these, and connect them with the laws of human nature . . .[20]

Mill lamented the fact that many still refused to recognize history as a valid science but rejected it as 'mere literature or erudition'.[21] This was the more regrettable in that sociology had to place especial reliance on history: it was only with the aid of history that doctrines and convictions could be tested and confirmed. A long succession of thinkers extending from Herder to Michelet had long since made of history a 'science of causes and effects'[22] – not because these historians aped the exact sciences in their methods of procedure but because they knew how to assign to the facts and events of the past their significance and proper place in the history of mankind's evolution. Through exposing the processes that produced the world of

---

[19] Mill, *A System of Logic Ratiocinative and Inductive . . .* [1843], 2 vols, ed. J. M. Robson and R. F. McRae, Collected Works of John Stuart Mill, 7, 8 (Toronto: University of Toronto Press, 1973–4), Vol. 2, p. 895.

[20] *Ibid.*, pp. 915–16.

[21] Mill, 'Guizot's Essays and Lectures on History' [1845], in *Dissertations . . .*, Vol. 2, p. 220.　　[22] Mill, 'Coleridge', p. 139.

the present and continued to characterize it, these thinkers made history as interesting as a novel and at the same time a means of foreshadowing the future and thus correctly preparing men for it. It was its hermeneutic–literary qualities which assured history of its place among the sciences.

A reader of Mill's *Essay on Liberty*, perhaps his most celebrated work, called it, with its merciless logic, a terrible book, 'so clear and calm, and cold'.[23] At first sight the *System of Logic* produces a similar impression: yet it also exhibits, especially in the passages on sociological method, traits that are distinctly autobiographical. For the inverse-deductive method which accords history so important a role in the logic of the social sciences allows literature and sociology to come together as it were through the back door. The sociologist placed all his hopes on an understanding historian who drew forth the lines along which history had developed and at the same time held them together as a narrator held together the threads of his story. When Mill said that if Bentham the dissenter and Coleridge the empathizer could only understand one another they would discover, not merely their own truth, but truth as such, there was concealed in this assertion a desire and a flavour of utopianism: and something of this desire and utopianism can still be detected even in his most abstract reflections on the methodology of the social sciences.

A partnership of thought, feeling and writing

Within the circle of his friends the outcome of John Stuart Mill's reading of Wordsworth was viewed with a somewhat critical eye: rigorous philosopher as he was, and by temperament and upbringing little likely to be drawn to poetry, he could only involve himself in confusion when he sought to effect an understanding between poetry and science. He had been and still was proud of his ability to prove everything, and with Carlyle, who doubted that science had anything at all to say about poetry, many asked themselves what poetry really meant to this patron saint of rationalism.

Even in Mill's panegyric of Carlyle's poetical history of the French Revolution there is an element of criticism: the author overdid his contempt for scientific method, analysis and generalizing conclusions; he had failed to grasp that we had need of general principles if we were to understand anything at all, or that perception itself was

[23] Caroline Fox to E. T. Carne, 25 November 1859; Fox, *Memories of Old Friends*, p. 322.

permeated by theory. In 1854 Mill noted in his diary that the Germans, and after them Carlyle, had perverted thought and language when they chose the artist as the symbol of moral and intellectual greatness: the artist had always to take second place to the philosopher and the poet to the scientist:

Philosophy is the proper name for that exercise of the intellect which enucleates the truth to be expressed. The Artist is not the seer; nor he who can detect truth, but he who can clothe a given truth in the most expressive and impressive symbols.[24]

It is noteworthy that in his autobiography Mill regretfully admitted he had formerly treated Bentham too harshly and Coleridge too benevolently.

Auguste Comte, said Mill, offered a warning example of a scholar who, the more he discovered feeling, the more he lost the capacity for systematic thought. If he had been a poet, the hatred of science which he gradually developed could have been forgiven him. As it was, they had to count it fortunate that there existed such positivists as Littré, who had still remained pupils of the earlier Comte who wrote the *Cours de philosophie positive*, for the sentimentality of the later Comte threatened positivism with ruin.

One rarely receives the impression that Mill really enjoyed the poetry he deals with in his treatises in such detail: it is a reasonable supposition that Wordsworth's commentaries helped him through his spiritual crisis as much as his poems did. As Mill himself wrote, in the last resort poetry was for him a kind of medicine: one took it, not because one enjoyed it, but because it acted as an aid and prophylactic. His decision to allow poetry a larger place in the culture of his age was taken on theoretical grounds, and his enthusiasm for it thus appears forced and occasionally comical:

After dinner Mr Mill read us Shelley's Ode to Liberty and he got quite excited and moved over it rocking backwards and forwards and nearly choking with emotion; he said himself: 'it is almost too much for one'.[25]

Nietzsche, who had seen through the later Comte, was not deceived by Mill either: Mill, he said, did nothing more than '*formulate* his moral sensations. Something quite different is called for: the capacity for one to have *different* sensations.'[26]

---

[24] Mill's Diary, 11 April 1854; *Essays on Literature and Society*, pp. 351–2.
[25] Kate Amberley's Journal, 28 September 1870; *The Amberley Papers: The Letters and Diaries of Lord and Lady Amberley*, ed. Bertrand and Patricia Russell, 2 vols, (London: The Hogarth Press, 1937), vol. 2, p. 375.
[26] Friedrich Nietzsche, *Nachgelassene Fragmente* [1880], *Sämtliche Werke*, Kritische Studienausgabe in 15 Bänden, ed. Giorgio Colli and Mazzino Montinari (München: Deutscher Taschenbuch Verlag, 1980), Vol. 9, p. 369.

Like Comte, Mill passed through severe spiritual crises, and, somewhat startlingly, did so at the same time; both believed their cause
lay in the exaggerated intellectualization of their lives and their
scientific occupations. They reacted with a rehabilitation of the culture of feeling and a dramatic change in their values: literature
gained increasingly in significance as compared with the sciences. In
both cases this process of the emotionalizing of their life and literary
enhancement of their work was accelerated and reinforced by a
relationship with a woman.

John Stuart Mill met Harriet Taylor in 1830: she was twenty-two,
he was twenty-four. As Mill wrote in his autobiography, Harriet was
married to an upright and honourable man who lacked, however,
any artistic or intellectual interests that could have made him his
wife's equal partner. To Mill, Harriet was a feminine genius, 'a
woman of deep and strong feeling, of penetrating and intuitive
intelligence, and of an eminently meditative and poetic nature'.[27] In
this she resembled Shelley, though she greatly excelled him in
reasoning power; she united in one person the virtues of Bentham
and Coleridge. And Mill was not the only one she impressed: Carlyle
called her a young philosophical beauty and a heroine of a novel
come to life.

Harriet, who had ambitions of her own, was not unreceptive to
Mill's advances, but none the less she stayed with her husband and
her three children. Without ever committing adultery, Mill and his
Platonica – another name given her by Carlyle – lived together for
long periods on the Continent, in England, and even in her husband's house: it was a strange, chaste *ménage à trois* in which Harriet
and Mill passionately debated philosophy and science together while
John Taylor, 'the greatest philosopher of the three',[28] kept silent. It
was inevitable that this relationship should irritate Mill's circle of
friends; and as a result of it he withdrew himself more and more from
all social obligations.

James Mill had died in 1836, and in 1849 John Taylor died: two
years later John Stuart Mill and Harriet were married. They lived
together for seven years, withdrawn from society and occupied with
projects they worked on together, often plagued with illnesses for
which Harriet sought a cure in the Midi, above all in Hyères. While
they were on their way for another stay there Harriet died, on

[27] Mill, *Autobiography*, p. 193.
[28] Jules Véran, 'Le souvenir de Stuart Mill à Avignon', *Revue des Deux Mondes* 107
(1937), p. 212.

3 November 1858 at the Hotel de l'Europe in Avignon; in the churchyard at the suburb of Saint-Véran Mill erected to her a monument whose inscription reads: 'Were there even a few hearts and intellects like hers, this earth would already become the hoped-for heaven.'[29] He purchased a house in Saint-Véran close to the churchyard and from then on lived in Avignon. Helen Taylor, his stepdaughter, became his assistant and confidante.

Mill's huge herbarium was already a source of admiration to his friends, and his love of botany now increased. In Orange he became acquainted with Jean-Henri Fabre, whom he esteemed as a practitioner of the inductive method and helped out of his financial difficulties when, as a consequence of having admitted girls to the classes in natural science, Fabre had been dismissed from his post at a *lycée* in Avignon; on 3 May 1873 Mill and Fabre, who were then working together on a *Flore de Vaucluse*, undertook an extended botanical excursion on which Mill contracted a cold and a fever. Four days later he died; in accordance with his wish he was buried, not in Westminster Abbey, but beside Harriet at Avignon.

The extent of Harriet Taylor's influence on Mill and what effect it had on his work is a matter of dispute. One thing, however, is certain: whatever influence there was, Mill rose well above it – a fact confirmed by many of his friends and by Nietzsche, who, pitiless as ever, spoke only of the 'philosophical chatter... of Mrs John Stuart Mill'[30] and compared her in this regard with George Sand.

To Mill, Harriet embodied poetic and artistic perfection: their earlier years of friendship were years of poetry, life with her was a 'partnership of thought, feeling and writing'.[31] When in 1832 Mill's article 'What is Poetry?' appeared it was generally ascribed to the influence of Harriet, since she had published poems and revues in Fox's *Monthly Repository*, while Mill was regarded as unreceptive to art. She undoubtedly influenced him on feminist questions and hastened his breach with Comte. When she came to know Mill's correspondence with Comte she wrote: 'I am disappointed at a tone more than half-apologetic with which you state your opinions. And I am charmed with the exceeding nicety, elegance and fineness of

---

[29] John M. Robson, 'Harriet Taylor and John Stuart Mill: Artist and Scientist', *Queens Quarterly* 73 (1966), p. 168.

[30] Nietzsche, *Nachgelassene Fragmente* [1884], *Kritische Studienausgabe*, Vol. 11, p. 100.

[31] Mill, *Autobiography*, p. 247.

your last letter... This dry sort of man is not a worthy coadjutor and scarcely a worthy opponent.'[32]

Even though Mill did laud Harriet's majestic intellect and call her the co-author of his books – from the *Principles of Political Economy* (1848), which they produced together, to the *Essay on Liberty*, which appeared a year after Harriet's death – her greatest importance for them lay in the humanity and poetical nature through which she supplemented and completed his abstract and scientific spirit. It was for this reason that Mill's recollection of his dead wife also took on a religious colouring – just as Comte had preserved the memory of Clotilde de Vaux in the religion of humanity and the cult that promoted it. When W. J. Fox received news of Harriet's death he wrote to his daughter that Mrs Mill's gravestone could bear the words: 'A greater than Laura is here.'[33] The cultivated of the time found it natural to associate the death of a clever and beautiful woman in Avignon with Petrarch. Comte had only a few years previously lamented the loss of his Laura: Clotilde de Vaux had played for him a role similar to that which Harriet Taylor played for John Stuart Mill.

Yet the differences between Comte and Mill must not be overlooked. Compared with Comte, to whom everything in the end became drama, excess and transfiguration, Mill still seems clear of mind even in his catastrophic phases. Mill's feelings when he thought of Harriet assumed a religious significance; Comte, on the other hand, dedicated to Clotilde a cult which he practised with every manifestation of mania – in the end he became the self-appointed high priest of humanity. Mill needed to celebrate no spiritual wedding to a woman he had lived with for many years and been married to for seven.

Apart from differences in temperament, reasons connected with their professional situation were also responsible for the different reactions of Comte and Mill. Comte never had a secure post and seldom one that brought him enough to live on: he remained all his life a solitary producer of theories for whom there were no critical colleagues but only enemies or disciples. Mill, who later became a Member of Parliament, always enjoyed a secure existence; and even though he had enemies as well as friends, the intellectual climate of England preserved him from too great excesses of thought and

---

[32] Harriet Taylor to John Stuart Mill, 1844; F. A. Hayek, *John Stuart Mill and Harriet Taylor: Their Correspondence and Subsequent Marriage* (London: Routledge and Kegan Paul, 1951), p. 114.

[33] *Ibid.*, p. 283, note 4.

action. Contrasted with the obstinacy of Comte, Mill's finesse, patience and deliberation shine all the more clearly: Comte had to become a fanatic, Mill could not possibly have done so.

In the essay on Coleridge Mill had complained that his age seemed unfitted to the production of strong and profound feelings. Philosophy counted as the domain of prosaic thinkers who had no suspicion of how complex and mysterious human nature could be. It was an era of compromises and half-hearted convictions. This, to be sure, was a characteristic of the English spirit in general, in which the healthy tendency to recoil from all extravagance was predominant: and it was so, not as a result of reflection or conscious insight, but as an almost instinctive reaction. In this sense Mill's utilitarianism and his calculated culture of the feelings could hardly be called opposites.

4

◁ ════════════════════════════════════ ▷

The unwritten novel: Beatrice Webb

James Mill, the foe of literature and the imagination, had so perfected his utilitarian methods of education – had done so, in fact, to
the point at which they became grotesque – that the satirist's fantasy
or novelist's invention could not exaggerate but only reproduce
them. It is not hard to recognize the elder Mill in the figure of Mr
Gradgrind in Dickens' *Hard Times* (1854): the merchant in whose
'matter-in-fact home'[1] numbers have taken the place of feeling and
affection. Looking back on his life, John Stuart Mill had once described himself as a 'reasoning machine'; Thomas Gradgrind regards
all children as 'reasoning animals' whose minds have to be formed
and disciplined by knowledge of facts. He could prove that the Good
Samaritan had been a bad economist, and he was shocked when, having asked what the fundamental principle of economics was, he
received the to him absurd reply: do unto others as you would have
them do unto you.

In this novel Dickens was, as always, not a distanced narrator but a
participating and sympathizing moralist: in *Hard Times* he opposed
to the precepts of political economy –that 'false science'[2] which destroyed sensibility and the imagination and made men into adding-
machines – the intuition of the heart. Though they were objects of
the economy, the proletarians were those who removed themselves
farthest from the axioms of economics once they had escaped from
the factory:

They sometimes, after fifteen hours' work, sat down to read mere fables
about men and women, more or less like themselves . . . They took De Foe

[1] Charles Dickens, *Hard Times* [1854] (New York: A Signet Classic, 1980), p. 19.
[2] Hippolyte Taine, *Histoire de la littérature anglaise. Dixième édition, revue et augmentée . . .
Tome cinquième et complémentaire: Les Contemporains* (Paris: Hachette, 1897), p. 49.

to their bosoms, instead of Euclid, and seemed to be on the whole more comforted by Goldsmith than by [the calligrapher and mathematician] Cocker.[3]

As the content and form of his writings bear witness, John Stuart Mill discovered many ways of freeing himself from the overpowering and oppressive influence of his father. He helped the culture of the feelings to regain its rights, and his autobiography as well as many of his essays belong, well written and punctiliously thought through as they are, to *belles-lettres* as much as to science.

When F. R. Leavis proposed that Cambridge should supplement the English curriculum with non-literary studies, he named Mill's classic essays on Bentham and Coleridge as examples: they were, he said, key documents of their time, and every student concerned with the Victorian era ought to have read them. What Leavis valued in Mill was less the amateur of poetry and poetical theory than the extraordinarily disciplined thinker, skilled logician and analyst: as such he could be of use to literary studies and criticism – disciplines in pressing need of working together with other disciplines if they wanted to be taken seriously.

The originality of Leavis' proposal lay not only in its elevation of the son of James Mill to the status of exemplary author and classic; Leavis saw in Mill's essays and autobiography the opening beat of a tradition of non-literary studies of the highest aesthetic rank that extended into the present day. In this sense Beatrice Webb's *My Apprenticeship* (1926) had to be read as a direct continuation of Mill's autobiography: it was the book of a sociologist and socialist that had become a classic of English literature. Following Herbert Spencer, Leavis saw in Beatrice Webb a second George Eliot: no more extravagant praise could be imagined, for to him George Eliot belonged to the 'great tradition'[4] of English literature and a study of her novels to the centre of any literary criticism occupied with the Victorian era. What drew him to Beatrice Webb above all was that throughout her life she saw herself as a frustrated poet, and a reading of her diaries led him to the conclusion 'that a literary training . . . would be very relevant to the essential qualifications of psychologists and sociologists'.[5]

---

[3] Dickens, *Hard Times*, p. 57.
[4] F. R. Leavis, *The Great Tradition: George Eliot, Henry James, Joseph Conrad* (London: Chatto and Windus, 1948).
[5] F. R. Leavis, 'Mill, Beatrice Webb and the "English School"', *Scrutiny* 16 (1949), p. 118.

Beatrice Potter was born on 2 January 1858. Her father, Richard
Potter, who had studied at the new London University and was sufficiently well provided for through an inheritance from his father,
originally intended to settle down as a landed gentleman in
Herefordshire. After the financial crisis of 1847–8, however, he had
to start earning his own living; his father-in-law made him a director
of the Great Western Railway, and he also became a partner in a timber
company in Gloucester from whose profits his income essentially
derived. The Crimean War made him rich when he was able to persuade both the British War Ministry and the French Emperor to
accommodate their troops in wooden barracks during the Russian
winter.

Beatrice has described in *My Apprenticeship* the multifarious undertakings and speculations which, under the impetus of the £60,000
the Crimean War had brought his firm, her father then launched
himself upon: among them was a project to dig a canal through the
middle of Syria as a competitor to the Suez Canal. The project was
abandoned when it was realized that it would have involved inundating
the holy places of the region and that the canal would have taken
forty years to fill. Richard Potter was a gentleman capitalist whom
his daughter remembered with great affection, but he was not a man
of firm principle and he lacked any feeling of responsibility for
furthering the public weal – a shortcoming of which his whole epoch
too was largely guilty.

But Richard Potter was amenable and pragmatic. When the right
to vote was first extended he became a champion of working-class
education and shocked his political friends with the suggestion that
if necessary they would have to persuade their daughters to participate in educating the masses. Potter was very markedly an *homme
à femmes*: he idolized his wife and loved his nine daughters; Beatrice
wrote that he was the only man she knew who sincerely believed that
women were superior to men – which had the paradoxical result that
in the beginning of their adult lives all his daughters were anti-
feminists. Beatrice recalled how, when at the age of thirteen she
asked her father if she might read *Tom Jones*, he praised Fielding's
wonderfully manly English and told her: 'If you were a boy I should
hesitate to recommend *Tom Jones*, but a nice-minded girl can read
anything; and the more she knows about human nature the better
for her and for all the men connected with her.'[6]

[6] Beatrice Webb, *My Apprenticeship*, with an introduction by Norman MacKenzie
(Cambridge: Cambridge University Press, 1979), p. 11.

The mother, who had borne nine girls, hated women; the greatest sorrow of her life was that her only son had died at the age of three. Beatrice was at that time seven. Her mother was interested in literature and had written a not very successful novel; in addition she was a fanatical champion of economic utilitarianism and a follower of Herbert Spencer, who was among the guests who frequented the Potter house. Certainly she had more faith in him than did her husband, who accompanied the philosopher on lengthy walks and usually responded to the emphatic enunciation of his theses and doctrines that attended them with the calm retort: 'Won't work, my dear Spencer, won't work.'[7]

Beatrice did not have a happy childhood; as the second youngest of the nine daughters she was largely ignored. Although the Potters lived more modestly than they in fact could have, Beatrice soon noticed that the Potters gave orders: there was no one who told *them* what to do. In the winter of 1873–4 she and her sister Kate accompanied their father on a business trip to the United States; here she began the diary that was later to become the most important source for her autobiographical writings.

For a long time neither among the rural society of Gloucestershire nor during the annual London season was Beatrice clear as to what she was really going to do with her life. Between 1876 and 1882 she spent her years in idleness; in 1882 her mother died, in 1892 her father followed: during these ten years Beatrice Potter became a social researcher.

First of all her position in the Potter home changed when she became a counsellor to her father and in practice a mother to her younger sister. She now began to observe the life of her own class with ever closer attention and wanted to learn more of the life and work of the classes of whom she as yet knew hardly anything. An opportunity of doing so soon presented itself. In November 1883, disguised as 'Miss Jones', the supposed daughter of a Welsh farmer, Beatrice visited certain poor relations of her mother who worked in the spinning-mill at Bacup, in Lancashire. She found the visit a moving experience, one less amusing and far more informative than she had expected; although she had joined the Charity Organisation Committee in London the year previously, and had already inspected the slums of Soho more than once, it was only now that she took her first real step towards participant social observation and research.

To the wider family circle of the Potters belonged a cousin of

[7] *Ibid.*, p. 26.

Beatrice's, Charles Booth, who, starting in 1886, for seventeen years
and largely at his own expense undertook one of the most monumental and successful inquiries ever mounted by the youthful craft
of social research: *Life and Labour of the People of London* (1902–3). Beatrice
became Booth's collaborator; and in 1887 her first publication
appeared within the framework of his inquiry. At the same time she
also started to work as a rent collector in London's East End. She
found the work hard, and when in 1885 her father became paralysed
and her sister, who was herself ill, needed Beatrice's help more than
ever, it seemed as if her career had ended almost before it had begun.
None the less she carried on: she continued her theoretical studies,
wrote an essay on Marx's theory of economics, which was not
published, and composed a treatise on 'Dock Life in the East End',
which appeared in the *Nineteenth Century*. She also continued her
observations of society by hiring herself out as a sempstress: her
experiences in this role were the subject of an article, 'The Pages of a
Workgirl's Diary', also published in the *Nineteenth Century*.

Politically Beatrice became a socialist; as a researcher she began to
reflect more and more on the possibilities of a science of society and
the conditions for creating one; the first large project of her own was
to be an investigation of the co-operative movement in England. In
1888 she heard for the first time of the Fabian Society, which had
been founded four years previously: it was a group of young radical
socialists who ought rather to have been called reformers, since, as
one of them, Bernard Shaw, expressed it, the society had 'turned its
back on the barricades and made up its mind to turn heroic defeat
into prosaic success'.[8] It had named itself after Quintus Fabius
Maximus, *qui cunctando restituit rem*, the Roman general who knew
how to wait until prospect of victory seemed certain. The most
prominent of the Fabians was Sidney Webb, who from humble
beginnings had, with the aid of grants and through surmounting for-
midable selection procedures, attained to a high official position.
Shaw called him the ablest man in all England.

When Beatrice met Sidney Webb for the first time in 1890 she had
behind her an unhappy affair with Joseph Chamberlain, who had
been mayor of Birmingham and who now impressed his stamp upon
the radical wing of the Liberal Party. By comparison with the attractive Chamberlain, Sidney seemed somewhat repellent; yet she found
his encyclopaedic knowledge, of which she had heard marvels, and
his selfless engagement in social questions impressive.

---

[8] George Bernard Shaw, Preface to the 1908 edition of *Fabian Essays in Socialism*, ed.
Shaw (Boston: The Ball Publishing Co., 1911), pp. xiv–xv.

Sidney at once fell in love with Beatrice, and courted her; she rejected him, and long continued to do so. He pressed her to agree, even if she did not love him, at least to work together with him as a colleague: if they were ordered correctly one and one made not two but eleven. Richard Potter died on 1 January 1892; six months later Sidney and Beatrice were married – she had concealed from her father her engagement to a socialist. Herbert Spencer, the apostle of individualism, had intended that Beatrice should take charge of his literary remains: when he learned of the marriage he discharged her from this responsibility. Beatrice closed *My Apprenticeship* with the following words: 'Here ends "My Apprenticeship" and opens "Our Partnership": a working comradeship founded in a common faith and made perfect by marriage: perhaps the most exquisite, certainly the most enduring, of all the varieties of happiness.'[9]

In this autobiography in which, as Beatrice Webb wrote, the love affairs are left out, the period of her secret engagement to Sidney is sketched only lightly: in their letters to one another and in Beatrice's diary, however, it becomes clear to how great a degree their relationship, begun so primly, was dominated on both a personal and a professional level by themes that had already played a vital role in the history of the social sciences and in the lives of such earlier social scientists as Auguste Comte and John Stuart Mill.

What we know depends on what we feel

In a letter to her father of November 1885 Beatrice refers to the growing number of women who were debarred from a matrimonial career and who 'seek a masculine reward for masculine qualities':[10] the future of such women seemed to lie in being active participants in the solution of the problems of society, and since the failure of her romance with Joseph Chamberlain she counted herself as one of them.

Sidney Webb had hardly met Beatrice before he was writing to her to say how much she had impressed him: he was in urgent need of a mentor able to translate the abstractions of socialist doctrine into the language of everyday politics for him, and he indicated that he would like Beatrice to take on this role. He went a little further and confessed that she had induced him to revise the views on women he had held hitherto. Beatrice replied in a business-like tone but also

[9] Beatrice Webb, *My Apprenticeship*, p. 414.
[10] Beatrice Potter to Richard Potter, November 1885; *The Letters of Sidney and Beatrice Webb*, ed. Norman MacKenzie, Vol. 1: *Apprenticeships 1873–1892* (Cambridge: Cambridge University Press, 1978), p. 48.

sounded a note of warning: women, she wrote, could be of most use when their motherly instinct was allowed full rein; on the other hand, the advantage of a friendship directed to working together could speedily be dissipated if at the same time the 'lower feeling'[11] was not suppressed.

Sidney replied with a long letter in which he did not conceal the differences of opinion that existed between them: they were, for example, not in agreement as to how the Poor Law should be reformed. He closed by expressing the hope that the last word had not been said on the nature of their personal relations. Though he was considered, and was glad to consider himself, obsessed with facts and unreceptive to the arts, he quoted poems to Beatrice and asked her, not without flirtatiousness, whether she did not also commend him for knowing his Rossetti.

On 23 May 1890 Beatrice and Sidney Webb travelled to Glasgow for a Co-operative Congress; in the evening they took a walk together through the streets of the city and, as Beatrice records not without irony in her diary, at last came to the decision to form a working partnership in which they would conduct social research together and pursue their mutual social–political goals. Beatrice made it clear that Sidney could expect nothing from her but friendship; he had to promise he would discontinue relations with her if they proved harmful to his ability to work. He was to think of her as of a married woman, the wife of a friend:

'That I can hardly promise' [Sidney replied]. 'But I will look at the whole question from the point of view of health: as you say, I will not allow myself to dwell on it. I will suppress the purely personal feeling. I will divert my imagination to strengthening the working tie between us.'

One grasp of the hand, and we were soon in a warm discussion on some question of economics. Finis . . .[12]

With that the critical twenty-four hours, as Beatrice called it, was past, but the problem of her relationship with Sidney was by no means solved. He complained of her intolerable superiority, her heartlessness, her blasphemous contempt for all human feeling. He begged her to come to him and talk with him about things more important than any scientific congress; she responded with a final warning: if he desired more than her friendship then that friendship too would be at an end.

[11] Beatrice Potter to Sidney Webb, 2 May 1890; Webb, *Letters*, Vol. 1, p. 133.
[12] Beatrice Webb, 23 May 1890; *The Diary of Beatrice Webb*, ed. Norman and Jeanne MacKenzie, Vol. 1, 1873–92: *Glitter Around and Darkness Within* (Cambridge, Mass.: The Belknap Press of Harvard University Press 1982), p. 332.

Sidney remained obdurate: in a long letter he gave free rein to his feelings, yet he was sufficiently cautious to stress how greatly his friendship with Beatrice had not only changed him but had above all enabled him to work better. And in doing so he cast a sudden light on how completely his personal situation was a repetition of another that had once before been of great consequence for the history of the social sciences:

Now you are to me the Sun and Source of all my work. Today I have slaved and toiled to catch up arrears, and the work was as nothing because it was for you. I took over another man's work, because selfishness had gone out of me. And tonight I was without an effort gentle and considerate and respectful to the stupidest London candidate on a small committee. I now realize what Comte was driving at by his apotheosised woman, I never understood Dante's life before. You are making all things new to me. You are simply doubling my force.[13]

It was an allusion Beatrice understood all too well, yet it is more than questionable whether it could have produced the effect Sidney had intended. She was familiar with the ideas of Comte through G. H. Lewes and through the writings of John Stuart Mill – she had read his autobiography with delight, the *System of Logic* and the *Principles of Political Economy* with strained application; but that she and her sister Margaret ordered Comte's collected works from the London Library was connected with the fact that at dinner parties and picnics they regularly encountered Frederic Harrison, who was from 1880 to 1905 president of the English Positivist Committee and was supported in his crusade on behalf of positivism by Mrs Harrison, who was 'always a "St Clotilde" to her Auguste'.[14] Beatrice had described how on long rambles in Westmorland she and Margaret, then twenty-five and twenty-one years old, engaged in vehement discussion of Comte, that frightful old pedant who wrote such dreadful French that between him and Voltaire there seemed to lie a deep gulf. Comte had driven religion out of the human intellect through the front door – but only to admit it into the house again by the servants' entrance: 'The man worships the woman. Who wants to worship any one, leave alone a woman?'[15]

Beatrice proposed a new concordat and Sidney Webb accepted it: like Comte, who had made women the guardians of morality, he obeyed the rules of conduct she laid down. And like Comte, too, he

---

[13] Sidney Webb to Beatrice Potter, 30 May 1890; Webb, *Letters*, Vol. 1, p. 142.
[14] Beatrice Webb, *My Apprenticeship*, p. 145. [15] *Ibid.*, p. 146.

learned that in the real world not everything can be reduced to syllogisms or understood by exertion of the intellect, that there exist imponderables which our reason cannot grasp but which are none the less of great significance for us. It was women not least who had taught Comte and Mill to cultivate their feelings; Sidney Webb sought to restrain Beatrice from committing emotional suicide: 'Even within positive knowledge there are more things to be taken account of than fall within logic and reason. Even 2 and 2 do not make the same to me now as they did six months ago! What we know depends on what we feel.'[16]

Sidney Webb and Beatrice were among the many readers Goethe found in nineteenth-century England, and both were familiar with G. H. Lewes' *Life of Goethe* (1855). In June 1890 Sidney wrote Beatrice a long letter in which he was outspokenly critical of Goethe, whose autobiography and *Wilhelm Meister* he had just reread: he called Goethe an egoist who had deserted from the great army of humanity and a man blind to reality who had been prone to errors neither Schiller nor Lessing had ever made; he deplored the cruelties to be found in *Stella* and in the *Wahlverwandtschaften*. The failures in his work and the blunders in his life were, he said, explicable from Goethe's desire to plan his life thoroughly and to subject it to the highest degree of self-control: he offered a warning example of how intellect by itself could lead man into error. The correct course was to recognize that instinct and feeling were equally significant motivations of human behaviour.

It was a curious letter betraying little knowledge of Goethe and no understanding of him at all: if one took it seriously one would have to call Sidney Webb's renowned intelligence into question. But it was in fact a letter that had nothing to do with Goethe: when he wrote of Goethe's lack of empathy and his overestimation of the intellect he was making an appeal to Beatrice: 'The roles are curiously reversed in some cases: just now I am feeling dreadfully like Friederike of Sesenheim . . .'[17] Beatrice Potter and Sidney Webb employed two differing languages in their letters to one another: Beatrice the language of reason and science, Sidney that of feeling and poetry. When on one occasion they spent an afternoon together in Epping Forest they at first conversed about socialism and economics, but then Sidney read Keats and Rossetti to her and found her so *ravissante* and angelic that he afterwards wrote her an impassioned letter that again imperilled their friendship.

[16] Sidney Webb to Beatrice Potter, 24 June 1890; Webb, *Letters*, Vol. 1, pp. 155–6. [17] Sidney Webb to Beatrice Potter, 29 June 1890; *ibid.*, p. 159.

In the meantime Sidney had read in a single night the 600 pages of Alfred Marshall's *Principles of Economics*, which he found impressive and superior to Mill, even if it was not that epoch-making work of political economy to the production of which he himself felt called. In her unwearying effort to keep their relationship on a practical level, Beatrice suggested they read Marshall together, for his theories presented her with great difficulties: 'In that case I shall be at your feet, and not you at mine, a wholesome reversal of the relationship – more in keeping with the relative dignity of Man and Woman . . .'[18] Sidney continued the language-game they were playing by replying to this suggestion: 'I shall be delighted to read the book with you chapter by chapter – not more than one a week however (with one bit of Browning?) . . .'[19]

It is astonishing how great a role literature plays in the letters of Sidney Webb, a man whose friends and acquaintances– Leonard and Virginia Woolf among them– later described him as a model example of the philistine. Astonishing, but at the same time understandable, for Sidney employed literature: as long as Beatrice forbade him open expression of his feelings towards her he had to find a medium in which he was able to speak of himself without uttering his own name. Literature was this medium, as he afterwards admitted: 'no novel interests me deeply unless I learn from it something about myself'.[20]

He discovered the supreme expression of feeling in the sonnets of Rossetti, and he thus sent Beatrice a volume of Rossetti's poems – without any inscription, so that she might read it openly. He recognized himself in many characters in novels: he had read only a couple of chapters of *Vanity Fair*, for example, when he remarked self-critically how selfish a man in love could be. Again and again he admonished himself not to be too sentimental and not to adopt the attitude of a Werther– very necessary counsel since Beatrice reminded him with cruel regularity that she would never be able to love him. It also seemed to him, to be sure, that literature was excellently suited to the delineation of the individual human psyche; but as a means of analysing society it was ineffective: 'Neither Dickens nor Thackeray, neither Tennyson nor Browning, ever thinks of a man as a citizen. He is a lover, husband, father, friend– but never a voter, town councillor or vestryman.'[21] Yet while Sidney Webb remained a lover

---

[18] Beatrice Potter to Sidney Webb, 11 August 1890; *ibid.*, p. 164.
[19] Sidney Webb to Beatrice Potter, 13 August 1890; *ibid.*, p. 171.
[20] Sidney Webb to Beatrice Potter, 14 March 1891; *ibid.*, p. 265.
[21] Sidney Webb to Beatrice Potter, 21 September 1890; *ibid.*, p. 194.

whose love was not returned literature was still of significance to him.

Resigned to living under the burden of unrequited affection, he began more and more to resemble Comte so far as his behaviour and way of life were concerned: he conducted himself like a Catholic, and more than once he prescribed for himself a reading of one of Comte's favourite authors, Thomas a Kempis – 'good old Thomas' – in order to be able to resume working. When he assured Beatrice of how important her friendship was not only for its own sake but even more for the impetus it gave to his work, since great thoughts always came from the heart, he was only repeating, though without saying so, that maxim of Vauvenargues which Comte himself had made his own. The six months of unsuccessful wooing of Beatrice had been a period of 'liberal education' for him, a *Bildungsroman* of the kind Comte too had lived through:

I am like Auguste Comte: as I cannot have what I want, I make a virtue of wanting only what I can have! But the friendship of Clotilde de Vaux was invaluable to Comte, in developing all the better side of his nature. We do not know the effect on her, but she can hardly have helped gaining. Let this be an omen.[22]

The omen was well chosen: Sidney Webb could have derived hope from the letters of Clotilde. Beatrice's resistance weakened: even if she still found Sidney hardly more attractive than she had when she first met him, she was now convinced that the scientific and political work they planned to do together would be advanced rather than hindered if they were married. On 20 May 1891 she agreed to marry Sidney – with the proviso that the wedding must wait until after the death of her father, who was to know nothing of their engagement. Sidney was thereupon transported into a condition he could describe only in French – '*délire, extase, ivresse*'[23] – even though Beatrice had assured him she would be marrying only his head.

Among the presents Sidney gave his *fiancée* was the poems of Matthew Arnold, and how diverse a role literature had played in the correspondence between them again became clear. Sidney sent the poems for emotional reasons: 'If any of these are not familiar to you, look at them now and again, they are sad but restful'[24] – to which Beatrice reacted with the following analysis: 'They are very beautiful and he is one of my favourite poets – full of reformed philosophical

[22] Sidney Webb to Beatrice Potter, 14 December 1890; *ibid.*, p. 244.
[23] Sidney Webb to Beatrice Potter, 23 May 1891; *ibid.*, p. 273.
[24] Sidney Webb to Beatrice Potter, 22 December 1891; *ibid.*, p. 359.

feeling but wanting in robust determination to make things better.'[25] From then on literary allusions gradually disappeared from Sidney Webb's letters.

Sidney had once assured Beatrice that together they could lift the world off its hinges. When he died in 1947 – four years after Beatrice – they had with an imposing quantity of publications and through their battles for social reform, their participation in politics and their propaganda in the salon, left behind them unmistakable traces in the public life of England and its institutions. They had determined the course of the Fabians and of the Labour Party, founded the London School of Economics (1895) and the *New Statesman* (1913), and travelled round the world twice. Sidney had been a minister in two Labour governments and, as Lord Passmore – Beatrice had refused the title – represented the Labour Party in the House of Lords. In 1932 they visited the Soviet Union and at the end of their lives became adherents of Soviet communism – a creed even the Stalinist purges could not make them renounce. They are buried in Westminister Abbey.

Philanthropy, social research, politics

In 1885 Sidney Webb became a member of the Fabian Society. Two years later Edward R. Pease, a co-founder and for many years secretary of the society, prepared for him a geological cabinet from which the stones and fossils were gradually removed to make room for documents and manuscripts.

The Webbs hoped that in the long run they could make out of their social research a species of descriptive science. Although sociology already existed, and both Sidney and Beatrice were familiar with its traditions, the discipline was none the less very far from possessing a clearly circumscribed subject-matter or having command of precise methods of procedure: even if he knew and respected his predecessors every social researcher had in a certain sense to create the discipline anew. This is what the Webbs did, and they found that Darwin and T. H. Huxley were just as important to them in the process as were those nineteenth-century writers who already called themselves sociologists. As Beatrice wrote in May 1900, the construction of the social sciences was the goal of their life.

[25] Beatrice Potter to Sidney Webb, 24 December 1891; *ibid.*, p. 360.

It was characteristic of the Webbs that they should shun theory and concentrate on comprehending the facts of society and describing them with precision: Beatrice felt a downright hatred for political economy because it had taken the eighteenth century's attacks on oppression and class rule and transformed them into a scientific discipline which had finally become the 'employers' gospel of the 19th century';[26] to Sidney Webb the current textbooks of economics were as obsolete as Buffon's natural history or Goethe's theory of colours because the economists refused to set about recording and classifying facts and reducing them to a systematic order. The same state of things obtained in sociology and academic psychology, in which fanciful definitions of the human mind led to abstract assertions that no longer had anything whatever to do with human reality. Spencer, who had laid so much weight on factual knowledge, was judged more leniently, but even towards him his pupil Beatrice remained a 'doubting Thomas'.[27]

Beatrice Webb trod the path, a not uncommon one in the nineteenth century, from philanthropy to social research. When she visited her poor relations in Bacup it became clear to her that there was only one way of understanding these people belonging to a different class from herself: one had for a time 'to adopt their faith and look at things in their light'.[28] One could not simply transfer to sociology the laws of other sciences, as Spencer had done, nor was there any hope of grasping the rules of social life by a process of intuition: such laws could be discovered only through painstaking labour with the aid of carefully prepared data. At the end of the nineteenth century the information needed for this undertaking was nowhere available: it had first to be assembled and arranged.

There existed no simple recipe for applying to the facts of social life the methods of assembling data and classifying it practised by the natural sciences. As with so many early social researchers whose aim was a scientific description of society, Beatrice Webb had concealed within her a detective and an ethnologist: she had spied on the spinning-mills of Lancashire and the sewing-rooms of London under an assumed name, and when she worked as a rent collector the tenants of her district seemed to her the 'aborigines' of the East End. All her writings are stamped with the pathos of a participant observation and experience at first hand – even the historical books, for

---

[26] Beatrice Webb, 18 August 1886; Webb, *Diary*, Vol. 1, p. 174.
[27] Webb, *My Apprenticeship*, p. 138.
[28] Beatrice Potter to Richard Potter, 9 November 1883; Webb, *Letters*, Vol. 1, p. 18.

which work in the archive took the place of the traditional field-work. This – together with the material independence the Webbs enjoyed – is also a reason why they were not easily impressed by the scientific work of the universities: Alfred Marshall, for example, was a professor at Cambridge, but, as Beatrice remarked, he lacked that experience of everyday life required to produce a whole man.

In the significance they accorded their own intuitions and the weight they laid on sympathetic shared experience the Webbs distinguished themselves from those 'facts-and-figures men' of the nineteenth century whose belief that data alone could constitute the basis of social research and social policy has been called 'Gradgrindism':[29]

Although Mr Gradgrind did not take after Blue Beard, his room was quite a blue chamber in its abundance of blue books. . . In that charmed apartment, the most complicated social questions were cast up, got into exact totals, and finally settled – if those concerned could only have been brought to know it. As if an astronomical observatory should be made without any windows, and the astronomer within should arrange the starry universe solely by pen, ink and paper, so Mr Gradgrind, in *his* Observatory (and there are many like it), had no need to cast an eye upon the teeming myriads of human beings around him, but could settle all their destinies on a slate, and wipe out all their tears with one dirty little bit of sponge.[30]

Throughout her life Beatrice Webb clung to the demand that sociological researchers ought to practise some other activity as well, as an aid to gaining a thorough insight into the realities of society: administration, as a kind of laboratory for sociological experiments, seemed to her especially well suited to this purpose.

The Webbs were at the same time concerned to enhance the scientific character of sociological research. Beatrice was always grateful to Herbert Spencer for teaching her to regard social institutions as though they were plants or animals, 'things that could be observed, classified and explained, and the action of which could to some extent be foretold if one knew enough about them'.[31] Comparative physiology, she noted in her diary in September 1883, would have to become the foundation of a scientific sociology; as a consequence she studied physiological textbooks, dissected and examined with the microscope, and at the same time read John

[29] Philip Abrams, *The Origins of British Sociology: 1834–1914. An Essay with Selected Papers* (Chicago: University of Chicago Press, 1968), p. 22.

[30] Dickens, *Hard Times*, p. 101.

[31] Beatrice Webb, 9 December 1903; *The Diary of Beatrice Webb*, ed. Norman and Jeanne MacKenzie, Vol. 2, 1892–1905: *All the Good Things of Life* (Cambridge, Mass.: The Belknap Press of Harvard University Press, 1983, p. 307).

Stuart Mill's *Logic*. When in 1895 the London School of Economics was founded its curriculum seemed to have been influenced not least by T. H. Huxley, who had seen in the youthful discipline of sociology the completion of the disciplines of natural history. Mathematics and biology were originally intended to count at the LSE as propaedeutic studies preliminary to the study of economics, though this plan was never realized. Even such a discipline as meteorology appeared briefly in the curriculum, only to vanish again. Yet Beatrice Webb clung to her original conception: she wanted to know whether the study of social institutions could be undertaken as impartially 'as the study of flora and fauna'.[32] To answer this question it seemed sensible to unite sociology with the descriptive natural sciences, and a donation from the Rockefeller Foundation in fact led to a proposal to institute a department of social biology at the LSE; this plan too failed to materialize, though such a department would certainly have accorded with the intentions of the Webbs, who had opposed to economics as a pure analysis of concepts and to a theory of politics their idea of the social sciences as those disciplines that concerned themselves with the assembling and classification of the facts of society.

All the writings of the Webbs are permeated by a tension between their objective of studying human institutions as scientifically, that is to say as calmly and objectively, as possible, and their desire to change existing society and to replace institutions founded on the profit motive with those orientated towards the common good. They combined within themselves a belief in the necessity and practicability of a concrete science of society on the basis of historical research, personal experience and statistical probability, with an awareness of being among the pioneers of social engineering.

Beatrice herself discovered an obvious compromise which could permit the emotional engagement of the early years of social research to be preserved into the age of social engineering: it lay in making a sharp distinction between the pure science and its application. Although, after their conversion to communism, the Webbs suggested to the Russians that they should employ the behavioural sciences for their political and propagandist goals, Beatrice still insisted in conversation with a Russian visitor in 1935, the year the Webbs' *Soviet Communism – A New Civilization?* appeared, that there was no such thing as a Marxist sociology but only a scientific one.

---

[32] Lord Beveridge, *The London School of Economics and its Problems 1919–1937* (London: George Allen and Unwin, 1960, p. 106).

The discoveries of science could be placed at the service of a political cause, but that did not mean that the practice of science had to become something cold and mechanical: on the contrary, it resembled rather a religious act. The revelation of natural laws was an expression of piety, one of the means by which the Kingdom of God brought closer its realization on earth. Scientific activity was both an intellectual and a moral process; in its highest form it demanded 'courage, honesty, good comradeship, an absence of vanity and spite – frequently the sacrifice of ambition, ease, health, and sometimes life itself'.[33]

Even in their textbook *Methods of Social Study* the Webbs adhered to the view that sociology was as much a biological discipline as botany or zoology; they expressly rejected Rickert's and Max Weber's conception of a specific science of culture. But this was hardly more than a declaration of political intent. Their studies of the British trade union and co-operative movements and of British local government clearly show that their sociology was biologically orientated only in a metaphorical sense: it was concerned with the origination, growth, modification and decline of specific social institutions. Since the Webbs did not consider themselves qualified to employ elaborate statistical methods they observed institutions from close to or worked within them, practised the gentle art of the interview and conducted extensive literary studies and investigations of archives. The Webbs were in no way realists in the epistemological sense, as H. G. Wells maintained: the categories with whose aid they classified the objects of their research were to them nothing more than words.

Even though they failed to share Max Weber's conception of sociology, they none the less stressed the need for sympathetic understanding in the social sciences and named Shakespeare and Goethe as examples of how far it was possible to develop the capacity to put oneself in the place of people of different origin and a different social class. In this sense the competent social researcher had also to possess the abilities of a novelist or a dramatist: an imperfect sympathy with the objects of his investigations could prove to be the greatest of all obstacles in the way of his scientific labours.

The Webbs have described in detail what they called the art of taking notes: they established the rule that each sheet of paper must con-

---

[33] Beatrice Webb, 17 September 1920; *Beatrice Webb's Diaries 1912–1924*, ed. Margaret I. Cole, with an introduction by Lord Beveridge (London: Longmans, Green and Co., 1952), p. 196.

tain notes pertaining to only one single event occurring at a definite time and place. Tens of thousands of such research notes were accumulated at their house in Grosvenor Road, London, where they arranged and rearranged them in an effort to discover ever new connections between the items of their material: this was the 'little-slips-of-paper-piled-topically-and-write-it-up'[34] method.

The 'Webb speciality' consisted in the investigation, at once historical and analytical, of the life-history of a social institution over three or four centuries. Because of the nature of the methods they employed in this undertaking it proved difficult at first to acquire assistants for their work of research and equally difficult to interest students in it later:

> We realize how difficult it is to convince students – especially those with a 'literary' rather than a 'scientific' training– that it is [through] just this use of such a mechanical device as the shuffling of sheets of notes . . . that the process of investigation often becomes fertile in actual discoveries.[35]

This too was why the Webbs tried to give an impression of the pleasure that could be gained from burying oneself in documents and from the sifting and sorting of writings pertaining to a specific problem: just as English socialism bore the stamp of the skilled political handicraft of a Ruskin or a Morris, so the sociologist was above all an intellectual workman, and the uniting together of hand and brain made sociological research an occupation thrilling and involving in a way no game or sport could ever be.

> This interest in the structure of society is enlivened by an exhilarating hunt for the human factor; the discovery of a leader or leaders; the becoming visible of this or that man's hand; the appearance in dry annals of pecuniary self-interest, personal ambition or personal vanity, just as much as of an enduring policy or a definite ideal.

Sociology was thus very far from having attained to the status of physics or chemistry, and it was certainly not at all like biology – it corresponded rather to the more literary pre-form of these sciences, the natural history of the age of Cuvier or Buffon.

With this devotion to and pride in the process of workman-like research itself there also went an interest in the practical application of the results of this research, for the Webbs were profoundly convinced that the social sciences needed to be and could be of practical

---

[34] T. S. Simey, 'The Contribution of Sidney and Beatrice Webb to Sociology', *The British Journal of Sociology* 12 (1961), p. 122, note 32.
[35] Sidney and Beatrice Webb, *Methods of Social Study* (London: Longmans, Green and Co., 1932), p. 94.

applicability; this was one of the reasons for the great respect they had for Masaryk, the sociologist who had become president of the Czechoslovak republic.

It was thus quite consistent that from being hesitant Fabians the Webbs should in the end become convinced communists and admirers of the Soviet Union. Within their conception of the process of sociological research, and their desire to employ the results of research for practical political ends, there had always lain concealed socialistic ideals, and the gigantic experiment in which the Soviet Union had been engaged since 1917 perhaps attracted the sociologist rather than the socialist in them.

Sociology and socialism

In the historical sketch which Sidney Webb wrote for the *Fabian Essays in Socialism* (1889) he described the utilitarian doctrine as the 'Protestantism of sociology':[36] the faith of the Gradgrinds, iconoclastic and hostile to tradition, that was first subjected to attack, not by the scientists, but by the artists. It was De Quincey and Coleridge, but above all Carlyle and Ruskin, who had called into question the cult of the middle class and prepared the way for Comte, John Stuart Mill, Darwin and Herbert Spencer. At the same time the idea of society as an organism had come to the forefront of the minds of professors of political economy, though it may not yet have penetrated their books.

In Sidney Webb's abstract the development of modern industrial society appears as a history of irresistible progress: everything in it leads towards and eventuates in urbanization, democracy, the study of political economy and socialism. The socialism the Fabians espoused was pragmatic, and constitutional rather than revolutionary; its goal was the introduction of nationalization wherever this was practicable. Their opponents spoke maliciously of 'gas-and-water socialism', but the Fabians themselves were not wholly averse to this description, since their desire was to translate the dogmas of economics and its doctrine of collectivism into the plain prose of vestrymen and town councillors.

In their deep-rooted distaste for theory these English socialists of the *fin de siècle* avoided any thorough study of Marx, and when they did study him it was usually with the object of refuting him. In April 1884 Webb reported in a letter to Shaw on a meeting held at the Karl

[36] Sidney Webb, 'Historic', *Fabian Essays in Socialism*, p. 40.

Marx Club, which later assumed the more appropriate name of the Hampstead Historical Society:

You were missing, and missed, at Mrs Wilson's economic tea party last Wednesday. We were 11, and you were the faithless Apostle. Mrs Wilson. . . read a most elaborate analysis of Ch. 1 of Marx, in English, over which she must have spent weeks. F. Y. Edgeworth, who was in the Chair, then opened the proceedings by expressing his intense contempt for Karl and all his works, and snorted generally on the subject, as Ricardo might have done to an errant economist of the period. The company . . . were speechless with amazement. . . I rushed in, and the rest of the evening was a kind of Scotch reel *à deux*, Edgeworth and I gaily dancing on the unfortunate K. M. . . . Now this sort of thing is demoralizing – I mean to me . . . But unless some utterly unscrupulous socialistic dialectician like yourself turns up here, we shall have discarded *Le Capital* within a month, and be found studying the gospel of Ricardo![37]

Sidney Webb was in fact anything but an admirer of Marx; the purchase of the second volume of *Kapital* seemed to him an exceptional waste of money, and Shaw asserted that Webb had skimmed through in an hour the first volume that had been lent to him and when asked expectantly what impression it had made on him had replied 'Scotland stands where it did'[38] – the first time he had ever quoted Shakespeare.

All this betrays little knowledge of Marx, let alone comprehension of him, and Shaw himself, who in the Fabian Society too swam against the current, came much closer to the source of Marx's influence when he declared that it rested less on Hegel's dialectic stood the right way up than it did on the tremendous quantity of facts and data which Marx had assimilated in the reading-room of the British Museum.

The Fabians did not constitute a party: they were intellectuals and scientists who trusted in the power of words and figures – in the heavy artillery of their books, as Beatrice once wrote. When in her diary she later looked back on her life's work she affirmed contentedly that she and Sidney had not only written history but had made history as well. Her direct involvement in politics notwithstanding, her primary goal had always been to influence the course of history by writing books. The public had to be shown that political convictions and political activity alone were not enough for the reform of society: rather, hard scientific work, the patient tracking down and

---

[37] Sidney Webb to G. B. Shaw, 4 November 1884; Webb, *Letters*, Vol. 1, p. 81.
[38] G. B. Shaw and Margaret Cole, 'Early Days', in *The Webbs and their Work*, ed. Margaret Cole (London: Frederick Muller, 1949), p. 6.

tireless systematization of the facts of society, constituted the foundation of any premeditated political programme. Empirical social research instead of sociological theorizing, the gradual improvement of concrete conditions of life instead of revolutionary propaganda and panaceas– it was in this that the scientific and political reformism of the Webbs found expression.

Sidney Webb had seen in every new printing of Mill's *Political Economy* (1848) a further step in the direction of socialism: he believed that the expansion of sociological knowledge brought mankind a step closer to domination of things and responsible control over its social destiny. His first tract for the Fabian Society was called *Facts for Socialists* (1887), and the title reveals how intimately united socialism and empirical sociology were for the Fabians.

The Fabians were middle-class theoreticians– a fact to which their motto 'Slow but sure' bore witness– *clercs* of the labour movement to whose service they dedicated their brains: and that they were 'intelligence officers without an army'[39] only enhanced their capacity for manoeuvre. The masses were to be served by an elite of selfless experts exercising their power in secret– yet not so much in secret that this exercise of power would lack its due of recognition. In this too the Fabians stood closer to Marx, and above all to Lenin's conception of a political party, than they themselves were willing to admit: when, in a letter to Upton Sinclair, H. G. Wells sought to play down the significance of Lenin by calling him 'just a Russian Sidney Webb',[40] he revealed little about Lenin but something about Sidney Webb and the motives that actuated him.

Methods of scientific work also constituted for the Webbs the foundation of their political activity: fundamentally they saw no difference between the two. Their primary goal was not to force unthinking people into socialist societies but 'to make the *thinking* persons socialistic':[41] to this end they evolved the techniques of 'wire-pulling' and 'permeating' that became notorious constituents of the Webb myth. While Sidney was principally occupied with research work, and then more and more also with practical politics, Beatrice made of her house a place where methodical social adventures were planned, the most important method being an elaborate

[39] G. M. Trevelyan, *British History in the Nineteenth Century*; Beatrice Webb, *Our Partnership*, ed. Barbara Drake and Margaret I. Cole, with an introduction by George Feaver (Cambridge: Cambridge University Press, 1975), p. 107.
[40] Beatrice Webb, 12 July 1918; *The Diary of Beatrice Webb*, ed. Norman and Jeanne MacKenzie, Vol. 3, 1905–1924: *The Power to Alter Things* (London: Virago Press in association with the London School of Economics and Political Science, 1984), p. 311.   [41] Beatrice Webb, 18 April 1896; Webb, *Diary*, Vol. 2, p. 94.

technique of seating arrangements at dinner. Disappointments and mistaken assessments on these occasions were not uncommon, to be sure: when she invited Balfour to dinner she seated him beside Charles Booth, yet the Prime Minister had in fact never heard of the man who had made so detailed an investigation of the life of the London worker. Balfour was the prototype of the 'private gentleman' who continued to determine the character of the British ruling class: he regarded all social and economic questions as 'ugly' and not worth concerning oneself with; when facts were cited or figures quoted he ceased to listen. What interested him was philosophy, literature and music, golf and motor-cars: and it went without saying that the Prime Minister to whom Charles Booth was an unknown knew every line of the plays of Shaw, whom he called the most significant writer of his time.

Before they began, late in life, to make propaganda for Russian communism the Webbs were certainly not fanatical advocates of any doctrine; but they were always fanatical advocates of a method and unshakable in the conviction of their ability to conduct politics on a scientific basis. To Virginia Woolf they appeared alien beings without illusions, passions or mysteries: one felt uncomfortable in their presence because their razor-sharp intellect kept constantly before one's eyes the extent of one's own stupidity. They resembled machines. Leonard Woolf described their omniscience and their merciless common sense: to Sidney especially, who said he never dreamed, doubt and indecision seemed to be things unknown – 'just as he had never had a headache or constipation'.[42]

In reality the certainty exhibited by the Webbs was, at least so far as Beatrice was concerned, much more the outcome of discipline than inherent in their constitution, and the basis of this discipline was strict control of the feelings – a control continually threatened by the desire, suppressed only with effort, to turn away from science and to devote themselves to literature.

Science and religion

When at the end of 1912 the founding of the *New Statesman* had definitely been decided on, Beatrice Webb saw not only the British labour movement but the whole of the thinking public entangled in a struggle in which words, ideas and temperaments contended: ought men to be ruled by feeling or by reason? It was a question that

[42] Leonard Woolf, *Sowing: An Autobiography of the Years 1880 to 1904* (New York: Harcourt Brace Jovanovich, 1975), p. 48.

had engaged her since she had first become involved in social work and one that was to continue to do so until her conversion to communism.

During a visit to Italy in November 1880, when she was 22 years old, she had attended a low mass at St Peter's; there she had become painfully aware that the days when she could honestly pray were apparently over. But the same intellect that had shaken her religious certainty also led her to the conclusion that behind the things knowable to us there was something absolute unattainable to human knowledge – a problem even the logic of a Herbert Spencer could not solve. She was convinced that her feelings were the better part of her nature, and could see that her emotional needs were satisfied by religion rather than by science. To such a view the *Zeitgeist* was unfavourable: more perhaps even than on the Continent the cult of science dominated in England; scientists constituted the leading element among the intellectuals and were in fact the idols of the day:

It was they who were routing the theologians, confounding the mystics, imposing their theories on philosophers, their inventions on capitalists, and their discoveries on medical men; whilst they were at the same time snubbing the artists, ignoring the poets and even casting doubts on the capacity of the politicians. [43]

In July 1882, while on a visit to Germany, Beatrice, her father, her sister and Herbert Spencer inspected Cologne Cathedral:

Even the philosopher does not criticize the interior, though he objects to the curved outline of the spires. 'In architecture what I require,' spoke he, 'is that the lines should be defined, that either they should be continuous or definitely broken.' When we entered service was going on. Father, Rosy and I, overpowered by the beauty of the building, sat and listened with solemn delight to the rhythmical chants of the vespers. 'This is excessively monotonous,' whispered the philosopher to me. 'I rather like it,' say I, venturing to disagree with him, though with a conciliatory smile. But feeling inwardly out of sympathy I move with Rosy to the seat lower down and join more completely in the service. This the philosopher observes, and when we meet again in the nave he remarks: 'The primitive man would here have a feeling of superstitious awe. It is only through the power of self-analysis and by tracing our feelings to their ultimate psychological cause that we are able to rid ourselves of it.' 'I confess to a certain amount of superstitious awe,' say I defiantly. 'I should be sorry that these cathedrals should pass out of the hands of the Catholic church with its beautiful ritual.' [44]

---

[43] Webb, *My Apprenticeship*, p. 131.
[44] Beatrice Webb, 2 July 1882; Webb, *Diary*, Vol. 1, pp. 52–3.

Her involvement in practical social work became for Beatrice Webb the most effective means of satisfying her emotional needs, philanthropic inclinations and scientific interests at one and the same time; and the physical exertion that such work also demanded often acted like a narcotic, permitting neither thought nor feeling and thus blunting the edge of a dilemma that continued to cause her a great deal of trouble. Sometimes she believed that active help for the poor could be at once a substitute for religion and a guard against the unfeeling analysis which science demanded of her. She admired those women who worked among the proletariat in the East End with unwavering enthusiasm and without any need to theorize – an activity that made demands on the feelings rather than on the intellect.

In all this the fact she was a woman played a decisive role. Philanthropic work was a feminine domain and as such was socially acceptable; social research was something else, though here women could, to be sure, derive advantage precisely from their lower status: since women were in many matters not taken seriously, and 'unemancipated females' simply had no attention paid to them at all, it was often easier for a woman to pursue such an activity as participant observation than it was for a man. This research in the midst of the real world always had about it a touch of the adventurous, yet there was for that reason always the danger that women who undertook it would not be taken seriously but would be repudiated as eccentric. On the other hand there existed a strong prejudice that women ought to be confined either to caring and tending activities or to social work, and that the only scientific subjects they should be entrusted with were those of a strongly affective character directly concerning women. When Beatrice Webb told Marshall of her plan to involve herself with the British co-operative movement he was decisively opposed to it and suggested that 'work among women' would be more appropriate. She herself often wondered whether her nature as a woman did not make her unsuited to analytical thinking.

In its outward aspect Beatrice Webb's life was a tireless endeavour to overcome such supposed constitutional disadvantages as these, which were in reality social prejudices: there were few men who emphasized the necessity and fruitfulness of 'hard thinking' in the social sciences with the determination and enthusiasm she did.

For the time was past when effective social reform could be thought through and realized by politicians, publicists or philanthropists alone. The poor had to be helped, their lives studied, the causes of poverty determined and effective measures for their removal proposed and put into operation: social reform and social policy had to be provided with a scientific foundation. It was precisely because she adhered to the ideal of 'pure' science that Beatrice Webb experienced her research undertaking as a mission in the religious sense and – however much she may have concealed it in public – as an activity that involved not only her intellect but her feelings as well.

Since the Webbs considered that their privileged social position obligated them to perform genuine work, they also always felt their scientific activities to be an expression of their ethical convictions and not only a means of realizing certain political goals. How profoundly they identified themselves with their work is revealed in the fact that Beatrice – who in later life asked herself whether it had been right to remain childless – always referred to the London School of Economics, the *Minority Report on the Poor Law*, the *New Statesman* and *Soviet Communism* as her four children. Virginia Woolf, who was otherwise repelled by the Webbs, was fascinated by that in them with which she could identify: the 'pathos ... of the childless couple'.[45] The Webbs had preserved their affection for one another and all their emotional energy for their work.

To espouse a kind of religion of science did not, however, imply being anti-religious: Beatrice accepted religion, and did so because the methods of science were incapable of teaching men anything to do with ultimate values – if science did claim such a thing it would reveal its bankruptcy. This had been the great error of the nineteenth century. One had to draw a sharp distinction between what one could prove and what one wanted to believe in.

For the great mass of mankind, however, the tension between reason and feeling was in no way abolished through this distinction. The age of science had alienated them from religion without offering them a substitute, for the blessings of the religion of science could be enjoyed only by those who practised it:

One wonders what will happen, when the religious feeling of the people is undermined by advancing scientific culture – for tho' the 'Co-op' and the chapel at present work together – the secularism of the 'Co-op' is half-unconsciously recognised by earnest chapel-goers as a rival attraction to the prayer-meeting and the bible-class.

[45] Virginia Woolf, 23 October 1929; *The Diary of Virginia Woolf*, ed. Anne Olivier Bell, assisted by Andrew McNeillie, Vol. 3: 1925–30 (New York: Harcourt Brace Jovanovich, 1980), p. 263.

One wonders where all this *feeling* will go and all the capacity for *moral* self-government.[46]

There was a scientist who had already recognized this problem in the middle of the nineteenth century and had proposed a solution to it: Auguste Comte. That he had developed positivism into a religion witnessed to his breath of vision, and demonstrated his superiority to such writers as Herbert Spencer, who had forgotten that man possessed religious needs which could not be satisfied by science and the intellect alone. What Beatrice Webb desired was the creation of a church in which the priests celebrated the rites of their religion for the purpose of mental hygiene – the more vague these rites were and the more mysteries they contained the greater their effect on the believers would be.

But as time passed and the collapse of capitalism came to seem to the Webbs inevitable and ever more imminent, as the Labour Party was frustrated in Parliament and the prospect of advancing the cause of socialism by means of 'wire-pulling' and 'permeating' diminished day by day, so the likelihood of establishing Comte's religion as the credo of Western industrial society also faded away. In the meantime, however, and without its founders having intended it, in the Soviet Union the Communist Party had become a religious order:

It has its Holy Writ, its prophets and its canonised saints; it has its Pope, yesterday Lenin and today Stalin; it has its code of conduct and its discipline; it has its creed and its inquisition. As yet it has no rites or modes of worship. Will it develop ritual as did the followers of Auguste Comte?[47]

It was a time when hordes of European intellectuals were visiting Moscow as communists and returning as enemies of socialism, and the Webbs too left on their pilgrimage to the USSR. As good scientists they did not undertake this journey without first having formulated certain hypotheses concerning the Soviet constitution which they then intended to test on the spot: among them was the supposition that the Communist Party was pursuing the same objectives as was the religion of Comte and resembled a religious order. The Webbs knew in advance that this hypothesis would be confirmed: and the fact, far from dismaying them, was what first made of them true adherents of communism – even the party purges, which

[46] Beatrice Potter to Richard Potter, October 1886; Webb, *Letters*, Vol. 1, p. 61.
[47] Beatrice Webb, 14 May 1932; *Beatrice Webb's Diaries 1924–1932*, ed. and with an introduction by Margaret Cole (London: Longmans, Green and Co., 1956), p. 307.

were then just beginning, were no longer able to deflect them from their convictions.

At the start of her autobiography, in 1926, Beatrice Webb had asked herself two questions: was a science of society and its organizations possible? and was religion as necessary as science, emotional beliefs as vital as intellectual curiosity? The Webbs themselves did much to establish sociology as a science, but over and above that they needed a religion: they found it in communism, and the 'culture of feelings' of which John Stuart Mill had once spoken now became a party matter.

Sociology and literature: autobiography as compromise

'The purpose of reading is above all to learn: now and then the growing youth will find a novel useful because it stimulates the imagination; but too much is unhealthy, for continual novel-reading ruins the unspoiled mind' – these precocious remarks, which might have come from an educational manual, were made by Beatrice Webb when she was eleven years old. Yet throughout her life she never lost the desire to write a novel: it was a concealed, and often repressed, motivation behind her sociological career.

Literature played an important part in Beatrice Webb's youth. She tried to translate passages from the *Faust* of her 'dear Goethe',[48] read *Wilhelm Meister* and Ludwig Tieck, and felt called to be a writer herself. With her cousin Margaret Harkness – who was soon to inspire Friedrich Engels, with whom she corresponded, to some surprising observations on literature and sociology – she talked about the novelists of the nineteenth century and the unexampled insight which they had into human nature. She was attracted most of all by Balzac, and for a time she harboured the intention of writing an essay on him and his skill in the analysis and description of society – a plan she abandoned when it came to seem to her too frivolous. She was convinced that such writers as Balzac would be of the utmost usefulness to the human sciences of the future – and especially to psychology, once this science had passed beyond the study of the primitive psyche to being a general science of human behaviour.

Certainly she was prey to doubts: convinced that she had taken the right path when she read Herbert Spencer and studied mathematics and geometry, she was at the same time unsure of the role literature ought to play in her education. She compared herself with Rosa-

---

[48] Beatrice Webb, 30 March 1879; Webb, *Diary*, Vol. 1, p. 31.

mund in *Middlemarch*, and was impressed by *Daniel Deronda*, in which George Eliot had depicted the priority of the emotions over calculating reason. It is therefore not surprising that she reminded others of George Eliot – her mentor Herbert Spencer, for example, and later F. R. Leavis, who was an enthusiastic reader of her diaries. It seemed to her that the desire on the part of the literary layman to write novels was actuated by the same motives as those that inspired the scholarly amateur's wish to devote himself to sociology or the humanities; and a certain indolence also played a role here, for there were sciences whose study demanded as little tedious preparation as did the writing of novels. This was certainly a bad misjudgment of such writers as Balzac and their way of working, just as it was a caricature of sociological research as Beatrice herself later pursued it: such assertions are an expression of her desire to combine her literary inclinations and her interest in science.

Within the disciplines that Beatrice also at first called the 'moral sciences', science and literature could not be rigidly separated from one another: it was not only what one wrote but how one wrote that mattered; how one researched was important, but so was the manner in which one presented the results of one's researches.

Beatrice envied those authors able to express hard scientific facts in clear and agreeable prose, and she set herself the task of discovering the secret of writing well. She had already accumulated experience in social milieux other than that of her own family, and thus it seemed to her strange to have to step back 'from life to grammar',[49] but she none the less compelled herself to undertake writing exercises in order to fashion for herself a smoother and more flexible style, and to this end she translated Chaucer into modern English. She complained of her lack of literary ability, although she was at the same time aware that the strength of her contribution to empirical social research lay in the manner in which she was able to present it: her collaboration with Charles Booth was so successful because he had command of a cautious, discriminating intellect with a feeling for detail, while she painted in bolder colours and was concerned 'more for the general effect of the picture than for *exactness* in representation'.[50]

The Webbs always regarded it as a favourable omen for their future work and life together that in his review of the first volume of Booth's inquiry he had remarked that Miss Beatrice Potter was 'the only contributor with any literary talent',[51] while after reading the

[49] Beatrice Webb, 2 January 1888; *ibid*, p. 237.
[50] Beatrice Webb, 15 July 1888; *ibid*., p. 253.
[51] Norman and Jeanne MacKenzie, Introduction to Part V; *ibid*., p. 316.

Fabian Essays Beatrice had found Sidney Webb's contribution the most significant because its author was the only one to possess a sense of history.

It would seem that, after the success of her article 'The Pages of a Workgirl's Diary', Beatrice had a sufficiently high estimation of her own literary talent, which lay especially in narrative ability and the capacity for pictorial representation, to venture on something bigger: in any event she now began, in collaboration with Auberon Herbert, who had also been active as a writer, to work on a utopian novel whose title, *Looking Forward*, suggests that it was intended as a companion piece to Edward Bellamy's *Looking Backward*. A diary entry of 30 September 1889 reveals how greatly she felt drawn towards literature:

This last month or so I have been haunted by a longing to create characters and to move them to and fro among fictitious circumstances – to put the matter plainly, by the vulgar wish to write a novel! In those early-morning hours when one's half-awakened brain seems so strangely fruitful, I see before me persons and scenes; I weave plots, and clothe persons, scenes and plots with my own philosophy of all things, human and divine. There is intense attractiveness in the comparative ease of descriptive writing. Compare it with work in which movements of commodities, percentages, depreciations, averages and all the ugly horrors of commercial facts are in the dominant place, and *must remain so* if the work is to be worthful.

But then I reason with myself: 'Who knows that you have any faculty for this new work? And grant you have, is it worth *your* while? Is it for that you have sacrificed your happiness?' . . . Still, I have in my mind some more dramatic representation of facts than can be given in statistical tables and in the letterpress that explains these – some way of bringing home to the hearts of the people, rich and poor, those truths about social organization that I may discover – illustrations of social laws in the terms of personal suffering, personal development, personal sin. But this must be delayed until I *have* discovered my laws, and as yet I am only on the threshold of my inquiry, far enough off, alas, from any general and definite conclusions.[52]

From now on her diary was the only place in which Beatrice Webb allowed herself the enjoyment of this deviation, the free play of her imagination: science had to precede art, for art could consist only in the perfected representation of facts already recognized by science. The ideal to be striven for was the welding together of science and art.

In 1894 there appeared *The History of Trade Unionism*, the first book Beatrice and Sidney Webb wrote together. Beatrice was discontented with this 'story' because it had not succeeded in presenting the his-

---

[52] Beatrice Webb, 30 September 1889; *ibid.*, p. 298.

tory and influence of the unions in a systematic way; and they at once began work on *Industrial Democracy*, in which they intended to avoid this error: the new book would contain a clearly formulated thesis capable of being examined and tested.

But the enthusiasm with which she had attacked this project soon faded: she complained that her spiritual needs were not being met and longed for other and higher forms of intellectual activity, for art and literature. Work on the book, which took shape only slowly, was dreadful drudgery: the same words and sentences kept appearing again and again, and the text presented no possibility of relieving the burden of scientific routine with occasional passages of narration.

It was therefore not to be wondered at that she should again toy with the idea of writing a novel once the tedious project she and Sidney were engaged on had been completed. This novel, which was to be called *Sixty Years Hence*, was imagined not so much as a utopia as a projection into the future of the processes of social evolution at present at work. Two themes stood at its centre: the final emancipation of woman and the victory of collectivism as an ideology permeating every institution. Beatrice wanted to be able at last to give her imagination full rein for once, without having continually to take account of prosaic facts. The reduction of myriad facts and details to readable form had grown disagreeable to her; if the novel she one day had to write showed she possessed no literary talent she would resign herself to taking up an old plan again and with equanimity completing her *History of Municipal Institutions*.

But the opportunity for writing this or any other novel never came. She and Sidney had hardly completed one project before they were engaged on another, and their long series of studies of English local government seemed as if it would never come to an end. The London School of Economics demanded all their attention, the *New Statesman* still had to establish itself, Sidney became increasingly active in the Labour Party and eventually as a Member of Parliament, and Beatrice too was involved in several committees, founded the Half-Circle Club for the wives of Labour politicians and continued to promote their ideological convictions through lectures and dinner parties even after 'wire-pulling' and 'permeating' seemed to be growing less and less effective as political strategies. Finally, it was a matter of self-discipline for her to conceal her literary inclinations, which Sidney too had repudiated as sentimental aberrations, and to confide her desire to write a novel solely to her diary.

That the Webbs had no interest in art and literature and set down

their 'solid but unreadable books'[53] mechanically once they had
assembled sufficient facts, soon became constituents of the Webb
myth which Beatrice and Sidney themselves did not do least to
nourish. Desmond MacCarthy, who had been a theatre critic before
he became responsible for literature at the *New Statesman*, recalled as
something that went without saying that he could never discuss
literary questions with Beatrice 'and certainly not with Sidney'.[54]
There was irony in the fact that when Sidney Webb was later
paralysed by a stroke and could neither write nor speak he continuously read novels – at the rate of one a day.

Bernard Shaw, who for long served as a ghost-writer to the Webbs
and helped to lend some agreeableness of style to the dryness of their
treatises, must have sensed something of the tension between
literary inclination and the stern duties of research that inwardly
agitated Beatrice; and Leonard Woolf clearly perceived it when,
though speaking of the blind spots in her intellect and her lack of
artistic ability, he emphasized at the same time that she also
possessed 'the temperament, strongly suppressed, the passions and
imagination, of an artist'.[55]

It became ever more apparent to Beatrice that working closely
together with Sidney Webb involved her in a certain risk: left to herself she would constantly improve as a writer, while as a co-author
she was gradually losing the art of writing altogether. She never
wrote in her own style but always in a mixture of her own and
Sidney's. Her desire to speak in 'my own words and sentences'[56]
again grew stronger: it was at length realized in her autobiography.
Even if she never wrote her intended novel this did not mean that
Beatrice Webb never gave in to her literary inclinations.

In January 1917 she set about composing the *Book of My Life* out of
material in her diary: instead of writing a textbook of sociology she
wanted to offer the products of her own experience and to describe
her apprenticeship in social research. It is noteworthy that in the
same diary entry of 17 May 1924 in which she extols the London
School of Economics as the greatest and most vital centre of
sociological research and teaching in the whole world, she describes,
as a compensation for this success, her dream of living a quiet life in
the country as a writer, 'alone with my thoughts and absorbed in the

[53] Beatrice Webb, *Our Partnership*, p. 15.
[54] Desmond MacCarthy, 'The Webbs as I Saw Them', in *The Webbs and their Work*,
  p. 127.   [55] Leonard Woolf, *Sowing*, p. 44.
[56] Beatrice Webb, 8 December 1913; Webb, *Diaries*, ed. Cole, vol. 1, p. 16.

effort of expressing these thoughts– past and present– in an attractive literary form'.[57]

She now became completely absorbed in creative writing, and in
this– except for occasionally offering advice on questions of style –
Sidney Webb had no part. With a frankness which she rarely
exhibited even towards herself Beatrice confessed that none of the
concrete problems she had for so long been concerned with– those
connected with the trade unions, municipal administration, the co-
operative movement, political organizations– any longer interested
her; she wanted neither to read about them nor to write or think
about them; what she was interested in was not states of society but
'states of mind'.[58] So captivated was she by her book, 'this child of my
old age',[59] that she doubted whether she would ever be able to write
another; and she had never felt such trepidation about any of her
publications, for autobiographies and memoirs resembled novels in
being evaluated by the critics as works of art and not as textbooks.

The autobiography was originally to be called *My Craft and My
Creed*: a title which is a clear expression of the tension between
reason and culture of the feelings, between Beatrice Webb's empirical
researches and her literary inclinations. In the end *My Apprenticeship*
was commended on account of its literary qualities even by those
who were no friends of the Webbs; and Virginia Woolf, who was
never to make any secret of her aversion to the bloodless and flesh-
less couple, saw, not without envy, that even the great Keynes sat at
Beatrice's feet. But she too found the autobiography interesting, as
she told Clive Bell in a letter of 9 April 1926; and two days later she
noted in her diary:

Mrs Webb's Life makes me compare it with mine. The difference is that she
is trying to relate all her experiences to history. She is very rational &
coherent. She has always thought about her life & the meaning of the world:
indeed, she begins this at the age of 4. She has studied herself as a
phenomenon. Thus her autobiography is part of the history of the 19th
century. She is the product of science, & the lack of faith in God; she was
secreted by the Time Spirit. Anyhow she believes this to be so; & makes herself fit in very persuasively & to my mind very interestingly. She taps a great
stream of thought . . .[60]

In *My Apprenticeship* Beatrice Webb represents her personal history
as a contention between an ego that affirms and an ego that denies–

[57] Beatrice Webb, 17 May 1924; Webb, *Diaries*, ed. Cole, Vol. 2, p. 27.
[58] Beatrice Webb, 10 July 1924; *ibid.*, p. 35.
[59] Beatrice Webb, 9 June 1925; *ibid.*, p. 62.
[60] Virginia Woolf, 11 April 1926; Virginia Woolf, *Diary*, Vol. 3, p. 74.

thus placing it in the genre of autobiographical writings whose celebrated model is *Rousseau juge de Jean-Jacques*.

The author of *My Apprenticeship* dramatizes her life with a sure sense for what is important in it – not least the question of her literary calling. More emphatically than in the diaries she again and again asserts that she was born without any literary taste: Racine and Corneille, whom she had to read for the cultivation of her French, taught her nothing about mankind and its problems, and their Alexandrines seemed to her merely laughable; the poems of Tennyson, who was the idol of the day, were to her the purest nonsense, and Shakespeare, whom her father admired, bored her. She was especially sceptical as to the value of poetry, and when she failed to understand this or that poem she would, like a little female Bentham, translate it into everyday prose – after which operation, she would complacently affirm, all meaning had departed from it. Goethe alone constituted an exception: he dominated her mind; she felt joined to him as to a friend and admired the richness of his experience, the certainty of his morality, the way in which he was able to unite art and science, and the self-confidence with which he applied both to the conduct of his life.

Precisely because her blindness to poetry is emphasized so dramatically in her autobiography Beatrice's later enthusiasm for literature, and especially for the novel, appears in all the more vivid a light. From a reading of her own diaries she concluded that in her youth she had probably been qualified less for empirical social research than for descriptive psychology, though she did not go on to ask whether this ability ought now to be put to the test in a novel or in behavioural research. Exposing the inadequacies of textbook psychology, she lauded the power of literature to elucidate reality in words that recalled the enthusiasm of Marx and Engels for Balzac and the 'glittering brotherhood of England's novelists':[61]

For any detailed description of the complexity of human nature, of the variety and mixture in human motive, of the insurgence of instinct in the garb of reason, of the multifarious play of the social environment on the individual ego and of the individual ego on the social environment, I had to turn to novelists and poets, to Fielding and Flaubert, to Balzac and Browning, to Thackeray and Goethe.[62]

Beatrice's disinclination had never been for literature as such: it had always been only certain authors whose work she found of no value.

[61] Karl Marx, 'Die englische Bourgeoisie' [1854], in Karl Marx and Friedrich Engels, *Über Kunst und Literatur*, ed. Manfred Kliem (Berlin, DDR: Dietz, 1967), p. 535.
[62] Beatrice Webb, *My Apprenticeship*, p. 138.

She learned nothing from Racine and Corneille, but French writers who, together with Voltaire and Diderot, imparted to her what she wanted to know included Balzac, who had portrayed the *Comédie Humaine* as a continuation of Buffon's natural history into the human domain, Flaubert, who regretted he was not a scientist and had urged that we 'love the facts for their own sake',[63] and Zola, the adherent of the experimental method.

What she prized above all was 'sociological novels',[64] and in the years following the First World War her diary is filled with references to contemporary authors whose works revealed sufficient sociological insight to excite her interest. To this group there belonged John Galsworthy and H. G. Wells, but also Santayana with his 'poetic prose',[65] Romain Rolland, the author of *Jean-Christophe*, Aldous Huxley, E. M. Forster, whom she advised in 1933 to abandon the essay and return to the novel, Somerset Maugham, Pearl S. Buck and Theodore Dreiser.

Set against these was a new school of novelists represented by Virginia Woolf; though technically very skilled, she was above all precious and clever and to anyone who desired to contend with the really pressing problems of the time of no consequence: 'Her men and women do not interest me – they don't seem worth describing in such detail.'[66]

For Beatrice Webb the autobiography had become a species of compromise through which she could unite her literary and her scientific inclinations. She planned further volumes; *Our Partnership* appeared posthumously in 1948, and sketches exist for a third volume with the working title *Our Pilgrimage*. At the same time she discovered that the social novel of the nineteenth century had in her own time found its continuation in the 'sociological novel': this was another species of work in which literature and the social sciences complemented one another. Beatrice Webb's attack on Virginia Woolf and her 'school' shows that she was aware from which literary direction the sociological novel of the twentieth century would be attacked: what she failed to see was that it was precisely the sociological novel which called into question the right of the discipline of sociology to exist.

[63] Gustave Flaubert to Mlle Leroyer de Chantepie, 8 September 1860; Flaubert, *Correspondance 1859–1871*, Edition nouvelle . . . par la Société des études littéraires françaises (Paris: Club de l'Honnête Homme, 1975), p. 46.

[64] Webb: Diary (typescript), 14 November 1933. [65] *Ibid.*, 29 April 1919.

[66] Beatrice Webb, 5 February 1927; Webb: Diaries, ed. Cole, Vol. 2, p. 131.

5

◁ ═══════════════════════════════════════ ▷

The utopian novel as a substitute for sociology:
H. G. Wells

In the 1920s Virginia Woolf proposed that English writers should be divided into two camps: among the *Edwardians* she listed H. G. Wells, Arnold Bennett and John Galsworthy; among the *Georgians* she counted E. M. Forster, D. H. Lawrence, Lytton Strachey, James Joyce and T. S. Eliot. She asserted with ironical precision that in December 1910 human character had sustained a decisive change, and with it all human relationships, religion, politics and literature had also changed. The *Georgians* were those who had taken cognizance of this transformation and had reacted to it with every exertion of their sensibility.

It was not hard to recognize where her sympathies lay. In accordance with her conviction that all novels 'begin with an old lady in the corner opposite',[1] she sketched through the example of Mrs Brown, whom she had met in a railway carriage, the distinction between the two groups of writers. The *Edwardians* looked out of the carriage; they described the factories gliding past, utopias, even the furnishing and upholstery of the carriage, but never Mrs Brown herself. Fundamentally they were not interested in human nature or the human character. In 1910 the most successful authors were Galsworthy, Bennett and Wells – but to ask them how to write a novel would be like asking a cobbler how to make a watch. The error of the *Edwardians* had been to accept the external world as given: the *Georgians*, on the other hand, asked themselves what reality actually was and saw in this question their characters' right to exist and the foundation of their literature.

Sharp though the division was between these two literary camps, Beatrice Webb had in fact anticipated Virginia Woolf in making what was at bottom precisely the same division – except that she

---

[1] Virginia Woolf, 'Mr Bennett and Mrs Brown' [A paper read to the Heretics, Cambridge, on 18 May 1924]; in *The Captain's Deathbed and Other Essays* (New York: Harcourt Brace Jovanovich, 1978), p. 102.

found herself in the opposite camp. In her terminology the Edwardians could be viewed as champions of the sociological novel: D. H. Lawrence had reproached Galsworthy that the people in his novels were not of flesh and blood but merely social characteristics; Arnold Bennett described himself as a philosophical observer who depended on the facts provided him by historians, sociologists and other writers, and confessed that the influence of Spencer's *First Principles* was visible in every line he wrote; and the concept of the 'sociological novel' might have been invented to describe the novels of H. G. Wells.

In 1910 there appeared Wells' novel *The New Machiavelli*, whose central figure Richard Remington, the career politician from humble beginnings, is a self-portrait of Wells. Other major characters in the novel include Oscar and Altiora Bailey: Oscar is depicted as an extraordinary 'dealer in exact fact'[2] and an uncommonly dangerous debater whose fund of political and sociological ideas is inexhaustible, and Altiora as being systematic even in those things that elude all systematization; and they immediately classify everyone they encounter into sociological types. Both are adherents of the nineteenth century's uncritical faith in science, such as had been propagated by Herbert Spencer. The Bailey's philosophy lacks all finesse: it is merely specialized, concentrated and accurate; the dinners they give are of a shameless frugality and they love all that is harsh and ugly. Everyone at once recognized them as the Webbs. They reacted calmly to the novel, and regarded the fact that they had become objects of caricature and satire as a sign of their fame and influence. But Wells' novel also demonstrated that social researchers such as the Webbs and sociological novelists such as himself were not necessarily in harmony with one another.

The Webbs counted Wells among the 'twelve wise men' with whom in 1902 they constituted a new club, the Co-Efficients, in which Wells soon assumed a similarly important role to the one he already occupied in the Fabian Society, where he contended for influence with the Webbs and with Shaw. When Wells' *Anticipations* appeared in 1901, Beatrice was impressed by the way in which he was able to unite imagination and factual knowledge so as to apply the methods of the natural sciences to the solution of the problems of society. Literature was always welcome to the Webbs as an instrument of propaganda – after the appearance of their *Minority Report of*

---

[2] H.G. Wells, *The New Machiavelli* (New York: Duffield and Co., 1910), p. 192.

the Poor Law Commission Beatrice sought to persuade Galsworthy, among others, to write something about it – and the utopian genre seemed to them especially useful, whether in the form of the novel or the drama. As Beatrice noted after reading Shaw's *Man and Superman*, there were theses, such as the breeding of mankind, which could not yet be treated with the aid of inductive procedures and for that very reason ought to be taken up by imaginative writers; in such instances literature was a kind of scientific trial rehearsal and highly welcome to social research:

We like him [Wells] much – he is absolutely genuine and full of inventiveness, a 'speculator' in ideas, somewhat of a gambler but perfectly aware that his hypotheses are not verified. In one sense he is a romancer spoilt by romancing, but in the present stage of sociology he is useful to gradgrinds like ourselves in supplying us with loose generalizations which we can use as instruments of research. And we are useful to him in supplying an endless array of carefully sifted facts and broad administrative experience.[3]

Wells' weakness lay in his lack of factual knowledge: he did not know how social organizations actually function. Moreover, as Sidney Webb pointed out to him in a letter of December 1901, he forgot that the ruling class of the future would consist not only of chemists and engineers but also of schooled administrators: experts in human organization whose sociology and economics would be no less scientific than chemistry or mechanics. People were not as easy to organize as machines: it required more imagination – and more poetry as well.

Wells saw in this criticism a challenge, to which he responded in 1905 with *A Modern Utopia* – a direct continuation of his *Anticipations* and, as he then believed, probably the last time he would be diverted from his true task of writing novels. The metaphysical scepticism which was the foundation of his thinking was, in his own mind, only a reflection of the economic and sociological conceptions of the age; his supreme objective was to discover a genre in which scientific discussion would be combined with imaginative story-telling. In his outline of a utopia the economic aspect constituted only a part of a general sociology: it was no longer a theory of trade based on bad psychology but a kind of physics applied to sociological problems. The Webbs found this utopia attractive, and they identified themselves without more ado with what Wells had called the 'Samurai', the social engineers of the future.

A political breach between Wells and the Webbs occurred,

---

[3] Beatrice Webb, 19 April 1904; Webb, *Diary*, Vol. 2, p. 320.

however, within the Fabian Society. A year after the publication of his *Modern Utopia* Wells argued, in the essay *The Faults of the Fabian*, that the society, which to his mind had been wasting too much energy on political and sociological research, should open itself up to an attacking style of politics, to propaganda instead of 'permeating'. His proposal to transform the respectable socialism of the Fabians into a militant movement could not have come at a better time: at the general election of that year the Labour Party had won fifty-three seats and appeared for the first time as an independent party in Parliament. A 'sudden outburst of interest in Socialism'[4] was the result. Wells found enthusiastic support for his ideas among the Fabians, especially the younger ones, but in the long run he was too little of a politician and too inexperienced in committee work – 'a novelist bombarding in vacuo',[5] as the malicious and politically more astute Shaw commented – to render his ideas sufficiently prac-ticable and translate them into action. He was convinced that the 'cold politeness'[6] of established institutions could only harm the world of literature, and thought a condition of anarchy the most appropriate for the ends of creativity. On 12 October 1906 he delivered a lecture on 'Socialism and the Middle Classes' in which – anarchistically inclined in regard to this question too – he attacked marriage in its traditional form and ridiculed the lack of ideas exhibited by the Webbs. In September 1908 he left the Fabian Society for good, declaring in his letter of resignation that from then on he intended to resume writing novels.

Even though there was never a complete breach between them, the Webbs' criticism of Wells now grew sharper and also more informative. Fundamentally it had remained Wells' goal to leave the society of the future to the natural scientists without paying any attention to the sociologists; he proclaimed a crude and dangerous gospel that threatened to diminish 'the demand for careful study of the facts of sociology and psychology'.[7] Wells, who pretended to himself that he was conducting his life according to Goethe's experimentalism simply in order to justify his libertinism, became

---

[4] Edward R. Pease, *The History of the Fabian Society* (New York: E. P. Dutton, 1916), p. 167.

[5] Norman MacKenzie, Commentary to the letter from Sidney Webb to H. G. Wells, 3 September 1906, in *The Letters of Sidney and Beatrice Webb*, ed. Norman MacKenzie, Vol. 2, 1892–1912: *Partnership* (Cambridge: Cambridge University Press, 1978), p. 236.

[6] H. G. Wells to Henry James, 25 March 1912, in *Henry James and H. G. Wells: A Record of Friendship, their Debate on the Art of Fiction, and their Quarrel*, ed. with an introduction by Leon Edel and Gordon N. Ray (Urbana: University of Illinois Press, 1958), p. 160.   [7] Webb, *Diary* (typescript), 22 August 1909.

increasingly unattractive to the Webbs, and, because he constituted in himself a treaty between a highly successful novelist and a natural scientist and thus forewent the mediation of sociology, a threat to social research. Though he knew nothing of the institutions of society, he was not content to be simply a writer but imagined he was free to dispense with the advice of social scientists: 'He thinks he *is* a scientist in sociology because he passed, not very brilliantly, the London University examination in chemistry and biology ... a veritable genius for pseudo-scientific story-telling ...'[8]

Even if he did laugh at the Webbs' deficiency of imagination, H. G. Wells did not leave the Fabian Society as a disappointed aesthete–on the contrary. He had slaved and written his way up from the lower middle class, and what he found objectionable in many of the older Fabians was their tendency to bourgeois complacency, their desire, which overshadowed everything else, for a political compromise that excluded all analysis and experimentalism in politics. He regarded his studies in the natural sciences as the decisive stage on his educational path, and experienced his zoological studies under T. H. Huxley as 'a grammar of form and a criticism of fact';[9] and it thus annoyed him that the nature of the socialist movement in England should be determined by poets and arts-and-crafts workers, by intellectual adventurers, teachers, churchmen and a pair of bureaucrats. There were no socialists with a scientific education: English socialism was still at the pre-scientific stage. When Wells set himself in opposition to the 'experimental dogmatism'[10] of the Webbs he did so not as a novelist but as a scientist.

Like many other writers who took a scientific interest in socialism, at the turn of the century H. G. Wells came to sociology. He became a founding member of the Sociological Society formed in London in November 1903 and belonged to its council as 'Mr H. G. Wells, Author of "Mankind in the Making" etc.': but, just as he had attached himself to the Fabians only to desert them again when his attempts at reform miscarried, so he seemed to want to employ the forum of the Sociological Society chiefly to point out to sociology what its limitations were.

On 26 February 1906, the year in which he attacked the Fabian Society, Wells delivered to a meeting of the Sociological Society held at the London School of Economics a lecture entitled 'The So-

---

[8] *Ibid.*, 25 October 1934.
[9] H. G. Wells, *Experiment in Autobiography. Discoveries and Conclusions of a Very Ordinary Brain (since 1866)* (New York: MacMillan, 1934), p. 161.   [10] *Ibid.*, p. 512.

Called Science of Sociology'. He claimed to be speaking not for himself alone but for many academics as well, of whose mood, he said, his lecture was a reflection. He not only contested the pretension of sociology to be a science in the narrower sense of the natural sciences, he maintained it was not a science even in the sense that modern history was a science, and that its inadequacies became palpable when it ventured to imitate the methods of the natural sciences.

He denied to sociology not only a cognitive but also an historical identity: Herbert Spencer and Auguste Comte were idols that ought finally to be toppled; one had to go back to Plato if one wanted to learn to think sociologically. In his lecture Wells revealed an astonishingly detailed knowledge of the sociology of his time: he appeared to be familiar with all the modern theoreticians, including of course 'Mr and Mrs Sidney Webb'; only the Germans were missing. According to Wells the failure of sociology could be foreseen merely from the fact that none of these authors could even reach agreement on what sociology actually was. All operations modelled on the procedures of mathematics – counting, classifying and measuring– could, he was convinced, lead only into error. Objective truth was to be found only in the uniqueness of the individual, and since so-called scientific method was only a means of 'ignoring individualities'[11] it had to be given up.

The valuation achieved through the methods of science, the analysis of large-scale phenomena, was necessary in such natural sciences as physics and chemistry, but even in biology it was dubious and in sociology it was completely out of place. When Wells derided Comte's and Spencer's conviction that everything could be investigated in the way the motions of comets or electric tramways are investigated, he pointed to those 'ologies' to which such analyses were unsuited – his literary public will have grasped the allusion to Dickens' grey and silent Mrs Gradgrind, who was so perplexed by her husband's 'ological studies'.[12] In sociology classifications were of no help:

We cannot put Humanity into a museum, or dry it for examination; our one single, still living specimen is all history, all anthropology, and the fluctuating world of men. There is no satisfactory means of dividing it and nothing else in the real world with which to compare it.[13]

For these reasons it was impossible to treat mankind as one treated an object of the natural sciences: a procedure was required that

---

[11] H. G. Wells, 'The So-Called Science of Sociology', *Sociological Papers* 3 (1907), p. 362.   [12] Dickens, *Hard Times*, p. 107.
[13] Wells, 'The So-Called Science of Sociology', p. 364.

involved a combination of science and art. Wells believed that this conception would find adherents even among sociologists; a sociology in which the subjective and the objective, beauty and truth, were united together would be neither art in the traditional sense nor science in the narrower sense, but a form of knowledge full of ideas and coloured by the personality: literature.

If one agreed with this point of view Comte and Spencer suddenly ceased to be sociological authorities and became pseudo-scientific mischief-makers; and a classification of the social sciences was replaced by a search for the forms of literary expression best suited to serving the ends of sociology. Two genres of this kind existed, one generally recognized, the other usually underrated: narrative historiography, of which Buckle, Gibbon and Carlyle were among the supreme exemplars, and the utopia.

The future destiny of a sociology conceived of as literature would be decided by the genre of the utopia. To Wells there existed in sociology no possibility of distinguishing between statements of what is and statements of what ought to be: in sociology ideas were facts, and the method appropriate to sociology was the working out of utopian ideas. If the Sociological Society was prepared to adopt this point of view, the synthetic framework for this discipline which 'Professor Durkheim, for example, thought necessary'[14] stood ready.

With the exception of narrowly historical works, all sociological literature that had stood the test of time was plainly of a utopian nature: Plato, More, Bacon and the literary elite of the French Revolution were among its contributors, as was Comte, who, though he spoke of science, facts and precise measurement, in reality constructed detail by detail his highly personalized occidental utopia – the only worthwhile gift he had ever given to the world. Sociologists could not avoid the task of forging utopias, and Wells imagined an enormous dream-book delineating the ideal society, the textbook of future sociology. Only one aspect of contemporary sociological research would find no place in this textbook: inquiry into how the existing institutions of social welfare could be improved.

Social emergency work of all sorts comes under this head. What to do with the pariah dogs of Constantinople, what to do with the tramps who sleep in the London parks, how to organise a soup kitchen or a Bible coffee van, how to prevent ignorant people who have nothing else to do getting drunk in beer houses, are no doubt serious questions for the practical administrator,

[14] *Ibid.*, p. 367.

questions of primary importance to the politician; but they have no more to do with sociology than the erection of a temporary hospital after the collision of two trains has to do with railway engineering.[15]

Sidney and Beatrice Webb's intention in founding the London School of Economics had also been to create an institution in which a scientific sociology would in the long run lead to more effective social and welfare work and to a reform of society acceptable to the Fabians politically: Wells, who neglected no opportunity for conflict, chose precisely this institution for delivering his plea on behalf of a literary and utopian sociology in which questions of practical social and welfare work should no longer play any role.

Even the vehement debate that followed his lecture, in which among others Shaw participated, could not deflect Wells from his prophecy that in future there would no longer exist a scientific but only a literary sociology.

During the years that followed there appeared in the *Sociological Review*, as the Sociological Society's journal was now called, an abundance of articles in which Wells could have seen a confirmation of his point of view. Large areas of modern literature were treated as descriptive sociology – quite apart from authors of the past such as Balzac, who counted in England too as the sociological novelist *par excellence*. Among British sociologists there were even bankers who expressed themselves like poets, and when the discipline again ventured abroad in the Garden City Movement and as municipal sociology, and sociologists began to resemble boy scouts rather than bookworms, Patrick Geddes, the leader of this movement, regarded the revitalization of sociology as a development that brought it closer again to literature, a realistic literature that had undertaken to depict life in all its abundance.

On the other hand, the sociological content of English literature from the middle of the nineteenth century was immense and still increasing; in the case of George Eliot it was so great that Herbert Spencer did not regard her novels as novels at all and excluded them from the rule that banned works of fiction from the London Library. Harriet Martineau, whose *Illustrations of Political Economy* was one of the great successes of the century, stood so completely under the spell of realism that she considered it impossible to invent the plot of a novel; and when, after having for many years depicted only factual events whose validity she had always tested, she was overcome by the

[15] *Ibid.*, p. 369.

desire to write a genuine novel she found the task difficult. Writers were convinced that they first had to acquire sociological knowledge before they could start writing, and the view was expressed in the *Sociological Review* that such authors as Galsworthy and Wells were in the first place sociologists and only afterwards novelists.

But there also appeared in the *Sociological Review* an article whose author thought it necessary 'to classify Mr Wells as an anti-sociologist'[16] – not because he perceived in him an almost personal antipathy to Marx and Comte, or on account of the pleasure Wells took in the irony with which a sociologist treated his own kind in Tarde's utopian novel, but because Wells remained a dreamer-up of catastrophes and believer in miracles instead of applying himself to the exact analysis of the structures and processes of society.

Just as his rank as sociologist remained a matter of controversy, so did Wells' reputation as a writer. While his approach to sociology was considered a step in the right direction, at the same time regret was expressed at his lack of sociological knowledge and reading-lists were drawn up for him: 'he really must read his Spencer'.[17] On the other hand his 'sociological cocktails'[18] were considered unpalatable, and such writers as Jorge Luis Borges expressed the hope that he would soon cease to be a sociological observer and return to being a simple story-teller who could write in the style of a Swift and of an Edgar Allan Poe.

While Wells wanted to turn sociology into literature his novels grew ever more sociological, in accordance with his own view that 'the modern novel . . . is the only medium through which we can discuss the great majority of the problems . . . raised . . . by our contemporary social development'.[19] In the end he debated the value of the sociological novel less with sociologists than with fellow-writers, and in a brief and decisive letter to Henry James of 8 July 1915 that was to bring about their final estrangement he distinguished between those authors who saw literature as an end in itself, like a painting, and those who regarded it as only a means to an end, like a piece of architecture.

H. G. Wells wanted his novels to produce some practical effect –

[16] S. K. Ratcliffe, 'Sociology in the English Novel', *Sociological Review* 3 (1910), p. 135.
[17] Unsigned review of Wells' *Mankind in the Making, Academy and Literature* 65 (1903), in H. G. Wells, *The Critical Heritage*, ed. Patrick Parrinder (London: Routledge and Kegan Paul, 1972), p. 92. [18] Wells, *Experiment in Autobiography*, p. 513.
[19] H. G. Wells, 'The Contemporary Novel', in *An Englishman Looks at the World. Being a Series of Unrestrained Remarks upon Contemporary Matters* (Leipzig: Tauchnitz, 1914), p. 163.

that too was why to many of his contemporaries he seemed to be a sociologist, and a fanatical one moreover.

The Sociological Society which Wells helped to found in 1903 was one of the first professional organizations of sociologists. With the exception of the newly created University of London, all endeavours to institutionalize sociology in the English universities came to nothing; it was only after the Second World War that it was gradually introduced in them, and not until the late 1960s did it enter Cambridge, where a visit from the American sociologist Talcott Parsons, far from facilitating its introduction, had only retarded it.

Paradoxically the late institutionalization of sociology in England was due to the early readiness of statisticians, officials and reformist politicians to apply sociological statistics to the solution of social problems: this infiltration of sociological knowledge into the administration made the security of sociology through an organized structure seem far less pressing a matter than it was on the Continent.

This fact also makes it comprehensible why the debate on the relationship between sociology and literature was conducted far less dramatically in England than it was, for example, in France. Although Durkheim's endeavour to secure a home for sociology in the universities was also only half successful, the introduction of sociology into the New Sorbonne none the less changed the curricula: the influence of sociology on the training of teachers seemed to threaten the hegemony of France's literary culture. In England, on the contrary, literary men and sociologists were not in competition for academic positions; and the intellectual differences between the two were, moreover, not so strongly marked as they were in Germany or France. But what especially blunted the controversy in England and thus always lent it something of the air of a game was the fact that the contestants usually came from the same milieu and had passed through a similar course of education. It was only in the debate over the two cultures that new and sharper lines of division appeared.

6

◁ ══════════════════════════════════════ ▷

Concealed sociology: English literary criticism in the nineteenth and twentieth centuries

The two cultures

On 6 October 1956 C. P. Snow published in the *New Statesman*, the weekly journal founded by Sidney and Beatrice Webb, an article entitled 'The Two Cultures'. When, three years later, he was invited to deliver the Rede Lecture in Cambridge, he expanded his article and spoke on the two cultures and the scientific revolution – thereby inaugurating a controversy whose slogans are still current and a focus of dispute today.

The two cultures which Snow confronted with one another were the culture of the literary men and the culture of the scientists. He seemed especially well qualified for the treatment of this theme: born in 1905, he was not only a trained physicist with considerable experience in scientific management and scientific policy-making, but also a writer who had in a series of novels treated the problems arising in connection with the exercise of scientific power and the ethics of science. Snow spoke of the cultures of the scientist and of the literary man as an anthropologist might speak of two hostile tribes: they were groupings whose differing values and norms of behaviour made communication between them virtually impossible and made every contact sooner or later degenerate into hostilities. In this division between the two cultures Snow saw the root problem of the Western world; and it had produced especially drastic consequences in England, where the tendency for social forms to crystallize was more pronounced than it was in Europe or the United States: in England there was apparently not a single area in which these two intellectual camps – almost indistinguishable from one another with respect to their social class, their intelligence and their material situations – were not still to be found.

Although Snow, who regarded science as his profession and writing as his calling, reproached the scientists for their literary philistinism as much as he did the humanists and artists for their dreadful ignorance of the science and technology of the civilization in which they lived, he left no doubt as to where his sympathies lay: it was on the side of the scientists, who for him were the embodiment of the future.

His chief reproach against the men of letters, however, was not that they were scientifically ignorant but that they were morally defective. Almost all the writers who, in his view, had set their stamp on the literature of the twentieth century – writers such as Yeats, Pound and Wyndham Lewis – were politically not merely idiots but villains: the view of life they embodied had accelerated an evolution that had finally resulted in Auschwitz. Anti-democratic attitudes were in the early twentieth century nowhere more common than in literature and the arts. Science, on the other hand, was at heart profoundly moral – and every scientist was at bottom an ethicist. From this it followed that the vital issue for Western civilization was that it should do away with the traditional predominance of literary culture and finally accord pre-eminence to the culture of science.

Snow was replied to by the literary critic F. R. Leavis in his Richmond Lecture of 1962. An academic outsider all his life, who achieved security only late on through a lectureship at Cambridge, Leavis was a merciless polemicist through need as well as by inclination, and when he attacked Snow he attacked not only the arrogance of the scientist but the English literary establishment as well. In Leavis' eyes Snow was devoid of all intellectual discipline; the vulgarity of his style was a reflection of the nullity of his arguments, and this 'spiritual son of H. G. Wells'[1] could quite simply have been ignored if he had not, like an evil omen, indicated the consequences threatening from the contemporary decay of culture.

To check this cultural decay the time demanded an assembling of all spiritual forces, the concentration of an experienced and creative intelligentsia into a vital 'English School' of which a fundamentally reformed university should be the centre: for to understand Western civilization, and the Industrial Revolution that had produced it, there existed no better instrument than literature.

This was precisely what Snow had denied: the literary intellectuals who stood alienated from the scientific culture of their time were in no position adequately to assess the origins and consequences of the Industrial Revolution, let alone to understand them. Such writers as

---

[1] F. R. Leavis, *Two Cultures? The Significance of C. P. Snow. Being the Richmond Lecture,* 1962. With a New Preface for the American Reader (New York: Pantheon Books, 1963), p. 40.

Ruskin, Morris, Thoreau, Emerson and D. H. Lawrence had consist-
ently closed their eyes to social reality: they were Luddites, out of
ignorance, who refused to understand that unhindered industrialization alone held out any hope for the world's poor. Snow the scientist
pronounced Leavis the literary critic incapable of understanding the
Industrial Revolution or contemporary society, and Leavis asserted
the same of Snow: thus they contended for an interpretative
privilege to which, since the middle of the nineteenth century,
sociology had laid claim.

In the contention between the two cultures a third, that of the
sociological intelligentsia, stood, a huge presence, in the background. Filled with anger, though not with surprise, Leavis saw the
sociologists weighing in on the side of Snow; while the latter observed
with pleasure that historians and sociologists were ever more firmly
refusing to be regarded as camp-followers of traditional literary
culture:

They argue that, though they are not scientists themselves, they would share
a good deal of the scientific feeling. They would have as little use – perhaps,
since they knew more about it, even less use – for the recent literary culture
as the scientists themselves. J. H. Plumb, Alan Bullock and some of my
American sociological friends have said that they vigorously refuse to be
corralled in a cultural box with people they wouldn't be seen dead with, or to
be regarded as helping to produce a climate which would not permit of
social hope.[2]

Though the themes which Snow and Leavis had struck up may have
sounded universal, and the social panorama which they spread out
before their readers may have extended far into past and future, this
dispute was also and not least a contention on a local level: for
Leavis, Snow embodied the old, encrusted Cambridge whose
ensconced academics he regarded as his enemies, while he himself,
he claimed, represented a new and the true Cambridge. At the end of
his Richmond Lecture he expressed the hope that the Cambridge of
the future might become a place in which that culture propagated by
the Sunday papers would no longer be regarded as an example of 'the
best that is known and thought in the world'.[3]

As everyone with a literary education would have at once
understood, with this quotation, which he did not designate as such,
Leavis had conjured up the historical context within which he wanted
to set his debate with Snow. Leavis had quoted Matthew Arnold, who

[2] C. P. Snow, *The Two Cultures and the Scientific Revolution* [The Rede Lecture, 1959]
(New York: Cambridge University Press, 1959), p. 9.
[3] F. R . Leavis, *Two Cultures?*, p. 50.

had already in the last quarter of the nineteenth century conducted a dispute over the two cultures with Thomas Henry Huxley; and in this contention too – though the participants may not always have been aware of it – the invisible third disputant, sociology, played a key role.

Literary criticism as a guide to living: Matthew Arnold

Matthew Arnold, who made so lasting an impression on the literary and social criticism of the Victorian age, was the son of an eminent Victorian, Thomas Arnold. Dr Arnold was born in 1795, and became headmaster of Rugby in 1827. Though he may have disappointed those who had expected him to reform the educational system of the public schools from the ground up, he was none the less the first to include such subjects as mathematics, modern languages and modern history in the curriculum of his school. In 1841, a year before his death, he was appointed Regius Professor of History of Oxford.

With the first excrescences of the Industrial Revolution before his eyes, Dr Arnold saw with trepidation how in his time working people were beginning to form organizations which seemed ready to resort to rebellion and murder; as a result he became the advocate of a state which was strong but aware of its social responsibilities, and of a church amalgamated with the state which was concerned less with preaching stabilizing dogmas than with acquiring its legitimacy through the active amelioration of social abuses. In the contention between the 'men of letters' and the 'scientists' in which Matthew Arnold was later to play a leading role he assumed an uncompromisingly conservative posture: he wrote to a friend that he would rather have his son believe the sun went round the earth than that his mind should be overwhelmed by the natural sciences.

Matthew Arnold, born in 1822, was a poet, critic, pedagogue and professor. For over thirty years – from 1851 to 1886 – he was active as one of Her Majesty's Inspectors of schools, and in 1857 he became Professor of Poetry at Oxford, where he was the first to lecture in English. Commissioned by the government, he undertook an extensive examination of the French, German, Dutch and other educational systems so as to pave the way for educational reforms in England.

Whatever Matthew Arnold did he did in the grand manner. He was and continued to be a poet whose strength was intuition and whose weakness was analysis; a scientist who rarely proceeded systematically and preferred to present his arguments by examples; a lover of dramatic gestures and forger of rousing slogans many of which are current in English even today. His diagnoses of the ills of society were as a rule acute and accurate, but his cures were mostly vague and indefinite. Relentless and repetitive, his style resembled that of a preacher hammering a single truth into the heads of his congregation: he himself called himself a simple, unsystematic writer without preconceived ideas; he did not wholly lack a sense of humour, but many of his writings are permeated by the just perceptible unintentional comicality of a writer who takes everything too seriously.

To Matthew Arnold, too, Wordsworth became the poet through whose life and work the mighty power of poetry could best be made manifest. In this there lay a certain paradox, for Wordsworth had never received in England the recognition he deserved: no sooner had he emerged from the shadow of Scott and Byron than Tennyson began to obscure his fame. As Wordsworth himself had soberly calculated, in an age in which Bentham determined England's philosophy of life his poems had not earned him enough money even to pay for his bootlaces.

Throughout Europe English policy was increasingly subject to criticism; English painting was at best provincial; the English had no music at all; but English science received recognition and, excelled only by Goethe, Wordsworth stood at the summit of European poetry. Wordsworth's poems showed how close human speech could approach to perfection and how it could become a medium through which man could come close to expressing truth. For Wordsworth the writing of poetry was a moral act, and the greatness of a poet was to be measured by the degree of seriousness with which he asked and answered the question of how man ought to live: a duty all the weightier in that the problems of the conduct of life were in England increasingly becoming the province of pedants and professionals – among whom were also numbered the adherents of the new social sciences.

Arnold warned against taking Wordsworth's commentaries and scientific-sounding arguments seriously, for, like other poets, he too lapsed into a kind of higher rigmarole when he became too philosophical: only his poetry contained reality, while his philosophy was as a rule only illusion. Wordsworth could not but experience difficulty in analysing his own poems, for they were as seemingly inevitable as nature itself; it was as though nature had taken his pen from him and written on his behalf. Whether or not this was an accurate characterization of Wordsworth, Matthew Arnold insisted in general that good writing was produced, not because men consciously and deliberately decided to produce it, but because they were constrained to its production out of an 'instinct of self-preservation'.[4]

For this perfect language called poetry interpreted life for us; it consoled mankind and sustained it in the world. Without poetry even the sciences seemed incomplete, and most of what in Arnold's time still counted as religion and philosophy would, he was convinced, in future be replaced by poetry. The strength of poetry resided in its power to interpret, to lay open the world: it was a power possessed in the first place by the lyric, but many prose works possessed it too. It could not be the goal of poetry to set down the solution to the secrets of the universe in black and white: it was concerned rather with establishing a meaning for man in the world and elucidating to him his place in it. Science never addressed the whole man; and therefore it was not Linné, Cavendish and Cuvier who had communicated to him a presentiment of where the secret of nature truly lay, but Shakespeare, Wordsworth and Keats, Chateaubriand and Senancour.

The more a scientist strove to make of himself a whole man, the more ardently did he yearn, in the midst of his arid activities, for a refreshment that poetry alone could furnish. As to what this poetical refreshment consisted of in the last resort, Arnold was deliberately vague: poets had command of a 'magical faculty',[5] and Goethe had, in his *Maximen und Reflexionen*, already said all that was to be said about it: 'The arts and sciences are attained by thinking, poetry is not: for poetry is inspiration.'[6]

Arnold was, however, very far from assigning poetry to the realm of the irrational: on the contrary, it was precisely its higher intellectuality that distinguished poetry from all the other arts, and only the fact that he thought emotionally divided the poet from the scientist. Arnold was highly critical of the creative outburst in English literature during the first quarter of the nineteenth century: the poets of

[4] Matthew Arnold, 'The Study of Poetry' [1880], in *English Literature and Irish Politics* (*The Complete Prose Works of Matthew Arnold*, Vol. 9), ed. R. H. Super (Ann Arbor: University of Michigan Press, 1973), p. 188.

[5] Matthew Arnold, 'Maurice de Guérin' [1863], in *Lectures and Essays in Criticism* (*The Complete Prose Works of Matthew Arnold*, Vol. 3), ed. R. H. Super, with the assistance of Sister Thomas Marion Hoctor (Ann Arbor: University of Michigan Press, 1962), p. 16.

[6] Matthew Arnold, 'On Poetry' [1879], in *English Literature and Irish Politics*, p. 348; Goethe, *Maximen und Reflexionen* (from *Wilhelm Meisters Wanderjahre*).

this era, he thought, knew too little but still went on madly writing. A mighty excitation of emotion, not of spirit, arose from the poems of Shelley and Byron; and in an age in which Goethe's Germany was grounding the strength of its culture in education and the faculty of criticism, even Wordsworth had very little interest in books.

Even if poetical inspiration rested less on analysis than on synthesis and presentation, the poet none the less had above all to know a great deal:

A poet ... ought to know life and the world before dealing with them in poetry; and life and the world being in modern times very complex things, the creation of a modern poet, to be worth much, implies a great critical effort behind it ...[7]

According to Arnold, true criticism was possible only from a position of impartiality. 'Disinterestedness' meant the search for 'the best that is known and thought in the world'[8] – independently of all practical or political considerations and free from any calculation of utility. Culture depended above all on discipline; yet discipline was very hard to achieve in England, because the country lacked a centre such as the Académie Française that could have watched over correctness of information, judgment and taste. In English poetry there was too much inspiration and not enough intelligence; and a host of prose writers existed who found it easy to write well because they were content to say little.

Poetry and criticism were activities that had almost nothing to do with aesthetics but very much to do with morality; Arnold, who always orientated himself by the life, character and actions of men, drafted something like an ethology on a poetic foundation, and understood the great poem as a dietetic of private as well as public life. In the light of such a claim, however, poetry and criticism were bound to enter into competition not only with science but with religion as well, especially since Arnold had asserted that, in his own day, the strength of religion resided in the fact that it was unconscious poetry. In Arnold's 'cultural arithmetic'[9] three-quarters of life consisted of morality of conduct, with science and art sharing the remaining quarter. Principles of right behaviour were among the most important themes of religion, which he characterized as

---

[7] Matthew Arnold, 'The Function of Criticism at the Present Time' [1865], in *Lectures and Essays in Criticism*, p. 261.   [8] *Ibid.*, p. 268.

[9] Fred A. Dudley, *Matthew Arnold and Science*, Publications of the Modern Language Association of America, 57 (1942), p. 275.

'morality touched by emotion':[10] in this way religion was secularized and society sanctified.

Arnold considered *Literature and Dogma* (1873) – an attempt at a better understanding of the Bible – his most important prose work. The first step towards a proper comprehension of the Bible lay in the realization that the language of the holy scriptures is not rigid and inflexible but fluid and approximative, not scientific but literary, and that consequently the Bible could be an object only of literary, not of scientific criticism. Only the nature of the *Zeitgeist* of the nineteenth century, which had elevated the natural scientist to the status of its idol and strove to subject every sphere of life to science, could explain why the theologians were increasingly renouncing all educative duties and merely seeking recognition as students of the Bible. The production of undoctrinaire essays no longer interested them: in future the dogmas of religion were to be presented, not in literary form, but with scientific exactitude.

With that, however, dogmatic theology abandoned the claim to be evolving the principles of the morality of conduct, for these were to be acquired, not through the procedures of science, but only by critically appropriating 'the best that has been said and thought in the world'.[11] Theologians wanted to be 'athletes of logic',[12] and in the process forgot that mankind did not long for logic at all, but for education and historical understanding. When St Paul employed such expressions as 'grace', 'rebirth' or 'justification' he used them approximatively, as though he was taking part in a conversation, making a speech or writing a poem, and not as though they were scientific terms. Paul employed no scientific terminology: the language of the Bible was a groping, poetical language, and theologians distorted the meaning of his sayings when they employed his literary phraseology as scientific terms.

It was a commonplace of anthropology that men clothed their dearest desires in legends and stories, and that these legends and stories thereafter determined their behaviour: a fact such as this required no further scientific investigation, for it was closer to actuality than any discovery of science, and religion was the firmest of all realities. Arnold compared his own time to the era in which Christ came to Judea: the Protestant dissidents were like the Pharisees, and 'our friends the philosophical Liberals, who believe

---

[10] Matthew Arnold, 'Literature and Dogma: An Essay Towards a Better Apprehension of the Bible' [1873], in *Dissent and Dogma* (*The Complete Prose Works of Matthew Arnold*, Vol. 6), ed. R. H. Super (Ann Arbor: University of Michigan Press, 1968), p. 176.   [11] *Ibid.*, p. 168.   [12] *Ibid.*, p. 169.

neither in angel nor spirit but in Mr Herbert Spencer'[13] corresponded to the Sadducees.

An admiring reader of the *Imitatio Christi*, Arnold thought that the gravest peril facing his age lay in the fact that the masses were gradually losing touch with the Bible. Among the forces responsible for this loss were not least the pseudo-science of Biblical criticism and the impertinence of those professors of theology who concealed their literary ignorance behind abstruse reasonings: like all who placed their faith in science, these Bible students too lacked a broad experience of the diversity of real life such as literature was well placed to communicate. Arnold quoted with approval Goethe's definition of superstition as the poetry of life – it was in precisely this sense that religion had to become superstition again.

By insisting on reading the Bible as a literary document and not as a scientific source Matthew Arnold reinforced the claim of literary criticism to be the only proper guide to living for his age: at the same time he thereby denied that natural science could make a similar claim.

The two cultures in the nineteenth century

The dispute between the two cultures goes back to before the nineteenth century, but it was only when the social and cultural consequences of the Industrial Revolution became perceptible, and the outlines of the new scientific and technological civilization became faintly visible against the skyline, and public education started more and more to affect larger segments of the population that it became a central topic of day-to-day politics.

When, for example, John Stuart Mill was elected rector of St Andrews University it was a matter of course that in his inaugural address he should broach the subject of the two cultures. He could rely on his hearers agreeing with him when he refused to regard the university as a place where men were instructed in a profession: no one was to receive there a training that would later enable him to earn a living. A university did not turn out efficient lawyers, doctors or engineers: it produced men capable of civilized intercourse with one another. Where contention arose was over the question of whether this general education should be predominantly literary or scientific. According to Mill the truth was, however, that every university education must pursue intellectual, moral and aesthetic

[13] *Ibid.*, p. 399.

goals simultaneously. Of these, the goal of aesthetic education was the hardest to attain, because in England art was not taken seriously but regarded as frivolous and a mere pastime: commerce and religious puritanism stood in hostile opposition to the cultivation of the feelings.

The contention over the two cultures came to a head in the dispute between Matthew Arnold and Thomas Henry Huxley, though it was a debate which, unlike that conducted in the twentieth century, was governed as a matter of course by the concept of fair play – a thing made easier by the circumstance that Arnold and Huxley respected one another and both dined at the Geological Society and belonged to the same club, the Atheneum.

Arnold had already touched on the theme of the two cultures in 1868, in his report to the Schools Inquiry Commission on the state of education on the Continent. True cultivation, he wrote, consisted in knowing mankind and the world: it followed that study of the arts and study of the sciences were of equal importance. Eight years later he laid before the Department of Education a general report in which this balance was already noticeably tilted: to be able to employ the discoveries of science properly mankind must be sufficiently secure in its morality, and this objective could not be attained without the aid of the humanities, poetry and religion. Overwhelmed by the increasing prestige and importance of the sciences, teachers especially were tending more and more to underrate the importance of literary culture and were thereby committing an error that would have serious consequences. In a characteristic turn of expression based on taking a current catchphrase and cunningly changing its meaning, Arnold insisted that the fruits of the sciences could be harvested only if what the political economists called the 'standard of living'[14] of all men was raised by the aid of literature.

Arnold delivered 'Literature and Science' as the Rede Lecture at Cambridge on 14 June 1882. A year later, during his tour of America, he delivered it again no fewer than twenty-nine times; he wrote to his sister that his audiences were wildly enthusiastic, especially in New England: everyone was interested in the problems of education, and the contention between literature and science was the theme of the hour. On his return to England he repeated the lecture, sometimes addressing an audience of as many as 2,500.

Arnold's Rede Lecture was not least a reaction to a lecture which

[14] Matthew Arnold, 'Reports on Elementary Schools, 1852–1882', in *Philistinism in England and America* (*The Complete Prose Works of Matthew Arnold*, Vol. 10), ed. R. H. Super (Ann Arbor: University of Michigan Press, 1974), p. 463.

T. H. Huxley had delivered at the new Birmingham Science College on 1 October 1880, on the theme of 'Science and Culture'. Huxley was not only a scientist but also a political advocate of science, and he fully deserved his nickname of 'Darwin's bulldog': no one excelled him in the skill and obstinacy with which he contended for the social recognition and propagation of the sciences. Huxley was convinced of the educative value of scientific knowledge simply because he saw in it merely the systematic extension of common sense: education was nothing more than the instruction of the mind in the laws of nature, and he who had enjoyed it was 'ready, like a steam engine, to be turned to any kind of work'.[15]

It was thus all the more regrettable that English educational institutions still gave priority to the cultivation of literary values and literary style: compared with the well organized armies of those who either clung to the educational primacy of the languages of antiquity or battled for the introduction into the universities of English and modern languages, the few advocates of the sciences appeared like guerrillas operating in enemy country, armed insurgents each of whom had to make his way more or less on his own resources.

But the situation was changing: industrialists who had likewise long spoken out against a higher valuation of instruction in science were abandoning this position as they came to notice the direct practical consequences science could have. That Huxley should have spoken on 'Science and Culture' at the Birmingham Science College in particular was a good omen in this regard, for Sir Josiah Mason, who funded the college, had stipulated that theology, party politics and 'mere literary instruction and education'[16] were to play no part in its curricula. This stipulation was the more welcome in that public opinion in England still regarded as educated only those who had studied Greek and Latin, while all the rest counted merely as specialists. But Huxley was in no doubt that the sciences were going to determine the modern world; and for that reason alone it was necessary to break the monopoly the languages of antiquity held in the schools and universities and to secure for the sciences the place there that they deserved.

Arnold's Rede Lecture reply to Huxley's lecture was anything but polemical: on the contrary, what was most noticeable about it was its conciliatory tone. Instead of attacking Huxley, whom he called an

[15] Thomas H. Huxley, 'A Liberal Education; And Where to Find It' [1868], in *Science and Education: Essays* (New York: D. Appleton and Co., 1893), p. 86.
[16] Thomas H. Huxley, 'Science and Culture' [1880], in *Science and Education*, p. 140.

'excellent writer and the very prince of debaters',[17] Arnold, who possessed only a rudimentary knowledge of the sciences, largely contented himself with rectifying terminology. He felt that one of the chief reasons why he had been misunderstood was Huxley's interpretation of the concept of literature in the narrowest sense, that of *belles-lettres*; 'literature', however, encompassed much more than that, namely everything that had been written in the letters of the alphabet or printed in a book. Literature included Euclid's *Elements*, Newton's *Principia*, and the writings of Copernicus, Galileo and Darwin.

On the other hand, the natural scientists could not be allowed to reserve the concept of science for themselves: provided they were conducted systematically and worked from original texts, literary criticism and the study of the languages of antiquity were also sciences. In this argument Arnold was following the German employment of the word '*Wissenschaft*', and he reproached Huxley with speaking always and only of 'science' in the limiting English sense, in which it meant only natural science. Once he had in this way broadened the concepts both of literature and of science Arnold did not find it hard to identify an area of agreement between Huxley and himself: literature and the natural sciences were both concerned with facts; both had to assume their appropriate places in school and university.

The danger, Arnold argued, lay in Huxley's determination that the natural sciences should predominate in modern education. It was of course important to grasp the results of the modern sciences: an adequate understanding of man and the world was no longer possible without it. But these disciplines furnished only instrumental knowledge: he who had a mastery of it could not systematically broaden it, but was and remained a specialist. Something restricted and narrow-minded adhered to the natural scientist who was no more than a natural scientist; and even Darwin had revealed such a narrow-mindedness when he had once confessed to a friend that scientific activity and the pleasures of domestic life were all he required – he felt no need for religion or poetry.

Such an attitude might be allowable in a born scientific researcher such as Darwin, though even within his own profession it constituted an exception, but as a rule of behaviour intended to apply to everyone it was unacceptable. For man was not content merely to know: he wanted to understand what he had learned and to grasp

[17] Matthew Arnold, 'Literature and Science' [1882], in *Philistinism in England and America*, p. 56.

what effect his knowledge had on how he acted. In every man there was implanted a profound longing for the good and the beautiful, an instinct for self-preservation directed not only to living on but also to living on in a right and proper way. Such fundamental needs as these could not be satisfied by the natural sciences.

Poetry and eloquence, on the other hand, were more than objects of the sciences: he who engaged in them participated in a 'criticism of life'[18] and gained for himself the principles of a guide to living which could help him to understand himself and to find his way in the world. Such a guide to living, a literary criticism understood as research into behaviour, spoke not only to the feelings and emotions; it alone was in a position to embrace and bring together the discoveries of the modern sciences, to recognize their meaning for the world of humanity, and to apply them to our sense of beauty and to our desire for the good life. And Arnold was addressing Darwin when, with ironical certitude, he asserted that the need for Greek art and literature was already to be discovered even in 'our hairy ancestors'.[19]

Huxley, however, had little reason to feel that Arnold's arguments really applied to him. It was with a shudder that he recalled the kind of scientific instruction normal in his youth:

I remember, in my youth, there were detestable books which ought to have been burned by the hands of the common hangman, for they contained questions and answers to be learned by heart, of this sort, 'What is a horse? The horse is termed *Equus caballus*; belongs to the class Mammalia; order, Pachydermata; family, Solidungula.' Was any human being wiser for learning that magic formula? Was he not more foolish, inasmuch as he was deluded into taking words for knowledge? It is that kind of teaching that one wants to get rid of, and banished out of science.[20]

Huxley's example recalls the opening scene of Dickens' *Hard Times*, in which Thomas Gradgind, 'a man of realities, a man of facts and calculations',[21] vainly tries to entice from the circus girl Sissy Jupe the scientific definition of a horse:

'Girl number twenty possessed of no facts, in reference to one of the commonest of animals! Some boy's definition of a horse . . . Bitzer,' said Thomas Gradgrind. 'Your definition of a horse.'

'Quadruped. Graminivorous. Forty teeth, namely twenty-four grinders, four eye-teeth, and twelve incisive. Sheds coat in the spring; in marshy coun-

---

[18] *Ibid.*, p. 68.   [19] *Ibid.*, p. 72.
[20] Thomas H. Huxley, 'On Science and Art in Relation to Education' [1882], in *Science and Education*, p. 170.   [21] Charles Dickens, *Hard Times*, p. 12.

tries, sheds hoofs, too. Hoofs hard, but requiring to be shod with iron. Age known by marks in mouth.' Thus (and much more) Bitzer.

'Now girl number twenty,' said Mr Gradgrind. 'You know what a horse is.'[22]

Huxley attacked those 'Goths and Vandals'[23] among his colleagues who wanted to banish everything from the curricula except the scientific disciplines; he was no Gradgrind and he knew that cultivation of the culture of feeling had an important role to play beside the training of the intellect in the development of the human spirit and that art and literature could never be replaced by the natural sciences. He attacked the overestimation of the languages of antiquity but was no opponent of an education in literature, for he thought the reading of great poetry, accompanied by a well-instructed literary critique, the best way to refinement of taste. Huxley agreed with Arnold that a guide to living was desirable if the end was the cultivation of the individual, but he doubted whether the principles for its creation were really to be found only in the writings of classical antiquity: an Englishman unable to educate himself with the aid of the Bible, Shakespeare and Milton would gain nothing from Homer and Sophocles, Virgil and Horace, either.

The debate on the reform of school and university education had, in Huxley's view, produced a false confrontation, for literature had hitherto played no role whatever in the university: Latin and Greek were taught merely to satisfy the needs of the pseudo-science pursued by grammarians and philologists. Huxley was a fervent advocate of the study of English literature, in which he found 'magnificent storehouses of artistic beauty and models of literary excellence'.[24]

Such opinions make it even harder to understand why Matthew Arnold thought he had to defend literature against Huxley, of all people. The title of his Rede Lecture, 'Literature and Science', is itself misleading, however: Arnold had to defend literature not so much against the natural sciences as against the rising science of sociology, and Huxley was also active in promoting the social sciences.

The interest Huxley took in the study of literature was not only aesthetic: he regarded the intellectual content of the great poetry of a nation as more important than its artistic form. It could be read as the decisive chapter in the story of the evolution of the human mind,

[22] *Ibid.*, p. 14.
[23] Thomas H. Huxley, 'On Science and Art in Relation to Education', p. 163.
[24] *Ibid.*, pp. 184–185.

and it revealed its interpretative power to its fullest extent only when it was viewed in relation to morality and politics and to such disciplines as physical geography. Like many of the educational reformers of his time, Huxley desired to promote the study of the sciences and of modern languages in both school and university at the expense of the languages of antiquity, especially Greek.

As soon, however, as one had become clear as to the role the natural sciences and a study of literature properly understood could play in modern education, it was all the more apparent that important spheres of instruction had hitherto been wholly omitted:

But there is a higher division of science still, which considers living beings as aggregates – which deals with the relation of living beings one to another – the science which *observes* men – whose experiments are made by nations one upon another, in battle-fields – whose *general propositions* are embodied in history, morality, and religion – whose *deductions* lead to our happiness or misery – and whose *verifications* so often come too late, and serve only 'To point a moral, or adorn a tale'[25] – I mean the science of society or *Sociology*.[26]

Like Matthew Arnold, Huxley had an altogether too low opinion of Comte, whom he called a 'speculative philosopher'[27] who continually contradicted himself; but that did not prevent him from speaking up on behalf of sociology as a science of social life: society was every bit as complicated as, if not more complicated than, the spinning-jenny, and like the latter it could not be improved by interference from those who had not taken the trouble to study the principles by which it functioned. In school as in university the pupil had to acquire a clear understanding of the essential conditions of life of modern technological–scientific civilization: he had to understand that social phenomena were merely an expression of natural laws. In his lecture on 'Science and Culture' Huxley proposed that the curriculum of the newly founded science college at Birmingham should be expanded by the addition of a new faculty:

This knowledge is only to be obtained by the application of the methods of investigation adopted in physical researches to the investigation of the phaenomena of society. Hence, I confess, I should like to see one addition

[25] Samuel Johnson, 'The Vanity of Human Wishes. The Tenth Satire of Juvenal Imitated, 219', in *Selected Poetry and Prose*, ed. with an introduction and notes by Frank Brady and W. K. Wimsatt (Berkeley: University of California Press, 1977), p. 63.

[26] Thomas H. Huxley, 'On the Educational Value of the Natural History Sciences' [1854], in *Science and Education*, p. 58.

[27] Thomas H. Huxley, *ibid.*, p. 49.

made to the excellent scheme of education propounded for the College, in the shape of provision for the teaching of sociology . . .[28]

The difficulty about the proposal was that there were insufficient teachers available for this new faculty.

It was from here that literary criticism, which Arnold had conceived as a moral science, was most dangerously threatened. Even though literary criticism might not be able to compete with the scientific disciplines in acuteness of method or rigorousness of procedure, it none the less had nothing to fear from them, since these faculties could do nothing towards promoting in man an understanding of himself or of the society in which he lived. Sociology, however, advanced precisely this claim, and the fact that such recognized scientists as Huxley were its advocates made it all the easier for it to present itself as a science. As Herbert Spencer's writings on education went far to demonstrate, sociology was threatening to become a discipline in direct competition with literary criticism.

For Spencer too considered that a guide to living constituted the heart of this science. 'How ought we to live?' was the question men directed to a discipline such as sociology. Spencer answered this question in the first instance by classifying all human activities according to their utility. The fifth and least important group under this classification included activities which men pursued principally during their leisure hours: among them were music, poetry and painting; and these ought consequently to occupy a correspondingly low place in school and university. The calamitous consequences of an educational ideal that gave preference to literary values over the acquisitions of the natural and social sciences were becoming ever more apparent:

When a father, acting on false dogmas adopted without examination, has alienated his sons, driven them into rebellion by his harsh treatment, ruined them, and made himself miserable; he might reflect that the study of Ethology would have been worth pursuing, even at the cost of knowing nothing about Aeschylus.[29]

These were the results of an ideal of education which made people blush because they pronounced 'Iphigenia' incorrectly, though they would admit quite freely that they knew nothing about the Eustachian tube or the function of the spinal cord, and through which a mother whose child had died from scarlet fever after too

[28] Thomas H. Huxley, 'Science and Culture', p. 158.
[29] Herbert Spencer, *Education. Intellectual, Moral and Physical* (New York: D. Appleton and Co., 1860), pp. 49–50.

much tuition would console herself with the reflection that before he died he had learned to read Dante in the original.

Spencer's sociology and teaching theories revealed even more clearly than did the writings of Huxley the extent to which Matthew Arnold's claim that literary criticism held a monopoly of 'criticism of life' was being contested; which made it all the more vital for him to demonstrate that his theory of culture could be an adequate instrument for analysing and at the same time correcting social evolution.

As early as 1861 Arnold had prophesied that the difficulty democracy would face in the future would be the discovery and preservation of ideals. He further foretold that, with advancing democratization, the state, which in North America had already replaced the aristocracy, would experience a considerable increase in the functions it had to perform – and this applied especially to the realm of public education.

In *Culture and Anarchy* (1869), his political credo, Arnold recommended 'culture' as the way out of the crisis of direction in which his age was involved: the impulse of man to self-perfection, and the inward-looking subjectivity of that self-perfection which was wholly indifferent to direct political action, was to act as a counterweight to the utilitarianism of his age, which had gone so far as to make some philistines suppose that the greatness of England depended on how much coal it produced. In an inwardly directed culture there was united together the scientific drive of man and his moral and social passion for doing good.

While the masses were indoctrinated and satisfied with the aid of a popular culture that was flooding over them like a deluge, Matthew Arnold adhered to his own ideal of culture not least because there were two goals he wanted to realize through it: the humanization of knowledge and the abolition of class. Arnold's diagnosis of modern society was merciless. In the paradisian centres of industrialism and individualism men stole the bread from one another's mouths, and as a school inspector familiar with the slums of the East End he was appalled at the multitude of the impoverished, degraded and ignorant he encountered there; he beheld 'children eaten up with disease, half-sized, half-fed, half-clothed, neglected by their parents, without health, without home, without hope'.[30] Spiritual anarchy and social unrest sustained one another, and the orders of society were lacking which had once, in times when cultural and political life

---

[30] Matthew Arnold, 'Culture and Anarchy: An Essay in Political and Social Criticism', *The Works of Matthew Arnold in Fifteen Volumes*, Vol. 6 (London: MacMillan and Co., 1903), p. 207.

were quietly concentrated together, taken their claim to leadership for granted and seen that it was in fact effective. Now, however, one had to ask oneself whether there was in the whole world another being as unintelligent and as incapable of seeing the world as it really was as an average upper-class Englishman.

To Arnold the aristocracy had forfeited its claim to leadership; the middle class, disqualified by those capitalists who might know how to produce an income but would not produce happiness for those forced to work for them, was in no position to replace it; the lower orders threatened unrest and rebellion. When he spoke of these three classes, Arnold spoke of barbarians, philistines and populace. This was not merely a 'humble attempt at a scientific nomenclature',[31] it was a complete moralization of politics, for any social reform could be only a cultural reform– an attempt to substitute for an 'Hebraic' philosophy of life concentrating on action an 'Hellenic' culture of thought and feeling. To Arnold, social reform on a large scale seemed premature if the individual attitudes of the people involved in it had not been rectified first; and the primary act must be the acquisition of firm and clear ideas: the 'mechanical details for their execution will come a great deal more simply and easily than we now suppose'.[32]

'Culture' was the attempt to acquire rational sense and to know the will of God through reading, observation and thinking – a goal which, as Arnold wrote to William Steward, a workman of Bedford, could not be attained through science but could perhaps be attained through poetry:

I agree least with your remarks on education. . . And as to useful knowledge, a single line of poetry, working in the mind, may produce more thoughts and lead to more light, which is what man wants, than the fullest acquaintance (to take your own instance) with the processes of digestion.[33]

In an age of expanding industry and growing urbanization Arnold's radical subjectivity appears as old-fashioned as it is moving – his writings are like lace covers on a steam-engine. But this poet and preacher was sufficiently realistic to recognize that his cultural ideals would have to be sustained by a higher authority if they were not to remain idle daydreams: culture required for its realization a strong state 'entrusted with stringent powers for the general advantage, and

[31] *Ibid.*, p. 89.   [32] *Ibid.*, p. 222.
[33] Matthew Arnold to William Steward, 8 May 1872; Arnold, *Letters 1848–1888*, collected and arranged by George W. E. Russell, 2 vols (New York: MacMillan, 1895), pp. 96–7.

controlling individual wills in the name of an interest wider than that of individuals'.[34] Arnold's readers were at once struck by the fact that, at a time when Marx was advocating the abolition of the state as an instrument of class domination, Arnold saw in the state the sole guarantor of a cultural and moral evolution of democracy.

When he read in Bentham's *Deontology* commendations of Xenophon and Euclid, while of Socrates and Plato it was said that under the pretence of teaching wisdom and morality they had talked only nonsense, Arnold was finished with Bentham. In the same way as he condemned Bentham he also condemned Comte: to Arnold sociology was an expression of that Jacobinism which furiously repudiated the past, produced abstract systems for renewing society *en gros* and drafted new doctrines determining the rational society of the future down to the smallest details. Comte, a 'grotesque old French pedant',[35] was one of the system-makers Matthew Arnold abhorred, and nothing could approach in ugliness the venues in which the adherents of the social sciences held their conferences: 'A great room in one of our dismal provincial towns; dusty air and jaded afternoon daylight; benches full of men with bald heads and women in spectacles . . .'[36]

In 1856 the National Association for the Promotion of Social Science was founded; it held a conference every year until 1884, and was disbanded in 1886 for lack of money. In his novel *Gryll Grange* (1861) Thomas Love Peacock made fun of sociology, which he caricatured as the science of pantopragmatics:

Nothing practical comes of it, and indeed so much the better. It will be at least harmless, so long as it is like Hamlet's reading 'words, words, words'. Like most other science, it resolves itself into lecturing, lecturing, lecturing, about all sorts of matters, relevant and irrelevant: one enormous bore prating about jurisprudence, another about statistics, another about education, and so forth . . .[37]

His advocacy of the cultural state and of a subjectivity protected by the state, his hostility towards systems and rejection of social planning, his anti-scientific posture and the over-riding educative value he accorded to literature seemed to make of Arnold a natural opponent of sociology and sociological positivism and a sworn enemy

[34] Matthew Arnold, 'Culture and Anarchy', p. 48.
[35] Matthew Arnold, 'A Word More About America' [1885], in *Philistinism in England and America*, p. 207.
[36] Matthew Arnold, 'Wordsworth' [1879], in *English Literature and Irish Politics*, p. 50.
[37] Thomas Love Peacock, *Gryll Grange* [1861] (London: MacMillan, 1896), pp. 52–3.

of Comte and his English disciples. It is indicative of the character of the English intellectual milieu and the close inter-connectedness of the English intelligentsia that Richard Congreve, the founder of English positivism, should have been one of Dr Arnold's most prominent pupils at Rugby. Huxley's definition of positivism as Catholicism minus Christianity had been corrected by Congreve: positivism, he said, was Catholicism plus science. This could only strengthen Arnold's abhorrence.

Among those who made merry over Arnold's hazy concept of culture, which was good enough only for reviewers and professors of *belles-lettres*, was Frederic Harrison: 'Culture, my friend, is an inspiration, a glow, an afflatus'[38] which could be detected only in the way poodles detect truffles. A positivist from the beginning, who deserted Congreve in 1878 and in 1910 became chairman of the London Sociological Society, Harrison, 'Auguste Comte's Horatio',[39] reproached Arnold with having offered only a travesty of positivism: in reality no one had been a more biting critic of Jacobinism than Comte. Arnold, he maintained, was an admirable lyric poet and an astute literary critic but a bad philosopher, whose guide to living – see things as they really are – was, as Kant had demonstrated once and for all, a demand for the impossible. The paradox was that, although they employed differing means, Matthew Arnold was fundamentally seeking to attain the same goals as were the positivist sociologists: 'Arnold, indeed, like M. Jourdain, was constantly talking Comte without knowing it, and was quite delighted to find how cleverly he could do it.'[40]

Harrison was in fact in complete accord with what Arnold had said in *Culture and Anarchy*: he believed every word, for it corresponded exactly to the credo Comte had proclaimed in the *Appel aux Conservateurs*. And he imagined how Arnold would some day encounter Comte in the Elysian fields: 'Ah, well! I see now that we are not far apart, but I never had patience to read your rather dry French, you know!'

Matthew Arnold became a sociologist against his will, and his literary criticism was a concealed sociology.

---

[38] Frederic Harrison, 'Culture, a Dialogue' (*Fortnightly Review*, 1867), in *The Choice of Books and Other Literary Pieces* (London: MacMillan, 1886), p. 101.
[39] Austin Harrison, *Frederic Harrison: Thoughts and Memories* (New York: G. P. Putnam's Sons, 1927), p. 221.
[40] Frederic Harrison, 'Matthew Arnold', in *Tennyson, Ruskin, Mill and Other Literary Estimates* (New York: MacMillan, 1900), p. 124.

F. R. Leavis: English as a guiding discipline

The debate between Matthew Arnold and Thomas H. Huxley made it clear that in the dispute over the two cultures the contention as to the relative educative value of the languages of antiquity and the natural sciences would be continued in a different arena, where literary criticism and sociology would contend over the claim to represent the guiding discipline for industrial society; this was a battle between two academic newcomers, for neither English nor sociology were established university faculties.

At Oxford and Cambridge especially, resistance to the introduction of a faculty of 'English studies' was still strong even at the beginning of the twentieth century on the grounds that it would mean the entry of dilettantism into the university: an Englishman did not need to be instructed in his own language, and his national literature was of no educative value. It is indicative of the state of things that the first professorships in English should have been established at the new London colleges: first at London University, founded in 1826, which later became University College, then at King's College, founded five years afterwards. University College was a centre of philosophical radicalism and of a secular education in which particular weight was laid on instruction in the natural sciences and modern languages; King's College was a rival foundation run by Anglicans and Tories in which secular education and religious instructions were intended to form a unity.

The expectations which these new institutions aroused is indicated in the fact that Thomas Carlyle intended to apply for a professorship at one of the two colleges, either in English or in moral philosophy: he was plainly of the opinion that the two faculties could in principle fulfil the same function. There was a widespread idea that literature above all was in a position to cure 'the soul-destroying evils of a rapidly changing society'.[41] The champions of the study of English saw in it not only a means of cultivating the feelings and emotions but in the end nothing less than a 'holy sacrament of the spirit'.[42]

'English studies' played an important role in adult education. The London Mechanics' Institute was founded in 1823; by 1850 there

---

[41] D. J. Palmer, *The Rise of English Studies: An Account of the Study of English Language and Literature from its Origins to the Making of the Oxford English School* (London: Oxford University Press, 1965), p. 31.

[42] Lionel Gossman, 'Literature and Education', *New Literary History* 13 (1981/2), p. 355.

already existed 500 comparable institutions. The mechanics' institutes were originally intended to give the worker an insight into the scientific principles that lay behind his work, but the institutes evolved a dynamism of their own that expanded their curricula considerably: political economy was soon one of the most popular subjects, and 'English studies' designed to improve the workers' ability to read and to assist them to a knowledge of English national literature also acquired importance. On the other hand, and quite contrary to the original intention, the scientific disciplines gradually retreated into the background: the scientific knowledge which the workers brought with them from school was too slight. The political function of the institutes, at which Dickens among others gave lectures, was a matter of controversy: 'The institutes were regarded as hotbeds of sedition, while others thought that giving education to working men was the only way of averting revolution.'[43]

Sir Josiah Mason's college in Birmingham, at which Huxley had delivered his lecture on 'Science and Culture', was in 1881 also expanded to include a faculty of arts, in which professorships in English and ancient languages and lectureships in French and German were established. 'English studies' played a further important role in the university education of women, who had long been permitted to study history and languages. In 1848 Queen's College for Women was founded, in which, as in comparable institutions, literature played a prominent role: it functioned as a medium for the culture of feeling and as a corrective to a scientific rationalism that was growing more and more estranged from real life. Since they had sufficient leisure and not too many social obligations to devote themselves intensively to culture women of the middle class were considered especially suited to the study of English; and there seemed also to be the tactical consideration that English could be employed as a buffer-discipline: women who devoted themselves to literature would abandon the thought of studying medicine or the natural sciences.

From 1880 onwards efforts were increased to introduce the study of English, 'the poor man's classics', into Oxford. A treaty of toleration with the languages of antiquity was necessary if this was to be effected, and a historical rather than a preponderantly philological orientation gradually came to prevail in the field of English studies. In 1894 the Oxford English School was founded, and during the first years of its existence four times more women than men were as a rule

---

[43] Palmer, *The Rise of English Studies*, p. 32.

enrolled in it. The study of English and the reading of the English poets were intended to meet some of the fundamental needs of men in the industrial age:

They need aesthetic culture ... They need moral culture ... They need political culture, instruction, that is to say, in what pertains to their relationship to the State, to their duties as citizens; and they need also to be impressed sentimentally ...[44]

In Cambridge the slow process of creating an English school was not completed until 1926, when it first became possible to take the final examination in English alone. While at Oxford the study of literature and language remained closely entwined together, at Cambridge a programme evolved called 'Life, Literature and Thought': here, unmistakably, was evidence that the idea of literary criticism as a guide to living such as Matthew Arnold had developed had now been accorded institutional security. But it was in a rebel against traditional academic Cambridge that Arnold's programme found its decisive continuation and enlargement: F. R. Leavis.

Even in a society of eccentrics F. R. Leavis remained an outsider all his life. Born in Cambridge in 1895, he attended none of the famous public schools but went instead to the Cambridge grammar school – an equally renowned institution, to be sure – and afterwards stayed at Cambridge to study history and English. This course offered no advantage in an institution that boasted of its cosmopolitanism and repudiated as provincial the town that gave it shelter. Leavis and his wife, Queenie Dorothy Roth, determined the nature of English literary criticism in the twentieth century, but she was never offered a firm academic appointment and Leavis obtained one only very late – in 1936, after Downing College had elected him a fellow. By this time both could look back on a series of important and influential publications: in the year 1932 alone, their *annus mirabilis*, there appeared F. R. Leavis' epoch-making reassessment of English lyric poetry *New Bearings in English Poetry*, Q. D. Leavis' weighty sociological study *Fiction and the Reading Public*, which describes the development of mass culture and the culture industry, and the first number of the magazine *Scrutiny*. Only in 1954 did Leavis become a member of the Cambridge faculty board, and he never received a professorial chair.

Leavis' literary criticism was at the same time a product of Cambridge and its English School and directed against them. Q. D.

---

[44] John Churton Collins, *The Study of English Literature* (London: MacMillan, 1891), pp. 81–2.

Leavis showed in many of her studies how careerism and intellectual indiscipline had destroyed the academic values which the university itself invoked; she recalled such outsiders as Alfred Haddon, who, unpaid and without public recognition, had established new faculties at Cambridge – ascetic and involved scholars who found in the university not an *alma mater* but rather a stepmother. To Leavis the academic was and remained an enemy who had to be defeated, and he was contemptuous of a system in which family background and personal connections counted for more than erudition, sensibility or honesty. This system obtained in the literary world of the *Observer*, the *Times Literary Supplement* and the BBC, all congregated in the capital, the Bloomsbury coterie, the universities of Oxford and Cambridge, and the British Council, which represented the system abroad. Leslie Stephen embodied the virtues of true English culture; the attitude and writings of his daughter, Virginia Woolf, were evidence of its decadence.

An Italian observer called Leavis a *puritano frenetico*: in regard to books which to him embodied the great tradition of English literature and which he revered like the Bible, criticism became reverential exegesis. Leavis was a strict educator and as a literary critic a teacher rather than a scholar; his English was far from elegant, and, betraying as it always did the style of the lecturer, was often difficult to read. Tact, delicacy and the ability to say the right thing without constant recourse to ponderous definitions were qualities he admired in Matthew Arnold and no doubt also claimed for himself. His fanatical demand for critical discipline was a reaction to the admission that the connoisseur of art often had to acquiesce in a *je ne sais quoi*; it is revealing how frequently in his writings emphasis in italics replaces argument and demonstration: 'She *was* a great novelist,'[45] he says, more in adjuration than proof, of George Eliot. What he prized in Eliot – and this too betrays how he saw himself – was a provinciality whose strength she employed without incurring its disadvantages.

Concerned less with being original than with preserving the purity of his judgment, Leavis often praised what others censured and rejected books – Fielding's *Tom Jones*, for example – which everyone else liked. He was insulting to those who declared themselves his allies without being asked to do so: when F. W. Bateson founded *Essays in Criticism* in Oxford as a scholarly counterpart to Leavis's admired magazine *Scrutiny* he was furiously repulsed by Leavis without ever learning why Leavis found him so unwelcome as a

---

[45] F. R. Leavis, *The Great Tradition*, p. 15.

confederate. Leavis was anti-Marxist when Marxism was fashionable, and he hated nothing more than making friends with the Establishment: this last led finally to a breach even with T. S. Eliot. In his uncompromising nature he resembled Wittgenstein, whom he considered a genius and with whom he maintained a distant contact. A stomach ailment compelled him to eat sparingly and at night he went for long walks in an effort to conquer insomnia – both were the result of a gas attack in which he was involved as a stretcher-bearer in the First World War. Although *Scrutiny* was a group undertaking, and he published books in collaboration with his wife, Leavis remained a solitary and, as a critic, isolated. Like Sainte-Beuve imprisoned in the routine of his *Nouveaux Lundis*, Leavis could also have said of himself that he was no lord or gentleman but a worker earning his wages; and in other respects, too, he was, as photos of him also reveal, in every way the opposite of a '*critique souriant*'.[46]

Between 1925 and 1927 Edgell Rickword produced the *Calendar of Modern Letters*, a magazine in which Leavis saw his own ideas of the nature of literary criticism partly anticipated. The *Calendar* published severe dressings-down of over-rated contemporary writers, not least among whom were such authors of sociological novels as H. G. Wells and John Galsworthy; these 'scrutinies' were afterwards collected and they gave their name to the magazine in which Leavis and his adherents advocated their uncompromising programme – praising without prejudice but at the same time prepared for any 'necessary work of destruction'.[47] Contributors to *Scrutiny* were above all youthful graduates of Cambridge, former pupils and at the same time critics of the English School who, like Leavis, worked without a firm academic position, a secure salary or payment for their contributions. *Scrutiny* soon acquired wide recognition – but official Cambridge, the quality Sunday papers, Bloomsbury and the British Council obstinately ignored it. Without any kind of subsidy *Scrutiny* appeared for more than twenty years before in 1953 it was compelled to cease publication; ten years later interest in it had grown to such an extent that Cambridge University Press published a reprint of it; Leavis wrote triumphantly that *Scrutiny* had now become classic and indispensable.

Although Leavis's forefathers were Huguenots he was the most un-French of critics. To those who reproached him with provinciality

---

[46] Charles Monselet, in his foreword to Sainte-Beuve's *Souvenirs et Indiscrétions*; Matthew Arnold, 'Sainte-Beuve' [1886], in *The Last Word* (*The Complete Prose Works of Matthew Arnold*, Vol. 11), ed. R. H. Super (Ann Arbor: The University of Michigan Press, 1977), p. 115. [47] F. R. Leavis, *The Great Tradition*, p. 23.

and also a certain Francophobia he retorted – citing Henry James as his witness – that he had no need to concern himself with a literary society which devoted its attention to an Alphonse Daudet while knowing nothing of George Eliot. The greatness of George Eliot and Henry James resided partly in the slightness of their resemblance to Flaubert, and Joseph Conrad was a more important writer than Flaubert because he cared not only about literature but about life as well. Allergic equally to academics and to every variety of *belles-lettres*, F. R. Leavis took literature in deadly earnest: life was too short, he once wrote, to examine Fielding in detail or to pay any attention at all to J. B. Priestley.

Every kind of fine writing, in literature or in literary criticism, that emphasized form at the expense of content counted with Leavis as irresponsible. It was because he always associated the aesthetic with the moral that Tolstoy was so great; it was because she enlivened her knowledge with fellow-feeling that one had to admire George Eliot; that a poet was sensitive was revealed in the fact that he complied with the claims of morality. Great novelists did not entertain the reader: they enlightened him as to the possibilities of life; the classics were authors who were both living and life-bestowing. Leavis read novels and poems as contributions to an exemplary anthropology: mankind could gain from them enlightenment as to its nature, its needs and its history.

Since literature was concerned with the possibilities of right living, literary criticism could be only a normative discipline: the standards it applied were moral ones, and its task was to interpret the values stored up in great literary works. Leavis' literary criticism, pursued so earnestly and with such rigour, was not a science of literature, and I. A. Richards, who had nursed Q. D. Roth's dissertation, was one of the earliest contributors to *Scrutiny* and counted as one of the forefathers of the New Criticism, suffered excommunication by Leavis when his psychological and semantic ambitions degenerated into pseudo-science. As early as in the *Principles of Literary Criticism* (1928) Richards had enunciated a programme with which Leavis was only partly in accord:

Mixed forms of writing which enlist the reader's feeling as well as his thinking are becoming dangerous to the modern consciousness with its increasing awareness of the distinction. Thought and feeling are able to misread one another at present in ways which were hardly possible six centuries ago. We need a spell of purer science and purer poetry before the two can again be mixed, if indeed this will ever become once more desirable. [48]

[48] I. A. Richards, *Principles of Literary Criticism* (New York: Harcourt Brace Jovanovich, 1928), p. 3.

What was bound to attract Leavis to such a programme was the inexorability, rigour and discipline it called for; what repelled him was its author's scientific optimism, which later went so far as to laud television as a 'heaven-sent instrument'[49] for the propagation of the Basic English he had helped to invent.

In Leavis' eyes a science was precisely what literary criticism was not. Since it was the critic's job always to be just to the individual author, discussion of theories or methods was absurd. Such wholesale designations as 'Romantic' were useless when poets as various as Blake, Wordsworth and Shelley were classified as 'Romantic'. Critics who hid behind categories of this kind were avoiding a moral decision: they were refusing to establish the value of each individual author. It is typical of Leavis that, when he speaks of the 'great tradition' of English literature in which he places Jane Austen, George Eliot, Henry James and Joseph Conrad, he declines to employ designations either of an era or a genre: the 'great tradition' is a normative category and the critic who employs it is not a classifier but a judge.

In the tradition of Matthew Arnold, Leavis conceived literary criticism as a guide to reading and to living. When he attacked the English culture industry he did so less from a feeling of resentment than from one of responsibility: Leavis was convinced that the spiritual future of England depended on a correct evaluation of great English literature, and talk of the 'bloody revolution'[50] needed in the encrusted realm of 'English studies' was almost more than a metaphor. In an age in which feeling for religion was growing weaker and weaker Matthew Arnold had preached the value of literary culture and education: it was in this spirit that Leavis – a puritan without religion, as he called himself – wanted to make of the reformed university a kind of community held together by a belief in the healing power of literature.

Sociology as a spur and a threat

The problem lay in the need to convert to such a belief not only scientists but also scientific policy-makers; and when Lord Robbins presented his *Report on Higher Education* the competition which literary criticism was faced with became clear:

---

[49] I. A. Richards, 'Complementarities', in *Uncollected Essays*, ed. John Paul Russo (Cambridge, Mass.: Harvard University Press, 1976), p. 262.

[50] Q. D. Leavis, 'The Discipline of Letters' [1943], in *A Selection from Scrutiny*, compiled by F. R. Leavis, 2 vols (Cambridge: Cambridge University Press, 1968), Vol. 1, p. 22.

Lord Robbins, surveying the needs of education at the university level, recognizes that the natural sciences must be complemented by the study of human nature and brings out the force of this recognition by pointing to psychology and the social sciences. These are disciplines; his concessive gesture towards Literature and the Arts makes it plain that they are to be regarded as pleasing adjuncts to what really matters – graces and adornments in the margin of life that shouldn't be discouraged: they contribute dignity and amenity.[51]

As was the case a hundred years previously in the contention between Arnold and Huxley it was apparent now too that the threat to literary criticism did not come from the natural sciences. The faculty of English stood at the other end of a scale that began with mathematics: there would never be in literary criticism a work corresponding to the *Principia Mathematica*. The Robbins Report was the product of a technological civilization in which the spirit of Bentham still lived on, the expression of a spiritual philistinism that wanted to employ the social sciences for the purpose of adapting mankind to the needs of the market-place and the culture industry. In the eyes of the philistine, whom Matthew Arnold had already seen through, English was merely a 'soft option'.[52]

Without any prospect of receiving recognition for it in the modern Bentham-world, literary criticism had to undertake a heroic attempt to present the deeds of creative writers not as a pastime but as a necessary activity upon which the survival and dignity of man depended. Without making any false claim to scientificality, literary criticism had at the same time to make clear that it was a discipline *sui generis*, a discipline in which doctrines, theories and general concepts counted for less than sensibility, awareness of responsibility and intelligence. In this discipline the literary tradition of a country consisted of more than its literary history: it was precisely because it took literature so seriously that it laid such great weight on extra-literary studies. Literary criticism could not compete with the natural sciences and it no longer needed to compete with philosophy and the languages of antiquity: what it had to come to terms with in a scientific and technological civilization was sociology.

Leavis and the *Scrutiny* circle did not simply reject sociology: of Q. D. Leavis, indeed, Denys Thompson said that she had filled the lacuna created by her renunciation of the Judaic tradition with

[51] F. R. Leavis, *The Living Principle: 'English' as a Discipline of Thought* (London: Chatto and Windus, 1975), pp. 19–20.

[52] F. R. Leavis, ' "English", Unrest and Continuity' [1969], in *Nor Shall My Sword: Discourses on Pluralism, Compassion and Social Hope* (London: Chatto and Windus, 1972), p. 108.

sociology, philosophy and anthropology. But the 'Leavisites' insisted that literary criticism was better sociology than sociology: for, while sociological experience must necessarily remain limited and no questionnaire could unlock human nature, such writers as Dickens offered in their novels an analysis of contemporary society whose liveliness and precision no professional specialist could equal:

Dickens was a great novelist, and, as such, an incomparable social historian. It is the great novelists above all who give us our social history; compared with what is done in *their* work – their creative work – the histories of the professional social historian seem empty and unenlightening.[53]

George Eliot was especially impressive in this respect: although pressured by positivists such as Frederic Harrison and sociologists such as Herbert Spencer, she stayed sufficiently clear-minded not to succumb to their suggestions. Sociological systems threatened an idolization of society to which the individual would in the end be certain to be sacrificed. Because in their analysis of society the individual received his due, George Eliot's novels were examples of an ideal sociology: in a book such as *Middlemarch* Beatrice Webb could have discovered all that she failed to discover in her arid sociological and statistical textbooks. On the other hand, Beatrice Webb was the George Eliot of the English social sciences and her autobiography, *My Apprenticeship*, a classic of English literature:

It is much richer in interest than Mill's *Autobiography*. The formative experience of Mrs Webb's early life was much richer. Her childhood was not an educational experiment, and she suffered nothing like the restrictive and starving intellectuality of Mill's upbringing. And as she describes her childhood, its milieu and its conditions, we recognize in the writer a potential novelist. In fact, it is not merely because she is a gifted and highly intelligent woman that, for all the differences of circumstances, she reminds us of George Eliot.[54]

When the second volume of Beatrice Webb's autobiography, *Our Partnership*, appeared posthumously, Leavis at once discussed it in *Scrutiny*. The book was not a classic of English literature, but the reviewer acknowledged that a good literary critic could have been made of Beatrice Webb.

He also approved of such social researchers as Mayhew, whose inquiries (*London Labour and the London Poor*, 1851 and 1862) confirmed the literary insight of a Dickens; and while he damned

---

[53] F. R. Leavis, 'Luddites? or There is Only One Culture' [1966], in *Nor Shall My Sword*, p. 81.

[54] F. R. Leavis, 'Mill, Beatrice Webb and the 'English School': Preface to an Unprinted Volume', *Scrutiny* 16 (1949), p. 114.

without mercy such writers as H. G. Wells who in their sociological novels sacrificed literature to sociology, he had praise for the anthropological eye of a T. S. Eliot, the sociological sensibility of a John Dos Passos and even for the light reading of a Thomas Love Peacock, whose ironical critique of nineteenth-century society also included a satire on the fashionable science of society.

In a lecture on 'Literature and Society', delivered before the students' union of the London School of Economics, Leavis treated ironically of an all-too-lively Romantic tradition which explained the work of the poet as a product of genius: 'Gifted individuals occur, inspiration sets in, creation results.'[55] Of greater importance was the search for the extra-literary conditions of literary production, the point of which was not the reconstruction of the economic and material context but the discovery of the spiritual tradition to which the writer concerned belonged. Neither Marx nor Wells could be of any use to literary criticism. Leavis was convinced that the social sciences had need of literary criticism, which would play the role of a universal propaedeutic in their utopian university, rather than the other way round: only the literarily cultivated in a climate of a living literary culture were really in a position to reflect on economic and social problems. Literature could be of use to sociology only if its literary qualities were taken seriously, not if it was misused as source-material.

For this reason Leavis – and the whole *Scrutiny* circle with him – was a sworn enemy of the sociology of literature, of which Levin Schücking's *Soziologie der literarischen Geschmacksbildung* (1931) counted as a warning example. If the sociologist wanted to profit from literature he had, for good or ill, to become a literary critic – which he could do all the more easily in that literary criticism rightly understood was concerned not only with literature but also with man and society, history and civilization: 'A review is necessary that combines criticism of literature with criticism of extra-literary activities. We take it as axiomatic that concern for standards of living implies concern for standards of the arts.'[56]

To Leavis English was a natural contact-discipline: a faculty whose inquiries were so far-reaching that an abundance of other disciplines could accumulate around it and thus create new inter-disciplinary crystallizations. When in 1963 he looked back on the period of more than twenty years during which *Scrutiny* had appeared, Leavis called

---

[55] F. R. Leavis, *The Common Pursuit* [1962] (Harmondsworth: Penguin, 1978), p. 183.
[56] The Editors [L. C. Knights and Donald Culver], 'Scrutiny – A Manifesto', *Scrutiny* 1 (1932), p. 2.

attention to the multiplicity of disciplines that had contributed to his magazine. They included sociology, economics, psychology and above all anthropology: of the contributors to *Scrutiny*, all of whom were former pupils of the English School at Cambridge, no fewer than five were anthropologists, and one of them wrote to Leavis from Africa to say how greatly *Scrutiny* and the literary criticism espoused in it had influenced him in his new profession.

The literary criticism espoused by Leavis also preserved its normative orientation in its contacts with other disciplines: collaboration was not sought with this or that faculty merely for the sake of collaboration; an attempt was made to identify those tendencies and orientations that broadly matched the position adopted by Leavis and in *Scrutiny*. The involvement of *Scrutiny* in scientific policy-making did not stop at the borders of literary criticism: thus, for example, a political economy that threatened to degenerate to mere monetary theory was countered with a true political economics that could serve the ends of social reform and social policy-making. Economics and ethics ought not of course to be confounded, but they should be made to relate to one another: this view led to a renewed commendation of the Webbs, whose 'monumental labours ... balanced studies of social and economic institutions in their every-day working'[57] could also be of the greatest assistance to members of other disciplines. In as much as the economics they practised was an analysis of institutions the Webbs were followers of Thorstein Veblen, whom *Scrutiny* treated as something of a sociological guide; and they were also exemplary in developing their theories not on an *a priori* basis but through cautious generalizations preceded by a detailed study of social actuality.

Sociology was already being referred to in the manifesto with which *Scrutiny* was launched: the anthropological procedure practised in *Middletown* was the method most likely to throw light on the state of contemporary civilization. Just as Veblen can be regarded as a sociological guide of the *Scrutiny* movement, so *Middletown* was a kind of model publication for it. Robert and Helen Lynd had published *Middletown* in 1929 as a study in contemporary American culture; it was a pioneer work that investigated the mutations of American society as reflected in an average town in the Middle West, the immediate model being Muncie, Indiana. The Lynds themselves described it as a work of cultural anthropology: they started from the

[57] Donald K. Kitchin, 'The Significance of Economics Thus Conceived', *Scrutiny* 2 (1933), p. 259.

presupposition that there existed in human societies basic modes of behaviour to be discovered everywhere, and that once these had been identified they would facilitate a clear description of a society's mutations. They offered this description in *Middletown*, which, together with its continuation, *Middletown in Transition* (1937), could also be read as a piece of descriptive literature in which census data played as large a role as quotations from the books of Sherwood Anderson.

The *Scrutiny* circle was impressed by the involvement and discipline with which the Lynds described in a concrete case the decay of a traditional social order and the rise of a new one; and this classic of descriptive social research concealed, moreover, a barely disguised repugnance for theoretical sociology. Sociological self-criticism stepped out into the open when, on the eve of the Second World War, Robert Lynd published *Knowledge for What?*, in which he compared the social scientist, who was coming more and more to resemble a technician, with a speaker delivering a lecture on navigation while standing in a ship already sinking. Lynd pointed approvingly to the sensibility of a D. H. Lawrence, who had described in his novels the consequences of the changes wrought by the industrialization of society. Works of literature made his own limitations clear to the sociologist:

Novelists, artists and poets provide valid insights into our culture that go beyond the cautious generalizations of social science and open up significant hypotheses for study.[58]

The *Scrutiny* circle regarded sociology as a synthesis of all the social sciences – a position comparable with that of literary criticism in the arts and one showing a curious parallelism to the conceptions of Durkheim. Like the *Année Sociologique*, moreover, *Scrutiny* resembled a research institute in which a distinct and morally legitimated research programme was taken and tested far beyond the borders of its own faculty. *Scrutiny* chose a certain sociology for its ally – and in doing so accepted as the criteria for its choice a particular perspective on the historical evolution of society.

The pastoral age and the world of the machine

Leavis's image of history exhibited Manichaean traits: England, the land that had produced Shakespeare, George Eliot and D. H.

---

[58] Robert S. Lynd, *Knowledge for What? The Place of Social Science in American Culture* (Princeton: Princeton University Press, 1939), p. 178.

Lawrence, had become for him the land of the welfare state, football and a literary culture determined by the Third Programme and the books section of the *New Statesman*. The Bentham-world as Dickens had depicted it in *Hard Times* seemed to have attained its completion in the world of the present: standardization and mass production were striding ahead, Americanization was accepted without resistance in all spheres of life, and the computer was beginning to write poetry. Next to *Middletown*, Q. D. Leavis' *Fiction and the Reading Public* was the guiding text in the description of the evolution of mass culture and the culture industry – although the author, overborne by nostalgia, had failed to take account of how greatly the reading of earlier ages (that of the eighteenth century, for instance) had also been determined by popular culture.

The way in which modern society was developing – which to Leavis, who sympathized with Spengler, bore all the stigmata of cultural decline – was accepted by scientists with indifference when not optimistically welcomed. Just as C. P. Snow had chastised the scientific ignorance and political perilousness of the men of letters, so Leavis attacked the immorality of the scientists and declared his solidarity with Blake's protest against the world of a Newton and a Locke. While denying to Marxism the ability to analyse the complex structure of modern industrial society, Leavis at the same time believed that only a form of economic communism would be capable of saving the world.

This view had less to do with an evaluation of Marxist theory than with a longing for a past era in which common property still played a role and man was still in harmony with his culture. The *Scrutiny* circle shared with Leavis an image of the world dominated by notions of decadence: technological civilization had destroyed the agricultural foundation of life and therewith also the basis for a civilization that could satisfy the needs of man. This image of life goes a long way to explain Leavis's hymns of praise for such a writer as D. H. Lawrence.

In the age of agriculture the English language had gained its strength from being at one with the life of the land: Shakespeare's theatre still addressed both the people and the cultivated. A subsistence economy and religion contributed towards making secure the peasant's condition within an agrarian society and guaranteed that men were content with life even if they were overworked and underpaid. This 'beautifully sufficient culture'[59] of a vanished pastoral age

---

[59] Denys Thompson, 'A Cure for Amnesia', *Scrutiny* 2 (1933), p. 5.

had been replaced by the world of the machine in which English once an expressive rural language, had declined into a mechanical idiom.

Not all of these assertions could endure historical investigation; Christopher Hill and Raymond Williams were among those who pointed out that Leavis' harmonious agrarian society was populated by beasts of burden unprotected by the law who were too much pre-occupied with securing mere survival to have time for rejoicing at the harmoniousness of their culture, which was in any case chiefly characterized by a high rate of infant mortality, chronic under-nourishment and illiteracy. But what Leavis and the *Scrutiny* circle were proclaiming was not the outcome of historical research but the enunciation of an image of the world designed first and foremost to strengthen the security of a group of academic outsiders: and such an image of the world also helps to explain the posture adopted by these literary critics towards sociology, the guiding discipline of Western industrial society.

Where their likes and dislikes lay was not hard to detect: they were hostile to every sociological theory, but they made use of the dis-coveries of empirical social research based on precise observation; they hated those sociologists who had made of themselves ac-complices of industrial society and admired those who had elevated themselves into its accusers. Like so many intellectual writers of the nineteenth and twentieth centuries they stood on the side of mechanical as opposed to organic solidarity, on the side of community and against society, so that, in respect of both its form of organization and its guiding ideas, the *Scrutiny* circle can be com-pared less to other groupings of literary intellectuals than to the various theoretical schools of sociologists. As a magazine Leavis' *Scrutiny* fulfilled similar functions to Durkheim's *Année Sociologique*, and the inexorable rigour of these literary critics' critical theories was equalled only by that with which members of the Frankfurt School attacked mass culture and the culture industry. A curious form of mimicry is apparent here: it is as though literary criticism, a nostalgic intellectual discipline gazing longingly back to the pre-industrial ages, wanted to imitate the key discipline of the industrial age: sociology.

The priesthood of the men of letters

During the nineteenth century the association between politics and morality, religion and science, science and literature grew increasingly attenuated. In all the countries of Europe a counter-movement thereupon set in: fuelled mostly by the intellectuals themselves, it demanded the formation of a new impartial intelligentsia capable of working against the current pernicious tendency to specialization and moral neutrality in public life. This movement was especially strong in England. Coleridge coined the concept of 'clerisy' and thereby inaugurated a debate that did not remain confined to England and which, *via* Julien Benda's *Trahison des clercs*, is still alive today. In this debate the literary and sociological intelligentsia play a significant role.

Coleridge distinguished from the other social classes of the country a class of those 'cultivating and enlarging the knowledge already possessed, and... watching over the interests of physical and moral science'[60] – educators who were to be distributed throughout the country so equally that no part of it would be without spiritual leaders or guardians. This class would constitute a kind of worldly church: not an *ecclesia* but an *enclesia* whose clergy would consist of churchmen and the cultivated of every scientific faculty. The influence of Kant is apparent when Coleridge stresses that mankind is threatened with a condition of overcivilization unaccompanied by a corresponding degree of cultivation: one of the tasks of the 'clerisy' would be to maintain an equilibrium between culture and civilization.

When Thomas Carlyle delivered his lectures on heroes and hero-worship he called gods and prophets, poets and priests the heroes of ages past – the idol of the modern world was the man of letters, who would remain a hero for as long as the art of writing and printing played a role in human affairs. The man of letters led an abnormal existence: he set down his inspirations in books and lived on what the public gave him for them. In the modern world the man of letters, an alienated hero, had become a leader and guide, and Carlyle found him embodied most impressively in Goethe:

'But there is no Religion?' reiterates the Professor. 'Fool! I tell thee, there is. Hast thou well considered all that lies in this immeasurable froth-ocean we name *Literature*? Fragments of a genuine Church-*Homiletic* lie scattered there, which Time will assort: nay fractions even of a *Liturgy* could I point out. And knowest thou no Prophet, even in the vesture, environment, and dialect of this age? . . . knowest thou none such? I know him, and name him – Goethe.'[61]

---

[60] Samuel Taylor Coleridge, *On the Constitution of the Church and State According to the Idea of Each* [1830] (*The Complete Works of Samuel Taylor Coleridge*, Vol. 6) ed. Prof. Shedd (New York: Harper and Brothers, 1860), pp. 50–1.

[61] Thomas Carlyle, 'Sartor Resartus' [1833], in Ben Knights, *The Idea of the Clerisy in the Nineteenth Century* (Cambridge: Cambridge University Press, 1978), p. 14.

Fichte's 'Gelehrter' became for Carlyle the 'literary man,' and Johnson, Rousseau and Burns were the 'men of letters' with whom he concerned himself – writers of the second rank, compared with Goethe, but because of the circumstances of their lives more familiar to an English public. The literary man, with his 'copy-rights and copy-wrongs',[62] was at once a profane and a sacred figure: someone who defrayed his living expenses with books and at the same time evolved in them a guide to living which mankind could follow.

To Carlyle his era seemed to be getting more and more out of joint: an indication of this was what the writers of books did in the world and what the world did to them. The writer was guided in his activities by the rules of no profession; no one asked whence he came or whither he was going. Like a pariah he wandered through a world which he could equally well mislead as enlighten; he was nothing but 'an accident in society.'[63] And yet books performed miracles in the way runes had done in earlier times. In the wretchedest lending-libraries of remote villages books determined the everyday behaviour of their readers, and the maddest views of life became practical realities. The art of writing united in the strangest way the distant past with the immediate present: 'All things were altered for men; all modes of important work of men: teaching, preaching, governing, and all else.'[64] The universities, in which knowledge had for long been handed on through spoken communication, had become collections of books, and in the church the true preachers and prophets were now those who could write books. Following Fichte, Carlyle saw literature as a kind of revelation: as Byron and Goethe, Shakespeare and Milton's cathedral music had shown, literature brought to light the god-like in the terrestrial and common.

The art of writing and printing could not be separated from the progress of democracy, and since the power of the writer was becoming an ever more public fact it could be expected that men of letters would soon organize themselves into a guild. The objective of such an organization could not be to secure the financial independence of writers through stipends or salaries – Carlyle considered it necessary, rather, that there should be men of letters who were poor, members of a spiritual order of beggars whose material poverty would enhance their spiritual influence.

It was through Darwinian eyes that Carlyle looked upon the literary world, in which – as in the rest of society – only the strong

[62] Thomas Carlyle, *On Heroes, Hero-Worship, and the Heroic in History*, ed. Archibald Mac-Mechan (Boston: Ginn and Co., 1901), p. 177. [63] *Ibid.*, p. 183. [64] *Ibid.*, p. 185.

could survive the struggle for the higher positions. He saw in this struggle the precondition of all progress, and to him too there occurred the question that became the central problem of the nineteenth century and its social sciences: ought this struggle to be regulated or should its outcome be left to chance?

Writers were burdened with what they had inherited from the eighteenth century, that era in which Pandora had shaken every evil out of her box. It was a sceptical age that wanted to know nothing of heroes and pictured the world as a machine, an age in which personal interests and motives, weavers' looms and parliamentary majorities set the tone. The era of Bentham and the utilitarianism of the steam-engine was an age in which heroism was blind and men acted like cogs and wheels in a contraption of steel. From this mechanical world the divine seemed to have vanished.

It was in the fact that men of letters were not organized that Carlyle saw the fundamental evil of an age suffering from both intellectual and moral scepticism which had brought forth such social pestilences as the French Revolution and Chartism; at the same time he had no doubt that men of letters would henceforth combine together to form a species of priesthood and bring to the world a new faith. The eighteenth century, the age of unbelief, had been an exception: 'I prophesy that the world will once more become *sincere*; a believing world: with *many* Heroes in it, a heroic world!'[65]

It was customary to reproach Carlyle with a lack of calmness in his thinking, which was always full of passion, and with allowing his intellect to be clouded by emotion, yet he foretold with precision the decisive role which the priesthood of the men of letters was to play in the modern world. Following Carlyle, Matthew Arnold described the social uprooting of the intellectuals as at once the precondition for and opportunity of the attainment of higher knowledge: intellectuals were aliens whose views were determined not by a particular class standpoint but by an unpartisan spirit and a desire for the perfecting of mankind; and with that, Julien Benda's *clercs* already come into the picture, as did Karl Mannheim's socially impartial intelligentsia.

Literary criticism and social planning

Among those who succumbed to the influence of Matthew Arnold was T. S. Eliot, an American from St Louis who, raised to respect

[65] *Ibid.*, p. 202.

religion, community and education, had– as he himself made a point
of stating– become in England a classicist in art, an Anglo-Catholic
in religion and a royalist in politics:

> Upon the glazen shelves kept watch
> Matthew and Waldo, guardians of the faith,
> The army of unalterable law.[66]

As to the poet's true position Eliot was at one with Arnold and
Shelley: he was the unacknowledged legislator of the world. But
Eliot was at variance with Arnold's attempt to see in poetry a kind of
'coffee without caffein',[67] a substitute for religion that could only
lead to a further diminution in the significance of religion. And he
commented ironically on Arnold's attempt to function as a critic of
society: like many others interested not only in literature but also in
ideas in general, Arnold had occasionally been assailed by the
temptation to set books aside so as first to put the whole
country in order.

In saying this, however, Eliot was not championing the principle
of *l'art pour l'art*: as he wrote in 1928 in the new edition of *The Sacred
Wood*, poetry always had something to do with politics, religion and
ethics, only he was unable to say precisely what. Sceptical towards
every species of interpretation, Eliot resisted accepting sociologists
as interpreters of poetry; in this he showed a similarity to F. R.
Leavis, who mounted so vehement an opposition to the sociology of
literature. On the contrary he warned the poet who reflected on the
use of his activities against 'involving himself in the tasks of the
sociologist'.[68] Poetry as such possessed a religious significance and
exerted its influence on society– for that very reason it must not be
misunderstood as religion and literary criticism must not be misunderstood as sociology.

When Eliot visited Paris for the first time in 1910 he stayed at 9,
rue de l'Université, close to the Sorbonne; it was also not far from
the Collège de France, where in January and February 1911 he attended
lectures by Bergson, whose evaluation of intuition was allied to his
own poetical tendency. Eliot's own declarations permit the reader to
perceive the influence of Bergson in 'The Love Song of J. Alfred
Prufrock'; but Eliot was also aware of sociology, and among those

[66] T. S. Eliot, 'Cousin Nancy', in *Collected Poems 1909–1935* (New York: Harcourt
Brace Jovanovich, 1948), p. 34.
[67] T. S. Eliot, *The Use of Poetry and the Use of Criticism. Studies in the Relation of Criticism to
Poetry in England. The Charles Eliot Norton Lectures for 1932–33* (Cambridge, Mass.:
Harvard University Press, 1933), p. 17.   [68] *Ibid.*, p. 147.

who appear to have exerted a particular influence on him in Paris was Emile Durkheim. The strongest influence of all, to be sure, was that of Charles Maurras, and Peter Ackroyd has pointed out that the current characterization of Maurras by means of the triad '*classique, catholique, monarchique*'[69] may have influenced Eliot's subsequent self-description.

There already existed in Eliot's early poetry a species of sociology of knowledge concealed behind all the irony and self-irony: an enduring tendency to render to himself an account of his own actions and position in the world. Leavis, who was among the first to recognize Eliot's poetic rank, also saw how great a role epistemological and metaphysical questions played in his poems: Eliot the critic seemed always to be commenting on Eliot the poet.

After 1928 – the period coinciding almost exactly with his conversion to Anglo-Catholicism – Eliot also became a social critic and social theoretician, though he was, to be sure, interested more in discussion of basic principles than in the solution of real social problems. The immediate occasion was the founding of the Chandos group, which took its name from the restaurant in London where its members were accustomed to meet. Founded after the General Strike of 1926, the group had defined its objective as the discovery of 'certain absolute and eternal principles of true sociology':[70] therewith was sounded the theme of a Christian sociology that now moved to the centre of Eliot's interest. In 1933 and 1940 he delivered lectures at the Anglo-Catholic Summer School of Sociology, and between 1938 and 1947 he was involved with The Moot, a group of clergymen, writers, scientists and politicians who met once a year to discuss questions of social planning and the creation of an elite in post-war England. The minutes and correspondence of the group show Eliot to have participated to the full in its deliberations.

He had always been sceptical as to the possibility of the individual intellectual's producing any real effect on society:

> No! I am not Prince Hamlet, nor was meant to be;
> Am an attendant lord, one that will do
> To swell a progress, start a scene or two,
> Advise the prince; no doubt, an easy tool,
> Deferential, glad to be of use,
> Politic, cautious, and meticulous;
> Full of high sentence, but a bit obtuse;
> At times, indeed, almost ridiculous –
> Almost, at times, the Fool.

[69] Peter Ackroyd, *T. S. Eliot* (London: Hamish Hamilton, 1984), p. 41.
[70] *Ibid.*, p. 222.

Now however, in time of war, the inclinations of the individual had to step into the background and intellectuals had to form themselves into a group. The differences which divided Eliot from the *Scrutiny* group as regards social criticism soon became evident. Leavis and his adherents continued to be petty bourgeois outsiders who reacted to the evolution of capitalism and state socialism by conjuring up a harmonious English agrarian society which had come to a definitive end in the last years of the seventeenth century: this social idyll, supported by no historical facts and serving essentially as a group-sustaining ideology, made of literary criticism a nostalgic discipline. The conservative social critic Eliot, on the other hand, whom Leavis repudiated as a vassal of the London Establishment, was decidedly more modern than the *Scrutiny* group: like other conservatives, Eliot had recognized that only a change in the traditional techniques for maintaining supremacy could ensure the continuing dominion of the political and cultural orthodoxy in England; and after the mechanism of naturally expanding markets had ceased to function the idea of social planning was accepted by these conservatives by compulsion, 'not for idealistic reasons'.[71]

At the end of the nineteenth century Matthew Arnold had perceived in the sociology coming into being on the continent of Europe the discipline which would stand in competition with a literary criticism that wanted to count as the guiding discipline for industrial society. But Arnold's fears were groundless: those constellations of social-historical study which were elsewhere creating the university faculty of sociology were very far from doing so in England, where sociological thinking had long since discovered a home in philanthropy and social work, in a row of already existing academic disciplines, in statistics and in political administration. While in such countries as France and Germany sociology had developed distinct yet varying profiles as a science both opposing and supporting the Establishment, and had then within each country gone on to splinter into separate schools, in England sociology was simply a constituent of social common sense: it had no need to secure its existence by becoming an independent academic faculty.

Marxism, with which sociology occasionally seemed to be a competing or contrasting discipline, had likewise failed to achieve a distinct profile in England: here even large segments of the working

[71] Harold Macmillan, 'Reconstruction' (1933), in Arthur Marwick, 'Middle Opinion in the Thirties: Planning, Progress and Political "Agreement"', *The English Historical Review* 74 (1964), p. 287.

class chose the Tories, the bourgeoisie was conservative, the socialists were reformers, and the beginning of the nineteenth century saw the gradual formation in the ranks of the upper middle class of that stable intellectual aristocracy typical of England which presented the paradox of an intelligentsia 'which appears to conform rather than rebel against the rest of society'.[72] This intellectual aristocracy had literature 'in its bones',[73] and its guiding discipline was literary criticism. Only a superficial observer could believe that there was no sociology in England: apart from the London School of Economics there was for decades no faculty of sociology, but lively sociological thinking lay concealed not least in literary criticism.

The stormy 1930s disturbed the imperturbable repose of English culture. Increasing international tension, and at home the breaking-up of the political and economic consensus, indicated that the capitalist system was about to collapse– a conclusion the Webbs also drew when, without ever having been Marxists, they threw themselves into the arms of Soviet communism. Unemployment, wage-cuts and strikes now made the class nature of English society stand out more sharply.

It was here that there lay the seeds of that development which was in the end to create a sociology in England as well, though, to be sure, its institutionalization had largely to wait until well after the Second World War. Compared with the construction of schools of sociology in America, France and Germany, however, English sociology always remained curiously pallid and lacking in distinct identity: the disciplines that came into being in England during the post-war years, and were its essential contribution to intellectual contention both at home and abroad, were so-called 'cultural studies', as represented by such names as Richard Hoggart and Raymond Williams. A brief characterization of what constitutes 'cultural studies' would amount to an abstract of English intellectual history since Matthew Arnold: they are a blend of sociology and literary criticism.

[72] N. G. Annan, 'The Intellectual Aristocracy', in *Studies in Social History: A Tribute to G. M. Trevelyan*, ed. J. H. Plumb (London: Longmans, Green and Co., 1955), p. 285.
[73] *Ibid.*, p. 251.

PART III

GERMANY

◁ ══ ▷

7

Prologue: artisan and poet too: W. H. Riehl

In the summer of 1856, while she was forging plans for her first novel, George Eliot reviewed two books by a German writer in the *Westminster Review*. She was fascinated by their literary quality, but informed her readers that the volumes were of significance first and foremost on account of their factual content and the philosophy of life that might be derived from it. The books concerned were *Die bürgerliche Gesellschaft* (1851) and *Land und Leute* (1853), the first two parts of *Naturgeschichte des Volkes* by Wilhelm Heinrich Riehl.

George Eliot employed her review to launch a vigorous attack on the English social novel. Although their authors claimed to be giving a realistic description of the people their accounts of the lower classes seemed to be remote from reality: the workers on the land, especially, resembled characters in an opera rather than hard-labouring people of flesh, sweat and blood. Unhappily, social science offered no possibility of correcting this false picture: carried away by the glittering success of the inductive method its adherents believed they could solve every social question with the aid of modern economics and all inter-personal problems with algebraic equations. Social reality suffered as much distortion from a romanticizing literature as it did from a science restricted to heartless calculations; literature, none the less, deserved more reproach, for when it was practised properly art came closer to life than did science: art was the best means of widening our experience and, taking us beyond our own personal relationships, of deepening our knowledge of our fellow men. The problem lay in the fact that sentimental literary men on the one hand and heartless theoreticians on the other gave a distorted picture of the life of the people, while those who knew of it from their own experience – parsons, farmers and mill-owners – handed on their valuable observations at best by word of mouth but did not write them down. This was why W. H. Riehl could serve as a model in England too: instead of being a romanticist he was a perceptive and scrupulously exact observer, constantly on guard against crude generalizations and those precipitate theories whose internal consistency is purchased with an obvious remoteness from reality. At the same time Riehl offered an example of how important form of presentation was for a properly understood social science. He knew what problems the substitution of scientific jargon for everyday or popular speech brought with it – the former might sound more exact, but it had paid for this exactitude by losing all trace of musicality and passion.

George Eliot, of whom it was said that she had brought the dead systems of Comte, Spencer and John Stuart Mill to life in her novels, saw in W. H. Riehl an artistic and scientific model. Quite in the manner of a Wordsworth, his works fulfilled the highest function of art by extending the reader's sympathies to encompass the life of simple people; on the other hand, his observations led to the enlightened conclusion that a modern social policy could be founded not on the doctrines of an abstract social science but only on an exact knowledge of social institutions. Richly illustrative and keenly observant, Riehl's books offered the best example there was of a descriptive social research with normative consequences.

Riehl made folklore into a German science, and what was German in him united him with Hans Sachs: he was artisan and poet too. In his *Wanderbuch* he revealed the working-secrets of how to study the people which meant above all things moving from place to place. As the founder of a discipline, however, he was in no way naive: he had at first had to struggle as a publicist and man of letters, and he was well aware that within what he called the state system of science a faculty such as that of folklore would have to fight for recognition. Yet the way in which the sciences were realigning themselves seemed to him propitious: history and the natural sciences were gradually emerging as the central powers of a new scientific constellation at the expense of philosophy, and all history was turning irresistibly into cultural history. Albrecht von Haller, Goethe and Alexander von Humboldt had promoted this development by bestowing on natural science the capacity to be literature – within the all-embracing cultural history of the future the itinerant poetry of folklore would constitute a kind of historical anthropology.

Even if, regarded as an autonomous science, folklore was not yet a hundred years old, its prehistory none the less reached back to the beginnings of literature. Herder could be counted among its founders, and he offered a clear example of the kind of prejudice with which the new science was confronted: 'The learned guild scented quite rightly in the latter the uncomfortable morning air of the new day just then dawning, and when Herder was called to a professorship at Göttingen declared he was not really a scholar but a mere belletrist.'[1]

It was, to be sure, propitious that, as Riehl was gratified to note, Germany was gradually growing weary of theoretical constructions– not least because the Weimar classics had shown that poets could also be scholarly, to the advantage of both science and literature. Certainly the conflict between science and literature, in which Riehl saw the 'token of entire periods of cultural history',[2] had not yet been finally decided; and it was also true that scientists were striving increasingly to become specialists and in the process more and more neglecting the art of presentation; yet at the same time the view was gaining ground that the truly great scientific epochs had been characterized by a cessation of hostilities in the battle between the scholar and the writer. A book, it was said, could be called successful only if it belonged not merely to science but also to literature, if the structure of its ideas and its style were welded together into a 'twofold art'.[3]

This at least was what Riehl had made into a maxim of his own writings when he exclaimed, in the roguish tone usually ventured on only by the happy outsider of the academic world:

As it is only through living a merry wandering life that I have wandered into bookwriting, so my books too must always be merry reading; they must have erudition but it must not wear a self-satisfied air, and even if the author has toiled slowly, testing and hesitating as he worked, he doesn't want the reader to notice any of this labour but think the book came to be of itself, written down quickly and boldly as chance dictated and as though on a country walk and always full of good humour and without the author having put on the cloak of learning first.[4]

Riehl's optimism was deceptive as to the future prospects of the folklore he was propagating: fundamentally the discipline was already antiquated at the moment of its birth. It bore too many of the traits of old-fashioned science to become a true key-discipline in the nineteenth century: far from distancing itself from its literary

[1] W. H. Riehl, *Die Volkskunde als Wissenschaft* [1858]. *Der Vortrag von Wilhelm Heinrich Riehl*, mit einer Einleitung von Max Hildebert Boehm (Tübingen: Laupp'sche Buchhandlung, 1935), p. 42.
[2] W. H. Riehl, 'Der Kampf des Schriftstellers und des Gelehrten' [1869], in *Freie Vorträge*, Zweite Sammlung (Stuttgart: Cotta 1885), p. 5.   [3] *Ibid.*, p. 4.
[4] W. H. Riehl, *Die Naturgeschichte des Volkes als Grundlage einer deutschen Social-Politik*, Vol. 1: *Land und Leute*, Vol. 2: vermehrte Auflage (Stuttgart and Augsburg: Cotta, 1855), p. xii.

preforms, it emphasized its poetical qualities; not only did it acknowledge the scholar as an author, it described the scientific writer as its ideal; it completely failed to separate fact from value-judgment, but adopted, consciously and with a good conscience, a normative orientation – for, as Riehl laid down, all genuine folklore was a moral sermon.

When the Nazis bewailed the degeneration of German sociology – Jewish and Marxist influence was held to be the cause – sociologists such as Max Rumpf, Gunther Ipsen and Hans Freyer, who allied themselves with W. H. Riehl and attempted to unite folklore with sociological theory, became objects of commendation: as a counter to the degenerate internationalism of the sociologists of the West a 'folkish' regionalism of the Riehlish stamp attained the status of a model.

Agreement with Riehl was far from complete, however. It was true that, even before the foundation of the Reich, he had travelled to Alsace and the borders of Germany and Hungary, yet it could not be overlooked that 'national frontiers and the struggles to which they give rise were not at the centre of his interests'.[5] It was also true that he rejected the neo-Kantian separation of nomothetic and idiographic orientations which Max Weber had unfortunately introduced into sociology, yet he persisted in a 'relativism of minutely descriptive cultural and musical history'[6] that did little to promote the expansionist goals of Greater Germany. What these reservations all went to show was that Riehl's was an aesthetic nature, not a political one.

However little one may agree with the motives that prompted such a verdict, it is certainly correct to say that there is no direct path leading from Riehl to the German sociology which at the end of the nineteenth and during the first third of the twentieth centuries possessed an international reputation. From Riehl's point of view this was not a truly great era of science, for it did not yet see an end to the struggle between the scholar and the writer: on the contrary it too was, with characteristic national deviations, marked by that contention between literature and a rising sociology which had produced such significant consequences for the politics of science in England and France.

[5] Max Hildebert Boehm, Einleitung, 'Die Volkskunde als Wissenschaft', p. 18.
[6] *Ibid.*, p. 19.

8

◁ ══════════════════════════════ ▷

Hostility to science and faith in poetry as a German ideology

When the Germans have reflected about themselves, one of the enduring themes of this reflection has been Germany's political and social backwardness compared with its Western neighbours; and if there exists anything that could be called a German ideology it consists less in attempting to trace the causes of this backwardness and pondering ways of ameliorating it than in playing off, with a mixture of pride and sorrow, Romanticism against the Enlightenment, the Middle Ages against the modern world, culture against civilization, the subjective against the objective, community against society and the heart against the head, so as in the end to attain to the glorification of German particularity and of the nature of the German. Whether one bewails the continual sundering of tradition in the spiritual life of the mysterious German nation, as Hugo von Hofmannsthal did, or whether one speaks of Germany as the land whose destiny was always hard, as Ernst Troeltsch did, such words are attended by a kind of proud melancholy and a confession to playing the role of the outsider – a role in which one is only too self-approving.

That subjective, inward Reich established by the philosophy of German idealism and the classic literature of Weimar did not only precede the founding of the political Reich by more than a hundred years, it was for a long time eagerly misunderstood as being itself a political act – that of renouncing politics altogether – and as legitimating a withdrawal from society into the sphere of private life.

Although reaction against the Enlightenment and its exaggerated expressions in literature, science and politics was universal throughout Europe, it was nowhere more resolute or sullen than it was in Germany. The German movement was 'not scientific in origin, it was directed towards the enhancement of life, subjective inwardness

and a new productivity, and poetry was its primary organ'.[1]
Humanity found its supreme expression in the poet, and the harmonious and perfect union of all the poet's possibilities in Goethe
made of him the chief witness of a philosophy of life which – to
follow Herman Nohl – in art preferred the genius to the rule, in
religion the prophet to the dogma, in morality the hero to the convention and in the sphere of law and the state the creativity of the
people to all systems and theories.

Even when priorities of this sort were reduced to brief encapsu-
lations, and it was well realized that the Germans were supposed to
be a peculiar people, they none the less produced a growing effect
beyond the borders of Germany and gave rise as much to envy as to
opposition. In De l'Allemagne (1810) Madame de Staël described the
writers of Germany as the most scholarly and thoughtful minds in
Europe; and to the French, whom he found too léger, and the
English, whom he found too calculating, Ernest Renan preferred the
bonhomie of the Germans: their ability not to lose touch with feeling
even when treating the most abstract problems, their capacity for
turning everything into poetry. In the praise bestowed by an admirer
such as Madame de Staël, to be sure, the disadvantages of an ability
so decidedly poetic become involuntarily audible: 'In France one
reads a book only so as to talk about it; in Germany, where most
people live alone, one wants the book itself to keep one company.'[2]

Only on a first, superficial glance is there any contradiction between Ernst Troeltsch's assertion that the essential medium of
expression of the German spirit is literature – and especially so since
the Germanic world was repressed back into a literary existence in
the eighteenth century – and Helmuth Plessner's complaint that
since the seventeenth century language has been literally useless to
the Germans, that all relationship between words, writing, literature
and the life of society has been lost to them. This contradiction is
resolved when we recall that the German movement was a movement of poets and thinkers but not of hommes de lettres and scientists.
In Germany, writing and reading are traditionally solitary acts, and a
literature consciously concerned with affecting society and firmly
anchored in it has always been counted superficial and un-German.
As regards both its production and its reception, something of the
anti-social adheres to the sphere of the poetical in Germany; and it is
significant that in the development of the realistic novel – the genre

---

[1] Herman Nohl, 'Die Deutsche Bewegung und die idealistischen Systeme', in Logos, 2
(1911/12), p. 350.
[2] Mme de Staël, De l'Allemagne [1810] (Paris: Flammarion, 1926), p. 127.

in which bourgeois society finds comprehensive artistic expression–German writers have contributed less than their European colleagues. It is thus only against the background of the political and social evolution of the belated German nation that the antithesis of poetry and literature, drawn with a sharpness unknown to England and France, becomes comprehensible, as it is also responsible for the specifically German tone acquired by contention over the social sciences – the more so in that the period during which sociology came into existence in Germany and the first serious attempts were made to consolidate and professionalize it coincided with that in which insistence on the special nature and situation of Germany was a central tenet of political ideology and propaganda.

Consciousness as fatality

When, after the end of the First World War, Friedrich Meinecke looked back on the three generations of scholarly policy-making that he associated with the names of Friedrich Theodor Vischer, Gustav Schmoller and Max Weber, he expressed the hope that this scholarly policy-making, 'which once overflowed with the values of "heart" [Gemüt] and with ideologies conceived in that spirit',[3] would now come down to earth and contribute to the rationalizing of German politics. This hope was delusory, just as no one had taken seriously Goethe's admonition, 'The Germans ought to refrain from saying that word "heart" for a period of thirty years; then "heart" will gradually reappear: at present it means no more than the indulgence of weaknesses, one's own and those of others.'[4]

Meinecke had underestimated the political danger represented by cultural pessimism and an ideology of 'heart': it was to attain to its full efflorescence in National Socialism. The ideological attack on political rationality, democratization and the effects of industrial society were paralleled in other European countries, above all in France and Italy; but the prophesies and condemnations uttered by the 'heroic vitalists'[5] were nowhere received with such enthusiasm as the works of Lagarde, Langbehn and Moeller van den Bruck were in Germany. That a man such as Lagarde could influence both Ferdi-

---

[3] Friedrich Meinecke, 'Drei Generationen deutscher Gelehrtenpolitik', *Historische Zeitschrift* 125 (1921), p. 283.

[4] Goethe, *Maximen und Reflexionen. Aus Kunst und Altertum. Fünften Bandes drittes Heft.* 1826, in *Sämtliche Werke*, (Zürich: Artemis/München: Deutscher Taschenbuch Verlag, 1977), Vol. 9, p. 535.

[5] Fritz Stern, *Kulturpessimismus als politische Gefahr: Eine Analyse nationaler Ideologie in Deutschland* (Bern/Stuttgart/Wien: Scherz, 1963), pp. i, 55.

nand Tönnies and the Thomas Mann of the *Betrachtungen*, both the George circle and Friedrich Naumann, with his idea of a socially aware, socially responsible Christianity, shows how widespread an effect this irrational, heroic vitalism had. Julius Langbehn, the 'Rembrandt German', had proclaimed that only a science of life could truly be called science, and this science stood in close proximity to art. With this the decisive catchword was uttered: in Germany science had to let itself be judged according to the canons of life, and the broad stream of hostility towards science which in the nineteenth century flowed through a country that had placed itself at the head of the scientific nations of Europe was – not least through the influence of Nietzsche – nourished by the suspicion that science had alienated itself from life and become hostile to it. 'And science itself, our science – yes, what, regarded as a symptom of life, is the meaning of science at all? To what end, worse *from what cause* – all science?'[6]

This climate of suspicion and criticism of science is propitious to a philosophy of the primacy of life, and it is very significant that, in the letter to Dilthey in which he says that philosophy 'is not science but life, and fundamentally has been life even where it wanted to be science',[7] Count Yorck distances himself from precisely Du Bois-Reymond in particular. For Du Bois-Reymond's celebrated *Ignorabimus* – an attempt to determine the limits of our knowledge of nature – in reality exalts immodesty to the status of a programme: it is an expression not of scientific scepticism but of scientific hubris. Du Bois-Reymond did not only believe he could indicate the precise limits of what is knowable – he attacked with all the more assurance the question of the possibilities of knowledge in general. His critique of Goethe was correspondingly severe, and he said he preferred Voltaire; to Doctor Faust, who confessed his inability to deprive nature of her veil with lever and screw, the physiologist and newly elected rector of Berlin University replied:

However prosaic it may sound it is none the less true that, instead of going off to court, issuing unsecured paper money, and ascending to the fourth dimension to encounter the Mothers, Faust would have done better to have married Gretchen, given his child a name, and invented electrical machines

---

[6] Friedrich Nietzsche, *Die Geburt der Tragödie. Versuch einer Selbstkritik* [1886], in *Sämtliche Werke. Kritische Studienausgabe in 15 Bänden*, ed. Giorgio Colli and Mazzino Montinari (München: Deutscher Taschenbuch Verlag, 1980), Vol. 1, p. 12.

[7] Graf Yorck to Dilthey, 6 October 1885; *Briefwechsel zwischen Dilthey und dem Grafen Paul Yorck v. Wartenburg 1877–1897* (Halle: Niemeyer, 1923), pp. 255–6.

and air-pumps; for which we would, in place of the burgermeister of Magdeburg, have been sufficiently grateful to him.[8]

Profoundly impressed by a scientist such as Helmholtz yet disappointed at Helmholtz's inability to accord the world of the spirit its rights, Dilthey adhered to his youthful impulse to understand life through life itself. In spite of Bergson, who in France remained a solitary figure, the maxim that thought cannot retreat behind life became a peculiarly German maxim, an actual 'protest of the empirical against empiricism'.[9]

That this programme was found inadequate is shown in the example of Walther Rathenau, who in 1913 complained in his confessional book *Zur Mechanik des Geistes oder vom Reich der Seele* that the philosophy of the age had deprived itself of life. The reason for this he found not least in the rise of the natural sciences, whose success had compelled all other disciplines to adopt mensuration and exactitude as well; the greater capacity for exercising criticism which they had acquired had been purchased at the cost of naivety, warmth and power of convincing, and they had thus become alienated from life. The age's fundamental error was to expect from science maxims relating to one's own will and desires and the formulation of ideals – to demand from the head what only the heart could give. To the calculating and plan-making mind Rathenau opposed the experiencing soul: the world should be to man not only a law-book but also a picture-book. For intellectual philosophy 'has behaved as though an oscillation theorist sought to explain with curves and diagrams the experience of a symphony, as though a meteorologist sought to encompass the feeling of a spring morning with weather-charts, as though a hydraulic engineer sought to calculate the sensations of the waves of the sea'.[10]

Science must not be expected to offer 'rules for living',[11] let alone a perfect reproduction of human feeling, of which only the lyrics of a Goethe or a Hölderlin, Eichendorff or Mörike were capable. In this the Germans enjoyed an inestimable advantage: nothing produced in France even in the time of the ancient Franks could compare with

[8] Emil Du Bois-Reymond, 'Goethe und kein Ende. In der Aula der Berliner Universität am 15 October 1882 gehaltene Rectoratsrede', in *Reden. Erste Folge: Litteratur, Philosophie, Zeitgeschichte* (Leipzig: Veit and Co., 1886), p. 430.
[9] Graf Yorck to Dilthey, 23 November 1877; *Briefwechsel*, p. 2.
[10] Walther Rathenau, 'Von kommenden Dingen' [1917], in *Gesammelte Schriften, 3* (Berlin: S. Fischer, 1929), p. 224.
[11] Walther Rathenau, 'Zur Mechanik des Geistes oder vom Reich der Seele' [1913], in *Gesammelte Schriften II* (Berlin: S. Fischer, 1929), p. 34.

German poetry, just as mechanization, hostile to life and alien to lyricism as it was, represented a profoundly un-German process which had in the end resulted in the deGermanization of Germany. Thus wrote the Jew, industrialist and politician Rathenau, and he came to the conclusion that the highest deed the intellect could perform was its own annihilation.

'Consciousness as fatality' was a catchphrase of the time, and Alfred Seidel, who gave his posthumously published book this title, embodied the self-destructive fanaticism with which such a conception of life could be lived and died for. Born in 1895 'a somewhat pitiable little youngest child',[12] Seidel early joined the *Wandervogel* and from 1915 pledged himself to the Free German Youth Movement; rejection of the sterile life of the university that attended it led, not to an enthusiasm for war, but to the evolution of an attitude hostile to all politics which made of the war-politics of the Reich no exception. Amid the confusion of the end of the war and the immediate post-war period he grew increasingly sympathetic towards the ideas of communism and towards a Communist Party 'clear and disinterested in its intentions, unconditionally helpful, unreservedly dedicated to its ideas, personally of an undemandingness almost Russian',[13] as Hans Prinzhorn described it.

At Heidelberg Seidel was initially closely associated with the George circle, but the contacts he made with the Heidelberg sociologists, and later those of Frankfurt, were to prove of greater significance: they included Alfred Weber, with whom he studied 'means of production and class struggle' in 1922, and more especially Karl Mannheim, whose sociological radicalism attracted him. In the course of a sociological evening which Weber had organized Seidel expounded in outline what was later to become *Bewusstsein als Verhängnis*:

> Convinced though he was of the rightness of his arguments he was none the less in no doubt as to how hard it would be to stand up to experienced professionals firmly established within a sociological system. He knew he would have not only to undermine the foundations of professional sociology but above all also to call radically into question the value of those profound perceptions introduced into this circle by Max Weber, who, dominant during his lifetime, had been almost deified since his death.[14]

None the less he did acquire the confidence of certain professional sociologists: Karl Mannheim went through a trial lecture with Seidel

---

[12] Hans Prinzhorn, 'Vorangestelltes Nachwort des Herausgebers', in Alfred Seidel, *Bewusstsein als Verhängnis*. Aus dem Nachlasse herausgegeben von Hans Prinzhorn (Bonn: Cohen, 1927), p. 12.　　[13] *Ibid.*, pp. 15–16.　　[14] *Ibid.*, pp. 19–20.

before the latter descended into the arena of the sociological even-ings, and Gottfried Salomon allowed him to deliver propaedeutic courses at the Frankfurt Sociological Institute.

Seidel seemed to gain a footing in the academic world only slowly. His book was accepted for publication, and he was to start work as a secretary to an acquaintance of Hans Prinzhorn's, but these events were no solution to the inner problems with which he wrestled: in November 1924 he took his own life. In his will he asked that *Bewusstsein als Verhängnis* should be printed: it appeared, edited by Prinzhorn, three years later.

Seidel counted himself as an analytical scientist, as one of the 'sadists of truth',[15] and he was bound to collide with the Georgeans, with whom he had initially sought contact; in the end they became his spiritual enemies. His concern was to prepare the path for a new religion and its prophets – yet at bottom he did not know what religion this would be. He had no wish to counter the faith in science and the glorification of consciousness which he found not least in the writings of the sociologists with the cheap solutions offered by George and his circle or the apodictic self-satisfaction of an Oswald Spengler: his problem was how – without lapsing into ecstaticism or the esoteric – the glorification of the intellect could be corrected rationally and faith in science corrected by scientific means. In his farewell letter to Hans Prinzhorn, dated 20 October 1924 from Erlangen, he again made clear how great a role was played in this struggle by sociology and especially by Max Weber, whose principle of value-freedom he had undeviatingly opposed:

I have not thought: the world-spirit, destiny, has thought in me. I know what devilish task I had to undertake. But all this has to be said in this age, it is the beginning of the great despair of Western culture which set in with Schopenhauer and Max Weber. The path can go only through this despair.[16]

Seidel had early on predicted that in Germany politics were going to turn savage and would demand clear-cut decisions: he would then stand on the side of the ruthless communists and pay heed to the devout fanatics, even if he would not be one himself. The alterna-tives were going to be Bolshevist terror or reactionary terror: he would stand on the side of Bolshevism. A little later he expressed the view that the most pressing problems of the future would probably be solved only by a species of national socialism. These were the alternatives from which Seidel fled.

[15] Seidel in a letter from Heidelberg of 11 March 1920; *ibid.*, p. 30.   [16] *Ibid.*, p 45.

Knowing only for living

Jules Michelet, at once the historian and the poet of the French Revolution, described how in the streets and squares of Paris one word, 'Nature', was in every mouth; and he associated the end of the Terror, which he denounced as anti-natural, with a decisive change in the political vocabulary: after 1795 'life' replaced 'nature'. In Germany there was embodied in this appeal to 'life' a critique of rationalism directed against the central ideas of the French Enlightenment of which the events of 1789 were seen as a logical consequence: here it was not nature but the frigid forces of reason to which the immediacy of life was set up in opposition. The 'ideas of 1914', first formulated by Johannes Plenge and later widely influential, that were led into the field against the slogans of the French Revolution derive not least from the conviction that there are limits to the burdening of the intellect: 'somewhere we must come to a halt so as to make ourselves deeper if our soul is not to be broken to pieces'.[17] With that comicality in which exaggerated pathos invariably ends, the same conviction led Stefan George's hagiographer Friedrich Wolters to assert that the age of logical gymnastics was over and the wrestling-match with the angel of life had recommenced.

To what extent this philosophy of living helped to prepare Germany's path to Hitler with the direct consequentiality imputed by Georg Lukács is a matter of dispute; what is indisputable is that it did promote an irrationalist reinterpretation of traditional rational values in philosophy. While in the case of Dilthey himself – who, though he did not desire to bring life before the judgment-seat of reason, did not desire either to have reason capitulate to life – an attempt is still made to mediate between science and intuition, after him, and not least within the George circle, this antithesis breaks forth with all possible acuteness.

Compared with the immediacy of experience the possibilities of knowledge in science here appear as of the second rank, if not quite immaterial. Dilthey had soberly maintained that thought cannot retreat behind life; with Gundolf and others this is transformed into a rule of conduct: acquire knowledge only to the extent required for living.

Only in exceptional cases is the critique of science that reached a high point in Germany after the First World War a critique of the

---

[17] Rudolf Kjellén, *Die Ideen von 1914: Eine weltgeschichtliche Perspektive* (Leipzig: Hirzel, 1915), p. 42.

natural sciences: with these the critics had as a rule nothing at all to do, quite apart from the consideration that they lacked all competence to judge the achievements of a Virchow, a Planck or a Helmholtz. Critique of science was for the greater part a matter for practitioners of the human and social sciences or of *belles-lettres*, and it was directed less against the procedures or discoveries of the natural sciences than against the tendency to transfer them to other disciplines and to infuse more and more domains of knowledge with the scientific spirit.

When Erich von Kahler's *Der Beruf der Wissenschaft* appeared in 1921 its title alone made it clear that it was a reply to Max Weber's *Wissenschaft als Beruf* of 1917; that it was published in Berlin by Georg Bondi nourished the suspicion – a suspicion its author certainly did not find unwelcome – that it constituted an official pronouncement of the George circle, something which Stefan George himself indignantly denied.

Von Kahler, who admired Max Weber, wished to be a follower of his, and regretted to find in him an opponent; he regarded the foundations of all disciplines as having been undermined and saw in the evolution of modern rational science a tragic process of self-destruction. Abstract systematics were visibly ceasing to be a means to knowledge, and '*life*' was slowly 'rising up chaotically'[18] in the perception of that world of experience which science could no longer regulate. Similar things could be read at that time in Gottfried Benn and others, though usually more in a tone of mean-minded cynicism. The universal feeling of discomfort could be reduced to the formula that the old science had abandoned the claim to direct mankind and had thus become meaningless to men. The outcome of the irresistible process of intellectualization was an increase in the significance of the irrational; new forms of knowledge had to be evolved; to be able to act men desired to unite feeling with knowing.

In the new science propagated by Erich von Kahler the separation of *research* and *presentation* was of decisive importance. With the old science all that was involved was a sufficiently scrupulous description of the course of the analysis; presentation and shaping of the material, on the other hand, were neglected and finally ceased to exist at all. The new science, however, would give precedence to presentation: no form of knowledge could be considered legitimate unless its results were presented so clearly it could afterwards be reproduced by the immediate understanding.

[18] Erich von Kahler, *Der Beruf der Wissenschaft* (Berlin: Georg Bondi, 1920), p. 21.

This strict differentiation between the process of research and the form of presentation led to a rigorous division into two of the scientific public: the process of research was an internal affair of the community of scientists; only the finished and perfected work should be made available to a larger public. The procedure by which knowledge was produced remained that of labouring, assembling, concentrating; the presentation and exposition of scientific discoveries came more and more to resemble the presentation of a work of art.

Arthur Salz in his turn published in 1921 a reply to Erich von Kahler, which he called *Für die Wissenschaft. Gegen die Gebildeten unter ihren Verächtern* (*For Science. Against the Educated among those who Despise it*). In Kahler's new science Salz saw at bottom nothing but an intuitive anthropology; yet, with a characteristic reversal of perspective, he too adopted the differentiation between mode of research and mode of presentation. As against the bestowal of an aesthetic form upon scientific presentation he proposed a sharp division between the *poet* and the *scholar*. To the poet alone it was possible or permissible to free himself from his social and political ties, 'to feel himself superior to the age, to the state, to society, absolute and unconditional, if he believes that these by no means easy renunciations will enable him to serve with a purer heart that for which he stakes his *life*, *his* gods, which are not the gods of any state'. [19]

To the scholar, however, who was in contrast to the poet a profane man, this possibility remained barred: every scientific discipline was too much an expression of its epoch for it to attempt with any prospect of success to appear superior to its age or its country of origin. Science was necessarily fastened to society, and Salz saw this fact in operation precisely in the 'new' science, whose champions were eager to escape their isolation and to combine together in a new community.

The revolution in science

In a critique of science whose principles at least did not contradict the convictions of the George circle the conflict between poet and scholar stood at the centre. This was a basic problem of the George circle: the poet could make of superiority to society the organizing principle of his own existence; if, however, he became a prophet and

---

[19] Arthur Salz, *Für die Wissenschaft. Gegen die Gebildeten unter ihren Verächtern* (München: Drei Masken Verlag, 1921), p. 58.

founder of sects who wanted to go beyond poetry to influence the sciences too, then he had to enter into forms of association capable of exerting a socially binding effect upon him analogous to that exerted by society or the state. What then threatened to happen was that the poet's charisma would become a matter of everyday and thus forfeit its legitimacy.

As a reaction to the cultural crisis that was also a consequence of the First World War there occurred a revolution in science – more precisely, in the human sciences: that, at least, was the dramatic way in which Ernst Troeltsch described the situation, and he stressed the aristocratic character of this revolution, which, greatly influenced by Nietzsche as it was, desired to get away from intellectualism and specialization, strove to get back into touch with life, and stood in opposition to the values of modern mass democracy. Even though it was limited to the human sciences, and was anchored predominantly in Germany, this movement signified the beginning of a fundamental change in the consciousness of modern man, which rose in revolt against democracy, socialism and the autocracy of reason. The new, visionary human sciences of a Bertram, Gundolf, Scheler, Spengler and Keyserling achieved 'a melding together of thought and plastic-sensual perception such as artistic Expressionism had striven inadequately to achieve through the medium of painting'.[20]

This claim on behalf of the human sciences was indeed of an unheard-of boldness: if, as a rule, the new human sciences were held to have fallen short when measured against the achievements of the arts, now they were asserted to possess expressive possibilities greater than those of art, or at least of one of the main streams of modern artistic endeavour, Expressionism. Wilhelm Worringer was the principal witness on behalf of this claim.

Worringer's starting-point was the crisis of Expressionism, which also had its positive aspects. Creative sensuality, which could no longer find complete expression in art alone, became sublimated, flowed into intellectuality and became mind. The creative energy of the epoch was no longer revealed largely in its painted devices but in its devices of thought, and no one need have cause to wonder if the so-called interpretative books of a Gundolf, Bertram or Scheler were greater works of art than those to be seen on canvas. Art was not being replaced by science, but science was beginning to become art. In this science man would discover the perspectives he needed to

---

[20] Ernst Troeltsch, *Die Revolution in der Wissenschaft* [1921], in *Gesammelte Schriften* (Tübingen: Mohr/Siebeck, 1925), Vol. 4, pp. 653–77.

find his way in the world: 'As creators we have grown poor, but our wealth is accumulating in knowledge.'[21]

It was as though art had taken a pause for breath, as though it had sacrificed 'sensual painting'[22] so as to assist in bringing to birth 'sensual thinking':

If Expressionism is an advance into new worlds of knowledge, an enlargement of our capacities for representation, then it is truly more legitimately at home in the new pictures in our minds than in those on our walls. True contemporary Expressionism lives not in the new optics of our eyes but in those of our mind.[23]

Troeltsch drew from such findings as these the optimistic conclusion that German science had emerged from its great crisis in a stronger and healthier condition: cured of the bad kind of historicism, science had been restored to the realm of life without thereby relinquishing its claim to rigorousness of method or systematism in investigation. With science having become also art and having effected a reconciliation with life, German science was experiencing a Renaissance.

Troeltsch had disputed and come to terms with Salz and von Kahler, and what struck him about these polemics was how slight the differences were between all these supposed competitors: Max Weber, whom Kahler had attacked so reluctantly and almost with a bad conscience, was anything but a typical champion of the old science, and the positions adopted by Kahler and by Salz, who was likewise close to the George circle, differed hardly at all. Troeltsch's diagnosis was, however, wishful thinking rather than an accurate description of the relations between the disciplines or of those between the sciences and the arts: there were faculties such as sociology and psychology which had as yet in no way determined what their disciplines specifically consisted of and which would be placing their barely achieved academic reputations considerably at risk if they promulgated claims legitimately maintained by the arts and by literature. In this context Worringer constituted something of an exception. As a rule neither painters nor poets had the least intention of admitting that artistic sensibility had departed into the sciences; intuitive knowledge and a living sense of individual and social reality were, as before, still at home in poetry. Evidence of the truth of this was provided not least by Dilthey, who had none the less been second to none in promoting the revolution in the human sciences.

---

[21] Wilhelm Worringer, *Künstlerische Zeitfragen* (München: Bruckmann, 1921), p. 26.
[22] *Ibid.*, p. 28. [23] *Ibid.*, p. 27.

Poetry in the age of science

In a letter to Count Yorck of February 1884, Dilthey wrote that he envied both the woodcutter and the physicist: both did a useful job, and every day and every week they could see what they had achieved. And yet Dilthey's objective was to protect philosophy against 'the radicalization that has occurred in the natural sciences'[24] and to preserve and strengthen the self-confidence of the human sciences in an age 'intoxicated with the natural sciences'.[25] His task was made harder not least by many practitioners of the human sciences themselves: as Yorck maintained, the philologists above all were natural scientists at heart who, when they became radical sceptics, did so because they lacked the practical experiment. The principle of 'divide and rule' must therefore also apply in the theoretical field: for the human sciences it meant not least an abandonment of the practice of imitating the disciplines of the natural sciences. The question, however, as to how sharply they could still be distinguished from the arts, and above all from poetry, then became unavoidable.

As early as in his inaugural address at Basel in 1867, when he spoke on 'The Poetical and Philosophical Movement in Germany 1770–1800', Dilthey emphasized that the view of life that dominated this epoch had been shaped by the great creations of the poets, which at the same time constituted the evolution of a new philosophy: the systems of Schelling, Hegel and Schleiermacher appeared as merely their logical and metaphysical continuation. The nation looked up to its poets as to its leaders; literature was, to a far greater degree than philosophy, the Germans' guide to living. Nowhere was this power of the poet, which raised him above those whose knowledge was scientific, more clearly evident than in the case of Lessing:

Poetry too expresses a general truth, as does science; but not in the form of an abstraction encompassing many individual cases but as the perception of a *single* life. It expresses it intuitively and thus with a wonderful power over the heart . . . And Lessing himself had to traverse a long path of scientific reflection in order to discover the perfect poetic expression of his life-ideal.[26]

To tread the path of science in such a way that it finally led to poetry – this was Dilthey's ideal. Because philosophical contemplation of

---

[24] Dilthey to Count Yorck, 1 November 1893; *Briefwechsel*, p. 165.
[25] Dilthey to Count Yorck, January 1891; *ibid.*, p. 118.
[26] Dilthey, 'Die dichterische und philosophische Bewegung in Deutschland 1770–1800. Antrittsvorlesung in Basel 1867', in *Die geistige Welt. Einleitung in die Philosophie des Lebens. Erste Hälfte. Abhandlungen zur Grundlegung der Geisteswissenschaften* [1923] (Stuttgart: Teubner/Göttingen: Vandenhoeck and Ruprecht, 1961), p. 17.

history had in Germany unfolded in the history of its literature, Dilthey wanted to employ poetics for the study of history, for poetry offered the invaluable methodological advantage 'of revealing with exceptional transparency the psychological processes in the products of history which brought them about. . .'[27] He also considered it one of the most important tasks of philosophy to re-establish the natural relationship between art, criticism and public.

But art, too, could not elude the changes occurring in the European *Zeitgeist*, which was becoming increasingly dominated by militarism and positivism. Art was becoming democratic, approaching close to reality, and beginning to resemble science; this was especially so in France, where the rise of socialism had been attended by the rise of a new literature: Balzac, Taine and Zola had probed reality with the scalpel of science. The epoch of 'ideals above time and place, Iphigenie, Wilhelm, Lothario'[28] seemed to be irrecoverably over; the artist's principal endeavour was to allow the ordering of reality to shine through the work of art so as to demonstrate how greatly his characters were determined by the nature of their epoch and the society in which they lived.

This approximation of poetry to science, which was the outcome merely of the importance which the scientific mode of thought had attained to in nineteenth-century Europe and was specific to this epoch, Dilthey regarded as a false evolution. The literature of realism and of naturalism had been prey to an illusion; it was no longer capable of penetrating the surface of the social structures beneath which the true nature of man could be seen lying unaffected. Mindful of the great achievements of the German movement in the Classic age and the realm of idealism, Dilthey urged German poets to forget their Romantic, Scandinavian and Slavic models: 'Only out of the depths of Germanic nature can there come to our poets an awareness adequate to the present day of what life is and what society ought to be.'[29]

This invitation of Dilthey's found its clearest echo in the George circle: its members distanced themselves from all literary groups or movements which 'pursued the exploration of the social classes or any other useful employment',[30] and Friedrich Wolters dubbed the

---

[27] Dilthey, 'Antrittsrede in der Akademie der Wissenschaften' [1887], in *Die geistige Welt*, p. 11.
[28] Dilthey, 'Die drei Epochen der modernen Ästhetik und ihre heutige Aufgabe' [1892], in *Gesammelte Schriften*, Vol. 6 (Stuttgart: Teubner/Göttingen: Vandenhoeck and Ruprecht, 1962), p. 245.   [29] *Ibid.*, p. 287.
[30] Friedrich Wolters, *Stefan George und die Blätter für die Kunst. Deutsche Geistesgeschichte seit 1890* (Berlin: Georg Bondi, 1930), p. 47.

three writers from whom the German poet had to keep his distance the 'god-deprived Frenchman'[31] Zola, the 'gloomy Norseman' Ibsen and the 'formless Russian' Dostoyevsky.

Dilthey's proposal to effect a marriage between the human sciences and poetry was not promoted by the tendencies towards becoming scientific existing in art: it was called into question by them. It was true that science could become poetic without sustaining any harm, but poetry abandoned itself when it adopted the aims and methods of science. Dilthey acted like a partisan of poetry in the territory occupied by science, and it was this role which permitted Hugo von Hofmannsthal to say in his obituary of the philosopher that there had never been a man who lived in an atmosphere more like the atmosphere of a poem. 'A German professor'[32] – that was the term von Hofmannsthal applied to Dilthey, and the designation was a perilous one in an age that could brand the professor as 'the German national sickness';[33] but Hofmannsthal warded off any resentment of the remark by adding, 'like Doctor Faust'.

Hofmannsthal himself saw himself as belonging to a scientific age in which there was hardly any room left for poetry and the poet was condemned to a marginal existence: 'He dwells strangely in the house of the age, under the stairs where everyone has to step over him and no one pays him any attention.'[34] None the less it was precisely the scholars who envied him this role, for at bottom they were frustrated poets shivering in the coldness of science, whereas to be a poet was – in the words of Hebbel's *Tagebücher* – 'to wrap the world around you like a cloak and warm yourself'.[35] It was precisely because he united thinking and feeling in what he did that the poet was superior to the scientific specialist not only in power of imagination but also in capacity for knowledge: he was the seismograph of the age and society in which he lived.

The Austrian Hofmannsthal confronted science and poetry with one another in a courteous, almost playful manner, not concealing his regret that the nation of Goethe should have abandoned the unity of poetical intuition and pretension to knowledge in which its strength had once resided. But already with Rudolf Borchardt, the friend and panegyrist of Hofmannsthal, the tone had become

---

[31] *Ibid.*, p. 54.
[32] Dilthey, *Von deutscher Dichtung und Musik. Aus den Studien zur Geschichte des deutschen Geistes* (Leipzig and Berlin: Teubner, 1933), p. x.
[33] Julius Langbehn, *Rembrandt als Erzieher. Von einem Deutschen* (Leipzig: Hirschfeld, 1890), p. 94.
[34] Hugo von Hofmannsthal, 'Der Dichter und diese Zeit' [1906], in *Reden und Aufsätze I (1891–1913)* (Frankfurt am Main: S. Fischer, 1979), p. 66.   [35] *Ibid.*, pp. 64–5.

shriller and the antithesis between poetry and science irreconcilable: science was not merely alien to life but hostile to it, and a deluded mankind called the process of its spiritual dissolution the age of natural science and had for long uttered the cliche '"science and technology" in the way they say Hansel and Gretel or Beethoven and Wagner'.[36] Poetry, on the other hand, was a primeval phenomenon and the poet the only imperishable thing the world produced; the poet created a work inaccessible to the intellect. Defensiveness against rationalism and exaggerated expectations of the power of poetry combined in Borchardt to produce an uncompromising state of mind which, in an age that demanded rational political action and a turning towards society if men were to secure their own decent survival, boasted of its abstinence from politics and celebrated retreat into subjective inwardness:

Poetry was everywhere and in everything except in what literature called poetry; the people was everywhere, only not where politics looked for it. Germany was anywhere but between the geographical borders of '97. Nowhere was it closer to me than within myself.[37]

One cannot justly associate Rudolf Borchardt with those who were shortly to drive him out of Germany: his tragedy, however, and the tragedy of others resides in the fact that before and during the Weimar Republic they championed causes that, far from hindering the Nazi seizure of power, perhaps even assisted it. In 1926 Hans Dahmen, who was not a member of the George circle but certainly sympathized with its aims, wrote a book called *Lehren über Kunst und Weltanschauung im Kreise um Stefan George* (*The Artistic and Philosophical Precepts of the Circle around Stefan George*). In many respects dilettante, commonplace in tone, obsequious and naive, it is not a good book, but for that very reason it is revealing as a document. Full of sympathy for his subject, Dahmen came to the precocious conclusion that philosophical insight was impossible unless it included the forces of feeling. He was painfully aware of an absence of these feelings in the sciences – with one exception. In Marburg he encountered a revered man with whom he spent many unforgettable hours in the psychological seminar, 'the friendly home of a science within which the heart does not languish'.[38] This psychologist was Erich Jaensch, who with incomparable resolution in 1933 led psychology, as a part of the German movement, over to the Nazis, who found

[36] Rudolf Borchardt, 'Eranos-Brief' [1924], in *Handlungen und Abhandlungen* (Berlin-Grunewald: Horen-Verlag, 1928), p. 147.   [37] Borchardt, 'Eranos-Brief', p. 160.
[38] Hans Dahmen, *Lehren über Kunst und Weltanschauung im Kreise um Stefan George* (Marburg: Elwertsche Verlagsbuchhandlung, 1926), p. 19.

'the combative mental attitude of the SA and SS. . . something completely familiar, comradely, inwardly related and congenial to me
from the very beginning'.[39]

If there was one author whom the German champions of scientific
scepticism and the propagandists of poetic intuition invoked as the
better alternative to rational knowledge, it was Goethe. The age of
technology and science could not be more scathingly damned than
by being called 'totally un-Goethean'.[40] But many Goethe admirers
were bad, or at any rate forgetful, Goethe readers; perhaps, too, they
would have liked to forget the words which Mephisto directed at
Faust and which in his *Zerstörung der Vernunft* Georg Lukács employed
as a kind of *leit-motif*:

> Verachte nur Vernunft und Wissenschaft,
> Des Menschen allerhöchste Kraft,
> Lass nur in Blend- und Zauberwerken
> Dich von dem Lügengeist bestärken,
> So hab ich dich schon unbedingt![41]

(Despise reason and science, the greatest strength man has, let the spirit of
lies fortify you in delusions and sorceries: then I have you, completely!)

[39] E. R. Jaensch, *Die Lage und die Aufgaben der Psychologie. Ihre Sendung in der Deutschen Bewegung und an der Kulturwende* (Leipzig: Barth, 1933), p. 123.
[40] Graf Yorck to Dilthey, 17 December 1890; *Briefwechsel*, p. 113.
[41] Goethe, *Faust. Der Tragödie erster Teil*, 1851–1855; Georg Lukács, *Die Zerstörung der Vernunft, Werke*, Vol. 9 (Neuwied and Berlin: Luchterhand, 1962).

9

A German speciality: poetry and literature in opposition

Enlightenment and industrialization, the advance of democracy and urbanization, the subjection of ever greater domains of experience to the ways of science, and the progress of technology evoked similar reactions everywhere in Europe. Since in the nineteenth century nothing could halt the triumphal march of the natural sciences, something stubborn and cranky, old-fashioned and reactionary came in this age to adhere to all criticism of reason and scientific scepticism. At the same time there occurred in Germany not only a division between science and poetry, but also an attempt, conducted with fanatical conviction though not always with convincing lucidity, to divorce poetry itself from other forms of literature. Similar attempts were also made in France and England, where as a rule whoever writes verse is accounted a poet, but in neither country did they make any significant mark. This is one of the screens with whose aid French and German intellectual culture above all can be distinguished one from another, and far-reaching philosophical options are as a rule to be associated with such assertions as Walter Benjamin's that France must be counted fortunate not to have accepted the division of poetry from other kinds of literature, or with the verdict of Stefan George – who none the less owed so much to the French and was an admirer of Mallarmé – that France may possess *littérature* but possesses no poetry.

In German, meanwhile, a further distinction was made – though without prospect of definitive terminological purity – between the writer (*Schriftsteller*) and the man of letters (*Literat*). Campe defined *Schriftstellerei* (writing) and *schriftstellern* (to write) almost neutrally as 'low but not for that reason objectionable words';[1] but Klopstock was, in his epigram '*Die Schriftstellerey*', already more hostile –

---

[1] Art. Schriftsteller, *Deutsches Wörterbuch von Jacob und Wilhelm Grimm*, Vol. 15 (München: Deutscher Taschenbuch Verlag, 1984).

'Germans, hesitate no longer to banish this word' – and '*Literat*' became in the end a favourite German polemical term, as it was for instance to Lagarde, who saw in the *Literaten* a water-weed to be exterminated, or to Max Weber, who described the *Literaten* as the authors of an irresponsible brand of writing that had degenerated into emotional nationalism, social–economic utopias and fun revolutions. It is significant that Max Weber counted the 'ideas of 1914' as belonging to the domain of the *Literaten*, and after the end of the First World War Ernst Troeltsch sighed with relief that the 'literary rodents'[2] had now vanished.

The most determined attempt to separate the poet from the writer was that undertaken by Stefan George and his adherents. This division applied equally to the distinction they made between the Germans and the French and to the order of rank they established within Germany: to Gundolf, for instance, the German language had since the death of Goethe become the spoil of literature, and George's own influence in linguistic creativity rested not least on his having again opened up the gulf between literature and poetry. As a *poet* George contrasted himself above all with the *writers*, and scholars were frequently denounced as *Cathedra-Literaten*. Within the George circle itself the differentiation between poetry and literature served to enhance group cohesion and counteract centrifugal tendencies: thus George criticized certain themes Gundolf had lectured on because he feared they involved a confounding of poetry and literature, and as prominently as in the first volume of the *Jahrbuch für die geistige Bewegung* he regretted their literary tone.

Between the new poetry represented by George and his circle, and any kind of literature, there was an unbridgeable gulf. The reason, Gundolf maintained, was that language was both a social and a natural phenomenon: in this sense literature belonged to society but poetry belonged to nature. As the prototype of the un-literary, indeed anti-literary, poet George embodied the religious man, a type radically different from other types of the species *homo sapiens*. This type was indifferent to the demands of everyday life; if money had to be earned to support existence any job would do unless it involved writing – the poets' hatred for the literary world derived its strength not least from the fact that in modern times literature had become a profession. Possessing neither profession nor civic status in the world, the poet appeared as an elemental being distinguished

---

[2] Ernst Troeltsch, 'Die Ideen von 1914' [1916], in *Deutscher Geist und Westeuropa. Gesammelte kulturphilosophische Aufsätze und Reden*, ed. Hans Baron (Tübingen: Mohr/Siebeck, 1925), p. 42.

not by what he did but by what he was: the true poet did not even need to write, let alone publish. The poetry he did produce, however, struck those capable of hearing it with the force of a revelation: 'Genuine verses are always a delineation of the primary rhythms of the world.'[3]

This may sound very exaggerated and immoderate – yet a great part of George's influence derived precisely from the unconditional and uncompromising way in which he composed his poet's existence. For he was by no means alone in holding the views he did, and he could count on agreement even outside his circle: Rudolf Borchardt, for instance, who saw through George yet continued to stick by him, who polemicized against him endlessly yet could not get free of him, was no less arrogant than George himself in the demands he made of the true poet or the privileges he demanded for him.

That the poetic must be divorced from the aesthetic just as much as from the literary went without saying. There were sufficient and more than sufficient literary men in the world, but true poetry, the mark and distinction of the human race, was threatened with extinction. Borchardt described how 'one afternoon in early summer, an afternoon clammily sultry as always in the channel of stifled air and heavy with the odour of the wistaria that fluttered on every house',[4] he discovered in the reading room of a university library the ancient little book that captivated and convulsed him because it opened his eyes for the first time to what poetry and what the poet is:

The poet was not a poet through art – there was no art of poetry. He was one as a man, through his humanity, language was poetry. Words were exclamations, not designations. His adjectives were cries of astonishment, his verbs were actions and commands. Style was not a production but a degree of intensity. The world of imagination belonged, like the world of the senses, to everyone. There it stood written.[5]

The book which Borchardt read was Johann Gottfried Herder's *Älteste Urkunde des Menschengeschlechts* (*The Oldest Record of the Human Race*), and Herder's conception of poetry as the mother tongue of the human species allowed him to define the poet in the manner of a human zoologist: he was *homo sapiens varietas poetica*, a being originating in a heroic world and fundamentally distinct from the rest of mankind in his 'need of solitude, need of staying silent, self-

---

[3] Friedrich Gundolf, *Briefwechsel mit Herbert Steiner und Ernst Robert Curtius*, eingeleitet und herausgegeben von Lothar Helbing und Claus Victor Bock (Amsterdam: Castrum Peregrini Press, 1962/3), p. 25.

[4] Rudolf Borchardt, *Eranos-Brief*, p. 157.   [5] *Ibid.*, pp. 157–8.

enrapture'.[6] Under no circumstances could he be compared with the everyday human being, who was *zoon politikon* and continued to vegetate in his community like a dog.

The poet and the poetical thus demanded to be viewed from the perspective of natural history, which would then make plain to what extent the poet had become an endangered species now that first religion, then the law and finally music too had declared their independence of him. The repulsive *Schriftstellerei* of a Flaubert or a Proust was a symptom of how far the poetical world had gone in decomposition, and his fear that the poetical, the primally human, could perish was eradicated for Borchardt only during those weeks he spent reading George and Hofmannsthal.

Borchardt's intelligence, however, would not permit him to emphasize solely the anthropological aspect of poetry to the complete neglect of its historical or social ties. In an address on the poet and history which he gave in 1927 at Freiburg University, he reminded his hearers that it was precisely poetry that had to depict the origin and evolution of man not only as an individual but also as a social being, and ventured on to the adoption of a standpoint that can only be called that of sociology of literature when he saw Eichendorff's and Rückert's capacity 'to hear the nightingale, to follow the swallow, to see the dewdrop suspended from the blade of grass'[7] as being connected with the existential form of Prussia as an agrarian state.

Less surprising but even more revealing of the relationship of literature to society, and thus also to sociology, was the description and designation of literature which Borchardt had already offered in 1902 in his address on Hofmannsthal:

It is wholly and solely an occasion for communication, and to him who has something to communicate it stiffens into a tribune set before an invisible multitude. It is a letter from the field written by a stranger to ten thousand strangers between the decampment and the battle; it is experience of typical circumstances and thus of typical validity; it is attack, defence, a will directed against institutions, as a pamphlet, as a discussion, as a coarse novel, as a shrill play; it is preponderantly nothing but observed life, news, perfunctorily disguised in fictions, of a closed existence, that of an East India soldier, a Brandenburg peasant, a Silesian weaver, a poor nobleman, a clergyman, a middle-class girl. Literature, which a hundred years ago possessed for such purposes only a single form, the bewitching form of the

---

[6] Borchardt, 'Über den Dichter und das Dichterische' [1920], in *Handlungen und Abhandlungen*, p. 79.

[7] Borchardt, 'Der Dichter und die Geschichte' [1927], in *Prosa IV* (Stuttgart: Klett, 1973), p. 212.

utopia, today, when it involves itself in our cities, is no less ethnography than when it tries to seize hold on Candahar and the East End.[8]

'Candahar' was indeed literature as ethnography, but 'the East End' was also literature as sociology. It was not least the decisive separation of poetry from literature that made possible such an equating.

When, during the First World War, Rudolf Borchardt, Hugo von Hofmannsthal and Rudolf Alexander Schröder founded *Hesperus* and formed themselves into a poet's society, Borchardt wrote to Hofmannsthal of what hung on the success of this society and its plans: 'Nothing more nor less than the rescue and security of the whole coming generation.'[9] And after the war he devoted all his energies to getting a new intellectual movement under way and promoting a spiritual reformation – through delivering lectures in a private house, where in a series of fourteen addresses he explained to his hearers the condition of the age.

Hofmannsthal was more sceptical, and though what Borchardt had to say on the significance of the poet and the function of poetry seemed to him desirable, he was unable to believe it could ever be realized. To Hofmannsthal, too, poetic contemplation was something higher than criticism, philosophy of history or aesthetics, namely 'life and the birth of life'[10] itself, as he wrote to Borchardt in a comment on Borchardt's essay on Alcestis; but in his own early essay on 'Poetry and Life' (1896) he had already come to the resigned conclusion that there was no direct pathway leading from poetry into life or from life into poetry. And later on, too, it always seemed to him strange and curious if life for once assumed in reality the appearance of a well-designed work of art.

This gentle resignation of Hofmannsthal's made the poet appear a more delicate creature than he did with the cutting and combative Borchardt – yet this did not mean any diminution in his significance or his value in the world. His work seemed less esoteric, yet the poet himself was still aware of being something special and that he could lay claim to a special form of society that would offer him security and promote his productivity. When in 1920 Hofmannsthal expounded his 'idea for an altogether independent monthly magazine that would oppose the sham taste of the epoch', his

[8] Borchardt, *Rede über Hofmannsthal* [1902], 2. Aufl. (Berlin: Hyperion, 1918), p. 38.
[9] Borchardt to Hofmannsthal, 15 August 1915; Hugo von Hofmannsthal und Rudolf Borchardt, *Briefwechsel*, p. 116.
[10] Hofmannsthal to Borchardt, 6 May 1913; *Briefwechsel*, p. 102.

foremost objective was to resist any attempt to be up to date. His future subscribers would form a closed circle in which 'a higher social world, a German spiritual community . . . is presupposed'.[11]

To enclose the higher spirituality of poetic creation in a higher form of sociability and in that way promote its effectiveness – this was a compromise between the asocial, indeed anti-social attitude which, according to a distinct German tradition, the true poet should adopt, and the matter-of-course sociability that distinguished the *homme de lettres* in France. The achievement of such a compromise was difficult because philosophical differences of this kind had their roots in the differences between the languages. Compared with intellectually sociable French, German was solitary, profound and monologic; it had always been alien to the French, whereas the Germans 'loved the French language with an insipid love'[12] and abused it 'with an insipid, misunderstanding hatred'.

It therefore constituted an appropriate distancing of himself from German ideology when, in that address made famous and infamous by its invocation of a 'conservative revolution', Hofmannsthal spoke not of *Dichtertum* but of *Schrifttum* as being the spiritual region of the nation. This address, delivered in 1927 at Munich University and dedicated to its rector, Karl Vossler, is permeated with a longing for what Vossler had called the sociability of forms of which the French had so easy a command. Within the French nation there had evolved even in literature a social element which was an ingredient of that 'tremendous gregarious susceptibility whose torments are endurable only through almost unlimited experience. . .'[13] The consequence was a high valuation of the writer, indeed even of the man of letters and the journalist, such as seemed unthinkable in Germany:

Nothing exists in reality in the political life of the nation that does not exist as intellect in its literature; its literature, full of life and devoid of dreams as it is, contains nothing that is not realized in the life of the nation. The man of letters . . . enjoys an incomparable distinction. The journalist, too, be he never so insignificant, can set himself beside Bossuet and La Bruyère, the schoolteacher is the companion of Montaigne. . .[14]

[11] Hofmannsthal, *Reden und Aufsätze II (1914–1924)* (Frankfurt am Main: S. Fischer, 1979), p. 127.
[12] Hofmannsthal, 'An Henri Barbusse, Alexandre Mercereau und ihre Freunde' [1919], in *Gesammelte Werke in Einzelausgaben*, ed. Herbert Steiner, Prosa III (Frankfurt am Main: S. Fischer, 1977), p. 437.
[13] Hofmannsthal, 'Das Schrifttum als geistiger Raum der Nation' [1927], in *Natur und Erkenntnis: Essays* (Berlin and Darmstadt: Deutsche Buch-Gemeinschaft, 1957), p. 170. [14] *Ibid.*, p. 172.

Germany presented the contrary picture: the 'rotation between the intellectual and the social' upon which everything depended in France was instinctively frustrated in Germany, where the chief aim was 'the refutation of the social'. Hofmannsthal, to whom the present was the responsible social life of the living and history the responsible social life of the nation, had it in mind to distance himself from this without becoming an outsider in relation to his language and his national literature. What he deplored in the case of Austria also applied to Germany: the absence of a class capable of responsible political thought and politically engaged but at the same time sufficiently independent not merely to pursue its own selfish ends. With Hofmannsthal, who was to so many the very epitome of the poet, the isolation of the poet was none the less ameliorated and the gulf between the remote and self-absorbed poet and the sociable *Schriftsteller* reduced; and this was also achieved, but on account of his origins and the heightened tensions of his time more decisively, by Thomas Mann.

Supporters and enemies of the Republic

The weighing of the world of the poet and that of the writer against one another, their rigorous separation and eventual melding together are enduring themes in the works of Thomas Mann, his reports on his activities, his attempts to determine his position. For many years he worked on a plan for a '*Literatur-Essay*', whose objective was to move the poet into proximity with the artist and charlatan and to present the writer as a responsible and aware contemporary who 'through his analyses is of more use than any poet in some conventicle mourning the ideals of ages long vanished';[15] the writer, not the poet, was for Thomas Mann the born social critic and moralist – and he was so, not through feeling and intuition, but through his intellectuality and sharpness of discernment. To Richard Wagner's apostate compound '*Literaturdichtung*' Mann opposed the man of letters as the artist of knowledge the model for whom was Nietzsche. He experienced no difficulty in taking sides in the contention between the analysing writer and the naive poet, even though he was aware that cleverness was badly paid and little admired. He himself admired it, to be sure, and did so not least in the new young generation of scholars, among whom he valued especially Ernst Bertram.

---

[15] Hans Wysling, '"Geist und Kunst": Thomas Manns Notizen zu einem "Literatur-Essay"', *Thomas-Mann-Studien* 1 (1967), p. 126.

Mann was aware what such an attitude signified in Germany: here the profession of writer enjoyed no tradition and even less recognition; literature would never be at home in Germany in the way it was in France. The German art was music, while with the French 'literature has no competitor as the national art'.[16] Wagner's contempt for the literary seemed very German and could count on being applauded; Mann contended that, on the contrary, it was unwise to open up an imaginary abyss between poetry and literature, since a strain of the literary was visible in every poet – a fortunate fact, since the literary spirit was 'the very highest revelation of the human spirit'.[17]

In his essay of 1913, *'Der Künstler und der Literat'* ('The Artist and the Man of Letters'), Mann did not merely affirm this attitude but sharpened it. Against the morally indifferent and irresponsible artist, the *Literat* now stood as psychologist and moral censor: *Literat* now meant what the French of the eighteenth century called a *philosophe*, an enlightened intellectual who furthered the Enlightenment mainly with the weapon of the pen. For what else was the Enlightenment but 'philanthropy and the art of writing',[18] the conviction that writing well meant thinking well and thus also acting well? Such a maxim as this was much less a German than a French or a European maxim: it could have come from Buffon or Matthew Arnold; and it was thus all the more meaningful that it should have been appropriated precisely by Thomas Mann, who had from his youth onwards turned 'more to the European–intellectual than to the German–poetic'.[19] He sounded engaged, unambiguous and sure of where he was going – and yet what he said was none the less an expression of inner insecurity and struggle, less a conviction and a manifesto than a piece of self-encouragement. For, as in his heroes, there existed in Thomas Mann himself a longing for the artistic, the amoral and the irresponsible, a discord between the addiction to myths of the Germans and the reason-obsessed clarity of the French, and between a commitment to the nation and a surrender to Europe – within him, the writer and the poet struggled with one another. Traces of this are to be found in those writings in which the singularities and enormities, the corrosive insights and grotesque misjudgments that characterize the *Betrachtungen eines Unpolitischen*

[16] Thomas Mann, 'Ein Brief zur Situation des deutschen Schriftstellers um 1910' [1910], *Thomas-Mann-Studien* 3 (1974), p. 9.   [17] *Ibid.*, p. 11.
[18] Thomas Mann, 'Der Künstler und der Literat' [1913], in *Schriften und Reden zur Literatur, Kunst und Philosophie, Das essayistische Werk* (Frankfurt am Main: S. Fischer, 1968), Vol. 1, p. 77.
[19] Thomas Mann, 'Einkehr', *Die Neue Rundschau* 28 (1917) p. 341.

(*Reflections of an Unpolitical Man*) are adumbrated almost playfully and as though to test them.

The early '*Gedanken im Kriege*' ('*Thoughts in Wartime*') of 1914 suddenly brings together art and war on the ground that both are united by the principle of order; politics now counts as 'an affair of reason, democracy and civilization',[20] and this triad is supposed to sound discordant for it is meant maliciously: morality is on the side, not of reason, but of the soul and of culture. And why is the example of Friedrich the Great so influential? Because he began as a man of letters and ended as a soldier. His earliest acts, Mann writes, were of a literary *habitus* and unmistakably marked by the spirit of the Enlightenment: abolition of torture, removal of censorship, sympathy for every measure that might promote a climate of toleration. In him there appeared 'embodied civility... come to power, literature in a silk dressing-gown'.[21] And this man of letters became an impassioned soldier who never again removed his uniform: in this Thomas Mann celebrated an ideal to which the *Betrachtungen* are also dedicated.

The *Betrachtungen* stand in the service of their time, they are 'armed service in the cause of ideas';[22] in them, one who was disabled in the war returns to his 'deserted work-desk'. At the same time, however, as regards their motivation, and to a large extent the unboundedly embittered tone that characterizes them, they are Mann's contribution to a fraternal conflict; and this contention with his brother Heinrich – the civilized man of letters (*Zivilisationsliterat*), unnamed but ever present – makes this gigantic polemic also a treatise on poetry and literature, and not only in the chapter entitled 'The Unliterary Land'.

The unliterary land is Germany: it had removed itself from the Latin West, which had always been literary and since the French Revolution had with increased vigour set about making the rest of Europe into a bourgeois civilization, which was to say a literary civilization. It was this that threatened Germany – the imperialism of civilization whose cleverest agent was the civilized man of letters. For to him the world of civilization was at one with the world of literature, while literature was an expression of 'uplifting and humanly decent rhetorical democracy'.[23] Whereas Mann formerly

[20] Thomas Mann, 'Gedanken im Kriege' [1914], in *Politische Schriften und Reden, Das essayistische Werk*, Vol. 2, p. 9.
[21] Thomas Mann, 'Friedrich und die grosse Koalition' [1915]; *ibid.*, p. 22.
[22] Thomas Mann, 'Betrachtungen eines Unpolitischen' [1918], in *Gesammelte Werke in Einzelbänden* [Frankfurter Ausgabe], ed. Peter de Mendelssohn (Frankfurt am Main: S. Fischer, 1983), p. 9.   [23] *Ibid.*, p. 55.

regarded it as complementary to the man of letters that he should be equated with the eighteenth-century *philosophe*, now, in time of war, he was for precisely that reason suspect and contemptible: for the German could not be a man of letters, and if he was one despite that, he had by that act expatriated himself, had become 'a Frenchman . . . a classical Frenchman, a Frenchman of the Revolution'.

At the same time Mann was far from wanting to persuade himself and others that he was in no way a man of letters but, on the contrary, the only thing a German writer could be in an age of patriotism, namely a poet. He openly admitted his cosmopolitan tendencies and how far he was from inhabiting the world of poetry; he could, he said, never hope to be a poet such as Gerhart Hauptmann. Mann laid claim to a divided nature similar to that endured by Nietzsche, who had taken the most German, most Goethean of all conceptions, the concept of life, and 'invested it with a new beauty, strength and holy innocence, raised it to the highest rank, to spiritual hegemony',[24] while at the same time being through his Europeanism as guilty as anyone of the intellectualization of Germany and of its permeation with literature. Mann did not ask for indulgence towards this divided nature, he demanded admiration of it: he was constitutionally a man of letters, and, as in the case of Nietzsche, to combat the world of letters required of him an exceptional degree of self-denial and discipline. He insisted that, though between the poet and the man of letters there existed differences of attitude and of intellectual predisposition, there existed no difference as to competence: the poet had learned to write as well and to make as many glittering phrases as the 'bourgeois rhetoricians'.[25]

Even as late as the immediate pre-war years Thomas Mann had regarded a union of philanthropy and the art of writing as a mark of distinction, as a sign of moral and political enlightenment in a writer worthy of emulation; now, in the last year of the war, he derided the '*belles-lettres* politicians'[26] who, modelling themselves on the French, wanted to turn Germany into a republic of lawyers and men of letters. The politicization of Germany during the years since 1860 was also attributable to non-political causes: responsibility lay with the rise of history and the natural sciences which had proceeded at the expense of poetry and philosophy. Politicization and subjection to science were only two sides of the same process – a process that was the more regrettable in that while the national culture of a country could be lived and experienced it could not be analysed or com-

---

[24] *Ibid.*, p. 82–3. [25] *Ibid.*, p. 161. [26] *Ibid.*, p. 231.

prehended through the methods of science. In France they even called the fishing-boats 'Pensée' or 'Honneur et dévouement moderne', and Germany too was on the way to that 'humbugging form of intellectualism... illustrated by ale-house signs bearing the legend "A l'Idée du Monde"'.[27]

The Betrachtungen eines Unpolitischen are a manifesto of the counter-Enlightenment. What lies at the bottom of them is the conviction that in the long run no state can be founded on the principles of the Enlightenment, and that a realization of the Enlightenment must eventually lead to the destruction of culture; for the Enlightenment meant over-estimation of reason exalted into a programme, whereas mankind's adherence to art proclaimed the power of feeling. As guardian of the soul's potentialities art was conservative, and so was the artist; and Mann seems to have been expressing his artistic convictions rather than a party-political opinion when he professed his intellectual inability to accord his support to the political Enlightenment: 'One may say that conservatism as such is a disposition, whereas progressiveness is a principle; and it is in this, it seems to me, that there lies the human superiority of the former over the latter.'[28]

Looking back on the Betrachtungen Mann afterwards emphasized their experimental nature: for him they were 'much more an experimental and psychological novel than a political manifesto',[29] and he was neither as fanatical an opponent nor as unconditional an adherent of the exaggerations and one-sided views that appear there as at first sight seemed to be the case. He did in fact quickly free himself from all this, and it was not long before he could proclaim his solidarity with the Republic and unreservedly confess to a renewed and profounder solidarity with the writer and the writer's profession.

His great lectures on Lessing of 1929 celebrate the 'classic of poetic understanding',[30] and the 'prudent poet'[31] who is, like Nietzsche, fundamentally not a poet at all: 'He is what the polite modern world lacking mythology and sensibility calls a writer. For the first time in Germany he embodies the European type of the great writer.'[32]

Such assertions as this seem unequivocal enough, as does Mann's

---

[27] Ibid., p. 304.   [28] Ibid., p. 401.
[29] Thomas Mann, 'Meine Zeit' [1950], in Politische Schriften und Reden., p. 328.
[30] Thomas Mann, 'Rede über Lessing' [1929], in Leiden und Grösse der Meister [Frankfurter Ausgabe] (Frankfurt am Main: S. Fischer, 1982), p. 10.
[31] Ibid., p. 11.   [32] Thomas Mann, 'Zu Lessings Gedächtnis' [1929], ibid., p. 28.

contention that the conflict between the realm of the poetic and the world of the writer belonged to the past and was now no more than an echo of a superfluous *querelle allemande* – yet even a Lessing could not be commended without some apologetic insurance, and so Mann hastened to attribute to Lessing's writings, which it had been insinuated showed un-German, Frenchified tendencies, qualities that brought them closer to his own people: 'something of Dürer's German masterliness'[33] adhered to them which could serve as a model for the overcoming of the perilous antithesis of intellect and feeling. And when he greeted his brother on his sixtieth birthday with the address 'On the Vocation of the German Writer in our Time' he emphasized in it that Lübeck Gothic could be united with Latinity, the German with the Romance, the sphere of the poet with that of the writer, and confessed his adherence to that species of German artistic mastery that reached out beyond the merely German to the European and the universally human. That the Prussian Academy of Arts should have called on Heinrich Mann to head what Thomas Mann called its *literary department* was a visible expression of this new-won though still threatened harmony: it signified 'an official recognition, incorporation and visible displaying of literature on the part of the new republican state'.[34]

But it is precisely the history of the department of the *poetic arts* (*Sektion für Dichtkunst*) – which was its real title – that demonstrated how lively the antithesis of writer and poet still was and what far-reaching ideological consequences it possessed. As early as 1924, Thomas Mann's homage to Ricarda Huch on her sixtieth birthday had elicited an open letter from Josef Ponten in which, while understanding Mann's demand that the importance of the antithesis between poet and writer should not be overestimated, he went on to accuse Mann of having himself taken sides on the issue, gone over wholly to the party of the writer and presented himself as the apologist of a culture of the intellect. Ponten wanted the sphere of the poet and that of the writer to be as distinct from one another as inner from outer, content from form, clarity from obscurity, tailoring from the garb of nature, instruction from revelation, time from eternity. As was proved by the case of Goethe, only the writer could become a poet – the reverse was impossible. Ponten invoked the

---

[33] Thomas Mann, 'Rede über Lessing', p. 14.
[34] Thomas Mann, 'Vom Beruf des deutschen Schriftstellers in unserer Zeit' [1931], in *Rede und Antwort. Über eigene Werke, Huldigungen und Kränze. Über Freunde, Weggefährten und Zeitgenossen* [Frankfurter Ausgabe] (Frankfurt am Main: S. Fischer, 1984), p. 346.

poet of *Buddenbrooks* and *Tonio Kröger*, of *Death in Venice* and *Felix Krull*, and sought to gain him for an ally; he distanced himself from Thomas Mann the writer, who was a theoretician and was more and more becoming an intellectual: as such he was tending towards such disciplines as history, political economy and political science, which, being incapable of interpretation or prophecy, were all backward-looking. If one confessed to being a man of letters one made of oneself an ally of pseudo-sciences which had yet to demonstrate any efficiency whatever:

> Natural *interpretations* are 'naturally' possible in these disciplines too, but how few have we been favoured with! What a poor showing have, e.g., our political economists put up, who have given us grandiose accounts of what *is* but not even one of whom has been able to tell us and Germany what *will be*. (How grateful we would have been to one who had told us how to save our halfpennies [*groschen*] in time.)[35]

Ponten's letter to Thomas Mann demonstrates the bitterness with which the contention between the poet and the writer was conducted in Germany – even monetary inflation has to be invoked to offer a new reason for preferring the poet's closeness to nature to the alienation of the writer.

The contention over the '*Sektion für Dichtkunst*' can – thanks to Inge Jens's scrupulous reconstruction of the events – be understood as a dispute between the poet and the writer. On one side there stood Thomas and Heinrich Mann, Alfred Döblin and Jakob Wassermann, while the other was headed by Erwin Guido Kolbenheyer, who conceived the poetic arts as being 'emotional direction and liberation of a people through the artifice of language';[36] Hermann Stehr, Alfred Mombert, Theodor Däubler, Wilhelm von Scholz and even Ricarda Huch were on Kolbenheyer's side, though not always from the same motives as his. In the last resort, however, the debate over the name of the department divided the '*Völkisch*' elements from the Republicans, the adherents of the Weimar Republic from its opponents. In 1931 Heinrich Mann was elected chairman of the department after Kolbenheyer and other '*Völkisch*' members had walked out: victory had, it seemed, gone to those who united with their commitment to literature a commitment to the German Republic.

---

[35] Josef Ponten, 'Offener Brief an Thomas Mann' [1924], in *Thomas Mann im Urteil seiner Zeit: Dokumente 1891 bis 1955*, herausgegeben mit einem Nachwort und Erläuterungen von Klaus Schröter (Hamburg: Christian Wegner, 1969), p. 118.

[36] Erwin Guido Kolbenheyer, 'Brief vom 24.12.1929', in Inge Jens, *Dichter zwischen rechts und links. Die Geschichte der Sektion für Dichtkunst der Preussischen Akademie der Künste* [1971] (München: Deutscher Taschenbuch Verlag, 1979), p. 111.

A year later – that is to say a year before the end of the first German Republic – Thomas Mann confirmed his position in two great addresses which celebrated 'Goethe as Representative of the Bourgeois Age' and described his 'Career as a Writer'. The form and objective of the second of these in particular, the Weimar lecture, were bound to appear as sacrilege to those who saw in Goethe the representative of the world of German poetry, for Mann began with Goethe's confession that he was really born to be a writer and then with the aid of this *leit-motif* set about putting a definitive end to the 'critical mania for drawing a schoolmasterly distinction between the sphere of the poet and the sphere of the writer'.[37] As before, in the case of Lessing, he did it by seeking to understand the spheres of the poet and of the writer as facets of a single author, forms of expression of one and the same creative individual; he also did it by reducing the writer's existence to an ordinary, everyday affair and yet affirming all the more decisively his commitment to it as the 'poet's earthly form of life'.[38]

Thomas Mann foresaw that this assertion would be bound to cause a scandal in Germany, and he hastened to acquit Goethe the writer of any suspicion of political renegadism or of that misdeed of the man of letters which Julien Benda had branded *trahison des clercs*. What was involved here, however, was less a vindication of Goethe – which would in any case have seemed forced if it had succeeded – than a speech for the defence by Thomas Mann in his own cause. For he was well aware that, with his partisanship for the writer and his gentle but obstinate irony at the expense of the poet's ingenuity, he had also adopted a political posture: for the Enlightenment against reaction, for the republic against the authoritarian state, for the socially responsible individual against the irresponsible detachment of the individual from the community. In this early development of a sense of the writer's responsibility and self-awareness which, interrupted only by the counter-experiment of the *Betrachtungen*, was accelerated and reinforced by his commitment to the Weimar Republic and his struggle against fascism, a significant role was played by Mann's perception of society and of sociology, as is shown above all in his attitude towards Max Weber.

[37] Thomas Mann, 'Goethes Laufbahn als Schriftsteller' [1932], in *Leiden und Grösse der Meister*, p. 181.
[38] *Ibid.*, p. 18.

10

◁ ═══════════════════════════════════════ ▷

Disciplines in competition: sociology and history

First delay and procrastination, then precipitancy, excess and a forced-up outbidding of competitors: these are the characteristics that mark the social and economic evolution of Germany in its transition to an industrial society. Something similar applies to the development of sociology: Treitschke's *Die Gesellschaftswissenschaft*, published in 1859, is a late arrival as a sociological treatise, but it is certainly one of the first doctoral theses (*Habilitationsschriften*) to be devoted to this theme and at the same time to embody an attack on sociology.

Treitschke saw himself confronted in the middle of the nineteenth century with a situation in which several disciplines or prospective disciplines were waiting to align themselves with the old political science or even to replace it: among them were the natural history of nations, social anthropology and sociology in the narrower sense. Such writers as Robert von Mohl, who maintained that sociology did not only have a right to exist but was actually a necessity, overestimated the role played by domestic economy in the life of society while at the same time inadmissibly diminishing the role of the state: starting from an erroneous, narrowly limited conception of the state they arrived at the conclusion that a science of society was needed, whereas between them political history and a correctly understood science of politics – one that was more than a mere compendium of prudential conduct and wordly wisdom – left no room for sociology. What made it worse was that sociology and socialism had much in common with one another, both being founded on the false doctrines of the French Enlightenment.

Treitschke conducted his polemic half-heartedly and as though with a bad conscience. In a series of letters he distanced himself from his 'unfortunate essay'[1] and was glad to have disburdened himself of

[1] Heinrich von Treitschke to Wilhelm Nokk, 26 December 1858; Treitschke, *Briefe und Gedichte*, Vol. 5 of *Aufsätze, Reden und Briefe*, ed. Karl Martin Schiller (Meersburg: Hendel, 1929), p. 391.

the 'unhappy subject'[2] for which he had at bottom been too young and too ignorant. One copy of the work – it is at present at Yale – he sent to Robert von Mohl, whom he had attacked but who was and remained his patron, with the dedication: 'To Herr Geh. Rath Robert von Mohl – with particular respect – the Author.'

In his attempt, carried out during the Nazi era, to determine the 'present tasks of German sociology', Hans Freyer pointed out that Treitschke and his competitors were in their fundamental positions entirely at one: what distinguished them all from the adherents of the social theories predominating in France and England was the deep-rooted conviction that bourgeois society was no more than an historical phenomenon, a state of transition, an analysis of which could in no way serve as the basis of a natural philosophy of human cohabitation. Bourgeois merchant-society failed to offer the Germans the foundations of a belief in progress that was blind to reality; it had, on the contrary, to be combatted and – by means of revolution if necessary – again done away with. 'With a superior realism',[3] said Freyer, German sociology set its face against the liberalism of Western European thought: its subject was 'the destiny of Germany in the age of bourgeois society'.[4] This diagnosis united together Treitschke, von Mohl, Riehl and Lorenz von Stein: under the influence of Hegel they all saw in the drifting apart of state and society the central problem of the epoch. Whether its solution would be better advanced by a renewal and expansion of traditional political science or by separating off an independent science of society was by comparison a secondary question.

In the nineteenth century the independent status of German sociology was not yet so perceptible as appears in Freyer's retrospect. Rather, sociology was accounted an Anglo-French discipline marked by an arrogant claim to knowledge and desire to effect change which it had inherited from the Enlightenment. For these reasons alone un-German, sociology also represented a threat, inasmuch as it assumed as a matter of course that bourgeois society was the standard upon which it had to base its analyses and was thus incapable of doing justice to the special features that characterized Germany and its evolution.

Rejection and reluctant acceptance of sociology

In his *Einleitung in die Geisteswissenschaften* (1883) Dilthey took up this argument and lent it a systematic foundation. What he called the

---

[2] Heinrich von Treitschke to Ferdinand Frensdorff, 11 November 1858; *ibid.*, p. 387.
[3] Hans Freyer, 'Gegenwartsaufgaben der deutschen Soziologie', *Zeitschrift für die gesamte Staatswissenschaft* 95 (1935), p. 123.   [4] *Ibid.*, p. 118–19.

'system of social ideas' was developed in the seventeenth and eighteenth centuries principally in England and France and since the French Revolution had been translated into social practice. At the same time an historical philosophy had evolved in Germany and had at once come into conflict with the social science of the West. Empiricism, namely 'loving absorption in the individuality of the historical event',[5] stood opposed to premature systematization; and if in France and England themselves resistance had sprung up to the attempts of a Comte, Buckle or John Stuart Mill to apply to history the methods of the natural sciences and in this way to found a science of society, this resistance none the less suffered from the disability that it was unable to evolve any basic principles but remained naive and dilettante: 'Opposition to exact science on the part of a Carlyle and other lively spirits was in the strength of its hatred as in the constriction of the language it used a sign of this state of things.' Something similar applied to most of the German reactions to positivism and empiricism, with Lotze's *Mikrokosmos* standing as an example: in the struggle against the ideology of science it sacrificed every scientific claim 'to a sentimental mood'[6] which desired 'to call back through science a contentment of the heart forever lost'.

Dilthey's goal was a scientific refutation of the ideology of science: he wanted to avoid the errors of Western social theory without succumbing to the danger of a flight into sentimentality that always existed in Germany. What was decisive for the nature of inner experience was not moods and states of feeling but the verifiable *facts* of consciousness: it was from these that one had to proceed if the humanities and the arts were to be developed as an independent system.

Even if Auguste Comte had laid the foundations of a true philosophy of the sciences, the total science of historical and social actuality devised by the French and English and called sociology by them none the less remained a chimera. Like philosophy of history, whose heir it was, sociology could never become a real science, and its already precarious position within the system of the established disciplines was made even more difficult by the rage for generalization that possessed the English and French. What these produced was nothing but metaphysical mist– and it lay at its thickest over the work of Comte, who with his pseudo-science also laid claim to be able to order the direction of society. Sociology presented itself as a

[5] Wilhelm Dilthey, 'Einleitung in die Geisteswissenschaften' [1883], in *Gesammelte Schriften*, Vol. 1 (Stuttgart: Teubner/Göttingen: Vandenhoeck und Ruprecht, 1962), p. xvi. [6] *Ibid.*, p. xvii.

new science, but in fact it represented nothing but the return of alchemy. Dilthey's views received support from Count Yorck, who equated sociological theory with modern political economy and none the less spoke of it only as 'this so-called science'.[7] Yorck evidences even more strongly than Dilthey himself a partiality for those writers – Treitschke for instance – who in the nineteenth century rejected English and French sociology and precisely by that act helped to found a *German* sociology. To Yorck 'the social' had become a mere fashionable expression, and in an age in which there were no longer any rulers but only administrators society was increasingly replacing the state, which survived only in the Catholic Church. On the other hand in Germany – as 'a sad privilege of ponderous subjectivity'[8] – universal problems were turning more and more into religious questions and thus creating the preconditions for a new Thirty Years War. In the face of such profound and far-reaching historical processes the analyses of a Comte appeared banal and Spencer's verbosity as the idle thoughts of an idle gentleman; that they were in practice the pupils of Spencer and had taken over his conception of science was by itself enough to disqualify the social democrats, as well as providing new proof of the odious proximity of socialism to sociology.

The sociology of Western Europe encountered *political* resistance in Germany because it did not merely accept the scandalous separation of society and state but actually welcomed it as a precondition of its scientific justification for existing; it provoked a *scientific* reaction because it misunderstood the nature of historical phenomena and promoted itself as competing with the science of history. Nietzsche's assessments of sociology, though they vary greatly, amount in the end to declaring it *culturally* disqualified.

Nietzsche, *'poète-prophète'*[9] and 'artist with scientific-historical annex', became the chief witness in the case against science in Germany. More poet than thinker, he was, for such readers as Ernst Troeltsch, one of those who broke the predomination of rationality through asserting the sovereignty of intuitive standards of feeling: 'to regain for the *man of knowledge* the right to *affects*'[10] was one of his

---

[7] Yorck to Dilthey, 7 March 1883; *Briefwechsel*, p. 32.
[8] Yorck to Dilthey, 10 March 1892; *ibid.*, p. 140.
[9] Friedrich Nietzsche to Heinrich Köselitz; Nietzsche, *Briefe (Januar 1885–Dezember 1886)*, in *Briefwechsel. Kritische Gesamtausgabe*, ed. Giorgio Colli and Mazzino Montinari Abteilung 3 (Berlin and New York: De Gruyter, 1982), p. 21.
[10] Nietzsche, *Nachgelassene Fragmente (Sommer 1886–Herbst 1887)*, in *Kritische Studienausgabe*, Vol. 12, p. 221.

maxims. The scientific philosophy of life, with its claim to universality, was a symptom of sickness and decay; 'the desire to render comprehensible, the desire to render practical, useful, exploitable'[11] was anti-aesthetic.

On the other hand Nietzsche was repelled by the Germans' hostility towards the Enlightenment, their attempt to substitute the cultivation of feeling for the cult of reason, their heartfelt wish 'to suppress knowledge beneath feeling altogether'.[12] A friend of France, Nietzsche wanted to criticize science like a Frenchman – he wanted, not to abolish it, but to make people laugh at its *tartufferies*.

On the other hand again, his critique of '*fait-alisme*',[13] his mockery of the 'delight in firm little *facts*' that ruled in France, makes Nietzsche sound like a restive reader of Durkheim who is protesting against having to regard the *faits sociaux* as things. Those he has in his sights are Comte, the Catholic visionary, and Mill, the typical shallow-pate, both of them representatives of a sociology whose mediocrity is precisely in accord with that of the mediocre-spirited who dominate in Europe. Just as the social question was a consequence of decadence, so sociology was as a discipline a creation of decay, an expression of a world view whose leading ideas were an outcome of the herd instincts. With the protestation that he himself at any rate was no *zoon politikon*, Nietzsche wrested himself free from the grip of the 'Herr sociologists of the future'[14] who were members of just that '*race moutonnière*' against whom he was defending his aristocratism. Like the '*Volk*, race, nation, utilitarianism and civilization, popular education, progress and the emancipation of women, sociology was among the modern ideas that Nietzsche pilloried: in an age in which the 'universities stand in the arts at the level of the male-voice chors',[15] and a professor was a being 'upon whose want of education and vulgarity of taste one can count until he proves otherwise',[16] every science, and sociology above all, was an obstruction to culture.

Politically suspect, declared impossible from an epistemological

[11] *Ibid.*, pp. 256–7.

[12] Nietzsche, *Morgenröthe. Gedanken über die moralischen Vorurtheile* [1881–7], in *Kritische Studienausgabe*, Vol. 3, p. 172.

[13] Nietzsche, *Nachgelassene Fragmente (Frühjahr 1884)*, in *Kritische Studienausgabe*, Vol. 11, p. 13.

[14] Nietzsche, *Nachgelassene Fragmente (November 1887–März 1888)*, in *Kritische Studienausgabe*, Vol. 13, p. 63

[15] Nietzsche, *Nachgelassene Fragmente (Frühjahr-Herbst 1873)*, in *Kritische Studienausgabe*, Vol. 7, p. 615.

[16] *Ibid.*, p. 614.

point of view, derided and laughed at from the heights of the higher culture and the arts: thus did sociology stand in Germany even before it had formed itself as a discipline or found a footing in the institutions of academia. And yet in all this criticism of sociology there lay a reluctant admission that one could not do without it. Treitschke, for instance, criticized such political scientists as Robert von Mohl who advocated the construction of an independent science of society, yet none the less ended by desiring a sociologizing of the classical sciences of state and politics. And when Nietzsche wanted to replace sociology with a 'theory of command structures'[17] and 'society' with a 'culture-complex'[18] he was at bottom only pleading for a sociology different from that of Comte, Spencer and Fouillé, for a sociology which has today partly accomplished the interpretative transformation he demanded and could call on him as its principal witness:

The interpretative character of all that happens.
There is no such thing as an event in itself. What happens is a group of phenomena *selected* and concentrated together by an interpreting being.[19]
Interpretation, *not* explanation. There is no such thing as a fact, everything is in flux, ungraspable, elusive; what is most enduring is our opinions. Introduction of meaning – in most cases a new interpretation over an old interpretation that has become incomprehensible, that is now itself only a sign.[20]

When, between 1904 and 1906, Dilthey planned a new edition of his *Einleitung in die Geisteswissenschaften*, he renewed his critique of Comte and Spencer, Schäffle and Lilienfeld, but clothed it in the assertion that hitherto sociology had not been 'a theory that includes the psychological life among the conditions of social relationships'.[21] But such a sociology did now exist – it was the sociology of Georg Simmel; and Dilthey expressly declared that Simmel was excluded from his critique. His reservations regarding the discipline remained; the procedures of sociology he accepted.

Georg Simmel: Impressionism in sociology

As in 1917 the beginning of the end was approaching Georg Simmel finally secured a professorship in the imperial German Reich – not in his beloved Berlin, nor in Heidelberg, Germany's secret capital at that time, but on the periphery, in Strassburg. Once again the man

[17] Nietzsche, *Nachgelassene Fragmente (Sommer 1886-Herbst 1887)*, in *Kritische Studienausgabe*, Vol. 12, p. 208.   [18] *Ibid.*, p. 470.   [19] *Ibid.*, p. 38.   [20] *Ibid.*, p. 100.
[21] Wilhelm Dilthey, *Einleitung in die Geisteswissenschaften*, p. 420.

of fifty-six had it demonstrated to him that, all his public success not-withstanding, in academic circles he had all his life remained an outsider.

Simmel saw an invaluable advantage in the constraint which sociology was still under to prove itself a science. He repulsed the reproach that it was not an independent discipline and that, since in the last resort its subject was the individual, it could be absorbed into, for example, psychology: the individual, he said, was not 'an object of knowledge but only of experience',[22] and sociology was concerned neither with the individual nor exclusively with such monolithic structures as state, family or class. Its concern, rather, was with making evident the reciprocal effects produced by individuals on one another, the patterns of private behaviour out of which enduring associations between individuals originated. Society was a process and sociology attempted to track down the patterns that constituted that process, the 'eternal flowing and pulsating'[23] that fettered individuals together. Simmel was what Trotsky, Georg Lukács and others saw him to be, the Impressionist of sociology. The education of the sociological eye seemed to him the most important aspect of a discipline which in its pure form was a kind of grammar: it demonstrated that social life obeyed regular laws even in those subtle ramifications that might seem to be the product of pure impulse.

In France and England social science begins with the construction of grand systems: but even Simmel's *Soziologie*, 600 pages long, is a mosaic of essays. It is not a textbook, and even when Simmel treats of fundamental questions he produces not a treatise but a *causerie*. Uniting cultural history and the history of art closely together, Simmel's sociology is perfunctory as regards form but permeated by a profound seriousness. He was aware of the tragedy that lay in the fact that in modern society equality could apparently be achieved only at the expense of liberty, liberty only at the expense of equality; and in this regard he called as witnesses such poets as Goethe, who had reviled as fantasists and charlatans those who promised the people equality and liberty at the same time.

Among Simmel's favourite topics was sociability, which he called the playful form of socialization: in sociability the sense of delicacy and tact – an aesthetic rather than any other quality – gained in significance in the measure that egoism retreated as the regulator of

---

[22] Georg Simmel, *Grundfragen der Soziologie (Individuum und Gesellschaft)* [1917] (Berlin and Leipzig: De Gruyter, 1920), p. 9.   [23] *Ibid.*, p. 13.

social life. Hovering between the merely practical and the purely individual, sociability constituted an ideal sociological world, a societal game. As a scientist Simmel felt at home less in the laboratory than in the salon, especially his own, whose sessions offered his guests a sociology *in vivo*: he was one of those sociologists in whose company people felt at ease.

Simmel's conception of sociology did not have to maintain itself against a critique of science from the standpoint of life: it was itself the expression and outcome of such a critique. Science was for Simmel only one variety of knowledge, and at bottom one for which on account of its autocratic character he felt little sympathy; it remained his optimistic conviction that 'the perfection of empiricism will replace philosophy as an interpretation, colouring and individual accentuation of reality just as little as the perfection of the mechanical reproduction of phenomena will the plastic arts'.[24] The basis of this optimism was the historical insight that life always rebels against being pressed into rigid forms. This rebellion was not always of equal force, to be sure; what happened, rather, was an oscillation between the desire for order and the impulse towards disorder, and each imposed its stamp upon individual epochs. This oscillation was of especial significance for sociology, for in the twentieth century 'life' had replaced 'society' as the characterizing concept of the epoch; with that there had appeared a growing repugnance for the closed system, and sociology had to confront problems deriving from a metaphysic of life.

The natural sciences were indifferent towards the objects of their investigations; they attained their position of supreme significance in the epoch of monetary economy, in which – objective, indifferent and thus characterless – the intellect ruled. The man dominated by reason gained more and more power compared with those who lived by their feelings and in accordance with their impulses: that was why Comte included bankers among the leaders of his future secular state, while on the other hand writers remote from economics, among whom Simmel accounted Goethe, Carlyle and Nietzsche, were marked by anti-intellectualism and rejected a world interpretation orientated solely by quantity and number. When, however, it came to expressing something about the ultimate values of mankind, art proved to possess a decisive advantage, in as much as

it every time poses to itself a single, narrowly circumscribed problem: a man, a setting, a mood – and then every expansion of them into the universal,

[24] Georg Simmel, *Philosophie des Geldes* [1900] (Berlin: Duncker and Humblot 1977), p. v.

every addition of great impulses of world-feeling, is felt as an enrichment, a gift, as it were an undeserved benefaction.[25]

In general, as he wrote to Husserl in 1911, Simmel saw in the difficulty of the problems that needed solving but never could be solved 'something marvellous';[26] and his definition of sociology as a science possessing no new subject-matter but capable merely of pointing out new paths, a science which refined its methods without ever constructing a system, has nothing resigned about it.

The influence of Nietzsche is visible everywhere here, and the sociologist Simmel, in whom many saw a secret artist, acknowledged with concurrence interpretations of his writings as works of art; and he was probably most moved by such judgments as that of Hugo von Hofmannsthal, who commended in Simmel an almost unexampled power 'of bringing the spiritual, the most impalpable, the most secret connections of intellectual reflection graspably close',[27] or by Rilke's confession after reading Simmel's comments on the *Stundenbuch* that they had revealed to him a new aspect of the path 'which I had been going along blindly'.[28]

By comparison with this the reactions of professional colleagues would have seemed to him secondary – those of sociologists especially so, since the discipline as yet possessed no distinct and recognized identity. Simmel evidenced great virtuosity in the way he varied his expressions of opinion as to the state of the sociological profession – being especially revealing when, as for example in his correspondence with Célestin Bouglé, a member of the Durkheim circle, he expressed them privately rather than in public. In the first letter, of February 1894, he lamented the insecure and uncertain condition in which sociology found itself; he thought it all the more vital that co-operation and contact should be maintained between 'the workers in this field'[29] – an expression Durkheim also liked to use. When Bouglé asked him what his further plans were he replied that he intended to devote himself wholly to sociological studies and

[25] *Ibid.*, p. viii.
[26] Georg Simmel to Edmund Husserl, 13 March 1911; *Buch des Dankes an Georg Simmel. Briefe, Erinnerungen, Bibliographie. Zu seinem 100 Geburtstag am 1. März 1958*, herausgegeben von Kurt Gassen und Michael Landmann (Berlin: Duncker and Humblot, 1958), p. 88.
[27] Hugo von Hofmannsthal, 'Brief an den Buchhändler Hugo Heller' [1906], in *Reden und Aufsätze*, Vol. 1, p. 376.
[28] Rainer Maria Rilke to Georg Simmel, 26 August 1908; *Buch des Dankes an Georg Simmel*, p. 122.
[29] Georg Simmel to Célestin Bouglé; *Briefe Georg Simmels an Célestin Bouglé*; Privatarchiv Bouglé, Bibliothèque Nationale, Paris. Zusammengestellt von Werner Gephart, Ms., o.J., p. 1.

would be engaged in no other field for the foreseeable future: the tasks of sociology were what lay closest to his heart. Just two years later he reported how interest in his conception of sociology was growing among students: they included Italians and Russians, Japanese and Americans. Translations of his writings were appearing in several languages. When, however, Bouglé asked Simmel in 1899 for a contribution to a congress, the latter's reply must have made him wonder whom the letter had come from:

I am sorry to say I cannot furnish the report for which you ask for the Paris congress. You should not forget that the *sciences sociales* are not my subject. My sociology is a wholly specialized subject of which I am the sole practitioner in Germany, and in regard to the other social sciences, which is what the congress is concerned with, I am only a layman and am thus in no position to offer a report on them. In general it somewhat saddens me that abroad I count only as a sociologist – whereas I am a philosopher, see in philosophy my life's task and practise sociology really only as a sideline. Once I have done my duty by it by publishing a comprehensive sociology – which I expect to happen in the course of the next few years – I shall probably never return to it.[30]

Troeltsch reports similarly, though in regard to a later date, that when conversation turned to sociological questions Simmel declined to talk about them: they no longer interested him.

Although Simmel himself was perhaps the last to be aware of it, what here emerged was the problematic position of a scholar who did not lack pupils but failed to institute a school. As Georg Lukács wrote in his obituary, Simmel was a transitional philosopher and as an Impressionist 'a Monet... who has as yet been succeeded by no Cézanne'[31] – and, as we may add today, would not be succeeded by one. He was, as Margarete Susman wrote, a solitary thinker, and was so not out of wilfulness but from the insight that saw in the unbridgability of their psychical solitude the only kind of common possession men could attain to.

As philosopher and artist–sociologist, Simmel saw in every work of art a piece of sociology and philosophy, and, like every writer who is a scientist and an artist as well, he therewith exposed himself to a twofold critique. To Rathenau, who censured his 'banking transactions with ideas',[32] Simmel was the embodiment of mere mind; to Emil Ludwig Simmel's tendency to conceal his analyses was respon-

---

[30] Georg Simmel to Célestin Bouglé, 13 December 1899; *ibid.*, p. 20.
[31] Georg Lukács in *Pester Lloyd*, 2 October 1918; *Buch des Dankes an Georg Simmel*, p. 173.
[32] Harry Graf Kessler, *Walther Rathenau: Sein Leben und sein Werk* (Berlin-Grunewald: Klemm, 1928), p. 31.

sible for the fact that this thinker 'would never be a great writer, because he has privatized his thought processes'.[33] Troeltsch rediscovered in Simmel's work the gossamer of an Indian summer 'in which countless trembling and shimmering threads fill all the air without beginning or end. . .'[34] He generously allowed that, as an ancillary science, Simmel's sociology had been of some assistance to the study of history, but its influence was essentially limited to that which it exercised on 'more refined journalism'.[35] Torn back and forth between science and art, Simmel had 'escaped the Scylla of sociological objectivism for the Charybdis of aestheticism, as so many do today'.[36]

Troeltsch's words sounded like an echo. In his *Philosophie des Geldes* (1900) Simmel had tried to show that the aesthetic viewpoint could be of use even in the analysis of sociological phenomena: Emile Durkheim at once reviewed the book in the *Année Sociologique* and mercilessly scourged 'this kind of bastard speculation which renders to us neither the fresh and vigorous sensations aroused by the artist nor the sober concepts for which the scientist seeks'.[37]

Max Weber: sociology as product of culture and art of maturity

If Georg Simmel cannot be regarded as a representative of that science assailed by the early critics of sociology in Germany, neither can Max Weber. The optimistic faith in progress of a Herbert Spencer was as remote and alien to him as was the grotesque and inflated systematism of Auguste Comte. Weber's concern was to accentuate the reverse and debit side of the process of civilization in the West, the side which bore the impress of the most fateful power of modern life, capitalism. A critique of science in the name of life could not be aimed at the works of Weber, who was more clearly and painfully aware than anyone of the limitations of reason and who saw 'the domain of what we can know' surrounded by 'unfathomable mystery'.[38] Life was irrational and fluid and, even though science had to cling to the rationality of its proofs and procedures, that which decided what was worth knowing was not science itself but life. Science was a product of culture: that is to say not a self-evident

---

[33] Emil Ludwig, 'Simmel auf dem Katheder' [1914], in *Buch des Dankes an Georg Simmel*, p. 155.   [34] Ernst Troeltsch, *Der Historismus und seine Probleme*, p. 572.

[35] *Ibid.*, p. 594.   [36] *Ibid.*, p. 581.

[37] Emile Durkheim, Review of Georg Simmel's *Philosophie des Geldes*, *Année Sociologique* V (1900/1), p. 145.

[38] Marianne Weber, *Max Weber: Ein Lebensbild* (Tübingen: Mohr/Siebeck, 1926), p. 340.

activity born out of nature but the outcome of a laborious penetration of an irrational universe in no more than the smallest segments.

In this sense rationality and objectivity were combat-concepts witnessing to the contention between man and actuality, to mankind's heroic effort to bestow meaning upon at least a portion of life. It was precisely because it was aware of its limitations that science had uncompromisingly to cling to its inner rationality and, because it saw all acquisition of knowledge embedded in a network of value-relationships, banish all value-judgments from the processes of its research.

The tragic aspect of such an attitude lay in its making of science both product and promoter of a process of rationalization and bureaucratization that would turn the world into a house of bondage in which mankind would in future live as the fellaheen once did in ancient Egypt. This process of increasing calculability, and with that the disenchantment of the world, was inescapable; he who welcomed it was unaware of what he was doing, he who sought to resist it was entangled in illusions.

Although it was a part of the process of rationalization, and even helped to advance this process, science was divided from faith only by a 'hair's breadth',[39] and as a profession it had to be practised quite otherwise than mechanically: passion and intoxication pertained to it, as did inspiration and a soul for which no arithmetical solution could be a substitute. But even though inspiration played no smaller role in science than it did in art, science was none the less imbued with the conviction that it could in principle render all things calculable and thus dominate them, and its goal remained the rationalization of the world. This conception of science was, as Max Weber himself knew from experience, already under attack from the younger generation at the turn of the century, and it was an attack that intensified after the First World War: 'The thought-structures of science constitute a subjective domain of artificial abstractions which think they can seize hold on the blood and sap of real life with their avid hands but ar enever able to catch up with it.'[40]

It was precisely because he was always conscious of the limitations of the intellect that Weber refused to distance himself from the

---

[39] Max Weber, *Die 'Objekivität' sozialwissenschaftlicher und sozial-politischer Erkenntnis* [1904], *Gesammelte Aufsätze zur Wissenschaftslehre*, Vol. 3, erweiterte und verbesserte Aufl., ed. Johannes Winckelmann (Tübingen: Mohr/Siebeck, 1956), p. 212.

[40] Max Weber, 'Wissenschaft als Beruf' [1917]; *ibid.*, p. 595.

intellectualism of science. He thundered against professorial prophecy but was offered the office of a prophet, he passionately propagated asceticism and by precisely that act acquired an empassioned following, he was hailed as a leader when he wanted only to be a teacher, and, although he sought above all to do justice to the demands of the day, visions of the future and long-range directives were expected of him. The recollections of those who knew him stress the sad–heroic quality that characterized him, a melding together of fact and individuality such as is to be found in his religio-sociological writings, where heroic Protestantism assumes the features of autobiography: this stylization of Max Weber was the work of Marianne Weber and Karl Jaspers, who saw in him 'the richest and deepest realization of the meaning of failure in our time' and a man 'who actively fulfilled his nature in its decline'.[41]

In a professional sense, Weber's asceticism betrayed itself not least in the attention he devoted to the tension between research proper and its presentation: he pointed to the perilous confusion that could result if one mistook 'the "artistic" form of *presentation* chosen in the interest of influencing the reader "psychologically"'[42] for something quite different, namely the logical structure of knowledge itself. One consequence of this insight was the rigidity that characterized his prose style – a rigidity which seemed to many of his readers and auditors not a defect, however, but an aspect of an attitude towards science to which Weber had had painfully to constrain himself. Helmuth Plessner probably fell short of the truth when he said that Weber ignored the questions of presentation in both his lectures and his books; Friedrich Meinecke came closer to it when he saw that Weber's neglect of form was the result of a conscious decision:

The neglect of form of which he was guilty in his scientific works was not merely a lack of elegance he believed he could permit himself so as to rush from one item of knowledge to another. For it deprives his discoveries of much of their persuasive power. And if neglect of form should gain ground in science in general we should be heading for the barbarization of science. In the case of Weber, however, it is wholly the result of a refusal to concern himself with form, not of an inability to do so.[43]

[41] Karl Jaspers, *Max Weber: Deutsches Wesen im politischen Denken, im Forschen und Philosophieren* (Oldenburg: Stalling, 1932), p. 8.
[42] Max Weber, *Kritische Studien auf dem Gebiet der kulturwissenschaftlichen Logik* [1906], *Gesammelte Aufsätze zur Wissenschaftslehre*, p. 278.
[43] Friedrich Meinecke, 'Max Weber' [1927], in *Max Weber zum Gedächtnis: Materialien und Dokumente zur Bewertung von Werk und Persönlichkeit*, ed. René König and Johannes Winckelmann (Köln and Opladen: Westdeutscher Verlag, 1964), p. 145.

Here it becomes clear what the price was that Weber had to pay for so decidedly renouncing the 'romanticism of the interested intellectual'[44] and, indeed, making opposition to it his guiding maxim. This interest of the intellectual seemed to him to pose a threat to every aesthetic phenomenon, and among the most decisive pieces of evidence as to Weber's kind of rationality is his fragmentary essay in musical sociology, in which it is probably not out of 'boldness'[45] but from an unconscious self-defensiveness that he declares that 'the strongest phenomena of feeling in human nature ... are to be rationally comprehended through being classified according to the concepts of history and sociology'. It must remain a matter of speculation how Weber – who is rightly counted as belonging to the Ibsen generation and who admired the Zola of *J'accuse* – would have written his book on Tolstoy or the comprehensive sociology of art which he planned to write.

With sociology itself Weber enjoyed a distant relationship; when he spoke of 'our' profession he meant political economy, and he was firmly against the creation of chairs of sociology:

For he did not conceal from himself the fact that this science is one that everywhere walks with the feet of others, and demands that these other sciences provide for it a good deal of the research it needs and an uncommon amount of critical attention. 'Most of what goes under the name of sociology is fraudulent,' he said in his valedictory address at Heidelberg.[46]

None the less sociology was – 'as an instrument of self-knowledge and disenchantment ... an art of maturity'[47] – of particular importance for the condition of life of modern man. Even more than was the case with other disciplines, sociology was obliged to guard itself against a scientism that promised everything and yet only led astray; Weber knew 'what monstrosities will be conceived if technologists schooled only in natural science should commit a rape on "sociology"'.[48]

For sociology and for the Republic

One can hardly refer to Max Weber's nervous crisis, which first declared itself in 1897 and was to have weighty consequences for his

[44] Max Weber, *Politik als Beruf* [1919], *Gesammelte politische Schriften*, Vol. 2, erweiterte Aufl., mit einem Geleitwort von Theodor Heuss, neu herausgegeben von Johannes Winckelmann (Tübingen: Mohr/Siebeck, 1958), p. 534.
[45] Karl Loewenstein, 'Persönliche Erinnerungen an Max Weber' [1920], in *Max Weber zum Gedächtnis*, p. 49.   [46] Karl Jaspers, *Max Weber*, p. 53.
[47] Helmuth Plessner, 'In Heidelberg 1913', in *Max Weber zum Gedächtnis*, p. 34.
[48] Max Weber, '"Energetische" Kulturtheorien' [1909]; *Gesammelte Aufsätze zur Wissenschaftslehre*, p. 402.

life and work, without drawing parallels with the cases of Auguste Comte and John Stuart Mill – parallels which extend into the details of their biographies and family life. A large role in this parallelism is played by the purity of a theoretical programme and the strategy of cerebral hygiene. Weber's case differs markedly, to be sure, in his not having succumbed to the temptation to give an aesthetic slant or religious interpretation to his scientific conceptions: he sought, on the contrary, to make of his epistemological rigorousness – the laboriously achieved outcome of his personal intellectual asceticism – the obligatory foundation of the work of sociology. The statutes of the Deutsche Gesellschaft für Soziologie, of which he was co-founder and 'comptroller', bear clear marks of his hand and his convictions. Paragraph 1 of these statutes lays it down that the advancement of sociological knowledge shall proceed through *purely* scientific investigation and inquiry and by supporting *purely* scientific undertakings; and as, in the seventeenth century, the Royal Society obtained the king's goodwill and the prospect of state aid by implanting the conviction that it intended to pursue purely scientific undertakings and would not involve itself in theology or metaphysics, morals or politics, so the Deutsche Gesellschaft für Soziologie promised to promote a scientific pluralism without 'advocating any kind of practical (ethical, religious, political, aesthetic, etc.) objectives'.[49]

Max Weber's reluctance to enter into questions of value thus became a rule of association, and science, whose rationality was for him in no way a matter of course but a transient product of culture continually exposed to the tempests of life, became in his hands a science of universal man. Speaking at the first congress of German sociologists, Ferdinand Tönnies, paraphrasing Goethe's *Faust*, asserted that mankind 'in its obscure impulses is none the less sufficiently well aware of the right path to know that reason and science represent the highest of all its powers',[50] and he later reproached Rathenau with having quite unjustly laid on science the blame for the mechanization of the world. Against those who in their battle against science and enlightenment wanted also to obstruct the progress of the social sciences Tönnies calmly maintained that this progress was irresistible: '*multi pertransibunt et augebitur scientia*'.[51]

---

[49] *Verhandlungen des Ersten Deutschen Soziologentages vom 19.–22. Oktober 1910 in Frankfurt a. M.* (Tübingen: Mohr/Siebeck, 1911), p. v.

[50] Ferdinand Tönnies, 'Wege und Ziele der Soziologie', *ibid.*, p. 22.

[51] Tönnies, 'Kommende Dinge?', Review of Walter Rathenau's *Von kommenden Dingen*, *Neue Rundschau* 1 (1917), p. 838.

Left in the lurch even by fellow professionals when it sought to claim its independence as a discipline, accepted by such allied disciplines as economics and history as at best an ancillary science, derided as a pastime for dilettantes or feared as a threat to German individuality, sociology none the less acquired increased significance in the Weimar Republic – and did so not least thanks to the cultural policies pursued by the minister and secretary of state Carl Heinrich Becker. Becker, whose ideas in the realm of educational policy were influenced by Weber and Troeltsch, regarded the First World War as a spiritual catastrophe, but saw in it an opportunity for a new cultural beginning, an attempt to make up the arrears in Germany's spiritual and political–moral development when compared with its neighbours to the west. Following a German tradition, Becker certainly saw the fundamental malaise of the age as lying in the first instance in the cultural overestimation of the intellectual and in the predominance of a 'rationalistic mode of thought which was bound to lead to egoism and materialism in their crassest form and has in fact led to them':[52] only within the sciences, and exclusively there, should rationalism rule. The principal task of the universities was to awaken the capacity for synthetic thinking in their students through the offer of branches of study which were by their nature not confined to a single discipline but embraced several domains of learning – a qualification possessed to a marked degree by sociology:

Germany has in regard to this science taken a back seat: for sociology, because it consists wholly of syntheses, is at variance with the German way of thinking. But that is why it is of all the greater importance for us as a means of education. Chairs of sociology are an urgent necessity in all higher institutions of learning. At the same time sociology, in the widest sense of the word, includes scientific policy-making and contemporary history . . . through sociological reflection alone can there be created in the intellectual domain a spiritual training which, transferred to the ethical domain, will then become political conviction. *Thus science becomes for us the path from individualism and particularism to citizenship of the nation.*[53]

A more dexterous procedure can hardly be imagined: for, while accepting arguments advanced by traditional anti-sociology, Becker develops out of them – taking as his starting-point the particular historical situation of Germany after its defeat – a *plaidoyer* for the enhancement of sociology in the interest not only of the German university but of a German nation that was from now on to regard

---

[52] Carl Heinrich Becker, *Gedanken zur Hochschulreform* (Leipzig: Quelle und Meyer, 1919), p. ix.   [53] *Ibid.*, p. 9.

itself as a democracy after the Western pattern. Some years later Becker enlarged the claims of sociology, which he too shared, and again employed the arguments of the discipline's opponents towards establishing the legitimacy of such claims. He associated a desire for synthesis even more firmly than before with a critique of the positivist tradition of thought, yet while the intellectual history of the nineteenth century made it difficult *not* to connect sociology with positivism or utilitarianism he declared sociology to be a discipline which formulated questions in a way that made it incompatible with positivism: the struggle for sociology was a struggle for a new, anti-positivist conception of science.

In the urge towards synthesis Becker perceived an urge towards form traditionally alien to the Germans, 'for form has never been among the strengths of the German; his impulse to truth in regard to the content is so great he can easily feel the form to be untruth, spurious, mere claptrap'.[54] The urge towards form as a reaction to an abundance of material hardly any longer susceptible to control was a more recent phenomenon in Germany. The examples Becker named – the books of the George circle, especially Bertram's *Nietzsche*, and the work of Spengler – were the same as those which for Ernst Troeltsch constituted the corpus of a new, revolutionary humanities, and Becker also agreed with Troeltsch in seeing the revolutionary element in these novel publications as lying in their dissolution of the boundary line between science and art. The pre-eminence of pure science was therewith abolished and intuition and private contemplation again came into their own and became an important ingredient of a new ideal of the humanities. And the new science which promoted and accompanied the formation of this new ideal was sociology. To cite Kierkegaard's question whether 'reason alone has been baptised and the passions are heathens'[55] would in any other European country have signalled the start of a well-rehearsed critique of sociology; to Becker it was a reason for holding the discipline in high esteem and for seeing in it an aid towards the democratization of the Germans.

This objective solves the problem of the paradoxes presented by Becker's mode of argumentation. If one bore in mind that Becker's political preferences were the opposite of Treitschke's, it was no longer surprising if the premises of classic anti-sociology were

---

[54] Becker, *Vom Wesen der deutschen Universität* (Leipzig: Quelle und Meyer, 1925), p. 41.
[55] Becker, *Das Problem der Bildung in der Kulturkrise der Gegenwart* (Leipzig: Quelle und Meyer, 1930), p. 23.

turned into a polemic in its favour: though the latter was still imbued with a considerable degree of intellectual aristocratism, an anti-democratic defence of the authoritarian state had been transformed into active support for the Republic.

Historical research and historiography

Among the firmest opponents of Becker's educational reforms and the most fanatical enemies of sociology was the historian Georg von Below, whose polemical writings prolonged the anti-sociology of the nineteenth century into the twentieth without a break. Below maintained that sociology as an independent discipline was something profoundly un-German, an importation from the West produced by 'coarse English naturalists'[56] and 'subtle French intellectuals', an 'abortion exciting disgust'. Comte especially was in no way the originator of a scientific movement, but merely a parasite who had shamelessly enriched himself with the labours of others. For the origins of sociology, correctly understood, lay not in France but in Germany; its founders were not the Western utilitarians and positivists but the German Romantics. A fact to be noted about German Romanticism was that the blow against rationalism and the Enlightenment was delivered not only by philosophy but also by the professional sciences and the arts; among the Romantics the more of a thinker a poet was, the greater his influence, and in the long run no division could be drawn between Novalis and Schlegel on the one hand and Savigny and Jacob Grimm on the other.

Romanticism corrected the errant course of the Enlightenment by restoring to poetry and the imagination their proper rights; by teaching that the individual was dependent on the spirit of the people, that is to say on the community, it led the way to the redis-covery of the individual. Whether one considered the historical school of law of a Savigny, the philology of a Jacob Grimm or the his-toricism of political economy – everywhere there was to be found sociological thinking: one could, indeed, almost equate Roman-ticism with sociology.

There was no discipline of sociology, but almost any 'real' dis-cipline used a sociological method. Becker's error lay in his regard-ing sociology not as a method or – which could perhaps still be maintained – as an analytical special science but as a general science,

---

[56] Georg von Below, 'Zur Geschichte der deutschen Geschichtswissenschaft II', *Historische Blätter* 1 (1921), pp. 173–4.

a subject for dilettantes, which for transparent political motives he wanted to promote. For sociology came into fashion in Prussia only through the revolution that advanced the Social Democrat deputy Hoffman to Minister of Education: it was he who pushed forward the creation of professorships in sociology, as did his successors Haenisch and Haenisch's secretary of state, Becker. It was, von Below maintained, thoroughly false to say that sociology was backward in Germany; on the contrary, human societal relationships had nowhere been so painstakingly investigated as they were within the German scientific tradition, which, in opposition to the positivism of the West, advanced a healthy realism. Sociology was at best a specialized science, as all disciplines were. Quite apart from the fact that no such thing as a universal science existed, sociology found it especially difficult to achieve a synthesis of the sciences. But Becker's objective was at bottom something quite different from this: he wanted to politicize and democratize the German state and had harnessed sociology to help him to this goal.

It is significant that with Georg von Below a historian became perhaps the sharpest critic of sociology in Germany. History and sociology had been competing disciplines since the middle of the nineteenth century; but whereas in France social history began, with the evolution of the *Annales* school, so to dominate the field that Fernand Braudel could afterwards say that social history and not sociology was the legitimate heir of Emile Durkheim, in Germany the conflict between sociology and history grew markedly more intense. German historiography had gained its cognitive identity through its preference for political history and its methodological identity through an idiographic execution emphatically legitimated by neo-Kantianism, and the energy with which it defended itself against any tendency to introduce sociological elements into it is demonstrated not least in the Lamprecht controversy. Karl Lamprecht and Kurt Breysig wanted history to approximate to an exact science – a path that could be pursued only via sociology. It is significant that a decisive role was played in the careers of both men by the concessions granted, against opposition from the representatives of the discipline, by the Education Ministers of Saxony and Prussia respectively: it can be no matter for surprise that it was C. H. Becker who in 1923 conferred a full professorship upon Kurt Breysig with the *venia*, scandalous to a traditional historian: 'sociology and general science of history'. Lamprecht considered the individual thing to be so irrational that it could be successfully reproduced only in art, while science – and thus history too, if it wanted to be a science at all – had to strive for a rational knowledge of the typical, of that which recurred regularly and conformed to laws. This rule applied to historical research – historiography, which for Lamprecht was comparatively a secondary affair, remained related to the arts.

Many historians felt obliged to agree with von Below in seeing in Lamphrecht and Breysig – these 'low empiricists and carters',[57] as Gundolf called them – only a kind of fifth column of sociology against whom it was necessary to wield the hatchet. The objections to the new version of cultural history were political and methodological; they included not least the reproach that an historical research which neglected historiography must in the long run lose its artistic dimension.

For at least since the rise of historicism and the historical speculations of the philosophy of life, the artistic character of history had been regarded not as a shortcoming but as the actual precondition for historical knowledge; in regard to which national differences – and again and again the antithesis between Germany and its Western neighbours – played a decisive role. The foolhardy thirst for the construction of scientific edifices for which Dilthey censured the French and English was bound to lead to the erection of gigantic but unstable systems, whereas a nose for detail and an empathy with the object unconfined by considerations of method had enabled the Germans to handle historiography as an art. For Dilthey the antithesis between the rage for generalization and artistic presentation was not least an expression of the relationship between sociology and history; although he had recognized and exposed the insufficiencies of Carlyle and the inadequacy of his reaction to the overestimation of rationality, Dilthey would have received Count Yorck's remark that his series of essays 'Poets as the Seers of Mankind' promised to become a counterpart to Carlyle's *On Heroes* as an act of support and encouragement. And it is characteristic of Yorck himself, who persistently sneered at sociology, that he should see in Ranke principally an aesthetician and poet, even if such a judgment did mingle praise with censure:

For Ranke was an aesthetician and a genuine contemporary and neighbour of Tieck: even his critical principles are of an ocular nature and provenance. The material of history, however, is to him a flux of forces that assume figures and forms. His historical personages are properly speaking *personae*, performers of historical roles. The poet remains hidden . . . As a historian

---

[57] Friedrich Gundolf to Ernst Robert Curtius, 8 May 1911; Gundolf, *Briefwechsel mit Herbert Steiner und Ernst Robert Curtius*, p. 196.

Ranke is wholly an eye; feelings and sensations, being purely personal things, he keeps to himself; his history is history seen, not history lived... Ranke is a great eye-piece to which nothing that has vanished can become *actuality*. But he is also the romantic sorcerer who brings the life of the past on to the stage and palliates truth into poetry.[58]

Yorck saw, too, that Ranke's confining himself to political history was more than a mere opting for politics: it was the expression of an aesthetic predilection for only those subjects which he considered could be dramatized.

Only a few decades later the struggle against the nineteenth century and its technological civilization, the defensive action against ratiocination and the accompanying enthusiasm for intuition and empathy, even led to a lack of historical knowledge being accounted a merit. Rudolf Borchardt had heard Treitschke speak – 'the deaf giant, his tight-shut eyes almost giving the impression he was also blind, stood and thundered hoarsely against the wall at the back of the wide auditorium, incomprehensible,, unforgettable'[59] – and, while to Yorck Ranke was the great eye-piece that allowed one to see history but not to experience it, so to Borchardt Treitschke appeared as a blind seer whose visions eluded all scientific criticism. In a dark age Heinrich von Treitschke's *German History in the Nineteenth Century* was a ray of light, not as a work of scholarship but as 'a great poetical deed, the only epic of the epoch... of perfect and ravishing poetic truth and without a shadow of historical insight, passionately loving and completely irrational, a composition compounded of faith and experience...'[60]

In just the same way, in the twentieth century Spengler's *Decline of the West* owed its tremendous success not least to the anti-scientific posture of its author, who expressed in the foreword to the first edition of 1917 the hope that his work 'might not be wholly unworthy to stand beside Germany's military achievements'.[61] Projected as a German philosophy, Spengler's morphology was intended to be anything but a piece of traditional philosophical scholarship: citing Goethe and Nietzsche as his models, Spengler shunned conceptual analyses and relied on a language whose aim was to lead the reader to re-experience what he had read. To treat history scientifically – i.e. as though it were a natural science – was in his view a contradictory proceeding: nature was susceptible to analysis, but

---

[58] Count Yorck to Dilthey, 6 July 1886; *Briefwechsel*, pp. 59–60.
[59] Rudolf Borchardt, *Eranos-Brief*, p. 152.   [60] *Ibid.*, p. 151.
[61] Oswald Spengler, *Der Untergang des Abendlandes: Umrisse einer Morphologie der Weltgeschichte*, Vol. 1, Gestalt und Wirklichkeit [1917] (München: C. H. Beck, 1924), p. xi.

history was closer to poetry than it was to science. Ranke had been aware of this when he had designated Scott's *Quentin Durward* as the true historiography. Discord between science and art, according to Spengler, was a mark of historically late ages; he left no doubt where his own preference lay as between scientific experience and experience of life, a systematic and a physionomical way of contemplating the world. At the same time, the dividing line between science and poetry was a fluid one: on one side of it there stood not only the natural sciences, sociology, psychology and rationalistic historical research, but also Ibsen and those other writers who, imbued with rationality, had long ceased to compose as a poet like Goethe composed but were capable only of constructing and interpreting. Goethe was again and again the admired model, for an understanding of the soul and psyche – whether of an individual or of entire cultures – was barred to the scholar and his modes of knowledge; poetry again came into its own where science had lost its powers: 'Critical research has ceased to be a spiritual ideal ... Two hundred years of orgies of scientificality – then one has had enough. It is not the individual, it is the soul of our culture that has had enough.'[62]

The penetrating military tone in all this was unmistakable, and the seductive power of Spengler's book lay not least in its having employed anti-scientific emotion to outbid the systematizing claims of science and the language of poetry to sing the praises of the man of action. Over a century before, the writers among whom Spengler did not wish to be numbered would have been called thoughtful but inactive: he called them 'rich in ideas but lacking in drive',[63] and desired for himself readers who preferred 'technology to poetry, the navy to painting, politics to critique of knowledge'.[64] The age of theorizing was past, and the future belonged to a conception of history which thought little of scientific experiment and relied instead on knowledge of mankind and physiognomical feeling, on illumination instead of on knowledge. When Max Weber called into question the tenability of Spengler's constructions of history the latter unhesitatingly confessed to being a poet.

Apparently from a combination of envy and a wish to distance himself from it, Weber had imputed to history the desire to embrace the whole of life; the whole of life was, however, imbued with irrationalities, and history was thus constantly in danger of becoming a species of poetry. If he was not to degenerate into a mere

---

[62] *Ibid.*, pp. 544–5. [63] *Ibid.*, Vol. 2, *Welthistorische Perspektiven*, p. 21.
[64] *Ibid.*, Vol. 1, p. 54.

archivist, the historian must of course have command of intuition and must employ it as a legitimate means of acquiring scientific knowledge; but Weber argued for a controlled intuition and that in history too research and presentation must be kept distinct from one another so that history should not become indistinguishable from the novel. What had happened in Germany was that historical research and historiography, far from coming closer together, had experienced a complete sundering, a schism, the causes of which were to be sought not least in the influence of the George circle.

By the beginning of the twentieth century sociology had taken its first small steps towards becoming a recognized and institutionalized profession in France, England and Germany. The successes which it had enjoyed were modest, but that meant no diminution in the number of its opponents. Quite independently of the national context, the *leit-motif* of all anti-sociologists was anti-modernism, a catchphrase sufficiently vague in meaning to embrace the most various and in part even antithetical positions and to enable them to be linked with one another in almost any combination; thus it was possible for one to take it for granted that sociology and socialism were only two sides of the same shield, while another protested that sociology was supposed to replace socialism. Whereas, however, in France the republicans' commitment to sociology made the harshness of the contentions that surrounded it understandable – for, as Georges Sorel's dictum that the members of the Académie Française, the sociologists and the heroes of national defence were equally useless made clear, the discipline counted as part of the establishment – in Germany its critics were often striking only at a scarecrow. This scarecrow was the sociology of Comte or Spencer, with its grandiose systematism, of which, however, there were very few representatives in Germany.

  German sociologists did not deny the national origin of their discipline: they were influenced equally by historicism and philosophy of life and inclined to be excessively modest in their self-examination. Simmel surrendered more than once to the temptation to make no clear distinction between science and life, art and science; and Max Weber's rigorism was the outcome of intellectual asceticism, not an expression of a devout belief in science. Of positivism, against which the Fronde of the German anti-sociologists organized itself, there was hardly a trace in German sociology; and how could one play off life against scholarliness or heroism against routine when one's opponent was, like Max Weber, 'a *true* masterful man and *hero* in

Carlyle's sense of the word . . . the aristocrat of democracy'?[65] In Germany the anti-sociologists promoted sociology, and the sociologists were themselves among the sharpest critics of their discipline.

[65] Gertrud Bäumer, 'Persönlichkeit und Lebenswerk von Max Weber' [1926], in *Max Weber zum Gedächtnis*, p. 118.

11

Remoteness from society and hostility towards sociology in Stefan George's circle

Resistance to civilization–mankind

The career of Stefan George is unique in the single-mindedness and deliberation with which a dandy and *Parnassien* became a prophet and his conception of art a rule of life. As Claude David has said, George conducted his life in the way a myth is constructed, composing it down to its smallest details. Every act in this composition was at the same time a strategic manoeuvre: the orthography and typeface he employed were intended as expressions of personality traits, so that George the law-giver would be as clearly distinguishable from Hugo von Hofmannsthal the man of the world as Roman is from Gothic.

That George could exert the influence he did without– according to Rudolf Borchardt – possessing a full command of the German language and could at the same time take in hand the rescue of the language, the purification of poetry and the rehabilitation of the poet presents no contradiction: he followed no rules but laid down laws, and it was not to his disciples alone that he seemed a hero and prophet. On meeting George for the first time Edgar Salin said he felt as Goethe must have felt on discovering Pindar; it was accounted an omen that George and Julius Caesar were born on the same day, and Kurt Breysig, whose pupils later went over to George, experienced a shudder of awe at the 'semi-divine personality of a man of such immeasurable force of being'.[1]

Friedrich Gundolf, who later did not so much reject George as suffer his rejection, emphasized George's otherness, a distant remoteness from the age and from society that made it impossible to speak

[1] Kurt Breysig, *Aus meinen Tagen und Traümen. Memoiren, Aufzeichnungen, Briefe, Gespräche*, aus dem Nachlass herausgegeben von Gertrud Breysig und Michael Landmann (Berlin: De Gruyter, 1962), p. 71.

of him with any pretence of scholarly objectivity: his humanity, unbounded by time, could only be sensed by intuitive faith, the power of his art only by him who despaired of the remoteness from art of the present day. George's humanity was of antiquity yet without any flavour of classicization; it belonged to no particular epoch, and his poems contained 'the reflections of a soul which has taken a passing flight to other ages and other climes and cradled itself there'.[2]

At the same time there was ample room here for misunderstanding, and the proclaimers of *l'art pour l'art* and the apostles of German subjectivity both unjustly laid claim to George. He was a man of action rather than of the *vita contemplativa*, harboured no theories but concentrated on practice, and it was precisely because he felt himself elevated above world and time that he wanted to exert an influence on his own time. George's remark to Kurt Breysig in 1916 that he himself might inherit the office of Bethmann Hollweg, the Reich Chancellor, was not meant as a joke, and Gundolf's expectation of the hero of whom the masses would desire to be nothing but an instrument was directed at Stefan George.

The depths of the impression George made and the extravagance of the reactions he evoked can be gauged from the letters and writings of Friedrich Gundolf. Judging German and other European literatures unreservedly from his personal experience, as early as September 1899 Gundolf designated George the 'index of culture'[3] whose work made any further poetry, philosophy or science seem superfluous. Whatever George's adherents created they owed to their association with their master, and after Gundolf had in 1910 completed his book on Shakespeare – it was to become the circle's compendium, as George's books themselves were its Holy Scripture – he confessed that he had 'written it as one possessed and... it is the product of a higher compulsion and of a will extending far beyond my own little bit of knowledge and ability.'[4] It was not only Gundolf for whom George was the incarnation of a better Germany; and by a better Germany was meant, not a resigned Germany which in the face of the demands of politics and everyday life had withdrawn into itself, but a combative Germany which regarded critique and reform

---

[2] Stefan George, 'Die Bücher der Hirten- und Preisgedichte, der Sagen und Sänge und der Hängenden Gärten' [1895], *Werke*, Ausgabe in vier Bänden (München: Deutscher Taschenbuch Verlag, 1983), p. 65.
[3] Gundolf to Karl Wolfskehl, September 1899; Stefan George und Friedrich Gundolf, *Briefwechsel*, herausgegeben von Robert Boehringer mit Georg Peter Landmann (München and Düsseldorf: Küpper, 1962), p. 39.
[4] Gundolf to George, 12 October 1910; *ibid.*, p. 206.

of language, poetry and poetic prophecy, as a long-term but for that reason all the more enduring means for the transformation and renewal of the nation. The *Blätter für die Kunst*, founded by George and Carl August Klein in 1892, saw its goal as being above all to restore to the Germans the lost figure of the poet. To George and his followers there were no poets in Germany but only scholars, officials and bourgeois who wrote verses; the worst, however, was the German man of letters— whether he presumed to produce poetry or with superficial essays and a shameless directness attempted to operate upon society as Heinrich Mann had done with his *Zola*. As 'artist, priest, prophet, ruler',[5] the poet was the sworn enemy not only of the man of letters, but – with a few exceptions – of the philosopher and scientist too; so strict was this divorce that one of the reasons for the estrangement between George and Ernst Robert Curtius was the latter's inability, originating in his Francophilia, clearly to separate the poet from the writer.

Gundolf, who later experienced difficulty in justifying his academic career to George, provided the clearest description of the anti-literary character of George's existence as a poet. In the last resort the poet embodied nature and the writer society: the poet represented values unbounded by time and elevated above such ideas of the day as change, evolution and progress; the writer was a psychologist, the poet a cosmologist, and they were related to one another 'as the seismograph is to the earthquake, the map to the landscape, the height of the barometer to the weather'.[6]

Whereas it was becoming increasingly fashionable to envision the poet too as existing within a relationship to society, Gundolf saw in him, embodied in George, a being independent of the *Zeitgeist* and in immediate touch with nature, a man in the strictest sense absolute and unconditioned. The true poet rendered a scientific investigation of man superfluous; in Gundolf's transfigured version, the German antithesis of cold reason and warmth-bestowing intuition remained alive:

In our over-wakeful, covetous, impudent, prying, prating and in its depths cold and cowardly world the poet is the guardian of the sacred flame or he is nothing ... he is the preserver of the mysterious warmth of life or he is an ornamental babbler.[7]

[5] Gundolf, 'Stefan George' [1927/8], *Beiträge zur Literatur- und Geistesgeschichte*, ed. Victor A. Schmitz and Fritz Martini (Heidelberg: Lambert Schneider, 1980), p. 235.
[6] Gundolf, *Stefan George in unserer Zeit* [1913], (Heidelberg: Weiss, 1914), p. 8.
[7] *Ibid.*, p. 20.

As prophet and poet only Nietzsche was in Gundolf's eyes the equal of George, both being united in their struggle against the delusion of the nineteenth century that the phenomena of society had anything at all to do with life and could even lay claim to impose laws upon it:

The writer as a servant of society: this was denial of spiritual freedom in an age when 'society' was no longer the bearer of the spirit, no longer an incarnate world-order ruled through and through by a 'God', a uniform fundamental force, but a network of relationships, objectives and interests.[8]

In language close in its pathos to the findings of the sociologist, Gundolf described that disenchantment and bureaucratization of the world which Max Weber had declared inescapable as a desacralizing and mechanization, a withdrawal of the gods from the affairs of the age. As a counter to society and history, but also to the German flight into subjectivity, the poet invoked the unchangeability of a myth whose end was to form the nation and the people.

Robert Montesquiou, the exemplary dandy, wanted his works – if he should ever resolve to publish them – to be printed in thirteen copies at most: twelve for his friends and one for the mob. In George's early attitude towards publication too there was something dandyish: the *Hymnen* and *Pilgerfahrten* were printed privately in only a hundred copies each, 'elevated even its smallest details above any consideration for the reading mob',[9] and it was only in 1898 that George's poems first appeared in public print, issued by Georg Bondi in three volumes. On 7 May 1909 he entered himself at the Pension Mozart at Wiesbaden as 'Stefan George, private person, Bingen', and in this single laconic phrase there is concealed more than a dandyish terror of the bourgeois: it is an expression of an attempt, extended into the private sphere because it denies the existence of the private sphere in the bourgeois sense, to lead the life of a poet in conflict with traditional conventions and in accordance with laws one has imposed on oneself. Among the principles imposed by George upon his circle was that of separating family affairs from affairs of 'state': he himself strictly declined 'to take cognizance of the families of our friends and the social and professional connections they maintain in accordance with the custom and habit of the bourgeois'.[10] Friedrich Wolters' official hagiography

---

[8] Gundolf, *George* [1920] (Berlin: Georg Bondi, 1921), p. 3.
[9] George, *Hymnen. Pilgerfahrten Algabal* [1890–2], Vorrede der Zweiten Ausgabe, *Werke*, Vol. 1, p. 8.
[10] Ludwig Thormaehlen, *Erinnerungen an Stefan George* (Hamburg: Hauswedell, 1962), p. 83.

of the George circle emphasized – as though it wanted to stress his immunity to everything societal – that it was precisely in Vienna, the 'city of the most frivolous and colourful sociability', [11] that George had passed his loneliest year, and maintained that the frivolity and superficiality of life in Vienna had been the decisive reason for the eventual breach between George and Hugo von Hofmannsthal.

Like Simmel, Breysig and Lukács, Hofmannsthal sensed the solitude and social remoteness that characterized George's lyrics:

> Die ihr mich schlinget in euren geselligen reigen
> Nimmer es wisst wie nur meine verkleidung euch ähnelt
> Spielende herzen die ihr als freund mich umfanget:
> Wie seid ihr ferne von meinem pochenden herzen!
> (You who wind me with you in your social dance
> Never know how I resemble you only in my outward garb
> You playful hearts who embrace me as a friend:
> How distant you are from my throbbing heart!)

It was precisely because this art was so timeless and so free of all social or historical reference that to Georg Simmel it represented the consummation of 'the poet's dominion over the world'. [12] It was precisely because it withdrew from everyday life that it determined the lives of a few of the elect even to their everyday behaviour; and Lukács, who saw in the man of George's songs the solitary 'man freed from every social bond,' [13] also saw that this was a lyricism, not of subjectivity, but of a particular kind of human relationship, that which George had in the *Jahr der Seele* called an inward sociableness.

This point of view was what determined the circle's aversion to or predilection for individual poets and certain genres. George was imbued with Mallarmé's longing for a language the mob did not understand, and his poetics, which consisted of aesthetic reactions rather than laid-down rules, anathematized any art which sought to achieve anything through consorting with social reality. Because their programme was not fidelity to reality but the restructuring of life through poetry George and his circle rejected the socially engaged art of a Zola, Ibsen or Dostoyevsky, just as, conversely, socialism seemed to them merely misdirected poetry. George's desire was to be unpopular because incomprehensible to the crowd,

[11] Friedrich Wolters, *Stefan George und die Blätter für die Kunst. Deutsche Geistesgeschichte seit 1890* (Berlin: Georg Bondi, 1930), p. 31.

[12] Georg Simmel, 'Stefan George: Eine kunstphilosophische Betrachtung' [1898], in *Stefan George in seiner Zeit: Dokumente zur Wirkungsgeschichte*, Vol. 1, ed. Ralph-Rainer Wuthenow (Stuttgart: Klett/Cotta, 1980), p. 32.

[13] Georg von Lukács: 'Die neue Einsamkeit und ihre Lyrik: Stefan George' [1911], in *Stefan George in seiner Zeit*, p. 137.

and Gundolf mocked at those men of letters who believed they had attained the summit of modernity because they had employed '*Kalisyndikat*' as a rhyme. The true goal was a conscious immersion in the evolution of poetry and the rejection of everything modern and fashionable: the proscribed genres included the story, the social drama and the novel – in short, all 'bourgeois interpretations of the events of life'. [14]

The circle's renunciation of all literary groupings or individual authors who made of social research an artistic creed led to a quarrel with contemporary naturalism. Gundolf counted it to the credit of naturalism that it had attempted to put aestheticism and the art of the epigone behind it and to lend a poetical voice to the world of the industrial society; none the less, one believed that 'all was done and mended when one had only overheard the most penetrating sounds of the present, especially the economic and social cries and sighs. . . when one has made of the necessity of the day the virtue of the evening'. [15] If this was what it did, naturalism was just as banal as those disciplines that sought to investigate industrial society and whose *chosisme* Gundolf indirectly criticized when he said of naturalism that its origin was 'service to the age, for the age, and that alone, whether it desired to accumulate things or eviscerate souls, practise sociology or psychology'. As Wolters, a disciple of Schmoller's, had maliciously observed, the miseries of the Silesian weavers had long since been paid for in the naturalistic boom.

The apologetics of Stefan George's adherents included the discovery, within the unholy mob he had anathematized, of above all the bourgeois and the bureaucrat, the objective being to emphasize that the poet's desire for unpopularity was in no way incompatible with the attitude of the people. The circle's declared turning away from all that had to do with the masses could in such George pupils as Klages expand to cosmic dimensions and in doing so neutralize itself; the invitation to forget that human beings exist at all or to take up the sword against 'this mouldy growth on a putrefying globe'[16] sounded murderous and never became influential. A different proposition, however, was the reaction of Gundolf, who was too rationally-minded for a flight into the cosmos but at the same time too intelligent and too much interested in demonstrating his

[14] *Einleitungen und Merksprüche der Blätter für die Kunst. Siebente Folge 1904* (Düsseldorf and München: Küpper, 1964), p. 34.
[15] Friedrich Gundolf, *George* [1920], p. 7.
[16] Ludwig Klages to Gundolf, 21 July 1903; Stefan George and Friedrich Gundolf, *Briefwechsel*, p. 136.

intelligence to be able to deny that abhorrence of everything to do with society involved not only a rejection of social science and a distancing of oneself from the bourgeois – George called them *Fettbürger* – but also led to a cold and arrogant distancing from those whose conditions of everyday life constituted what was called the 'social question':

Whoever has regarded this 'people' on a Sunday afternoon in cities great or small, and has done so with his eyes open and not befogged by humanitarian, social or progressive catchphrases, loses all desire to engage in any intelligent relationship with it, to appeal to it with 'ideas', to seek to 'educate' it. [17]

The resolute distancing of oneself from society led in the end to an inability to write of the people too except in inverted commas.

The first volume of the *Blätter für die Kunst* contained an epigram in which service to art was allied with rejection of state and society; a training as a poet consisted in renouncing all connection with contemporaries and abjuring the 'drearily sophistical Anglo-American principles and utilitarianism "of applied reason"'. [18] The objective of poetry was not to bring something about, it was the perfecting of the poet's own beauty and being. In the face of such a sacred and necessary egoism, social reality appeared unsubstantial and ineffective:

We felt how insignificant all the wars between nations, all the sufferings of the classes become before the awe at the dawning of the great days of renewal: how all the burning questions of societies fade into unsubstantial darkness when after each eternity a redeemer reveals himself to mortals. [19]

What Stefan George and his following resisted was what they called civilization–mankind: weary of so-called progress, they desired no new victories of technology over nature but, as Gundolf wrote, victories of human nature over technology. Just as history ought to transform itself back into myth, so man ought to liberate himself from society and sociology become a science of universal man. What scientific technological civilization threatened to accomplish was deadening of soul and Americanization– in short the 'ant-hillization' of the world– whereas man was not an 'inter-social ant or drone' but his own law and form.

---

[17] Friedrich Gundolf, 'Wesen und Beziehung' [1911], in *Beiträge zur Literatur- und Geistesgeschichte*, p. 173.
[18] *Einleitungen und Merksprüche der Blätter für die Kunst. Neunte Folge 1910*, p. 51.
[19] Stefan George, *Tage und Taten: Aufzeichnungen und Skizzen* [1933] (Düsseldorf and München: Küpper, 1967), p. 79.

Only to a first, superficial glance could it appear than in its repulsing of industry and the world of work, of science and technology pursued as though in a factory, the George circle was playing off culture against civilization, the heart against the head, community against society – that its opposition to the hated nineteenth century was an expression of a self-alienation which had in the familiar German manner eventuated in political resignation and a cult of subjectivity. The George circle was not merely a community of opposition, it was also a union of minds; and a divorce from everything that had to do with the state in the traditional sense was an inescapable precondition of the creation of the poet's state: 'Thus, even above the empires bounded by race and economics, unconstrained by tolls or mountains, there stands in the free and open space of its self-created atmosphere the Spiritual Empire...'[20]

How great the influence of this poet's state was can best be shown, not from the confessions of one of its members, but from the evidence of an outsider: from Thomas Mann, who had in the *Betrachtungen eines Unpolitischen* referred to George as a German phenomenon largely out of a sense of duty but three years later, when he was already on the path to acceptance of the German Republic, suspected that 'truth and life'[21] might reside in the sphere of Stefan George:

I do not know where else than in this teaching of the body and the state there can be found a positive contrast to the hopelessness of the civilization of progress and of intellectualized nihilism. I cannot be prevented from holding this view by the fact that I too am among those it denies.

The George circle

Kurt Breysig, follower and critic of Stefan George, met and talked with his students, first at Schönhausen, then at Lichterfelde; Kurt Hildebrandt wrote of this circle that it went without saying that it evinced not a trace of organization. This 'went without saying' expressed something fundamental to George and his disciples: changes to society should be the result not of planning but of the impetus imparted by a sense of life, communities should be constructed not according to the dictates of interests but through the

[20] Friedrich Wolters, 'Herrschaft und Dienst' [1909], in *Stefan George 1868–1968. Der Dichter und sein Kreis. Eine Ausstellung des deutschen Literaturarchivs im Schiller-Nationalmuseum Marbach a.N.* (Stuttgart: Turmhaus-Verlag, 1968), p. 249.

[21] Thomas Mann, 1 August 1921; *Tagebücher 1918 bis 1921*, ed. Peter de Mendelssohn (Frankfurt am Main: S. Fischer, 1979), p. 543.

pull of sympathy and appeal. The question remained as to how such an anti-organizational attitude could be organized, how moods and experiences, insight and intuition, could be perpetuated.

The George circle assumed its definitive form only gradually: *Der Siebente Ring* (1907), Gundolf's *Gefolgschaft und Jüngertum* (1909) and Wolters' *Herrschaft und Dienst* (1910) mark the changes of regime which led to the construction of the inner circle of disciples. As early as 1904, however, it was said in regard to a book exhibition of the Society for the *Blätter für die Kunst* that people falsely regarded it as a kind of secret society, whereas it was in truth no more than a loose association of the artistically inclined possessing no statutes of any kind and co-opting others of like mind merely by affiliation. When Ernst Kantorowicz described anyone influenced by the George circle as being encircled, he expressed in that description the idea of an organic growth to which the circle owed its natural survival. Such social mechanisms for preserving and extending the circle as election and formal membership were considered taboo, and it was more than a mere flourish and gesture when the Georgeans wanted to differentiate themselves from the literary world in this respect too. For, taking Mallarmé's *cercle* in the rue de Rome as his model, George had recognized what binding forces lay concealed within the true poet: 'The reason o poet that comrades and disciples are so glad to call you master is they cannot imitate you yet you are able to do such great things through them.'[22] Hugo von Hofmannsthal had an intuitive grasp of this structural principle of the circle when Carl August Klein told him about the *Blätter für die Kunst*: as he wrote with his familiar transparent irony, he very much welcomed the combination of 'exclusivity and lack of programme'.[23]

At this time George still spoke of the community around the *Blätter* as of the members of a family: the circle of friends was designated a *state* only from about 1907 by Friedrich Wolters, and from the first this had a Platonic ring to it; it also recalled Schiller's aesthetic state, which was to be discovered in a few select circles. Fundamentally, what formed itself around the *Jahrbuch für die geistige Bewegung* was a state within a state, a spiritual realm which, as George wrote to Wolters in February 1918, had or wanted to have the whole world for its enemy. The investigations of Norbert Fügen showed that the 'state' possessed between twenty and forty members; more than half came from large towns or cities, many of them belonging to

[22] Stefan George, *Tage und Taten*, p. 55.
[23] Hugo von Hofmannsthal to Carl August Klein, 26 June 1892; *Briefwechsel zwischen George und Hofmannsthal*, Vol. 2 (München and Düsseldorf: Küpper 1953), p. 22.

the educated middle class, with a large contingent of South German aristocrats and ennobled bourgeois. Though the George circle was orientated against economics, rationality and society, the concept of the state could, in the view of Claude David, justly be applied to it: one ground for saying so was the existence of a subtle hierarchy, determined always by the judgment of George himself, in accordance with which every so-called pillar of the 'state' was allotted his appropriate place. The relationship between the ideal and the real state remained problematic, it is true; in the last resort the Georgeans could never definitely decide between the alternatives of Sparta or Athens. The younger men lived in quasi-celibacy – at least so far as spiritual ties were concerned – and the separation of family affairs from affairs of 'state' assumed the traits of a *rite de passage*:

> Neugestaltet umgeboren
> Wird hier jeder: ort der wiege
> Heimat bleibt ein märchenklang.
> Durch die sendung durch den segen
> Tauscht ihr sippe stand und namen
> Väter mütter sind nicht mehr . .

(Each one here becomes reborn in a new shape: where he was born, home, is only the echo of a fable. Through mission and benediction you exchange family, rank and names; father, mother are no more . .)[24]

The circle was not spared mockery from without: as early as 1901 Hofmannsthal called the community of the *Blätter* 'a half-dressed-up half-philistine association not lacking presumption, a *cénacle* not without ill-will towards all who do not go along with them',[25] while Borchardt – pulled continually back and forth between revulsion for and admiration of George – saw at work in the circle's founder the 'true Mohammed instinct of the political prophet'.[26] But Hofmannsthal also admired how well the members of the circle could be trusted to expose their individuality only in their subjective attitudes; and when he, Rudolf Alexander Schröder and Borchardt were struggling to establish the magazine *Hesperus* all felt envious of George, whose firm and undisputed command held together a fundamentally deplorable band.

Although George set great store on differentiating between the poet and the founder of a religion the cultivation of the circle was an altogether religious procedure, and the circle itself understood itself

---

[24] Stefan George, '*Der Stern des Bundes*' [1914], Drittes Buch, *Werke*, vol. 2, p. 162.
[25] Hugo von Hofmannsthal to Graf Kessler, 16 August 1901; *Stefan George 1868–1968*, p. 70.
[26] Rudolf Borchardt to Hugo von Hofmannsthal, 23 July 1911; *Briefwechsel*, p. 49.

to be an *ecclesia invisibilis*. Something secret and mysterious had always to adhere to it, and George was uncommonly annoyed when E. R. Curtius ventured to speak of a secret France. 'In France nothing is secret – everything is public'[27] was George's response: what was assembled around him was 'the secret Germany'.[28] None the less the *ecclesia invisibilis* of the Georgeans in fact had about it as much of the French *chapelle*, the demonstrative academic–cultural defensive alliance congregated around a patron, as it did of the informal, indirect and thus all the more influential coterie of an *invisible college*. Fundamentally all such designations were interchangeable for the circle and were frequently borrowed from models and sympathizers – as, for instance, the *Jahrbuch für die geistige Bewegung* was an imitation of Albert Verwey's magazine *Die Bewegung*, whose title George had found so attractive. But whether the circle was orientated towards pedagogy rather than religion, whether it was a sect or a society – all this was of secondary significance beside the fact that Stefan George alone decided on the admission of new members, that he alone knew who belonged to the circle at any given moment, that he alone laid down the rules and decreed expulsions. Resignations did not occur, and when Kurt Breysig charged that George too had been deserted by some of his pupils the latter retorted that they had always been figures only on the periphery of the circle. Without enduring, binding and thus verifiable basic principles ever having been laid down, there ruled within the circle, accepted and promoted by its members, a spirit of orthodoxy that had to be preserved until the final victory of the Georgean cause – what Gundolf described as a spirit of peculiarity and the peculiar that would later on count as normal, just as the original 'coterie language'[29] of the *Jahrbuch* might then appear quite natural.

Exclusivity, absence of programme and a communality expressed in language and attitude rather than formal membership and articles rendered the circle capable not only of political manoeuvrability but also of political reversionism: adherents of George were later among Hitler's admirers as well as among his victims, and George was as right to emphasize his distance from Wilhelmine Germany as Rudolf Borchardt was to emphasize the acceptance of the George circle by the Prussian state. The undisguised ridiculing of Weimar democracy

[27] Stefan George to Friedrich Gundolf, 26 October 1916; *Briefwechsel*, p. 288.
[28] George, 'Das neue Reich' [1928], *Werke*, Vol. 2, p. 205.
[29] Friedrich Gundolf to Leonie Gräfin Keyserling, 10 January 1912; Gundolf, *Briefe. Neue Folge*, ed. Lothar Helbing and Claus Victor Bock (Amsterdam: Castrum Peregrini Presse, 1965), p. 101.

on the part of George and his followers, moreover, did not hinder C. H. Becker, one of the circle's sympathizers, from trying to enlist its members in the republic's official cultural life and scholarly policy-making.

Socially disengaged on principle and inimically-minded towards their own society to the point of denying and demonizing it, George's adherents constituted an alliance of an incomparable firmness of cohesion, a state within the state which exercised great influence in the Weimar Republic and especially in the domain of the university. At the same time, the stabilization of the circle's attitudes and actions in the long term was made possible only through its fixation upon Stefan George, the poet who was at once *vates* and *princeps*. George had at one time proposed to Hugo von Hofmannsthal a salutary dictatorship whose sphere should hardly be confined to the taste and temperament of the Germans; after Hofmannsthal's refusal George had to exercise this dictatorship alone. The unlimited authority accorded him explains how a circle can hold together without organization or rules; why he was accorded it, how he acquired his legitimacy as poet and policy-maker, can be explained only by viewing George's dictatorship as the epitome of Max Weber's conception of a charismatic ruler.

Poetry and scholarship

Though he was continually scolding the professors Stefan George was all his life besieged by them, and the George circle, which wanted to sow distrust of university scholarship, became an influential academic lobby in Germany. To the respect accorded him by scholars – when he asked George for a copy of his poems Heinrich Rickert emphasized that he was not a worthy old gentleman nor a typical professor and that there were some things human of which he was not wholly unaware – George responded with disrespect and mockery. Of an essay about him by Simmel he asserted he understood not a line, and to Simmel and Dilthey, who would both have gladly listened to all he had to say, he revealed only as much as, they being scholars, it was right for them to know. Only when occasionally a scholar advocated ideas sympathetic to the circle's own conceptions and thus attracted attention was the mockery tainted with a trace of jealousy – as happened, for instance, in the case of Bergson, whom in a characteristically indecisive polemic George called a Goethe of evolution. Friedrich Wolters, who glorified George and his circle but could analyse their sympathizers and opponents with a cold accuracy, saw through Simmel, Breysig and Dilthey, who lauded George, as outsiders in the border region between art and science who were in the long run unable to do justice to the phenomenon of George either as scholars or as connoisseurs of art. In the years before the First World War many a professor may have found Gottfried Benn's vision turn into reality for him in the auditoria of Germany:

And if one day your entire auditorium should rise up and bellow in your face it would rather listen to the darkest mysticism than to the gravelly grinding of your intellectual acrobatics, and kick you in the backside so that you flew from the rostrum, what would you say then?[30]

Mockery of professors and rebuking of academics did not, however, exclude a high estimation of the scholarly virtues, which George demanded of his disciples and the absence of which he bitterly bewailed: 'That I, the most unscholarly, should preach to you the German scholar: caution + conscientiousness!!'[31] How far this estimation of scholarship and scholarly procedure went can be shown through the example of philology: Norbert von Hellingrath's edition of Hölderlin was regarded as admirable because the editor understood his trade to be to serve the subject in hand; Wilamowitz and Vossler, on the contrary, were regarded as pernicious because they ventured on revaluations from a personal point of view, offered a 'Plato for servant-girls'[32] and in general pursued scholarship as 'the systematic defilement of great things'. As tools of trade certain scholarly procedures were indispensable – scholarship as an interpretation of man and world that had no desire to stand in the service of poetry was superfluous and dangerous.

For the rest, George and his circle's critique of science and scholarship, starting from Nietzsche's dictum that 'the problem of science . . . cannot be recognized in the context of science',[33] again took up motifs which were already audible in the nineteenth century and even more strongly so at the beginning of the twentieth. Their aversion to the stupid nineteenth century differed little from the attacks on it by a Léon Daudet; George saw it as an epoch that had decisively affected the contemporary attitude of mind, and threatened his disciples that he had first to kill the nineteenth century in each

---

[30] Gottfried Benn, *Ithaka* [1914], *Gesammelte Werke*, ed. Dieter Wellershoff, Vol. 6 (Wiesbaden: Limes, 1968), p. 1471.
[31] Stefan George to Friedrich Gundolf, 6 April 1900; *Briefwechsel*, p. 50.
[32] Friedrich Wolters, *Stefan George und die Blätter für die Kunst*, p. 487.
[33] Friedrich Nietzsche, *Die Geburt der Tragödie* [1872, 1886], *Kritische Studienausgabe*, Vol. 1, p. 13.

one of them if he was to make them educable. Against a background of a diffuse critique of reason and an enthusiastic glorification of the achievements of insight and intuition in the field of knowledge an assault was made on the inductive method and the erudition of the lecture-hall; the sciences were in general regarded as a product of late ages in which men had lost the almost instinctive certainty in knowing, feeling and willing which they once possessed and were obliged to avail themselves of the crutches of reflection. Criticism of the language employed by individual advocates of George's scholarship that came from outside the circle – occasionally also from within it – were answered with the assertion that what was involved here was, as was painfully obvious to the initiated, an atrophying form of poetry, the utterances of those who at least still had experiences even if they could no longer adequately express them.

George himself regarded the mysteries of antiquity as the epitome of higher wisdom. As he himself said, what was merely a matter of knowledge was alien to his nature: the humanly vital was his province; not only did he consider scientific progress a chimera, but the scientific ethos itself seemed to him fundamentally perverse. Against the communal world of a scientific community he set the aristocraticism of the solitary sage: 'One knowledge the same for all is fraud.'[34] Thus, as Kurt Hildebrandt wrote, in the George circle the errors of heroes counted for more than the truths of the mediocre, and the most resounding triumph of research was held in lower esteem than the minutest poem. That learning could not penetrate the depths of all that could be known and experienced, that science was incapable of teaching men how to live–'irresolvable is the meaning of men's lives'[35] – was common property among the Georgeans, even if there were great differences between those who, like Gundolf and Wolters, wanted to exhaust the possibilities of rationality and those who, like Klages, wagered on the powers of the irrational.

The achievements of science – which, since Kurt Hildebrandt was the only member of the circle to have concerned himself with the natural sciences, could as a rule mean only the humanities and social sciences – were not assessed by their empirical content or theoretical soundness but compared with the awakenings of mystical experience or the raptures engendered by poetry: only the latter permitted

[34] Stefan George, *Der Stern des Bundes.* Drittes Buch, *Werke,* Vol. 2, p. 167.
[35] *Ibid.,* p. 172.

entry into that higher world of cultivation that George had already proclaimed to Hofmannsthal. The enhancement of its reputation on the part of science at the expense of poetry that characterized scientific–technological civilization, the academic career of anyone who, dependent upon himself alone yet capable of deeper insight, could have become a poet, was lamented in the George circle as a sign of spiritual and moral atrophy. In addition to this, the masses of material produced by the individual specialized sciences was hardly any longer capable of being shaped into comprehensible form, so that their mode of presentation was increasingly declining in significance compared with their mode of research. On the other hand the most various attempts were being made to approximate poetry to science: absurd tendencies that led to an art that was nothing but a superficial quasi-science bringing forth caricatures of nature and society.

Friedrich Wolters, who produced the above diagnosis in his description of the George circle, saw in it no occasion for resignation, however. Even though he misunderstood Du Bois-Reymond's *Ignorabimus* as a critique of the natural sciences – it is in fact an incredibly self-confident support for scientific hubris masked as modesty – and quite wrongly associated it with the catchphrase 'the bankruptcy of science', he correctly observed that the critique of science was to an increasing extent being conducted by scientists themselves and that the so-called scientific revolution derived not least from impulses originating in the George circle. For this reason Wolters could designate it a realistic task of the Georgeans not only to participate in the reform of education so needful in Germany but to exert a decisive influence on the direction this reform took: for the bankruptcy of those who had wanted to raise their sons to be not poets but, with the aid of a rational pedagogy, men of science, was plain and obvious – the outcome of these misdirected endeavours was the 'Ullstein German'.[36] The *Blätter* community was not under the illusion that it could mass-produce poets; neither did it have any desire whatever to do so. But there existed a need to promote in men the ability to dream which a mechanic could perhaps do without but even a merchant could not. The goal of all education was the 'man capable of poetical excitation'.[37]

Hofmannsthal and others were struck by the extent of George's influence among the younger scholars of his time, an influence greater even than among the poets. One might try to become a kind

---

[36] Wolters, *Stefan George und die Blätter für die Kunst*, p. 521.   [37] *Ibid.*, p. 523.

of academic Stefan George, while as a poet one could be only his disciple, not his likeness and image. In the 'Attempt at a Self-Critique' which he prefaced to the 1886 edition of the *Birth of Tragedy*, Nietzsche regretted that what he had to say in that book he had not dared to say as a poet: 'It ought to have *sung*, this "new soul" – and not spoken!'[38] George took up this lament in the poem on Nietzsche in the *Seventh Ring* and thus laid a heavy burden of self-justification upon all those who, desiring to abandon poetry for science and scholarship, had forsaken George for a post in academia:

> Warum so viel in fernen menschen forschen und in sagen lesen
> Wenn selber du ein wort erfinden kannst dass einst es heisse:
> Auf kurzem Pfad bin ich dir dies und du mir so gewesen!
> Ist das nicht licht und lösung über allem fleisse?[39]

(Why inquire so much of distant men and read so much in books when you yourself can find out such a word that one day it could be said: I was this to you and you thus to me! Is this not light and alleviation from all labour?)

George had directed these lines at Gundolf, and when Gundolf made scholarship his career he asked George not to reproach him for his 'intellectuality',[40] explained that among his principal activities would be the public reading of poems, and in his scholarly publications distanced himself from the world of traditional science and scholarship. He placed value on mode of presentation and not merely on increase of knowledge, and – in, for instance, the foreword to *Shakespeare und der deutsche Geist* (1911) – defined method as inner experience. Things of the past he treated in a way that revealed their relationship to the life of contemporary man. When George had later sundered himself from Gundolf the implication was clear: the professors had ruined Gundolf.

The number and names of George's pupils who were awarded professorships in the humanities was impressive: in this they had the support of such cultural politicians as C. H. Becker, who in 1920 wanted to bring Gundolf to Berlin, used his influence to facilitate Kurt Hildebrandt's being called there, and would gladly have seen Friedrich Wolters a member of his ministry. From 1911 there appeared in the *Blätter* publishing house or from Georg Bondi the 'Scientific Works from the *Blätter für die Kunst* Circle', and from 1921 Ferdinand Hirt brought out the 'Works of Research and Investi-

---

[38] Friedrich Nietzsche, *Die Geburt der Tragödie, Kritische Studienausgabe*, Vol. 1, p. 15; Stefan George, *Der Siebente Ring*, Nietzsche, *Werke*, Vol. 2, p. 12.
[39] George, *Der Siebente Ring: Gundolf, Werke*, Vol. 2, p. 104.
[40] Gundolf to George, 10 November 1910; *Briefwechsel*, p. 211.

gation from the *Blätter für die Kunst* Circle' – impressive documents of the scientific policy-making objectives of a group which subordinated science to poetry.

The George circle and history

A text of Percy Gothein, who is to be accounted a member of the third generation of the George circle, shows how deeply rooted in the Georgeans was the idea that science had to be assessed according to the lights of poetry. The age in which this view was still dominant was the turn of the eighteenth and nineteenth centuries, when the greatest scholars were under the influence of Romanticism and of their experience of Goethe:

When this age of the scholarly founders was past and those that came afterwards dwelt further from the wellspring, scientific endeavour too withered into unfruitful specialization, for science does not live by its own resources but needs repeated spiritual fructification from without. All the scholars of the first generation wrote poetry in their youth, as even Mommsen did, and if their poems are not of the first order but conceived in the post-Goethean manner, they none the less exercised a fructifying effect on their lives that is not to be under-rated. What matters is not so much the poems themselves as the fact that the scholar who has to deal with the poetry of earlier ages is himself and from his own experience familiar with the poetic sphere. [41]

That Gothein should have alluded to Mommsen in this context was no accident, for to the Georgeans it was in the learned historiographer rather than the writer that, in the science-intoxicated nineteenth century, the spirit of poetry had remained alive:

The true task of the poet, from a new view of the world to acquire a new power of utterance, was in the nineteenth century more nearly accomplished by the three great historiographers Ranke, Mommsen, Burckhardt. Science, to be sure, always lies within that which an age presupposes to be ultimate truth, while the seer is precisely the transformer of this truth: but if one later takes a bird's eye view of the epigone period of German writing, Ranke's pictures of the Reformation, Mommsen's Roman history and Burckhardt's Renaissance will (regardless of whether they have since been 'superseded' scientifically) be seen to have most readily retained their power of mythical illumination, while the plays, novels and poems of even the most talented writers have long since been the concern only of the psychologists or the literary historians. [42]

It was for this reason that historiography became the Georgeans' favourite discipline, and they in turn influenced it not least through

---

[41] Percy Gothein, *Das Seelenfest. Aus einem Erinnerungsbuch* (Den Haag, 1955), p. 53.
[42] Gundolf, *George*, p. 10.

the biographies in which in a high reverential tone they sympathetically describe the life and work of great figures of poetry and history. Just as Gundolf, who could, to be sure, express himself very sarcastically regarding the biographical method and fashion, in his *Shakespeare* defines method as inner experience and thus emphasizes its untransferability, so the biographies originating in the George circle are dominated by the conviction that the only way to an improved science lies through the deliberate violation of the polished procedures of science as it exists. Ernst Bertram's *Nietzsche*, which announced itself in its sub-title as an 'Attempt at a Mythology', provoked dissent through its conception of history as the 'science and utterance of the soul' and stressed the value of legend through its confession of a disbelief in science and, indeed, in philosophy as well. George himself counted Ernst Kantorowicz's book on the emperor Friedrich II among his favourite biographies, and the contentions Kantorowicz was involved in with his guild make clear where the potentialities and limitations of a historiography in the spirit of Stefan George lay.

At the seventeenth Congress of German Historians, held at Halle on the Saale from 22 to 26 April 1930, Kantorowicz spoke on the 'Limitations, Potentialities and Tasks of the Presentation of Medieval History'. The lecture aroused great interest among both Kantorowicz's professional colleagues and the general public, so that the national edition of the *Deutsche Allgemeine Zeitung* of 26 April published a long extract from the report of the proceedings which was very probably 'discussed and decided on by the circle, if not by Stefan George himself'.[43] Part of Kantorowicz's intention was a reckoning with the critics of his book; but at the heart of his lecture there stood the official proclamation of the principles of a new kind of historiography.

Inspired by Konrad Burdach's observation that one could write history neither as a George pupil nor as a Catholic, Protestant or Marxist, but only as an unprejudiced scholar, Kantorowicz reproached positivist historical research with invading the domain of art when it sought to impose its ways of working upon historiography too. What was here called to account was the type of the historical reporter able to render a report on every epoch and every event with perfect equanimity and free from any kind of personal perplexity: 'a highly suspect type and one whose promotion would

---

[43] Eckhart Grünewald, *Ernst Kantorowicz und Stefan George. Beiträge zur Biographie des Historikers bis zum Jahre 1938 und zu seinem Jugendwerk "Kaiser Friedrich der Zweite"* (Wiesbaden: Steiner, 1982), p. 91.

in fact seem superfluous nowadays, since there is in cosmopolitan Ullstein-Germany truly no shortage of him'.[44]

With this Kantorowicz went far to equate the distinction between historical research and historiography with the distinction between cosmopolitanism and nationalism, and thus promoted what was at first sight a contention of interest only to historians to the rank of a political polemic. Taking as his starting-point certain passages from Gundolf's book on Julius Caesar, Kantorowicz assigned historical research and the historical *belles-lettres* flourishing in Germany indifferently to the camp of cosmopolitanism, whereas in the opposing view it would, in the words of Eckart Kehr, be more appropriate to make a sharp distinction between historical *belles-lettres*, 'the historiography of mass democracy',[45] and 'the theoretical work of the universities'. But this was only a sideshow in the conflict which Kantorowicz had seized the opportunity of igniting: what was of decisive significance was the alignment of positivist methodical historical research with cosmopolitan science, while historiography was, as an art, assigned to the national literature and, if written by a German, capable of being produced only from a German perspective. The historiographer Kantorowicz took his stand against the positivism of a form of research in which national feeling was sundered from feeling for truth, and thus defended those works of history proceeding from the George school whose authors wanted them to be accounted not works of analytical science but works of art.

The example of Kantorowicz shows that the ideas of the George circle touched on questions central to what the science of history in Germany understood itself to be; it also makes clear what narrow limitations were placed upon anyone who wanted to work as a professional scholar and at the same time remain a Georgean. This conflict became visible very early on in the person of Kurt Breysig and the conception of history which he represented.

Breysig's basic convictions, the fundamental tenor of his life and work, made of him an admirer and adherent of George almost by nature; added to which was his reverence for Nietzsche, at whose bier he had in 1900 pronounced the funeral oration. Yet what he saw in Nietzsche, whom he precisely equated with Comte, was above all the founder of social science – without, however, adding that

[44] *Ibid.*, p. 92.
[45] Eckart Kehr, 'Der neue Plutarch. Die "historische Belletristik", die Universität und die Demokratie' [1930], in *Der Primat der Innenpolitik. Gesammelte Aufsätze zur preussisch–deutschen Sozialgeschichte im 19. und 20. Jahrhundert*, herausgegeben und eingeleitet von Hans-Ulrich Wehler (Berlin: De Gruyter, 1965), p. 276.

Nietzsche, the mocking foe of *homo sociologicus*, had become a sociologist against his will.

With a number of former pupils of Gustav Schmoller – Friedrich Wolters, Berthold Vallentin, Friedrich Andreae, Kurt Hildebrandt and others – Breysig formed in Berlin the *Freier Bund bauender Forscher*, a group which was aware that its methods of scholarly critique and practice were indebted to George. Breysig and his pupils parted company when, in the first volume of the *Jahrbuch für die geistige Bewegung*, Wolters published his 'guiding principles': an attack on positivist science and scholarship which provoked opposition from Breysig. He too, who had once described himself as 'a happy child of nature from the university of life',[46] was not one to place absolute faith in science; he knew how much scientific research had suffered under the increasingly numerous type of the scientific official and administrator; but he also saw in science a creative force and he resisted the presumption of the artist in his attitude towards the researcher. He did not want to abandon science, he wanted to create a better science. Faced with the choice, Breysig's pupils went over to George, who in conversation with Breysig denied he had exerted any direct influence upon them. For Breysig this only made things worse: he had to recoil from a personality whose emanation defeated all argument.

Breysig wanted to cultivate history not only academically but also as a science of life. At the same time he resisted the division of science into two great zones such as Dilthey and the neo-Kantians had undertaken: there was only one science, and history was part of it. This conviction bestowed upon his ambitions something quixotic and almost tragi-comic – 'To me the history of mankind is short: large format but only two thin volumes'[47] – and rendered him receptive to every analogy that offered itself: he transcribed Nernst's law of chemical mass and Bohr's theory of electrons into sociological laws, and contrived a fantastic comparison between the motions of electrons and the marriage contracts of the Australian Aborigines. In the eyes of many of his contemporaries, therefore, Breysig remained a dilettante in every field; and since many regarded sociology as a discipline for dilettantes it was not surprising that, together with Georg Simmel, he should have been the first to deliver lectures on sociology at Berlin University, or that in 1925 he became a member of the Deutsche Gesellschaft für Soziologie and in 1929 a

[46] Samson B. Knoll, 'Kurt Breysig: Eine Einführung', *Kurt Breysig und Stefan George: Gespräche. Dokumente* (Amsterdam: Castrum Peregrini Presse, 1960), p. 52.
[47] Breysig, 7 June 1896; Breysig, *Aus meinen Tagen und Träumen*, p. 94.

member of the Institut International de Sociologie. He was influenced by Gabriel Tarde, and even Emile Durkheim once sent him a student – though it later emerged that he did so in error.

Although their theoretical positions should not be considered identical, Lamprecht and Breysig both reveal how the need for causality makes itself felt even in the science of history. Lamprecht's motto, *scire est per causas scire*, must have sounded to every Georgean like a declaration of war, a renunciation of all teleology and reliance on statistics that could without exaggeration be described as the systematic removal of the individual from the field of science.

At the end of the nineteenth century almost all historians wanted to be Rankeans: Lamprecht could triumphantly claim that he had talked with Ranke shortly before his death and that the latter had on that occasion praised his book *Deutsches Wirtschaftsleben im Mittelalter*. Lamprecht's opponents found this episode distressing, and they considered it tasteless and presumptuous when Lamprecht and his few followers wanted to be known as Young Rankeans. How inapplicable this honorary title was was shown, apart from any other consideration, in the fact that Lamprecht could not write: his style, characterized by Georg von Below as *Hetzjagdstil* – a style of precipitate haste – proved the rightness of Buffon's dictum *le style c'est l'homme même*. Whoever denied that historical and natural-scientific thinking differed in principle was a dilettante. All those who escaped into the phraseology of natural science were dilettantes. Their home was 'this science with the ungratifying name'[48] – sociology. It was against this science, which was also the product of a false conception of history, that the George circle directed its attacks.

[48] Heinrich Rickert, *Die Grenzen der naturwissenschaftlichen Begriffsbildung. Eine logische Einleitung in die historischen Wissenschaften* [1902] (Tübingen: Mohr/Siebeck, 1913), p. 255.

12

◁ ══════════════════════════════ ▷

Stefan George, Georg Simmel, Max Weber

Georg Simmel and Stefan George

The critique of science practised by the George circle found in sociology a rewarding target. In this discipline the presumption of the natural sciences rose to the height of claiming to understand even man and the human community through the rules of a universally applicable method that were as rigorous as they were remote from life. If there existed any scientific discipline to which the Georgeans felt themselves drawn it was an idiographically executed history, and that this competing discipline was at pains to deny sociology the status of a legitimate academic subject served to strengthen their attitude of hostility towards sociology. Yet the George circle's relationship with sociology was characterized by ambivalence rather than by uncompromising rejection. German sociologists – mostly philosophers or political economists who in any case rejected this label – were themselves outspokenly critical of the new discipline, while on the other hand a tradition of anti-sociological thinking grounded in the science of history and methodologically orientated towards historicism had led to the production of a German style in social science which the Georgeans did not find wholly alien to them. Thus it came about that there were on one side – for example in group sociology and the sociology of religion – attempts at applying and asserting some elements of the Georgean view of life, while on the other the Georgeans owed to sociology certain decisive elements of their philosophy of history and society. George's followers rejected sociology as a discipline but they profited from the work of individual sociologists; they employed sociological principles of interpretation without taking over the methods of sociology; the pessimistic, even tragic tone that permeated the works of a Simmel or a Weber was often an expression of their own disposition and did not as a rule mean that the presuppositions or consequences of sociological thinking had any share in it.

Of those scholars who were not themselves members of the George circle none stood closer to it than Georg Simmel, who for a time described his own work as a philosophical–sociological parallel to Stefan George's poetry. With Kurt Breysig, Simmel was among the first to pledge himself to George, and in the lecture-hall he lauded him and Rodin as the greatest artists of the age. Dedicating the later editions of his *Geschichtsphilosophie* to Stefan George, 'poet and friend', and his book on Goethe to Marianne Weber, Simmel was a mediator between poetry and science who exerted an influence on George and upon whose attitude towards knowledge and way of thinking George exerted an influence: so intimate were the conversations the two conducted together in Berlin over the years that Simmel found even Gundolf's participation in them an annoyance.

The quality which alienated Simmel from everyday academic life and blocked his university career was what made him a preferred conversation partner for George and his disciples: the courage for intuition that made his writings seem like works of art. When Simmel emphasized the advantages art possessed over philosophy and valued art as a productive detour to scientific knowledge, when he lamented the neglect of the concept of fate in modern thinking and maintained the significance of the heroic against the anti-individualist currents of the age, he must have seemed to the Georgeans to be one of them. Even George himself learned from him, and how productive discussion with Simmel was manifested itself, even if usually in a concealed fashion, in many passages of George's works – for example in the epigram '*Nordischer Meister*' in *Der Siebente Ring*, which reflects the contention between George and Simmel over the person and work of Rembrandt. Nietzsche formed a bond between Simmel and George, just as, all their differences notwithstanding, he also formed a bond between George and Max Weber. George's 'inward sociability'[1] sounded like a *leit-motif* of Simmel's sociology. Simmel and George shared the same feelings with regard to the era preceding the First World War, which Romano Guardini called the end of modern times – they both felt discomfort and displeasure at the advancing process of civilization, though they differed in the way they expressed their reaction to it.

[1] George, *Erinnerungen an einige Abende innerer Geselligkeit (Überschriften und Widmungen)*, *Werke*, Vol. 1, p. 142.

To the astonishment of the art historian Georg Dehio, Simmel comported himself before the Strassburg minster in the same way Herbert Spencer had done in Cologne cathedral: not reverentially but analytically; continually driven by an inner tension from contemplation of it to conceptualizing about it. Every amelioration of this, in the eyes of the Georgeans, pernicious impulse to conceptualize was recorded with hopeful attentiveness, as in Gundolf's letter to George of 13 November 1910: 'In general I think I perceive in Simmel, in his writings as well as in himself, traces of cosmic influence: he is growing more mature, fuller, almost more bodily. I believe we shall yet live wholeheartedly to rejoice not only in his humanity, for which I am again and again compelled to feel reverence, but even in his teachings.'[2]

Betwen Gundolf and Simmel there were striking similarities; they can be expressed in such catchphrases as 'metaphysics of the individual' or 'secular metaphysics', and led Simmel, for example, who had himself written about Goethe, ungrudgingly to recognize Gundolf's *Goethe* as the authoritative book on the subject: Gundolf, he said, had here achieved what Dilthey, who lacked the reach, had always tried to achieve. Yet even Gundolf felt obliged to distance himself when it became apparent that Simmel was always going to prefer knowledge to will, conceptual encompassment to devout contemplation. Among the George circle they pronounced that Simmel's punishment in Hell would be that 'seized with a fearful hunger for the body he would everlastingly be allowed to embrace only the images of concepts'.[3] Friedrich Wolters, in whose imagination this punishment originated, was alluding to a concrete instance: for the second *Jahrbuch* one of Simmel's pupils, Herman Schmalenbach, who was later professor of philosophy at Göttingen and Basel, had composed an essay with the title 'The Images of the Concept'. George indignantly repudiated the essay: its theme was self-contradictory, 'for the concept as such is unevident, abstract, at bottom destructive, the image concrete, shaped, creative'.[4] Schmalenbach reacted as did many whom George rejected: undeterred in his inclinations he wrote about George and his circle, and to facilitate analysis of it evolved the new sociological category of the 'league'

---

[2] Gundolf to George, 13 November 1910; *Briefwechsel*, p. 212–13.
[3] Edith Landmann, *Gespräche mit Stefan George* (Düsseldorf and München: Küpper, 1963), p. 110.
[4] *Stefan George: Dokumente seiner Wirkung*. Aus dem Friedrich Gundolf Archiv der Universität London herausgegeben von Lothar Helbing und Claus Victor Bock, mit Karlhans Kluncker (Amsterdam: Castrum Peregrini Presse/Publications of the Institute of Germanic Studies, University of London, No. 18, 1974), p. 235.

(*Bund*), on which he published a long essay in the *Dioskuren* in 1922.

The decisive, elemental distinction between Simmel and George was, as Michael Landmann correctly pointed out, that to the former everything was concept, while to the latter everything was substance: it was a difference to which Simmel's sociological interest contributed, even if it does not account for it altogether. Simmel avowed how similar the claims advanced by sociology as a discipline were to the demands the masses had been making with greater urgency since the nineteenth century, but at the same time he distanced himself from the proximity to socialism in which sociology must unavoidably be placed. This was for him sociology's tragedy, and when he quoted Schiller's 'Seen by himself each man is fairly prudent and sensible: once they are *in corpore* each becomes a blockhead' he left it in no doubt that he agreed with him.[5]

George was less inclined to a wholesale condemnation of modern civilization than many of his disciples were, and Simmel's ambivalence made the latter's sociological findings useful to him. Estrangement arose between them when George's pedagogic tendencies increased, his poetry became more didactic and the circle of friends evolved into a 'state'; on the other side, Simmel gained, if late in the day, a degree of recognition as a university teacher and this alienated him more and more from George. It is significant that George composed the epigram 'The Teacher of Wisdom' (*Das neue Reich*), which is aimed at Simmel, after Simmel, already called to Strassburg, was at pains to distinguish the influence he was able to exert there from George's esotericism and elitism:

> Seit dreissig jahren hast du gepredigt vor scharen
> Wer steht nun hinter dir? 'Kein einzelner – die welt.'
> O lehrer dann hieltest du besser die türen geschlossen
> Du hast für nichts gewirkt als für ein blosses wort.[6]
> (For thirty years you have preached before multitudes.
> Who now stands behind you? 'Not a single individual – the world.'
> O teacher, then you would have done better to keep your doors shut.
> You have worked for nothing but a mere word.)

Simmel's attempt to evolve a sociological aesthetics is an exemplary instance of what united him with George and what finally separated them. The Georgeans would accept an attempt at an aestheticizing

---

[5] Friedrich Schiller, *Gedichte. 3. Buch – Votivtafeln* [*Werke, Nationalausgabe*, ed. Norbert Oellers, 2. Band, Teil I] Weimar: Hermann Böhlaus Nachf., 1983), p. 323; Georg Simmel, *Grunfragen der Soziologie*, p. 41.

[6] George, *Das neue Reich: Der Weisheitslehrer, Werke*, Vol. 2, p. 233.

of sociology, even if they were not particularly interested in it: what they could not endure was the claim also to direct the eye of sociology upon creations of art. Simmel, however, desired both, and thus his combination of aesthetics and sociology was in the end rejected by a poet such as George no less firmly than it was by Emile Durkheim the sociologist.

Stefan George and Max Weber

In 1926 Hugo von Hofmannsthal read Marianne Weber's book on Max Weber; he counted the biography among the finest books of the year and was profoundly impressed by the 'remarkable and passionate man'[7] Max Weber. A year later, in the address he delivered in Munich on 'Literature as the Spiritual Region of the Nation', Hofmannsthal contrasted two figures who might seem to be possible leaders of the Germans in an age of productive anarchy. One was a poet even if he did not confine himself to writing poetry; genius and usurper in one, revolutionary in his Germanicism because he sought to disregard the mighty power of social forms, 'perhaps... more a prophet than a poet... a dangerous and hybrid nature, at once lover and hater and teacher and seducer'.[8] Language was to him a magical force which he pressed into his service, he bore many along with him and, refusing as he did to accept a place in the existing order but creating his own order, he affected all who came into contact with him. The poet of whom Hofmannsthal spoke could not have been Stefan George – if only because Hofmannsthal spoke of the poet's making use of the literary forms of the drama and the novel – but no one could have been more like him than Stefan George. 'Wholly contrasting with him in his basic disposition'[9] was the other figure, disciplined instead of self-vaunting, 'as constrained to the point of torment as the former is free to the point of derangement'. He was a man of science for whom the preservation of the intellectual heritage had become a dark destiny; a man passionate and heroic in his endeavour to make a science that had detached itself from life into a standard for morality. The 'hubris of desiring to rule' that characterized the former was here countered by the 'hubris of desiring to serve'. The scientist of whom Hofmannsthal spoke could not have been Max Weber, and yet it was only the personality of Max Weber that could have been painted in the dark and tragic

[7] Hugo von Hofmannsthal to Josef Redlich, 8 November 1926, *Briefwechsel* (Frankfurt am Main: S. Fischer, 1971), p. 78.
[8] Hofmannsthal, *Das Schrifttum als geistiger Raum der Nation*, p. 177. [9] *Ibid.*, p. 179.

colours Hofmannsthal chose. Both figures were, as Hofmannsthal said, only shadows and silhouettes, yet they acquired flesh and blood if one thought of Stefan George and Max Weber.

Marianne Weber has depicted at length in her biography how Weber came to be acquainted with George and what his attitude towards him was. Heinrich Rickert had drawn Weber's attention to George as early as 1897, in Freiburg, and had even recited George's poems to him: but he did so without result, for Weber, who was then at the height of his scientific creative powers, was able to see in them nothing but evidence of an artisticality and aestheticism quite alien to him. Only when he became ill did things change in this regard: Weber reacted to his nervous breakdown exactly as Comte and Mill had done before him. 'Secret chambers of his soul hitherto closed'[10] were opened up: 'Artistic images taking the feelings to ever new depths now found entry.' He now read poetry, and also read it aloud, but he did not allow it to overwhelm him and repeatedly reassured himself and others that he found the emotional world of a Stefan George or Rainer Maria Rilke remote and alien. In 1910 Gundolf, who had become a friend of Weber, brought George to meet the Webers in Heidelberg: they received him as one they hoped to teach not to learn from, and they were disquieted by the contradiction between George's simplicity as a person and the pathos of his poetry. Even before he came to know him personally Weber had expressed himself at length in a letter on his view of George's poetry and his poetical mission. He saw in George's lyrics the possibility of the representation of states of feeling that had nowhere before found utterance: it was this that made even their Dantesque pathos endurable. What he found objectionable was that George had not remained an aesthete but wanted his poetry to produce a practical effect: the aesthete who had fled from the world now sought to rule it, and the goal of all poetizing was the self-deification of the poet who felt called to be a prophet:

The path to this is either through ecstatic rapture or through contemplative mysticism. George and his school has, it seems to me, chosen the first path, because only this path permits the employment of the Dantesque means of expression proper to him. But this path – and this is his fatality – never leads to a mystical experience . . . but always only to the orgiastic booming of a voice which then seems an everlasting voice; in other words, never to *content* but only to a passionate twanging of harps. One promise of a tremendous, redemption-guaranteeing experience is outdone by another, even bigger one; new bills are repeatedly drawn on what is supposed to be coming,

[10] Marianne Weber, *Max Weber: Ein Lebensbild*, p. 463.

although the fact that they cannot be redeemed is perfectly obvious. And since it is in the end impossible to enhance further this purely formal prophethood, the poet is constantly in search of the postulated content of his prophesying without ever being able to seize hold on it.[11]

Unlike Comte and Mill, Weber desired to see in the poet only an artist, the annunciator of inner experience and of states of mind the man of science was unable to express; but he denied to the poet the possibility or the right to be prophet or seer. He was none the less impressed by the seriousness and sincerity with which George and his adherents pursued their mission; and he was as indignant at Rudolf Borchardt, who had polemicized against the George circle in the *Süddeutsche Monatshefte*, as he was impressed by Hofmannsthal, whom he met in Vienna in 1917 and who spoke well of George and Gundolf even though he knew they had by then repudiated him.

Marianne Weber depicted in George and Weber 'the polar potentialities of humanity';[12] this polarity divided them, but it did not actually set them at variance with one another. The scientific mode of knowledge here came into conflict with the artistic, but while Weber knew how to value George's existence as a poet, George, though he maintained it was remote from his understanding, could in fact respect the profound seriousness and attitude towards life that lay behind Weber's defence of rationalism. Marianne Weber characterized Weber's debates with George as warm, sympathetic and, all the differences between them notwithstanding, marked by a comprehension of one another. Yet George considered even an instructive contention profitable only over a short period, and after June 1912 he and Weber never saw one another again; Marianne reports, however, that as late as 1917 Weber read in Oerlinghausen from George's poems and Gundolf's book on Goethe.

It is instructive to note how close together the Georgeans brought George and Weber in precisely the secular domain: in his *Erinnerungen* Kurt Hildebrandt described their political positions as being almost identical – which was certainly not the case – and saw the ground of their separation as lying above all in Weber's envy of George's charisma. The desire which animated the Georgeans in this endeavour becomes clear when Hildebrandt laments the fact that Weber and George could have complemented one another as Goethe and Schiller did: the remark contains a criticism of Weber, who defined the goals of his political actions with too precise an application to contemporary reality, but it also contains a concealed

[11] *Ibid.*, p. 466–7.   [12] *Ibid.*, p. 468.

criticism of George, whose poetical political utopias could have produced a greater practical effect given the assistance of the realism
and sureness of eye of a Max Weber.

If Weber was confused by the singular combination of personal
modesty and poetical pathos which he found in George, the
Georgeans in turn found Weber no less irritating. The champion of
value-freedom had more of the tribune than the scholarly bureaucrat about him, and when Edgar Salin became acquainted with him
in the Campagna he described him, not as an academic instructor or
a colleague, but like a figure out of Böcklin:

A giant striding across the plain with great heavy paces. His sombre glance
directed more within himself than on the autumnal landscape or the
wanderer at his side – his brow furrowed by gloomy thoughts – his beard as
though charged with all the currents and impulses of the soul. The huge
slouched-hat with the broad brim might give the impression of an artist, but
the bearing was that of an unfortunate warrior from another country driven
hither by an adverse fate. There was no trace of the south in him. Germanic
traits seemed clearly to have been mingled with Slavic; neither in his coun-
tenance nor his movements nor his speech was there a glimmer of Romance
blood. [13]

It was a discourse of Salin's which, at one of the sociological discussion evenings at Heidelberg at which the Georgeans and
Weberians disputed with one another, provoked Weber to a lengthy
polemical statement of the potentialities and limitations of the
science of history. Anticipating ideas he was later to develop in the
lecture on 'Science as a Profession', Weber unfolded his concept of a
value-free science which impressed many of his hearers, Gothein,
Gundolf, Alfred Weber and Jaspers among them. Salin asked him
how, given so narrow a scientific perspective, he rated Mommsen's
Roman History, and Weber did not hesitate to deny Mommsen's work
the character of a work of science; whereupon Salin replied: 'In that
case I don't know of what mortal use your science can be or why we
should interest ourselves in it.' [14] The point of this contention
becomes apparent when we remember that Talcott Parsons, the
American sociologist who not only introduced Weber's work to the
United States but was responsible for Weber's becoming, via this
detour, a classic of German sociology graduated under the George
adherent Edgar Salin.

What attracted the Georgeans was Max Weber's personality: an
inter-weaving of life and work which, all his asceticism as to values

[13] Edgar Salin, *Um Stefan George. Erinnerung und Zeugnis* (Düsseldorf: Küpper, 1954),
    p. 108.   [14] *Ibid.*, p.111.

notwithstanding, throws autobiographical traits into clear relief in
Weber's historical analyses as well as in his work on scientific theory
and methodology. Weber's scholarly and scientific sobriety was not
an inborn characteristic but a rule of life attained to and maintained
with effort, and it was precisely the fact that he so decisively
repudiated the fashionable cult of personality that made him himself
the object of just such a cult – not only in the case of Marianne
Weber and Karl Jaspers but also with such members of the inner
George circle as Friedrich Wolters, who revered in Weber one of the
'noblest bearers of the *Zeitgeist*'[15] and saw united in him the virtues of
Simmel and Dilthey. Bewitched by George, the Georgeans as a
whole respected Weber rather than revered him; profoundly
impressed by the fact that his thought and action always cost him
something, they saw in him a Prussian puritan who fought for every
advanced position out of a sense of duty and was among those who
deprived the world of magic because the thought of any connection
with a higher world filled him with fear.

When the Georgeans confronted the poet with the sociologist
they beheld a paradox: while the poet renounced the cult of the ego
and assembled a community about him, while he wanted to create a
school so as to guarantee the survival of a poetical tradition, Weber
stubbornly clung to his isolation, the social scientist resisted the
absorption of the individual into the alliance and had a fellow feeling
for everyone, even a Don Quixote, who sought to assert himself
against institutions.

Both George and Weber seemed called upon to become leader-
figures in an age that lamented its deficiency in leadership: but
George, who had at least considered a direct involvement in politics,
in the end shrank from it; Max Weber failed to find the support a
leading role in politics would have demanded.

Weber, who had a high opinion of Zola, was by no means opposed
to a poet's being involved in politics: his suspicions were aroused,
however, when he saw poetry itself being used for the achievement
of objectives that lay outside the legitimate sphere of art. His revulsion for the latter-day prophet could only increase when he saw a
poet, of all men, step forward as seer, proclaimer of truth and charismatic leader, when what the age required was practical expertise and
a sober understanding of what was politically possible. He denounced as Romantics those who sought to oppose conditions and
developmental tendencies that could in no way be ameliorated: in

---

[15] Friedrich Wolters, *Stefan George und die Blätter für die Kunst*, p. 471.

the Calvinist sense he accommodated himself to a reality that it was beyond the power of man to transcend.

In as early a document as the report he presented to the first meeting of the German Sociological Association at Frankfurt am Main in October 1910, Weber suggested that the future work project of the German Sociological Association should include an investigation of co-operative movements, with special emphasis on artistic and literary sects. What is already hinted at here Weber himself later spelled out when he accounted the 'sects sustained by artistic cosmic feelings'[16] among the most interesting subjects for sociological investigation, and named Stefan George and his circle as an example of such a literary sect which also laid claim to be an incarnation of the divine. At the same time he pointed out that the Georgean lyric found the social environment appropriate to it in the modern metroplis, whose product it was. Simmel, too, had argued that this was the case, and George himself did not remain unaffected by this point of view.

The most far-reaching analysis of the George circle, however – and the one that wounded the members of the circle most deeply – was to be found in Weber's remarks on the charismatic leader. Even though Weber chose a man of letters such as Kurt Eisner as an example of the charismatic personality who becomes a model and leader on account of qualities that count as being more than ordinary, the reader was bound immediately to conjure up the figure of Stefan George; and how could the circle around him be better described than as 'an emotional communization',[17] that is to say what Weber called the oligarchic community? That the charismatic leadership annunciated, created and demanded obedience to new commandments, that there existed no hierarchy in the strict sense and the leader intervened only in each individual case – all this was contained in the programme of the George circle and was realized in the everyday life of the 'state' to which it was applied and whose conduct was orientated by it. Pure charisma was to Max Weber typically alienated from reality; because charismatic subsistences were determined absolutely by their detachment from the everyday world, disdain for economy had to be an element of their programme.

[16] Max Weber, 'Rede auf dem Ersten Deutschen Soziologentage in Frankfurt 1910', *Gesammelte Aufsätze zur Soziologie und Sozialpolitik* (Tübingen: Mohr/Siebeck, 1924), p. 446.

[17] Max Weber, *Wirtschaft und Gesellschaft. Grundriss der verstehenden Soziologie* [1921], 4., neu herausgegebene Aufl., besorgt von Johannes Winckelmann (Tübingen: Mohr/Siebeck, 1956), Kap. III: Die Typen der Herrschaft, §10. Charismatische Herrschaft.

Independence of means could be the existential basis of charismatic groups, and it was

conceivable in the case of a group of disciples primarily artistic that elevation above the economic battle is accounted normal through limiting those who are truly called to the 'economically independent' (that is to say, *rentiers*: as in the circle of Stefan George, at least according to the original intention). [18]

This provided a sociological explanation of the alienation from the ways of the world exhibited by George and his pupils: it was neither a whim nor the expression of a point of view that might be amenable to correction, but a necessary precondition for the creation of a circle at all and for the survival of a group orientated by poetical-prophetic pronouncements and revering in George its charismatic leaders. That Max Weber regarded charisma as the antithesis of enduring institutions, and set in opposition to it a professional training, was bound to intensify even further the conflict between prophetic poetry and sober analysis of the world.

Attempts were made, both from within and outside the George circle, to refute and correct Weber's economic analysis of the class situation of the circle's members. It was hinted that the Georgeans lived directly on their income and not by investing it and living off the interest; and Leopold von Wiese emphasized that the members of the circle had been not petty bourgeois *rentiers* but either of the upper class or people of reduced circumstances. The reaction within the George circle itself consisted less in an attempt to criticize the empirical accuracy of Weber's analyses than in taking issue with the tone of voice in which he had spoken of George and his disciples. It was found improper and spiteful and, what weighed the most, to reveal for the first time a betrayal of his own ideals on Weber's part: in his remarks on the George circle there could no longer be any question of a science free of value-judgment, and even those who had long refused to accede to George's harsh verdict on it now came to regard it as a 'poor Heidelberg scarecrow'. [19] While the Georgeans had formerly joined with Weber in revulsion at the men of letters of the lecture-hall, they now found his so-called analyses to be mere abuse of men of letters: after this blunder the 'objective science' of Max Weber could make even less claim to be serving the living spirit. The problem George's adherents faced was the same as that faced by the French and English men of letters: while they combatted soci-

[18] *Ibid.*, p. 142.
[19] Kurt Hildebrandt, *Erinnerungen an Stefan George und seinen Kreis*, p. 125.

ology as an expression of philistinism and dilettantism, as the embodiment of fake science and hubris in the realm of knowledge, at the same time they were able to formulate their philosophy of history, social criticism and visions of the future only with the aid of sociology.

In his introductory essay to the first volume of the *Jahrbuch für die geistige Bewegung* (1910) Karl Wolfskehl discussed the George circle's intention to exclude from its purview all questions pertaining to society or the state, and countered the reproach that such a limitation meant losing touch with real life with the question of what sense there could be in maintaining contact with a society which

itself lacks all the natural relationships out of which a people articulates itself into the living bodily expression of a common soul, which laboriously conceals in inherited forms of organism its inability itself to create new forms, a society that dares not venture to discover a plastic expression for any of its common needs, which was not robbed of divinity, deprived of all life, as soon as it assembled itself together. . .[20]

This was not the language of sociology, but it was, in a different idiom, an expression of the attitude critical of, indeed hostile to, society adopted by many sociologists in Germany, and Wolfskehl plausibly named the 'observations and conclusions of present-day social science' as the source of his remarks.

Two years later, in the introductory essay to the third volume of the *Jahrbuch*, an attempt was undertaken to designate the various decisive perspectives under which contemporary society had evolved. Among them were tendencies towards Catholicization, which, because they rejected Protestantism as the source of a bourgeois society orientated towards liberal utilitarianism, the Georgeans welcomed with particular enthusiasm: capitalism, industrialization and modernization were, in their view, fruits of the Protestant spirit against which Catholicism might serve as a bulwark. This close connection between Protestantism and capitalism, however, was, the Georgeans underlined, 'not a malicious supposition but something demonstrated irrefutably in the classic work of Max Weber'.[21] The third volume of the *Jahrbuch*, with which Simmel too was profoundly annoyed, led to a contention between Weber and George and Gundolf, the cause of which lay not so much in the latters' adoption and interpretation of the Protestantism thesis as in

---

[20] Karl Wolfskehl, 'Die Blätter für die Kunst und die Neuste Literatur', *Jahrbuch für die geistige Bewegung* 1 (1910), p. 12.
[21] 'Einleitung', *Jahrbuch für die geistige Bewegung* 3 (1912), p. vii.

Marianne and Max Weber's suspicion that certain disapproving remarks by the Georgeans, contained in the same introduction, on the modern woman's efforts at emancipation were directed at the Weber household. George denied this in conversation with the Webers; but, as Marianne Weber writes, the Webers received this assurance only as an expression of George's opinion, not as proof that their suspicions were unfounded.

Likewise in 1910, Gundolf had opined of the maxims of the *Blätter für die Kunst* that they were marked 'by an almost statesman-like insight into the games of hide-and-seek the *Zeitgeist* plays with itself, full of sound human understanding and good humour'.[22] This remark claims for the Georgeans a sociological, if not meta-sociological, competence which they in fact possessed. Some of George's pupils were closely associated with sociology: Wolters was a favourite pupil of Breysig and of Schmoller, and in 1908 Georg Bondi published in Berlin a *Festschrift* dedicated to Schmoller – *Grundrisse und Bausteine zur Staats- und Geschichtslehre* – all the contributors to which, namely Breysig, Wolters, Berthold Vallentin and Friedrich Andreae, were, if the expression is not taken too narrowly, Georgeans. The Georgeans were attentive and approving readers of Tocqueville, and Stefan George even recognized – after his own fashion, as Salin emphasizes – the significance of such a writer as Keynes. And it was precisely because George feared the victory of the 'Anglo-American model ant'[23] that sociology – which was moreover still a young discipline 'and therefore not yet so ploughed up or so enmeshed in a thick network of concepts and causes as the others'[24] – was useful for acquiring knowledge of this danger.

And even if Salin declined to discuss in the *Archiv für Sozialwissenschaft und Sozialpolitik* an essay emanating from the centre of the Georgean 'state', 'Rule and Service' by Friedrich Wolters – he no doubt rightly assumed that the journal would in any case refuse a review of such a publication – close contact remained with Simmel and Max Weber. There was also Alfred Weber, under whom Kafka graduated; unlike his brother he was not without artistic gifts, and, strongly sympathetic towards George and his circle, he pursued a critique of modern capitalism and its inimical effects on culture. That Alfred Weber should have reproached academic sociology with having lost itself in systems and catalogues, and desired to restore it to being an

[22] Friedrich Gundolf, *Das Bild Georges*, p. 139.
[23] Edith Landmann, *Gespräche mit Stefan George*, p. 34.
[24] Erich von Kahler, *Der Beruf der Wissenschaft*, p. 74.

existential science, must have made him seem to the Georgeans an adherent of their own principles.

When Friedrich Gundolf delivered his inaugural lecture at Heidelberg, Stefan George and Max Weber were among the audience. Gundolf never wearied of speaking to George of Max and Alfred Weber as scholars sympathetic to the ideas of the circle. 'Of all the professors, the two Webers seem to me to have felt most a sense of the deeper life,'[25] he wrote to George in November 1910, and he added: 'not only as knowledge, as in the case of Simmel, but as wanting and willing'. And a year later, when Gundolf discussed 'questions of the year-book (not the Year-Book itself)'[26] with Max Weber, he immediately felt obliged to inform George how astonished he had been 'at the abundance, the seriousness and the force of this man'. The mediating role Gundolf played – and was permitted to play so long as George was interested in it – did not affect his rejectionist attitude towards sociology, to which he denied on principle the status of an independent discipline. His jeering remark that sociology was not a science but a Jewish sect may have been aimed at Simmel; but it also struck at Max Weber, who had so often described the George circle as a sect. Weber's protestations that the expression was value-free when he employed it did nothing to assuage the indignant Georgeans, who saw in it a war-slogan that called the legitimacy of their poets' 'state' into question. Gundolf was, to be sure, sufficiently his own man to feel free to jeer at sociology and its exalted claims – and not least at that species which obtruded itself in the guise of philosophy of life. In April 1913 he drew the attention of Countess Keyserling to a course of lectures:

In addition they are now haunted by a Viennese friend and patron of Bergson named Biach, which seems to be an Hebraic combination of a German sigh (*Ach*) and the Greek *bios*, life: that is why he is a biologist or what in today's circumstances one can only be, a sociologist.[27]

Gundolf's distancing of himself from sociology did nothing to diminish his high opinion of Max and Alfred Weber – on the contrary, it permitted him a sovereign appropriation of many of their ideas and convictions; so that in 1927 Hildebrandt could assert with astonishment that Gundolf was now writing him letters in which he advocated a value-free science quite in the manner of Max Weber. It

---

[25] Friedrich Gundolf to Stefan George, 21 November 1910; George and Gundolf, *Briefwechsel*, p. 213.　　[26] Gundolf to George, 5 Decemebr 1911; *ibid.*, p. 229.
[27] Gundolf to Leonie Gräfin Keyserling, 18 April 1913; Gundolf, *Briefe. Neue Folge*, p. 119.

is to be doubted whether Gundolf went quite that far – what is beyond doubt is that, however much George may have influenced it, his own conception of the nature of science received its definitive form through his contention with Max Weber.

After the departure of Else Jaffé and Countess Keyserling, Gundolf described Heidelberg as an abode of duty through which he had to replace with achievement and good works what he had been denied by grace, and this finds its reflection in his letters and in his conversations with Max Weber as an attempt 'to dig out the instinctual foundations of creative German theology, which are at the same time the instinctual foundations of the entire Enlightenment',[28] in the history of German culture from Luther to Lessing. Gundolf's attempt to comprehend the history of culture and religion through anthropology is the result of an extremely fruitful engagement with Weber's sociology of religion, which also led him to abandon the too narrow perspectives of a study of history confined principally to the realms of literature and poetry.

Gundolf's efforts, within the framework of the contention surrounding the *Jahrbücher*, to give a precise shape to his own conception of science reveal everywhere the influence of Max Weber: it is visible in Gundolf's rejection of aestheticism in art and of scholasticism in science, as it is in the warning he utters against the workaday trivialization threatening science. His endeavour to cure 'cerebral mechanization'[29] through 'sensual contact with substance' may, to be sure, have seemed illusory to Weber, and his devaluation of the conceptual at the expense of experience and intuition indicates the point at which even Gundolf and Max Weber had to part company. Gundolf wrote that the separation of thought and life was the curse of the epoch, but Weber saw in it a destiny that could be eluded neither through intellectual formulae nor through the rules of life of a literary or artistic sect: it had to be endured. To appeal to Plato, with his unity of knowledge and experience in which instinctual functions were extended into the realm of cognition, was, in Weber's view, nostalgia and self-deception; and he could hardly have been impressed by Gundolf's reference to Bergson, in whose work, Gundolf said, concepts sprouted forth as if from a 'tree of life nourished by dark juices'.[30]

Gundolf's contention by letter with Karl Vossler, who had criticized his book on Julius Caesar, was – in the year in which Marianne Weber's biography appeared – also a debate with Weber

---

[28] Gundolf to Leonie Gräfin Keyserling, 29 May 1911; *ibid.*, p. 79.
[29] Gundolf to Friedrich von der Leyen, 8 July 1911; *ibid.*, p. 89.   [30] *Ibid.*, p. 90.

and a rejection of sociology. In Vossler's proposal that such phenomena as fame and genius should be referred to social and psychic factors Gundolf could sense the growing danger which literature was facing from the ever more clearly emerging sociology of knowledge – Karl Mannheim's essay on the 'Ideological and Sociological Interpretation of the Creations of the Mind', which was also published in 1926, seemed to him like a call to battle.

Gundolf was familiar with mistrust of one's own feelings, and spoke of the desire 'to exhibit a cool head rather than a warm heart',[31] yet he continued to maintain that even in the realm of science the search for truth was not enough: *veritas* must be joined with *verecundia*, a judicious awe of those mysteries out of which truth was born. For reverence and respect seemed to Gundolf to be more gravely threatened than was the capacity to criticize, and when he saw in the existence of a single poet – who was now again distinguished from the writer – a surer guarantee of human dignity and the future of culture than he did in that of a thousand scholars, he was echoing the credo of a community from which George had expelled him.

However much Gundolf might, directly or indirectly, want to distance himself from Max Weber, however vehemently he might mock at the scarecrow objectivity which was often nothing but our grandfathers' subjectivity, he none the less spoke of Weber's 'grand sociology'[32] even when he distanced himself from it, and he left it in no doubt that Weber was one of those heroes to whose witness and survival so large a part of his own work was dedicated:

I am very sad at the death of Max Weber; although I shared few of his opinions, I know of no one left in the old world that is now going under, and of which he was a part, of an elevation, force and nobility equal to his.[33]

With Alfred Weber, who was with Gothein one of the most decisive advocates of his admission to an academic post, Gundolf enjoyed a relaxed relationship that occasionally verged on condescension; he also no doubt regarded Weber's cultural critique, whose acerbity he once ironically contrasted with the milder tone of the *Jahrbuch*, as an almost worthless attempt to employ the methods of sociology to outbid some of the assertions of the George circle. He accorded Alfred Weber respect, but no more than respect. When Max Weber's brother was sixty years old Gundolf dedicated a poem to

---

[31] Gundolf to Karl Vossler, 4 May 1926; *ibid.*, p. 215.
[32] Gundolf to Herbert Cysarz, 14 November 1926; *ibid.*, p. 220.
[33] Gundolf to Kurt Osswald, 23 June 1920; *ibid.*, p. 178.

him that was not much better than a piece of occasional verse written in an album:

> Ohne uns von deinen vielen
> Wegen eines zu bezielen
> Lass uns dankbar dich begleiten
> Mit und in dir durch die weiten.[34]

(Without directing us to any one of your many paths, let us gratefully go on ahead with and through you.)

But when George Bondi published a book of Gundolf's poems in 1930 – Karl Wolfskehl objected to the narrowness of the selection Gundolf had made – the slim volume contained a poem on Max Weber which, while its poetical quality can likewise not be considered very high, betrays in its choice of words and in its rhythms how great the impression Weber made on him must have been:

MAX WEBER

> Die jahrzehnte die uns jetzt gebrauchen
> Soll kein schwelgerischer dunst durchrauchen.
> Einer zwang die schönen und heroen
> Mit dem wort aus liebe fluch und drohen
> Noch in heilsgesicht und fernensage.
>
> Du warfst in die trümmer deiner tage
> Heut, entledigt der geputzten schilder,
> Dich mit nacktem herzen quer durch bilder
> Deines grauns und hoffens .. branntest, sprengtest
> Dich in jede not .. ob du verengtest
> Deine herrliche weite für die wichte
> Ob du überschwangst in weltgeschichte,
> Dir entrückt, und niemals auf der lauer
> Deines glücks noch bang um eitle dauer.
> In den wust gehäufter unratmassen
> Trotzte sich dein wille, um zu fassen,
> Um zu wissen, um zu büssen deine
> Schaffenslust im opfertod der scheine.
> Du, versucht wie keiner aus den schwärmern
> Vom geraun der himmel, und den wärmern
> Festen, mären, räuschen zugedrungen ..
> Von sirenen mehr als wir versungen:
> Huld und macht! Zu künden und zu üben
> Deine huld und macht im leichten trüben,
> Vor dem flor des schau-spiels, über schwünden

---

[34] Gundolf to Alfred Weber, for 30 July 1928; *ibid.*, p. 225.

Wehrtest dir als billigste der sünden. . .
Du zerrissest eher die behänge
Die zu schön sind und das gottgepränge
Das beschwichtigt, eh der kampf begonnen.

WAHRHEIT nach dem untergang der sonnen,
Abgerungen den erwürgten wähnen,
Ungelohnt vom Drüben, und mit tränen
Die der mann verbergen muß dem nächsten . .
Wahrheit im getümmel der behexten
Die sie lernen, um für neuen glauben
Sie zu tauschen oder zu zerklauben . .
Wahrheit ohne rast auf mürben kissen
Ohne wiederkäun der fertigen bissen . .
Wahrheit als die blöße noch der würde,
Auf dem nacken wuchtend jede bürde
Der gestürzten götzen und die völle
Des gehöhlten firmaments als hölle,
Trugst du aus dem grund durch tausend türen,
Führer, frei vom lug wohin sie führen.
Und wir, zweifelnd jeder ständigen mitte,
Segnen, vor den zielen, solche schritte,
Vor den sätzen, deine lautre stimme,
Dein ermutend lächeln der im grimme
Wach beschwingten treue . . und wir wagen
Deinethalb die antwortlosen fragen.[35]

Thus the dilemma confronting the Georgeans is here repeated: sociology might be a petty bourgeois discipline but he who embodied the potentialities of the discipline most convincingly was anything but bourgeois. In retrospect it has been justly observed how disproportionately slight the influence of Max Weber was in the 1920s, and that during this period there could be no question of designating him a classic of sociology. Among those who came to recognize his quality early and never harboured any doubt of it were the Georgeans: to them Max Weber was more than the classic writer in his discipline, he was – all differences notwithstanding – a great human being.

[35] Friedrich Gundolf, *Gedichte* (Berlin: Georg Bondi, 1930), pp. 23–4.

◁ ══ ▷

13

Weberian motifs in the work of Thomas Mann

Middle-class novel and truth-game

In his Munich lecture of 1917 on 'Science as a Profession' Max Weber described how in the modern world the ultimate and sublimest values had increasingly disappeared from public life, to survive either in the form of world-renouncing mysticism or in the fraternalism of direct relationships between individuals. Art, too, was no longer monumental, but had become increasingly intimate, so that 'today it is only within the smallest community, from man to man, in *pianissimo*, that something still pulsates which corresponds to that which in earlier times as a prophetic pneuma passed in a storm of fire through the great communalities and welded them together'.[1] It was not in Weber's nature to call to mind that other mode in which knowledge of the world and distancing from the world were fused together and sympathy, love even, was refined to extremely indirect forms of expression: irony.

Irony was the stylistic device employed by Thomas Mann, and perhaps he wrote no more ironical or self-ironical book than the *Betrachtungen eines Unpolitischen* (1918), a 'truth-game'[2] and piece of experimentation in which engagement is ingeniously combined with detachment. It is also the book in which Thomas Mann's relationship with Max Weber begins to sound for the first time like a *leit-motif*, a roguish quotation, that recurs in altered form in subsequent passages in his works.

The *Betrachtungen* was bound to produce an ironical effect, if only because Mann, who was here writing against the Western democracies with their bourgeois and *citoyen* ideals, was also the author of

---

[1] Max Weber, *Wissenschaft als Beruf, Gesammelte Aufsätze zur Wissenschaftslehre*, p. 612.
[2] Thomas Mann to Karl Kerényi, 7 October 1936; Karl Kerényi and Thomas Mann, *Romandichtung und Mythologie: Ein Briefwechsel* (Zürich: Rhein, 1945), p. 57.

Buddenbrooks, a middle-class novel as he himself had called it in a letter to his brother Heinrich of November 1913. Thomas Buddenbrook appears in it not only as a symbol of the German middle class but as the embodiment of the modern bourgeois as such. The achievement-orientated moralist was for Mann the hero of the modern world, and he stressed how deeply not only *Buddenbrooks* but also *Fiorenza, Königliche Hoheit* and the figure of Gustav von Aschenbach in *Der Tod in Venedig* were impressed with his empathy and poetical sympathy with this type:

I set some store on confirming that I acquired the idea that the modern capitalist businessman, the bourgeois with his *ascetic* concept of professional duty, is a creation of the Protestant ethic, of puritanism and Calvinism, entirely on my own account, without having read it, through direct insight, and that it was only afterwards, not long ago, that I noticed that learned thinkers had also been thinking and saying it. Max Weber in Heidelberg and Ernst Troeltsch after him have treated of 'the Protestant ethic and the spirit of capitalism', and the idea is taken to an extreme in Werner Sombart's 'The Bourgeois', which appeared in 1913 – in which the capitalist entrepreneur is interpreted as a synthesis of hero, merchant and citizen. That he is to a great extent right is shown in the fact that I had as a novelist given shape and form to his teaching twelve years before he himself exhibited it: supposing, that is, that the figure of Thomas Buddenbrook, the anticipatory embodiment of his hypothesis, exercised no influence on Sombart's thinking.[3]

This was a bold claim to priority based on chronology which Georg Lukács took seriously when he spoke of the 'Buddenbrookizing'[4] and 'Aschenbachizing' of some of the leading sociologists of Mann's time such as Rathenau, Max Weber and Ernst Troeltsch. It is true that Mann himself to some extent withdrew this claim to priority: the reason he and a succession of social scientists with him had made the connection between the Protestant ethic and the spirit of capitalism their theme was that they had all read an author who stood at the centre of their thinking: Friedrich Nietzsche. Nietzsche was to so great a degree an enduring theme of Thomas Mann's thinking that he could write of Ernst Bertram's book on Nietzsche that he was 'devoted to it as a sibling of mine'[5] – by which he meant the‍ *Betrachtungen*. The relationship with one another of two readers of Nietzsche, the traces which the thinking of Max Weber left in the work of Thomas Mann, demonstrate again how rich in tension the

[3] Thomas Mann, *Betrachtungen eines Unpolitischen*, p. 145.
[4] Georg Lukács, 'Auf der Suche nach dem Bürger' [1945], in *Thomas Mann* (Berlin, DDR: Aufbau-Verlag, 1953), p. 22.
[5] Thomas Mann, 11 September 1918; *Tagebücher 1918–1921*, p. 3.

relationship of the social sciences with the poetic imagination has been in Germany.

It is not merely an ironical distancing from the social sciences and from psychology that characterizes the *Betrachtungen*: the book is permeated by a retreat from the realm of the social in general, a decisive taking of sides with the individual against society which from the beginning allows Mann to define irony as a personal, not a social ethos. He resolutely rejects an art that is open to misuse as an agent of social–political reform. Rousseau stood at the beginning of that evolution that led to the identification of democracy with politics as such and degraded poetry to social literature; the nature of Germany, however, resisted the politicization of every ethos, a process of Latin origin, and, accepting the authoritarian state as the only form of state suited to it, espoused culture as against civilization, soul as against society, art as against literature and music as against politics. While in France a social mathematics obtruded even into the novel and the drama, the German was by nature protected against any temptations of this sort:

> He will never agree that society is the same thing as 'life', never rank the problems of society above the moral, the inner experience. We are not a social nation, nor a mine of information for idle psychologists to pick up.[6]

The German would become an exemplary human being and the German nation an exemplary nation because here human being and nation were not merely social but also metaphysical entities. 'The social realm is a very questionable domain morally; it has the atmosphere of a menagerie',[7] Mann says, with that pessimism which is in his eyes the only appropriate attitude when dealing with questions of importance; and he proffers the authoritarian state in the German mould as a model for the Western democracies in which the state is suffering more and more from the loss of its metaphysical character and society is becoming ever more homogeneous. Conflict between individual and society seems to Mann unavoidable, and he aligns himself with the programme of the counter-Enlightenment because the social life glorified by the Enlightenment 'is and remains the sphere of indigence, compromise and irresolvable antinomies'.[8] The *Reflections of an Unpolitical Man* is an anti-social pamphlet and an anti-sociological tract as well: when Mann explains the increasing sacralization of society as following from a decline in the functions

---

[6] Thomas Mann, *Betrachtungen eines Unpolitischen*, p. 35.
[7] *Ibid.*, p. 252.   [8] *Ibid.*, p. 256.

of the state, and appeals to the political science of an Adam Müller as a model, he certainly places himself within the tradition of carping at and criticizing Western social science out of which there emerged a specifically German tradition of sociology; and yet not only his later position but that which he already adopts in the *Betrachtungen* resembles the attitude of the man in one of Tallemant de Réaux's *historiettes*, who made a long speech full of conviction, but at the end of it, as though against his will, could not prevent himself from saying, 'Cancel all that!'

For Thomas Mann is writing in the first instance not for a certain circle of readers but above all against a reader who probably never in fact read the *Betrachtungen*, against his brother Heinrich, the civilized man of letters; and the book is permeated with a fraternal hatred which can never belie the fact that it must therefore also be directed against his own origins and his own nature.

Heinrich Mann had taken up the position of the enlightened man of letters against which his brother mounted his attack in the essays 'Intellect and Action', 'Voltaire-Goethe' and 'Zola', published between 1910 and 1915. In these essays the French appeared as the enviable chosen people because they were able to feel so secure in their literary instincts; the man of intellect was embodied in the man of letters, and the novel was the art-form of democracy – struggling democracy in the case of Balzac, democracy triumphant in the case of Zola. Zola furnished Heinrich Mann with all those catchphrases that were bound to provoke Thomas Mann – not least the characterization of democracy as an applied science of man, a sociology or anthropology *in vivo*.

How greatly Thomas Mann was affected by this is shown, all else apart, by his having brought Goethe to the field to combat his brother's Zola: a work of art, he said, could certainly produce moral results, but to make a moralist of the artist was to trespass on the artist's preserves. Democracy extolled as applied sociology was thus a 'state for novel-writers',[9] humanized and capable of literature, amusing and entertaining, populated by easily manageable men of letters who could if need be compose treatises on political economy with such facility that you might imagine they had never done anything else. Offering itself in this fashion, the social–critical novel had become a firm constituent of democracy; what had been lost on the way, however, was art, and the social involvement of a Zola demonstrated above all that he was finished as a writer. The civilized

[9] *Ibid.*, p. 301.

man of letters was an enlightener and an author, a democrat, revolutionary and *romancier*: in short, a kind of honorary Frenchman; and in attacking in the *Betrachtungen* the civilized man of letters Mann attacked that civilization in which literature was regarded as being self-evidently a constituent part of political power, namely France.

The reduction of the world to a domain of the bourgeois and of literature was the work of the French. An *entente cordiale* of civilization had fallen in and attempted to play the First World War as an outsized Dreyfus affair. In this situation, to recommend France and French *esprit* as a model for the Germans to copy constituted high treason, and the intellectual collaborators with the enemy were proposing that the Germans should adopt social science and the social-critical novel at precisely the moment when a fundamental shift in opinion on this matter was beginning to take place in France: Mann cited Charles-Louis Philippe, who in 1905 had rejected the *roman à thèse* on the grounds that it was no more than the misuse of a literary genre for the pursuit of social and psychological studies.

Hôtel de la Civilisation

Among the French writers of whom Thomas Mann spoke with respect was Romain Rolland. The author of *Jean-Christophe* was a significant figure for his own country: but his novel must also appeal to the Germans, for it was not a typical French social novel but a psychological novel of the German kind, which had, moreover, a German musician as its hero. Towards the conclusion of the *Betrachtungen* Mann quotes with endless delight long passages from those sections of *Jean-Christophe à Paris* which deliver an annihilating critique of the Third Republic from a French viewpoint; he cannot resist repeatedly citing Rolland's own words, so greatly do 'these pages swarm with judgments that accord with the basic motifs of the present book'. [10]

If after reading Thomas Mann's book we go on to read *La Foire sur la Place* and *Dans la Maison*, which two volumes together constitute *Jean-Christophe à Paris*, we are even more astonished at the similarities between the German essay and the French novel, and it becomes clear that Mann has borrowed motifs of his critique of France from Romain Rolland even where he does not actually refer to him: thus Rolland's mockery of the French Navy Ministers who – to ennoble the fleet and out of aversion to war – named their battleships *Descartes*

[10] *Ibid.*, p. 560

and *Ernest Renan* may have inspired Mann's cutting remark about the French trawlers that went hunting for fish with the watchwords of the Enlightenment inscribed on their bows.

But how could a German partisan of the counter-Enlightenment have concealed his delight at a French novel in which a German, Christoph Krafft, having arrived in Paris after a long train journey in the company of dull Frenchmen, seeks a cheap hotel within reach of his modest purse and finally discovers in a dirty side-street the even dirtier accommodation he can afford and finds it is called the Hôtel de la Civilisation! How could Thomas Mann have refrained from quoting whole pages of a book in which the civilized men of letters of a shabby Paris, one and all unmusical and devoted to the 'spirit of cerebral prostitution',[11] are as 'mendicant friars and Jesuits of reason'[12] upholders of democracy's reign of terror! How could Mann have described better the vices of a republic which was in reality a disguised aristocracy:

The customs of the court dominated this republic without republicans; there were socialist newspapers, socialist deputies who lay on their bellies before kings passing through, lackey-souls that stood at attention before titles, gold-braid, decorations; to keep them on the leash all one had to do was to throw them a couple of bones or the Legion of Honour.[13]

Mann could have quoted further passages and would no doubt have done so if he had not been a reader not only of Max Weber but also of Emile Durkheim: for the strategy of ruling employed by this oligarchy of intellectuals and men of letters disguised as a republic also included stuffing the leaders of the proletariat with an indigestible quantity of education and thus stupefying and bewildering them, in which process the university extension courses providing instruction in physics, biology and sociology played an inglorious major role. And Romain Rolland's characterization of the Parisian intellectual culminated in the assertion: 'Even the daintiest notions had to be spiced with sociology: at that time everything employed the cloak of sociology.'[14]

To criticize the Third Republic above all on account of its educational policy, and to condemn sociology because it had become a kind of state religion in place of Catholicism, counted among the standard arguments of the polemic mounted against Emile Durkheim and his school by his own compatriots. But Rolland

[11] Romain Rolland, *Jean-Christophe*, Vol. 2: *Jean-Christophe à Paris* (German ed., Frankfurt am Main: Rütten and Loening, 1922), p. 91.
[12] *Ibid.*, p. 153.   [13] *Ibid.*, p. 162.   [14] *Ibid.*, p. 136.

pretended to be expressing the thoughts of a German. He sensed that from the viewpoint of a conservative German the intellectualism of the French republicans and their addiction to sociology would seem one and the same thing. Thus the arguments once deployed against Durkheim to denounce his sociology as nothing but a laboriously disguised Germanist discipline were now reversed: *morbus germanicus* on the French side of the Rhine, sociology was accounted *morbus gallicus* on the German. This was not the least of the reasons why *Jean-Christophe* constituted so important a source for Mann's anti-sociological pamphlet.

Maurice Barrès, who in his contention with the *durkheimiens* and the educational policy they pursued had become a sociologist against his will, also plays a role in the *Betrachtungen*. In the first place Barrès could be sure of Mann's sympathy in his struggle 'against the malicious thirst for destruction of the reigning apothecary-atheism';[15] but in the course of this he also referred to the figure of Homais in *Madame Bovary* and thus to an author who had never wearied of making merry at the expense of Comte, the founder of sociology. In addition there existed similarities between the author of *Der Tod in Venedig* and the author of *La Mort de Venise* to which Mann's attention was drawn only by a third party, but which thereafter seemed to him all the more manifest. Like Thomas Mann, Barrès came from the tradition of late nineteenth-century decadence, which both overcame in a spirit of eager experimentation; that they were both nationalists enabled them to understand and respect the position of the other which each was obliged to combat. Catholic politics and Protestant moralism were hostile to but not competitors with one another. Finally, Barrès and Mann were writers, and the solidarity of men who lived by writing bound them together beyond all their political differences.

Max Weber set to music

That he belonged to the profession of writer whether he wanted to or not was responsible for the contradictions in Thomas Mann's position: considerations of political tactics would have demanded that he promulgate his views as being those of a German poet, but artistic rectitude compelled him to formulate them as the philosophy of life of a European writer. He was and remained the author of *Buddenbrooks* and thus the author of a novel – that un-German genre

[15] Thomas Mann, *Betrachtungen eines Unpolitischen*, p. 165.

whose scandalous tendency, joyfully emphasized by his brother Heinrich, was to ally itself with the political and social ideals of odious democracy. Like Stefan George, Mann too cited Nietzsche, who would rather have sung than spoken: that Nietzsche to whom he was constantly appealing yet who through his Europeanism was more greatly to blame than any other for Germany's turning to intellectualism and literature. It was almost in the sense of agreeing with him that Mann recorded that George had rejected *Buddenbrooks*: 'This is still music and decadence.'[16] He confessed that as a novelist he was an analyst of the decadence of bourgeois society who had perhaps written the first and only German naturalistic novel.

None the less, *Buddenbrooks* was a profoundly German book, 'not an extravagant work of art but life';[17] and when a French reviewer declared it to be untranslatable Mann regarded this as having quashed once and for all the suspicion that he had been under of political and artistic intellectual collaboration.

On the evidence of *Buddenbrooks* Mann was compelled to confess that he was also a European and a man of letters of the Western pattern: but at the same time he emphasized that he had always given preference to the ethical over the aesthetic, and had always been a burgher rather than a Bohemian. Yet in his time he experienced the evolution of the burgher not so much to bourgeois as to artist, for 'what I was involved with was the psychological and human; I took the sociological and political along only half unconsciously, I was little concerned with it'.[18] Against aestheticism he set his being as a burgher, but against the sociological interpretation of life typical of the burgher he set his being as an artist: whatever might be said of his 'artistic labours' they were 'always excellent scores'.[19]

Mann had contrasted music, as the Germans' fervent means of expression, with the superficial social literature of the French; *Jean-Christophe* appealed to him as a German musician's struggle against the sociological intellectualism of the Third Republic. And yet it was precisely in the case of music that his inclination for the social, for the sociological, for the motifs of Max Weber was shown to be irrepressible, for he also accounted German music from Luther through Bach to Max Reger – music as counterpoint and grand fugue – as 'Protestant ethics expressed in sound'.[20] This observation alone suffices to show that for the author of *Buddenbrooks* and the *Betrachtungen* Max Weber was more than merely a sociologist against whom one could half-seriously establish priorities in intellectual property.

[16] *Ibid.*, p. 105. [17] *Ibid.*, p. 88. [18] *Ibid.*, p. 139. [19] *Ibid.*, p. 318. [20] *Ibid.*, p. 320.

And his high opinion of Hans Pfitzner was only superficially and in an almost absurd sense connected with the fact that Pfitzner had dedicated one of his chamber works – *Two German Songs* for baritone with male chorus *ad lib.*, after texts by Kopisch and Eichendorff, Op. 25 – to Grand Admiral Tirpitz, whose naval policy Mann too said he admired; where the true affinity lay becomes visible in Mann's portrait of Palestrina:

Palestrina is the man of the pessimistic ethos. If the world 'goes forward' in a direction in which one has absolutely no faith, although one recognizes such progress as necessary and ineluctable and is even compelled by one's nature to promote it, then it is impossible to give in to one's feelings: the sense of the age assumes a personal ethical character, it is a matter of 'thy earthly course', it is a matter of 'be thou perfect'; it is a matter of holding *on* – I do not say holding out.[21]

This however was – at the heart of what Thomas Mann found congenial to him – nothing other than Max Weber set to music.

Citizen of this world

Max Weber had objected against aesthetics that it suppressed the question of 'whether the realm of art is not perhaps a realm of diabolical rule, a kingdom of this world and thus in its profoundest depths anti-godly and in its profoundly felt aristocratic spirit anti-fraternal'.[22] This is a sentence that could be discovered, without the alteration of a single word, in the works of Thomas Mann from *Tonio Kröger* to *Doktor Faustus*: it points to an elective affinity which makes the continuing influence of Max Weber in Mann's writings and letters seem only too comprehensible. To detect this elective affinity we need only to reread the *Protestant Ethics*, in which Keats and Matthew Arnold, Heine, Gottfried Keller and Gustav Freytag are among Weber's authorities – and then take up *Death in Venice*, a novella admittedly autobiographical but defiantly revelatory whose Protestant character Mann never tired of stressing. Gustav Aschenbach, a self-portrait of the author, fits into the universe of Max Weber more comfortably than any other of Mann's characters: a foe to idleness of any kind, imbued with the spirit of service and self-control, Aschenbach's favourite expression is 'hold out'.

Gustav Aschenbach was the poet of all those who work at the edge of exhaustion, of the overburdened, of those already worn out but who still hold themselves erect, of all those achievement-orientated moralists who,

---

[21] *Ibid.*, p. 421. [22] Max Weber, *Wissenschaft als Beruf*, p. 600.

though slender of growth and slim of resources, none the less through spasms of will and prudent husbanding create for themselves, at least for a time, the effects of greatness. There are many of them, they are the heroes of the age.[23]

Thomas Mann made the acquaintanceship of the 'renowned Prof. Max Weber'[24] on 9 November 1919 in the house of the barrister Max Bernstein in Munich; a month later, on 28 December, he met him again: 'Weber polemicized against Spengler and proved to be the excellent, skilful and lively speaker he was reputed to be.'[25] Weber too referred to this evening, in a letter in which he expressly mentioned the presence of Thomas Mann and said how much he enjoyed the conversation at dinner; on 29 January 1920 he wrote that in future he and Marianne wanted to draw more young people and writers into their circle, Thomas Mann in particular.

When in a lecture Weber adopted a critical attitude towards the murder of Kurt Eisner by Count Arco, rightist students demonstrated against him and the rector had to have the course discontinued. Erika Mann was in Weber's audience and she reported home about the scandal. Thomas Mann was unable to conceal a certain *Schadenfreude*: 'At bottom I am gratified at the students' nationalist anti-revolutionary sentiments' he wrote in his diary for 21 January 1920.

Remarks of this kind, however, are already somewhat backward-looking, for almost immediately after finishing the *Betrachtungen*, which appeared during the last year of the war, Mann experienced a change in many of his opinions. Towards the Europeans he continued as before to present himself as a German, but towards the Germans he now disclosed his European inclinations with less reserve. The Zolaesque, the social propagandistic, was still as alien to him as before, and he felt drawn no less intensely to the myth, to music, to the individual. The unrest in Munich made him no more sympathetic towards the politicizing men of letters than he had been, yet now he already counted Heinrich Mann as being among the type of the European writer who was more important than dramatist or story-teller. He evinced an energetic effort to understand the social domain better, an effort that finds convincing

[23] Thomas Mann, 'Der Tod in Venedig' [1913], in *Frühe Erzählungen* (Frankfurt am Main: S. Fischer, 1981), p. 569.
[24] Thomas Mann, 9 November 1919; *Tagebücher 1918–1921*, p. 317.
[25] Thomas Mann, 28 December 1919; *ibid.*, p. 352. (The following reference to Max Weber's reaction comes from M. Rainer Lepsius and alludes to Weber's correspondence with Mina Tobler).

expression in his diary entries on his reading of Balzac. *César Birotteau* left him feeling cool towards and amused by 'the French social genre',[26] yet a little later he notes concisely: 'Have again given up reading Balzac as being too social.'[27] A year later his judgment of Balzac's *La Fille aux yeux d'or* was precisely that of the French literary men of the right who lauded Balzac as a legitimate social scientist: 'The sociology of Paris that forms the introduction is magnificent.'[28] Sociology surfaces in passages scattered throughout Mann's works – not least in the *Magic Mountain*, where Settembrini's 'Society for the Organization of Progress' plans the publication of a comprehensive *Sociology of Suffering*, one volume of which is to be devoted to an examination of the theme of suffering in the masterpieces of world literature. The model for this is obviously the five-volume *Sociology of Suffering* published by Franz Carl Müller-Lyer between 1908 and 1913; but such borrowings have nothing to do with the substance of the discipline – as little as have the references in the *Betrachtungen* to the Swedish sociologist Gustav Steffen or to Bogumil Goltz, who was quite rightly mocked as a little, a very little, Carlyle. Of more significance is his collaboration in the writing of *Doktor Faustus* with T. W. Adorno, whose 'extremely progressive, subtle and profound artistic–sociological critique of situations'[29] Mann admired.

The revision of his own opinions which Thomas Mann undertook is clearly visible in his lecture 'On the German Republic' (1922): it concerns not least his relationship with his brother and thus with the profession of writer, and at vital points of the argument reaches back, either openly or in the form of allusive quotation, to Max Weber's sociology of religion.

In a sketch of his brother composed in 1925 for an American public Thomas Mann called the novel the art-form in which the poetic and the skill of the writer can succeed most easily – thus a genre to which both brothers could lay claim. Of all German writers Heinrich Mann was the one most involved with the social, a concept Thomas Mann could now employ without *rancune* while being at the same time intent on preserving his distance from it:

There are metaphysical, moral, pedagogic motives and interests – in short those belonging to the inner man – which are dear to us others: the novel of development, evolution and confession has always been the specifically

---

[26] Thomas Mann, 15 June 1919; *ibid.*, p. 265.
[27] Thomas Mann, 2 July 1919; *ibid.*, p. 277.
[28] Thomas Mann, 26 April 1920; *ibid.*, p. 426.
[29] Thomas Mann, 'Die Entstehung des Doktor Faustus. Roman eines Romans' [1949], *Rede und Antwort* (Frankfurt am Main: S. Fischer, 1984), p. 157.

German variety of this literary genre. In the case of this author alone, and attended by so much artistic polish only in his case, has the moral element borne from the first not the stamp of 'inward asceticism', to employ a term from the philosophy of religion, but that of political and social-critical expansion.[30]

At bottom nothing had changed in his inner artistic relationship with his brother: now, however, a tone of impartial cordiality ruled between them, and there is a certain irony in the fact that Thomas Mann employed concepts familiar to Max Weber to distinguish his own innerworldliness from his brother's orientation towards society. When on the occasion of his brother's birthday on 27 March 1931 he addressed the Prussian Academy of Arts on 'The Vocation of the German Writer in our Time', he spoke of a youthful project the two brothers had pursued during their time together in Rome: they worked on an endless series of pictures called 'The Life-Work' or 'The Social Order', a frieze depicting 'human society in all its types and groups... from Pope and Emperor to Lumpenproletarian and beggar – nothing was spared in this *trionfo* of social ranks, we had time to spare and we amused ourselves as we could'.[31] Heinrich Mann's 'Germanised-Latin social spirit' was already apparent in this still almost childish undertaking, yet his brother's music and metaphysics no longer represented an antithesis to it: for whereas Thomas Mann had formerly set music in opposition to politics and Richard Wagner to Emile Zola, now the fresco that was the work of both brothers was to him a product of the same century, the nineteenth, which had been the century of the *Rougon-Macquart* but equally that of the *Ring des Nibelungen*.

The sphere of the poet and the writer could now easily be united with the social sphere – indeed with that of the social sciences – and when the Prussian Academy of Arts instituted a section for the poetic arts Thomas Mann energetically advocated that, in addition to poets, critics, essayists, historians and cultural philosophers should also be accepted into it: 'If Max Weber were still alive it would be absurd to leave him out of the literary academy, and such figures as Gundolf, Ernst Bertram, and even Alfred Kerr in the long run belong in it without any doubt.'[32]

[30] Thomas Mann; 'German Letter VI', *The Dial*, October 1925', in ' "German Letters". Thomas Manns Briefe an "The Dial" (1922–1928)', *Thomas-Mann-Studien* 3 (1974), p. 51.
[31] Thomas Mann, 'Vom Beruf des deutschen Schriftstellers in unserer Zeit', *Rede und Antwort*, p. 346.
[32] Thomas Mann, 'Rede zur Eröffnung der "Münchner Gesellschaft 1926" ', *Nachträge, Gesammelte Werke in dreizehn Bänden*, Vol. 13 (Frankfurt am Main: S. Fischer, 1974), p. 597.

While the sociologist was thus becoming a man of letters, on the other side representative writers were increasingly emphasizing their interest in society and in social problems. In the *Betrachtungen* Mann had still polemicized against those who forgot Goethe's ethos of personal cultivation and misunderstood him as a social writer. He wrote the *Betrachtungen* as the catastrophe of the First World War was coming to an end; a year before the Nazis assumed power he saw in Goethe the representative of the bourgeois era and again justified his association of Protestantism with the bourgeois ethos by referring to Max Weber: 'For love of toil and labour, the ascetic faith in them, has also been characterized as a psychic accessory of the bourgeois ethos by a sociology which sees the bourgeois ethos as grounded in Protestant religion.'[33]

Mann transforms Novalis' reproach that in Goethe's *Wilhelm Meister* all that is left in the last resort is economics into an unconditional commendation of Goethe's modernity, and later on repeatedly quotes as a kind of *leit-motif* Maurice Barrès' view of Goethe's *Iphigenie* that it was a civilizing work which 'defends the rights of society against the arrogance of the spirit'.[34] Mann sang a hymn to what he called Goethe's citizenship of this world and his late Saint-Simonianism, his inexhaustible interest in the proposed cutting through of the isthmus of Panama and in the Suez and Rhine–Danube canals, 'the optimistic pleasure he took in the civilizing advance of technology and increasing ease of communication'.[35] Behind this outlook there lay the concept of 'commerce' which had been decisive for the golden age of capitalism; but while the older Goethe understood the heroism that marked the early stages of industrialization and tried to appropriate it, he also sensed how this capitalism was bound to end. It was Goethe who inspired the Weber reader Thomas Mann to a vision of the society of the future:

The new, social world, the organized world of unity and planning in which mankind will be liberated from sub-human and unnecessary suffering, from suffering that violates reason's sense of honour – this world is coming; and it will be the work of that great sobriety which all minds that are of any account, all that repudiate an outmoded and apathetic petty-bourgeois state of soul, already profess today.[36]

Since Novalis' interpretation and critique of Goethe's *Wilhelm Meisters Lehrjahre*, opinions on the *Wanderjahre* have been divided too.

[33] Thomas Mann, 'Goethe als Repräsentant des bürgerlichen Zeitalters' [1932], in *Leiden und Grösse der Meister* (Frankfurt am Main: S. Fischer, 1982), p. 157.
[34] Thomas Mann, 'Goethe und die Demokratie' [1949]; *ibid.*, p. 340.
[35] Thomas Mann, 'Goethe als Repräsentant des bürgerlichen Zeitalters', p. 178.
[36] *Ibid.*, p. 179.

Written between 1820 and 1829, it is filled with an air of serious and seriously intentioned didacticism; the connection between piety and utilitarianism is, in the American section especially, brought clearly to light, and the anarchic capitalism of the early textile industry is depicted with the same involvement and precision as is the domain of the machine which, as Goethe put it, would never again be banished from the earth. Goethe had read Franklin's autobiography in 1810 and 1817, and its traces are visible everywhere in the *Wanderjahre*. It was therefore logical that the *Wanderjahre* should become a key text, not only for Thomas Mann, but also for Max Weber, for whom Franklin's autobiography had been an important source:

The idea that modern professional work bears an *ascetic* stamp is likewise not new. That limitation to a specialization, with the abandonment of Faustian universality it involves, is in the modern world a precondition of useful activity of any kind; that today 'deed' unavoidably involves 'renunciation': *Goethe* too, at the height of his practical wisdom in the *Wanderjahre* and the end he bestowed on the life of Faust, desired to teach us of this ascetic fundamental motif the bourgeois lifestyle must possess if it wants to constitute a style and not the absence of a style. To Goethe this realization constituted a renunciatory farewell to an age of full and fair humanity that the evolution of our culture would no more repeat again than it would the heyday of antique Athens. The Puritan *wanted* to be a professional man – we *have* to be one.[37]

Delivered a year before the Nazis assumed power, Mann's address on Goethe was a despairingly optimistic attempt to conceal the threatening evil; yet his communist utopia too bears, almost against his will, traits of the horror ahead: it reflects the termination of the process of bureaucracy and rationalizing, and his organized world of unity and planning is nothing but the fellaheen state which Max Weber, the greatest of sober thinkers, saw irresistibly on its way.

When on 15 April 1937 Thomas Mann delivered the after-dinner speech at the banquet to celebrate the fourth anniversary of the Graduate Faculty of the New School for Social Research in New York – the University in Exile founded by Alvin Johnson to provide possibilities of work in the United States for social scientists driven out of Germany – he was regarded as a great writer with a world public who was employing in exile the weapon of the word in the struggle against Hitler's Germany; hardly anyone would have supposed him to harbour any deeper solidarity with the social sciences.

[37] Max Weber, *Die protestantische Ethik und der Geist des Kapitalismus* (Tübingen: Mohr/ Siebeck, 1934), p. 203.

And yet his confession that he was a political–social man constituted a dramatic recantation of positions he had held before.

The same year brought him a further opportunity of emphasizing how close his views were to those of Max Weber. To an inquiry by Pierre-Paul Sagave, who after the war published a study of the German social novel, Mann replied:

I have hardly any direct relations with the church, even with the Protestant church, and I imagine nothing of this kind appears anywhere in my life's work. On the other hand, I have throughout my life felt myself to be a Protestant in as much as I feel that Protestantism is the basic element of German culture itself and regard even Goethe and Nietzsche as being essentially Protestants. I would like also to direct your attention to the figure of Thomas Buddenbrook in my youthful novel, in whom this element probably appears most strongly, if in an ethically secularized form. I myself spoke, in the book 'Reflections of an Unpolitical Man', of the specific relationship existing between this figure and certain sociological theories which, advanced principally by Max Weber, seek to demonstrate the connection between Protestantism and bourgeois capitalism.[38]

Protestant ethics and the spirit of capitalism– this is the self-selected formula which serves to characterize a significant part of the work of Max Weber. It also marks the work of Thomas Mann, who– not least in his letters to Karl Kerényi – repeatedly describes the secularization and disrespectful profanation of religion as one of his fundamental tendencies. What in the polemical climate of the *Betrachtungen* appeared as a contest over priority was transformed in the age of the Weimar Republic and under the pressure of solidarity in exile into a realization of a significant elective affinity.

The Thomas Mann Archive in Zürich contains Mann's copy of the third volume of Weber's essays on the sociology of religion, dealing with the Judaism of antiquity. It is immediately obvious that this is one of the principal sources for Mann's *Joseph and his Brothers*: the volume has been worked through from cover to cover, exclamation-marks abound, selected passages are written out, errors of punctuation and grammar are corrected, and only at the point at which Weber refers to Joseph's 'coy virtue'[39] does there writhe in the margin an ironical question-mark.

---

[38] Thomas Mann to Pierre-Paul Sagave, 23 February 1937; Thomas-Mann-Archiv der ETH Zürich.

[39] Max Weber, *Gesammelte Aufsätze zur Religionssoziologie. III: Das antike Judentum. 2.*, photomechanisch gedruckte Aufl. (Tübingen: Mohr/Siebeck, 1923), p. 59 (Thomas Mann's copy in the Thomas-Mann-Archiv der ETH Zürich).

There is a brief breathing-space in the *Betrachtungen* in which polemics fall silent and pure admiration holds sway: it is where Mann recalls 'Eichendorff's elevated and free and lovingly conceived novella',[40] *Aus dem Leben eines Taugenichts*. It was, as Joseph von Eichendorff had called it, a well-bred novel, and Thomas Mann loved it because it lacked all ambition for psychological analysis or will to social criticism. The 'good-for-nothing' was the antithesis of the achievement-orientated moralists to whom Mann – who had proclaimed the ethical command to produce and complete to be the maxim of his creative work – felt so closely related: he envied the good-for-nothing as Aschenbach had longed for idleness and escape from routine.

Without being a Bohemian, the good-for-nothing was however not only useless but wished 'to see the world too as being useless':[41] he was convinced that he could be happy only if he ceased to bother about earning a living. Mann called him a symbol of the German and approvingly quoted his words: 'I am at home nowhere. Wherever I go it is as though I had arrived too late, as though the whole world had failed to reckon on my appearance.'[42]

But this approval remained an episode, for Thomas Mann knew only too well that the good-for-nothing was in no way the exemplary German, the typical representative of the nation arrived too late. He had in any case already conferred the title of exemplary German upon another: upon his own creation Thomas Buddenbrook, who, anything but a good-for-nothing, was the personification of the Protestant ethic of achievement. In the figure created by the Catholic Baron von Eichendorff Mann saw embodied a German utopia: in Thomas Buddenbrook, on the other hand, he saw embodied German–Protestant reality, the unrivalled analyst of which had been Max Weber.

---

[40] Thomas Mann, *Betrachtungen eines Unpolitischen*, p. 375.
[41] *Ibid.*, p. 378.   [42] *Ibid.*, p. 379.

14

◁ ══════════════════════════════════ ▷

The German spirit in peril: E. R. Curtius, Karl Mannheim and T. S. Eliot

An organon of the new incarnation

The confrontation between the literary and the sociological intelligentsia in Germany reached a climax in the debate on the claims and legitimacy of sociology conducted between 1929 and 1932 by Ernst Robert Curtius and Karl Mannheim. To understand the situation in which the disputants found themselves we must first understand what preceded the controversy and what followed it, and we must also take account of what was happening in France and England.

In 1928 Karl Mannheim had delivered to the sixth meeting of the German Sociological Association in Zürich a sensational report on 'Competition as a Cultural Phenomenon', which had provoked both vehement opposition and enthusiastic agreement; in 1929 his principal work, *Ideology and Utopia*, appeared; in 1930 Mannheim, a Hungarian Jew, was appointed to succeed Franz Oppenheimer at the Johann-Wolfgang-Goethe University at Frankfurt.

In the same year as it appeared E. R. Curtius published in the *Neue Schweizer Rundschau* a scathing critique of *Ideology and Utopia*: his review was called 'Sociology – and its Limitations'. Curtius launched his attack with a glance at France:

The intellectual history of the French Republic includes some memorable battles over sociology. Sociology of positivist origin offered itself as an excellent instrument for the moulding of public opinion. If it had been scientifically demonstrated that when the Red Indian performed his cultic dances he was identifying himself with a parrot the budding popular educator was immune to the sorcery of the mass. Sociology functioned as the official ideology in the *Kulturkampf* waged by red France against black. The sarcasms of a Péguy gave it a thorough drubbing, and the leading intelligentsia of France has deserted it. Today sociology is no longer a party matter or a war-doctrine in France; it has become what it always should have been: an honest specialized discipline.[1]

Without alluding to his name, Curtius was seeking to prevent the introduction of sociology into the schools and universities of the Weimar Republic as a kind of moral doctrine after the manner of Emile Durkheim: such a notion was dangerous politically and must in the long run also call into question the status of sociology as an academically recognized discipline. It had always been perturbations of mind, Curtius maintained, that had provoked imperialist claims on the part of the individual sciences: sociology constituted no exception, but the claims it advanced seemed in the light of the political and social situation existing in Germany especially threatening.

In Mannheim's difficult and opaque book, Curtius said, there lay concealed a number of problems of the highest immediate interest: they involved the function of mind and spirit and the continuance of tradition. He attacked Mannheim with the weapons of the sociology of knowledge itself when he contended that what Mannheim presented as objective knowledge was in reality only a personal confession: the basis of this confession was an unexampled perplexity with life which sought a way out of a crisis of all values and convictions in a flight into the future. A modern man as the sociology of knowledge depicted him had as his only principle the unmasking of all values and traditions, which were to him either ideologies or utopias but in any case nothing but differing sorts of fiction. Curtius' sociological analysis of Mannheim's intellectual position culminated in his relegating it to a certain social stratum; what found expression in *Ideology and Utopia* was the nihilism of the uprooted intellectual.

Curtius also resisted seeing the historical circumstances under which Mannheim had written his book as being unique: there had always been crises of values and there always would be, but systems would with equal rapidity change so as to clarify and overcome them. The reason Mannheim asserted the uniqueness of the present age was only too obvious: it served to justify the claim advanced by sociology to be a uniquely relevant contemporary science with incomparable diagnostic capacities and therapeutic potentialities.

As a personal confession Mannheim's book would have been disquieting but no cause for public concern. *Ideology and Utopia* was,

[1] Ernst Robert Curtius, 'Soziologie – und ihre Grenzen' [1924], in *Der Streit um die Wissenssoziologie*, Vol. 2: *Rezeption und Kritik der Wissenssoziologie*, ed. Volker Meja and Nico Stehr (Frankfurt am Main: Suhrkamp, 1982), p. 417.

however, more than that: it was the prospectus of a discipline which 'is taught and demands a hearing in German schools and universities as the most modern "central science" '.[2] As the Romanist and literary scholar Curtius saw more clearly than many of Mannheim's own colleagues, it was thanks to Mannheim that in Germany sociology was no longer a sociologists' debating club: it was setting about acquiring a firm body of theory and developing a definite pro-gramme of research; it was laying claim to public attention and sup-port and had acquired the courage for a comprehensive diagnosis of the contemporary world. It was in this that Curtius saw the danger proceeding from sociology: he hoped that German youth – and, as though to remind himself against whom he was writing, he repeated in parentheses '*German* youth' – would not let itself be deprived of its sense of idealism and greatness through the misrepresentations of sociology. In an age of diminishing religious, spiritual and moral capital, a partisan sociology was attempting to dispose of its op-ponents by branding them as Romantics. This involved a grotesque self-overestimation, and Mannheim would have done better to have conceived the sociology of knowledge as Scheler did, as a kind of ancillary discipline to philosophical anthropology, which could in turn form the basis of a new metaphysics. Mannheim's sociology was on the whole guilty of encroaching on domains that belonged legitimately to the realm of philosophy – for only philosophy could decide questions of values.

In his reply to Curtius's attack, which appeared in the same journal, Mannheim interpreted it as a positive sign: sociology, hitherto an outsider and intruder in Germany, had finally entered public awareness. With Weber, Troeltsch and Scheler German sociology had not only experienced a belated breakthrough but had at the same time attained if not surpassed the level of achievement of the sociologies of the West. Although Mannheim maintained that the extreme claims Curtius attributed to sociology had not been for-mulated by him in the way stated, his reply was anything but defensive.

For to describe sociology as an 'instrument for expanding con-sciousness and soul',[3] and to see in it the 'organon of the new incar-nation', was to accord to sociology the almost exclusive right to be the rule of conduct for modern society. And to assert that in all this Marxism acted as a ferment was particularly scandalous; for,

[2] *Ibid.*, p. 422.
[3] Karl Mannheim, 'Zur Problematik der Soziologie in Deutschland' [1929]; *ibid.*, p. 429.

Mannheim maintained, it was only by contending with Marxism that sociology had been in a position to react to the expansion of the potentialities of thinking and scope for action that had taken place more adequately than with mere aesthetic visions and gestures. His choice of words makes it clear that at this point Mannheim was criticizing Stefan George and his circle. Already, in the early twenties, he had described in letters from Heidelberg how greatly the town was dominated by the polar antithesis of the sociologists and the Georgeans, two groups whose typical representatives were Max Weber and of course Stefan George himself. Their confrontation was also a confrontation between university and poetic community, the Protestant cultural tradition and Catholicism, and quite generally the division between scientific and literary culture. Mannheim's account is founded essentially on Max Weber's analyses of George and the George circle. He speaks ironically of George's new man and of the new impetus the myth had received in Germany through him: the Georgeans were isolated intellectuals who solved the problem posed by their psychical homelessness and alienation from the world by closing their eyes to political and social reality, refugees from the world who had found asylum in 'life's quiet bay'[4] of Heidelberg. The Georgeans had obstructed a clear view of actuality; here too sociology constituted a necessary corrective.

With the assertion that the present day presented an incomparable, historically unique state of affairs, and that sociology offered the only orientation adequate to confronting it, Mannheim was in accord; at the same time he therewith rejected Curtius' claim that the structural situation of German sociology could be compared with and assessed by that of the discipline in the French Third Republic. With an irony supposed to express composure but which in retrospect seems evidence of a frightful clear-sightedness, Mannheim sought to react to this attack by one he supposed to be a guardian of academic morals by saying: 'Above all, however, we have no desire to be martyrs.'[5]

The heresy of sociologism

This contention between E. R. Curtius and Karl Mannheim excited great interest beyond the borders of Germany; it was not the least of

---

[4] Mannheim, *Heidelbergi Levelek | Heidelberger Briefe| II; Tüz (Bratislava), 1. April-15. April-15. Mai 1922*, p. 95. I thank Erzsébet Vezér, Volker Meja and Nico Stehr for their assistance in procuring this text, and Bálint Balla for translating it.
[5] Mannheim, 'Zur Problematik', p. 433.

the factors which inspired Pierre Viénot to produce a book whose title was to become a catchphrase of political diagnostics: *Incertitudes allemandes* (1931). Viénot found that Germany had always suffered from the sickness of national introspection, yet the twenties had been the high point of historical relativism: Mannheim was to Viénot an extreme representative of an awareness of this crisis and thus a representative of modern Germany against whom old and everlasting Germany had risen up in the person of Curtius. But even if one sympathized with Curtius one had to recognize that Mannheim's diagnosis was a more accurate assessment of the currents of the age. Mannheim was an intellectual ascetic and stamped with the pathos of rectitude; not a nihilist, he none the less promoted nihilism through the uncompromising way in which he traced the origin of dominant ideas back to the interests of distinct social classes.

Mannheim's true antagonist Viénot saw not in E. R. Curtius but in Stefan George. George and his circle embodied an idealism that had come into existence as a reaction to the materialism of the Wilhelmine era; against Mannheim's cold and uncompromising intellectualism the Georgeans set the warmth of sympathetic understanding, against his dispassionate analysis a moral posture, against his destruction of values the preservation of everlasting values. Germany had therewith entered into a confrontation between two conceptions of life which, though it had always been present, could in the political circumstances of the thirties have catastrophic results. On one hand Germany too was participating in the continuing process of rationalization taking place: to many the dominance of the *esprit de géometrie* had become, as it had to Alfred Seidel, a fatality. The counter-reaction had been no less vehement; and to the Frenchman Viénot it seemed as though Germany was now collectively taking the path of a Maurice Barrès which, starting with the cult of the ego, ended in an unconditional faith in the national community.

Curtius' book *Deutscher Geist in Gefahr*, which appeared in 1932, was a sharper answer to Mannheim's rejoinder but at the same time also an answer to Viénot. 'Demolition of culture and hatred of culture'[6] were the catchphrases with which Curtius launched his attack: Germany had had a great culture – in 1800. The tragedy was that a process of increasing subjection to science had rendered these

---

[6] Curtius, *Deutscher Geist in Gefahr* (Stuttgart and Berlin: Deutsche Verlagsanstalt, 1932), p. 11.

cultural values dilute and shallow and suppressed them from general awareness. But certitudes still existed in Germany – and a recollection of values which it would be rewarding to revive.

The heart of the matter for Curtius was the fact that the concept of culture itself had ceased to be a value and now merely designated the sociologically conditioned form in which the other cultural values were transmitted. A clearer proof of the decadence of the German spirit there could not be: for Curtius regarded the interest of sociology as 'formally the most universal but so far as substance is concerned the poorest degree of interest a subject can embrace'.[7]

Significantly, Curtius pronounced this verdict in the course of a eulogy of Hugo von Hofmannsthal, who, after the narrowing of the George circle into a sect, had been the only one in a position to proclaim the unity of nation and culture. To the Romanist Curtius Hofmannsthal seemed to be the writer who could have achieved in Germany what was a matter of course in France: the embodiment and fostering of national values in literature. Hofmannsthal's Munich address of 1927, 'Literature [Schrifttum] as the Spiritual Region of the Nation', was to him 'the last memorable event of German culture'.[8]

Political hatred of culture could appear openly, as in the USSR, or concealed, as in Germany. In the latter case it disguised itself and wore the academic gown of an oppositional science. Curtius was here alluding to sociology; and when he confronted Hugo von Hofmannsthal and Karl Mannheim with one another he was thus reiterating a confrontation applicable throughout Europe: on one hand the poet who with the power of the word preserved traditional values, on the other the sociologist who with his jargon destroyed them. Generalizations of this kind must, to be sure, have been difficult for Curtius, for, though a firm opponent of the sociology of knowledge, he was an equally firm adherent of philosophical anthropology, which pointed the way to a new metaphysics; and his antipathy towards Mannheim only served to enhance his admiration for Max Scheler – who had, however, been not only a philosopher but also a sociologist and, together with Leopold von Wiese and Hugo Lindemann, had directed the Institute of the Social Sciences of Cologne University.

Curtius removed the contention surrounding sociology from the realm of everyday political problems and put it into the perspective

---

[7] Curtius, 'Hofmannsthals deutsche Sendung' [1929], in *Kritische Essays zur europäischen Literatur* (Bern: Franke, 1954), p. 158.
[8] Curtius, *Deutscher Geist in Gefahr*, p. 19.

of universal history. Under this perspective the contention constituted a reiteration of the struggle over primacy of values in which
collective and individual had been engaged at least since the time of
the Greek sophists. It took a dramatic turn in the French Revolution, whose outcome was the politicization of society; and this
formed the soil which nourished sociology. Following Carl Schmitt,
Curtius could accept the desire of sociology to gain recognition as an
academic discipline; what he rejected was its claim to be the universal central science of the modern world. This claim constituted
sociologism – 'the utopian interest–ideology of sociology clad in
theoretical form'[9] – and it was a creed that had to be contested.

With this Curtius had taken sides in the dispute between von
Below, Tönnies and C. H. Becker over the introduction of sociology
as a subject of academic study; he took the side of Becker and
Tönnies, though at the same time he guarded himself against the
imperial claims of one discipline, which seemed to him to be
threatened not only by Mannheim's sociology of knowledge but also
by Hans Freyer's programme for a sociology as a science of reality.
What he wanted above all was that sociology should be accepted as a
study course for post-graduates and that admission to it should be
dependent on passing an examination in history.

A sociology with modest academic aspirations of this kind need
have no fear that it would fail to exercise influence. Curtius indirectly supported Mannheim's assertion that belated German
sociology had long since caught up with, indeed outstripped, the
professional competition from the West. Although it had originated
in France with Comte, and had been mightily developed by
Durkheim and Lévy-Bruhl – 'both, however, probably immigrant
Jews'[10] – sociology had exerted no lasting influence on the consciousness of the French; and although in sociology, as in other disciplines too, the amateur had preceded the professional and Balzac
had been the supreme, the 'revelatory, dionysian *poet* of society',
which he loved and hated as one loves or hates a woman, as a rule the
cultivated Frenchman lacked the slightest feeling for sociology – in
this matter he could learn from the Germans.

In an account of Curtius' contention with Mannheim, who was
later to be reviled by the Nazis as a Hungarian Jew, it would not be
proper to suppress Curtius' clearly expressed views on the relationship
between sociology and Judaism. Sociology exercised a great power
of attraction on those who felt bound to society as such rather than

[9] *Ibid.*, p. 81.   [10] *Ibid.*, p. 83.

to a particular state or nation: it was this that explained its proximity to socialism as well as to Judaism. But whoever desired to set Jew and German in opposition to one another forgot that there also existed a German Judaism whose 'nobility of blood and spirit'[11] was embodied in Friedrich Gundolf. Curtius saw in the fact that so many Jews were prominent in sociological research a challenge to the sociology of knowledge; at the same time he therewith made it clear where the moral and cognitive limits of the discipline lay: non-Jews would have analysed Jews if the Jews had not analysed themselves.

Three years later Curtius found the position he had adopted in 1929 confirmed by the sociologists themselves. In his struggle against the exaggerated claims advanced by sociology he had always been able to call on the testimony of such people as Ernst Troeltsch, but now the distinction between sociology and sociologism was proclaimed *ex cathedra* – by Theodor Geiger, in Vierkandt's new *Handwörterbuch der Soziologie*.

It was thus all the more astonishing that in *Ideology and Utopia* Karl Mannheim could preach the heresy of sociologism as though it were an article of faith. Curtius repeated his attack of 1929, but he did not leave it at that. For Mannheim's article '*Wissenssoziologie*', which also appeared in Vierkandt's *Handwörterbuch*, showed that in the interval he had drawn closer to philosophy; conversely Curtius had, as he impressively demonstrated, not only acquired a profound knowledge of existing sociology but felt for it a greater degree of sympathy than he had done three years previously: 'I do not consider it impossible that Mannheim and I, who are both subject to the living laws of the sociology of knowledge and must obey them unquestioningly, will grow even closer together.'[12]

None the less, Curtius continued to maintain the primacy of philosophy: it alone could offer mankind that comprehensive orientation which Mannheim unjustly claimed for sociology. The foundation of this claim was, moreover, destructive in its nature and led to a perilous glorification of revolution which shifted Mannheim singularly close to the circles around the right-wing *Tat* magazine.

Impartial intelligentsia and perspectival humility

Looking back on the 1920s and the early years of the 1930s, we cannot today be in any doubt that with Karl Mannheim there opened up in Germany the opportunity of a new orientation and stabilization

[11] *Ibid.*, p. 85.   [12] *Ibid.*, p. 92.

for sociology that was brought to nothing by the victory of National Socialism. Dirk Käsler and René König have convincingly demonstrated that Mannheim appeared to be called to overcome the stagnation which the discipline was caught in and to become the 'social "leader" of a sociology orientated towards social science'.[13] The four great essays alone – which appeared between 1926 and 1929 – make clear the extent to which Mannheim's sociology was bound to polarize adherents and opponents of the subject: he ventured on an ideological and sociological interpretation of the products of the mind and on a reconstruction of conservative thinking in Germany, investigated the problem of the differences of the generations, and had the courage to emphasize the importance of competition in the intellectual domain.

The claim advanced by Mannheim's sociology to be able to subject the products of the mind – including, that is to say, the productions of science and the phenomena of the arts – to an objective inspection that was every bit as justified as the traditional subjective inspection was calculated to excite disquiet in Germany; its attempt to refer the intellectual and spiritual to the social would be bound to seem a betrayal of the spirit and an assault on traditional values. That Mannheim appealed among others to Dilthey in the course of this placed him in a certain competitive situation – for it had been precisely Dilthey who, upon the appearance of Gundolf's book on Shakespeare, had exclaimed that he now felt as though he were standing on the mountain gazing into the Promised Land.

Mannheim's programme of a sociology of knowledge would have struck the Georgeans above all as hubris, and the closing words of his lecture on competition can be read as an attack on the views of George and his circle: 'He who would like to have the irrational where the clarity and austerity of reason must still *de jure* rule is afraid to look the mysterious in the eye where it truly belongs.'[14] Mannheim was familiar with the Georgeans' aversion to sociology from his time at Heidelberg, and it was Norbert Elias, later Mannheim's assistant at Frankfurt, who intensified a certain objective of the sociology of knowledge when he described it as an

[13] Dirk Käsler, 'Der Streit um die Bestimmung der Soziologie auf den Deutschen Soziologentagen 1910–1930', in *Soziologie in Deutschland und Österreich 1918–1945* (Kölner Zeitschrift für Soziologie und Sozialpsychologie, Sonderheft 23), ed. M. Rainer Lepsius (Opladen: Westdeutscher Verlag, 1981), p. 230.
[14] Mannheim, 'Die Bedeutung der Konkurrenz im Gebiete des Geistigen' [1928/9]; in *Der Streit um die Wissenssoziologie*, Vol. 1: *Die Entwicklung der deutschen Wissenssoziologie*, p. 369.

intellectual revolution which deemed the mystery of creative man no vaster than the mystery of man as such.

However much Curtius may in 1932 have expressed the hope that he and Mannheim might draw closer together, there was little sign in Mannheim of a willingness to revise his original opinions. In the same year as *Deutscher Geist in Gefahr* appeared he delivered a lecture on 'The Tasks of Sociology at the Present Time' to a conference of German sociology professors in Frankfurt-am-Main; the brochure of the same name, printed in the same year and comprising a mere sixty pages, is perhaps the most self-confident utterance on the nature of his subject any sociologist had hitherto given vent to in Germany.

That he could concern himself with the state of sociological instruction and had good grounds for thinking that his outline of a sociological curriculum would find broad agreement among his professional colleagues, Mannheim considered a sign of the discipline's maturity. Even journalists and politicians in Germany now had to argue sociologically if they wanted to obtain a hearing; sociology no longer needed to struggle for recognition – its concern now was whether it was to become a practical everyday science or the property of scholastics. The struggle for sociology had achieved its end: no one any longer contested its right to consider itself a specialized science. It was on this foundation – and in an age which pressed for syntheses in every sphere – that the discipline's claim to be a universal science could be reiterated with greater prospect of success.

Sociology of knowledge was a necessity as a self-correction of philosophy; as a theory of ideologies it performed a pedagogic function; in sociology the Enlightenment was brought to completion, it was 'the life-orientation in keeping with the needs of the man of industrial society, whether this society has its organizational basis in capitalism or in socialism'.[15]

Many passages of Mannheim's brochure read like a reply to E. R. Curtius even when he is not being directly addressed, and this produces a striking crossing of arguments between the Romanist and the sociologist. Since French literature was 'an uninterrupted discourse on man ... a course of instruction in anthropology',[16] and

---

[15] Mannheim, *Die Gegenwartsaufgaben der Soziologie. Ihre Lehrgestalt* (Vortrag, gehalten am 28. Februar 1932 bei einer Tagung reichsdeutscher Hochschuldozenten der Soziologie in Frankfurt a.M.) (Tübingen: Mohr/Siebeck 1932), p. 41.
[16] Curtius, *Die französische Kultur: Eine Einführung* (Berlin and Leipzig: Deutsche Verlagsanstalt, 1930), p. 96.

thus at bottom something like a jargon-free sociology, many French people believed that as an academic discipline sociology was superfluous: as a consequence they all too often contented themselves with impressionistic findings instead of producing realistic analyses. While Curtius thus denied the French the capacity for sociological insight and in this matter recommended to them the Germans as a model, Mannheim depicted France as a paradise in which sociology was taught even in the *écoles normales primaires* and some knowledge of sociological civics was taken for granted. In Germany on the other hand – according to Mannheim's wilful interpretation – Romanticism had only awakened interest in mind and historicism and historicism had produced a 'metaphysics of uniqueness'[17] that had almost become a constituent of common knowledge.

In one thing alone were E. R. Curtius and Karl Mannheim at one: their estimation of Balzac. But whereas to Curtius Balzac seemed something of an exception among his compatriots, to Mannheim he was the embodiment of that sociological keen-scentedness the possession of which the Germans could only envy the French:

The man of industrial society requires a sociological orientation even if he intends to make his way purely as an individual and pursue a 'career' involved with society only to a limited extent. Thus even a character in Balzac will acquire the insight that in modern society one can rise to the top only when one has studied with the closest attention the laws of the society in which one intends to rise. Balzac's novels themselves are an attempt to produce such a sociological natural history of bourgeois society. Their particular charm, however – to dwell on this point for one moment more – is that in addition to this they have a sense of the visions and vagaries which, in spite of all its rationality, or precisely within this element of rationality, are to be found in this society's actual existence.[18]

Curtius had always excluded from his critique of Mannheim the latter's analysis of the intelligentsia: it seemed to him novel and unique in Germany, comparable only with Charles Maurras' *L'Avenir de l'intelligence*. The reference to Maurras was more than incidental: in 1921 Curtius had himself written a little book on the *Syndicalism of the Intellectual Workers in France*, and his contention with Mannheim acquires an additional penetrating edge from the perspective of this early publication.

What attracted Curtius to France was the absence there of that intellectual crisis which everyone affirmed existed in Germany. The traditionalism of the French demanded that disputes be conducted

---

[17] Mannheim, *Die Gegenwartsaufgaben*, p. 12.   [18] *Ibid.*, p. 41–2.

in sanctioned and traditional form – which at the same time took the edge off them. The French, so Curtius already believed in 1921, explained crises sociologically, that was to say with reference to the social reality that surrounded them; the Germans, on the other hand, at once betook themselves to philosophy of history and started haggling with the cosmos when faced with the merest domestic problems. While the Germans, under the influence of their sociologists, believed in the illusion of an impartial intelligentsia, the French organized themselves and formed on the right the Parti de l'Intelligence led by Maurras and on the left the Parti des Intellectuels led by Anatole France.

In France it was realized that a concentration of intellectual energies demanded first and foremost the disciplining of the intelligentsia, and it was not without some sympathy that Curtius followed the obstinate efforts being made to unite the organizable intellectuals in the CTI, the Confédération des Travailleurs Intellectuels, and those who resisted organizing in a looser association, the Compagnons de l'Intelligence. He also cited with approval the Saint-Simonian formula according to which the task of *belles-lettres* was to strengthen social cohesion. Among the neo-Saint-Simonians who gathered around the journal *Producteur* were Alfred de Tarde and Henri Massis – frequently named by Curtius – who, under the common pseudonym Agathon, had lent vigorous weight to the opposition of the literary intelligentsia to Emile Durkheim and his school. Curtius could see very well that the desire of the French intellectuals of the right to arrive at a new form of understanding of community could be comprehended as a contribution to a sociology of knowledge: he grasped the syndicalism of the French intellectual workers as an attempt to overcome the irresistible process of intellectualizing and rationalization by going above and beyond it and making productive use of the energies released by it. If one wanted to invoke similar endeavours in Germany one could think of Max Scheler and of the phenomenological school.

This early interest in the syndicalist endeavours of the French intellectuals is reflected in Curtius' critique of the concept of the impartial intelligentsia – a 'Cloud-Cuckoo-Land',[19] as he called it – in the course of his contention with Karl Mannheim. In voicing this critique he was not alone. The circle around Stefan George, it is true, produced analyses of the age identical with Mannheim's conception of the uniqueness of the contemporary era; it is also true that in the

---

[19] Curtius, *Deutscher Geist in Gefahr*, p. 101.

same circle there was talk of the 'free space of a self-created atmosphere';[20] and Hofmannsthal too described in his Munich lecture of 1927 a socially unencumbered intelligentsia animated by the desire for a new synthesis. These were all expressions Mannheim himself employed, but the inferences that were drawn from them were totally different from those which he drew.

While Mannheim saw the independence of the intelligentsia as accidental and the uncompromising relativism of their values as an expression of their honesty, the Georgeans maintained that the creation of values was as much a commandment of the hour as was the uniting into circles of a few who were held more tightly together by unanimity of soul than were the members of any formal organization.

To Mannheim's all-embracing suspicion of ideology George's adherents opposed the demand for 'perspectival humility';[21] Gundolf regarded impartial historical judgments as lies and condemned relativism as the atheism of modern times, a symptom of a feeble age that had lost sureness of instinct in knowledge of the grand values. In Gundolf's contention with Georg Misch over the correct interpretation of Dante there emerges clearly the kind of resistance which Mannheim's sociology of knowledge was bound to provoke:

When you say that access to Dante can be obtained only via the Middle Ages I would assert that the path to the Middle Ages is above all through Dante. A work of art is something self-enclosed and self-sufficient, a centre out of which the paths lead to the historical peripheries and not the reverse. But this centre can be experienced only primarily, out of one's own heart, as a *human* experience become form, and the historical, i.e. the relative, can never provide us with the key to the human, i.e. to the substantive: only to the extent that the historical is human in the sense that it is capable of being still experienced today do we possess any path to it at all. . .[22]

It was in a fashion similar to this that Thomas Mann had in the *Betrachtungen* opposed any attempt to see through art and the artist: the consequence of such an attitude was not the cultivation of culture but a progressive disintegration. It was not only to the Georgeans that sociology of knowledge was bound to seem a product and a hastener of the hateful process of civilization.

---

[20] Friedrich Wolters, 'Herrschaft und Dienst' [1909], in *Stefan George 1868–1968*, p. 249.   [21] Ernst Bertram, *Nietzsche*, p. 5.
[22] Friedrich Gundolf to Georg Misch, 12 November 1910; Gundolf, *Briefe. Neue Folge*, p. 72.

To understand the nature of the contention between Curtius and Mannheim we must understand Curtius' relations with the George circle. George's vehement criticism of Curtius subjected these relations to a degree of strain; and before Curtius could become a Georgean they were broken off. In 1916 George wrote a furious letter to Gundolf in which he reproached him with having accorded approval to Curtius' book *Die literarischen Wegbereiter des neuen Frankreich*, which was originally to have been published by Georg Bondi. Curtius had, he said, allowed himself to be influenced by the chatter of the French without inquiring into essentials; he had been regaled with problems which he had attacked without any restraint: 'Curtius is a passing guest at many places indeed – it will be many years yet before he finishes filling himself unnecessarily until he can take in nothing more. He would do better to choose remotely distant subjects!'[23] Curtius was simply foolish, he took a false view of things, and to speak of the secret France was a scandal in the George circle, which wanted to embody the secret Germany. The decisive difference between the Georgeans and Curtius was revealed in the latter's analysis of the Dreyfus affair: he misunderstood its significance because he was stuck on the suggestions of Péguy. George had made it clear, not least in his mocking rejection of Gundolf's francophobia, that during the First World War he had not thought of concealing certain francophile tendencies in himself; and Curtius's French leanings, only too understandable in a Romanist, were not what George had principally against him. His critique was of a more fundamental nature: 'What an error to mix up spiritual and political things in this way.'[24]

What Curtius held against Mannheim George had once reproached Curtius with: recollection of this fact makes it understandable why, in his critique of Mannheim, Curtius should not have denied his affinity with the sociology of knowledge or concealed his desire to meet his opponent half-way. Curtius was himself at once a frustrated sociologist of knowledge and an unfaithful and outcast Georgean.

In a kind of *curriculum vitae* first published in 1945 and included in the *Kritische Essays zur europäischen Literatur* in 1950, Curtius maintained that in the humanities there existed no methods that went beyond immature schooling – except perhaps one, which could not, however, be taught: 'instinct and intelligence working together'.[25]

[23] Stefan George to Friedrich Gundolf, 26 October 1916; George and Gundolf, *Briefwechsel*, p. 287. [24] *Ibid.*, p. 286.
[25] Curtius, 'Anhang' [1945], in *Kritische Essays zur europäischen Literatur*, p. 433.

This may remind the reader of T. S. Eliot's concise formula that there exists only one method: that of being very intelligent. Yet Curtius appealed to someone else – to Max Scheler, the greatest thinker of the epoch who had established metaphysically the connection between love and knowledge. Once, when phenomenology was under discussion, George had described Husserl as harmless but Scheler as suspicious because he encroached upon the preserves of the circle: by appealing to Scheler Curtius distanced himself from George, yet at the same time approached him as closely as he could be approached from outside the circle. His adherence to objective science, his desire to recast 'experience . . . in the fire of creation . . . into the steel structure of knowledge',[26] recalls in its choice of metaphors Max Weber and in its attitude another who had freed himself from George: Kurt Breysig. In this Curtius revealed his proximity, not only to the philosophy of Max Scheler, but also to the sociology of Karl Mannheim.

It was also in 1932 that Max Rychner's 'German Chronicle' appeared as part of a regular series in T. S. Eliot's journal *The Criterion*. As Pierre Viénot had done for the French reader, Rychner with subtle Swiss irony drew the attention of the English public to the apocalyptic tone in which the Germans discussed the crises that affected them and their awareness of these crises. A symptom of the latest German crisis was the amount of attention suddenly being devoted to sociology, and the symptomatic figure in regard to this sociology was above all Karl Mannheim. Rychner made a bold assertion: with a promptitude that would have delighted Hegel, intellectual radicalism had produced the antithesis to analytic sociology – a national irrationalism better known as national socialism. Here was where Curtius had stepped in, and Rychner explained to the English reader that the best way to understand the background to the German crisis was to read *Deutscher Geist in Gefahr*. The new humanism which Curtius propagated was likewise a convincing way out of the danger threatening Germany.

That Curtius should have been presented in *The Criterion* in this fashion was no accident: in 1927 he had translated *The Waste Land*, and he himself wrote for *The Criterion*; and after Eliot had read 'Humanismus as Initiative', which later became the fifth chapter of *Deutscher Geist in Gefahr*, he described it enthusiastically as 'one of the best and most reasonable expositions of a "humanist" attitude that I have ever read'.[27]

[26] *Ibid.*, p. 435.   [27] T. S. Eliot, 'A Commentary', *The Criterion* 12 (1932), p. 74.

Impartial intelligentsia and 'clerisy'

When, in 1933, Karl Mannheim was removed from Frankfurt University at the behest of the Nazis, he emigrated to England. At first he was a lecturer at the London School of Economics; afterwards he moved to the Institute of Education at London University, where he later became professor of pedagogics. He died on 9 January 1947. In an obituary notice in the *Times* two days later he was described as having found his way into the English mind and spirit in an astonishingly short space of time, and in the end to have become in many respects more English than the English.

This obituary was referred to in a letter from a *Times* reader that appeared on 25 January 1947:

It would be impossible to improve upon your obituary notice of Professor Karl Mannheim, within the limits which your correspondent has set himself. There is, however, one piece of testimony which I should like to add, as it will otherwise escape the appreciation of posterity, however attentively his books may be read in the future. This concerns the remarkable influence which Mannheim had come to exercise, within the short period of his residence in this country, upon men of his own generation, not all engaged in the same studies, who had the benefit of his acquaintance. In informal discussion among a small group he gained an ascendency for which he never sought, but which was, on the contrary, imposed upon him by the eagerness of others to listen to what he had to say. His interests were so wide as to touch those of men practising a wide variety of intellectual activities; his personal charm, and his kindly curiosity in human beings, drew such associations closer. In conversation, he was never desirous to impose a doctrine, but always primarily to state a problem and to elicit the reflections of his auditory. In consequence, his talk was always a stimulant to original thought; and many are aware of a debt to him, whose points of view are very different from his, and whose indebtedness will not be immediately apparent to those who will know both Mannheim and his friends only through their published works.[28]

The author of this letter was T. S. Eliot.

When Q. D. Leavis's *Fiction and the Reading Public* appeared in 1932, Eliot considered it worthy of an editorial comment in the *Criterion*. Mrs Leavis had characterized her own methods as anthropological, and Eliot remarked in approval that literary criticism did indeed need to turn to anthropology – if one understood by anthropology not only individual and social psychology but also such disciplines as economics and sociology, which critics had too long neglected.

[28] T. S. Eliot, Letter to the Editor, *The Times*, 25 January 1947, p. 7.

It was thus not only interest in the work of a colleague but also interest in the union of literary criticism and sociology that directed Eliot's eyes to Curtius' *Deutscher Geist in Gefahr*. Of the essays that comprise the book two attracted him particularly: 'Sociology or Revolution?' and 'Humanism as Initiative'. What exercised Eliot was that Curtius was concerned 'with the views of a contemporary sociologist named Mannheim, of whose work I am ignorant, and who has hitherto been only a name to me',[29] for in this debate problems of particular importance to Eliot himself were ventilated. The issue was the overestimation of change at the expense of permanence, of critique of values at the expense of the preservation of tried and tested evaluations. On which side Eliot's sympathies lay was clear, but it was also clear that Mannheim's views, which Curtius had challenged for the purpose of his polemic, had impressed him.

Mannheim's emigration to England had given his work a new direction. His interest in the sociology of knowledge was undiminished, but now the foreground was occupied by the political question of what a science such as sociology could do to ensure the survival of democracy after the breakdown of the Weimar Republic. In 1935 Mannheim had published *Mensch und Gesellschaft im Zeitalter des Umbaus*; five years later *Man and Society in an Age of Reconstruction* appeared, translated by Edward Shils and twice as large as the German original. In an introduction written for this new edition Mannheim dealt with the crisis of liberalism and democracy on the Continent and in England, thereby enunciating a *leit-motif* of his future labours which was, from an English point of view, to reflect anew on the German experience and on the basis of this experience to try to find a better solution to the problems facing England and the Western democracies. Mannheim now, in fact, became in many respects more English than the English, and when in 1937 the *Prager Presse* asked him, together with other intellectuals, which books had especially influenced him he mentioned 'the venerable scholarly couple Sidney and Beatrice Webb... [who] even in their old age gave us an exemplary description and analysis of Soviet Russia'.[30] His previous work, and his new labours so decisively directed to the problems of the Western democracies, made it only too understandable that the sociologist Mannheim should be co-opted into the Moot – the group of theologians and writers, clergymen and

---

[29] T. S. Eliot, 'A Commentary', *ibid*.

[30] Kurt H. Wolff, 'Karl Mannheim', in *Klassiker des soziologischen Denkens*, ed. Dirk Käsler (München: Beck, 1978), Vol. 2, p. 344.

officials, who from 1938 to 1947 met regularly to discuss the relationship between Christianity and society.

Problems of planning, the class-affiliation of the intellectuals and the function of elites were Mannheim's central themes; and they were very familiar to T. S. Eliot, who wanted to pursue further the idea of the 'clerisy' evolved by Coleridge and was familiar with corresponding French conceptions that had their home in the circle of ideas around Julien Benda's *La Trahison des clercs*. What attracted Eliot to the Moot, which Mannheim characterized as an order, was not least the 'significant disagreement'[31] that kept discussion alive; it was an association that would in the long run produce more effect than any political party – one of those elite groups modern democratic society had need of if it wanted to elude the universally threatening danger of totalitarianism.

So far as the surviving documents allow us to reconstruct them, at the centre of the Moot group discussions stood the debates, conducted orally and by letter, between Mannheim and Eliot. When Mannheim spoke of an impartial intelligentsia and impartial intellectuals he originally had in mind – on account of his first emigration – the scattered *intelligenzija* of Budapest rather than German professors and *Literaten*; yet the term, which had also been employed by Alfred Weber, quickly acquired a more general meaning: it was a Continental version of the problem of the elite, which could be fruitfully compared and collated with those ideas of Coleridge and Matthew Arnold with which Eliot was associated.

Mannheim's notes 'Topics for the next meeting of the Moot', written in 1941, initiated an intensive debate with Eliot. Mannheim spoke of a new mentality, a peculiar kind of religious experience and a strong sense of solidarity that had developed among the victims of Fascist dictatorship. Typically, and especially in Germany, such profoundly affecting experiences led to a kind of flight from the world; now, however, it was the task of those emigrants who had fled to the Western democracies to devote all their attention and energies to the question of how European society was to be reconstructed after the war. Mannheim maintained that a revitalizing of the English ruling class was needed: the creation of an emotional solidarity that

[31] T. S. Eliot, Notes on Mannheim's Paper [Papers for Moot], 10 January 1941, p. 2. Moot Materials 1939 to 1949. Quoted, as are all the Moot Materials, from the copy in the Sozialwissenschaftliches Archiv der Universität Konstanz. I am grateful to Thomas Luckmann and Ilja Srubar for making it possible for me to see this material. I also thank Mrs T. S. Eliot for permission to quote from T. S. Eliot's Moot contributions and from his letter to J. H. Oldham of 2 May 1949.

could be engendered and perpetuated less on the level of a formal organization than through informal collegiality.

Eliot, who admired Mannheim's capacity for synthesis, found no difficulty in acceding to such ideas; and they were the more significant to him in that they could easily be concerted with a programme for a Christian sociology. Eliot set great store on designating the 'clerisy' – 'those individuals who originate the dominant ideas, and alter the sensibility, of their time'[32] – as an elite, not as a class: the class in which he was born was precisely that from which the 'cleric' had to emancipate himself and, in full awareness of what he was doing, become an outcast and outsider. To Eliot the decisive distinction between the 'clerisy' and all other classes was that classes transmitted culture whereas the 'clerisy' created it. The possibility of human intervention here reached its limits, to be sure: 'Culture might be described as that which cannot be planned, except by God.'[33].

Mannheim reacted to such notions with the mild reproach that Eliot was employing an over-simplified sociology that had come into fashion under the influence of Marxism. His letters to Eliot always included something instructive, but Eliot as a rule made no use of this aid. Mannheim suspected that Eliot's 'clerisy' was associated with some such idea as elites within the elite – a construct with which the average sociologist could not have all that much sympathy since it was hard to measure. To Eliot, on the other hand, Mannheim's concept of the intelligentsia was conceived too narrowly, since it applied as a rule to a definite group at a definite time in a definite country. He also resisted Mannheim's desire to identify his concept of class with Marxist conceptions. None the less Eliot and Mannheim were agreed that the concept of *intelligenzija* was calculated to form a bridge between their individual ideas.

The magnitude of Mannheim's influence in England – an influence that was made even greater through its having originated in a quite different cultural clime – can also be demonstrated elsewhere than in his relationship with T. S. Eliot. As Alec R. Vidler wrote:

I have felt towards Karl more like a grateful and enthusiastic disciple than I have towards anyone else I can think of. I suppose many things combined to make his a mind from which I had an immense amount to learn, and from which it was very delightful to learn because of his generosity in imparting.

[32] Notes on Clerisy by T. S. Eliot, 5 September 1944, p. 3.
[33] Comments by T. S. Eliot on Michael Polanyi's Notes on the Clerisy, 22 November 1944, p. 2.

His nationality, his upbringing, his experience were so different from mine that he came to me as from another world that seemed much more real and rich than that tired and stale one with which I was familiar. His ways of thinking and feeling were unlike those to which I was accustomed among Englishmen, especially academic Englishmen . . . [34]

It is true that in his *Idea of a Christian Society* (1939), an attempt to develop a Christian ethic in Matthew Arnold's sense rather than a party programme, Eliot had already declared his desire to proceed in a way different from that of the sociologist or economist; yet he had at the same time confessed to having been profoundly influenced by a succession of social scientists. Among them were such Christian sociologists as Tawney, but they also included Karl Mannheim, towards whom Eliot still felt indebted ten years later in his *Notes Towards the Definition of Culture*. In the same year he wrote to J. D. Oldham, who had in mind the idea of composing a biography of Mannheim:

All I can testify to, perhaps, is the strength of the impression which he did make, upon one who knew him primarily through our meetings at the Moot, and secondarily through social meetings at his home. At the Moot, as we all know, he was a brilliant expositor of ideas: what made his conversation so impressive was, to me, the relation between his ideas and his personality. I mean that his thought was real, because it was the expression of an interior debate in his own mind and heart. It always seemed to me that the mind of Mannheim was devoted to order, to system, to the effort to bring the irresponsible conflicts of society within the control of reason; whereas his heart was devoted to freedom and tolerance; and that the development of his thought was a continuous effort to reconcile these two directions. Hence his thinking had the mark of sincerity: he was trying to solve problems because it was necessary for his own life to solve them, not trying primarily to convince others, or to compel admiration by the mere demonstration of a flawless argument. [35]

Beyond this, Eliot valued in Mannheim the man of the world who set store by good manners and was at once religious and a sceptic, a gourmet and a connoisseur of art who could comment on a poem of Eliot's in a fashion that showed he knew something about poetry.

The *Scrutiny* group, on the other hand, denied to Mannheim any aesthetic judgment whatever: his lack of artistic sensibility was demonstrated by his liking for such an author as Noel Coward. In

---

[34] Rev. Alec R. Vidler to J. H. Oldham, 2 May 1949, p. 2. I am grateful to Dr Vidler for permission to quote from this letter.
[35] T. S. Eliot to J. H. Oldham, 11 April 1949, p. 1.

1947 *Scrutiny* lamented the still growing 'baneful influence'[36] Mannheim was exercising upon the English mind with his un-English ideas: the clinical, military and mechanical metaphors alone that preponderated in Mannheim's writings betrayed that he was among the pillars of the Bentham world, and the sociologism he championed was calculated to make men forget they were not only social beings but unique individuals as well.

This critique makes it sound as though its author had been reading Curtius. Mannheim's sociology no longer imperilled the German spirit, but the reservations expressed in the *Scrutiny* circle showed very clearly how influential Mannheim had become in England – so influential, in fact, that to an attentive observer his debate with T. S. Eliot could seem a continuation of that dispute which had made such an enduring mark on the intellectual life of England in the nineteenth century and afterwards:

Had Eliot developed his criticism of Mannheim more fully, we might consider this clash as important in twentieth-century intellectual controversy as, according to John Stuart Mill, the contest between Coleridge and Bentham had been for the nineteenth century.[37]

[36] G. H. Bantock, 'The Cultural Implications of Planning and Popularization', *Scrutiny* 14 (1947), p. 171.
[37] Russell Kirk, *Eliot and his Age: T. S. Eliot's Moral Imagination in the Twentieth Century* (New York: Random House, 1971), p. 325.

◁ ═══════════════════════════════════ ▷

15

Epilogue: sociology in National Socialist Germany and afterwards

National Sociology

In 1932 the *Westdeutsche Akademische Rundschau*, the 'Official Organ of *Kreis V* of the *Deutsche Studentenschaft*', published an attack on E. R. Curtius' new book by Erich Jaensch. In Jaensch's view Curtius had, with his thesis that the German national movement was a threat to the spirit – he was referring to the section of *Deutscher Geist in Gefahr* headed 'Nation or Revolution?' – placed himself in conflict with large segments of the German people. Curtius' distorted description of the grand lines of development that would lead out of the miserable present in Germany into a glittering future was the outcome of a false perspective: wearing the spectacles of the *homme de lettres* he sought verification of his rash assertions in literature instead of analysing reality itself – a procedure always hazardous but in times of great historical change misguided in principle. As a literary historian and Romanist Curtius was the last person to be able correctly to evaluate a revolution that could be compared only with the Renaissance.

Men of letters whose personal profile was drawn 'as it were in pen and ink'[1] might be of use in a country such as France, where political movements were always attended by a literary mirror; in Germany they were useless, and from the point of view of the German movement perhaps even harmful.

The psychologist Erich Jaensch was also a sworn enemy of sociology. He harboured a traumatic recollection of the time when Becker was minister and the leading idea in educational policy had – or so he asserted – been to suppress psychology and transfer its teaching and research tasks to sociology. The arguments Jaensch presented against sociology were not of the kind usually brought

---

[1] Erich Jaensch, 'Deutscher Geist in Gefahr? Zur Auseinandersetzung mit dem Buche von E. R. Curtius', *Westdeutsche Akademische Rundschau* 2:13 (1932), p. 1.

forward during the Weimar era and the Nazi era that succeeded it: he maintained that, while a discipline such as psychology pursued the ideal of a rigorously objective scientificality, sociology was a discipline open to any political option and could thus be politically motivated and corrupted in any way one chose. As his chief witness to the truth of this assertion he later named Erich Rothacker, who had published an article on 'National Sociology' at precisely the moment of Hitler's assumption of power: 'Among the few genuine grains the blind hen democracy discovered during its brief period of rule is *sociology*, or the *idea of establishing sociological chairs*.'[2] Rothacker treated sociology ironically as a contemporary science which desired always to be practical and available to the driving forces of political momentum. His choice of words suggests that he had sociology of knowledge above all in his sights when he cynically maintained that historical revolutions would undoubtedly cause sociology to alter its basic orientation. That sociology had long been so closely associated with Marxism was due less to a natural affinity between the two than to the boundless corruptibility to which the discipline was prone. The National Socialists had nothing to fear from sociology, but they could, if they wanted, expect a few things from it: 'The favourite, Marxism, has long since been overtaken by the Fascist runner.'

The discipline of the outsiders

It was only long after the 'economic miracle' that German intellectuals began to ask themselves seriously what the twelve years of National Socialism had meant for the German universities. It was painful to remember these years, but even more painful would have been the presence and undiminished influence of those who had every reason to forget and to remember nothing.

Those who had emigrated and those who had collaborated with the regime were in agreement that sociology had vanished in Nazi Germany, though there was disagreement as to the reason it had done so. Most of the *emigrés* expressed the view that a sociological research which must unavoidably have exposed to the public gaze the lies of the Nazi leadership would have been a serious threat to the brown despots and was on that account suppressed; those intellectuals who had remained in Germany – and there were many social scientists among them – asserted, on the other hand, that the Nazi

---

[2] Erich Rothacker, 'Nationale Soziologie', *Westdeutsche Akademische Rundschau*, 3:1 (1933).

regime had nothing to hope and nothing to fear from a discipline that was already intellectually exhausted at the end of the Weimar Republic: sociology had allegedly already destroyed itself before 1933, and the Nazi era was represented as a period in the history of the social sciences simply too uninteresting to be profitably recalled.

This strange consensus between *emigré* and Nazi collaborator has been shaken in recent years, and younger social scientists and historians especially have refused to accept unquestioningly the thesis that sociology ceased to exist under the Nazis. Their questions have effected a dramatic change in our picture of the history of German sociology in the first half of this century.

There is no question but that the Nazis so weakened the discipline of sociology that after 1933 it quickly withered away intellectually as well as morally; responsibility for this process lies however first and foremost with the fact that the Nazis persecuted communists, Jews, social democrats, liberals and even conservative groups and thus at the same time persecuted the sociologists who belonged to these groups. Individual sociologists were persecuted and the discipline was '*gleichgeschaltet*', but it was not proscribed as such. It is significant that Adolf Hitler, whom Theodor W. Adorno once called the sworn enemy of sociology, very nearly became a colleague of Adorno's, for in February 1932 there was the serious intention, approved by Hitler, of appointing the future Führer a professor of organic sociology and politics at Braunschweig to assist his application for German citizenship.

Most of the emigrant sociologists believed that their discipline could flourish only in a democratic environment: they trusted that a kind of inner morality in the social sciences would make it impossible for them to be used or misused for totalitarian ends. Because they underestimated the complexity of the National Socialist system of government they succumbed to the illusion that that which is morally unequivocal must be structurally simple. On the other side, the collaborators with and followers of the Nazis asserted that with the political end of the Weimar Republic sociology too had come to its intellectual end. However absurd and cynical this argument may sound it was not only the followers of the Nazis who put it forward.

The Weimar Republic contained a multiplicity of parties and a multiplicity of sociologies. Regional centres existed – above all Heidelberg, Frankfurt and Cologne – but no national centre; it is striking that Berlin never became anything like the capital of sociological teaching or research. As a discipline sociology achieved only an indistinct identity: there were few chairs of sociology and nothing but sociology. Although the 1920s saw some advance from hostile competition between isolated sociologists to a knowledge-promoting concentration of rival groups of theorists the predominant feeling was one of fragmentation: anything like a solidarity of discipline was hard to detect among sociologists. Some of them developed private languages no one else could understand; with others monologue was answered with monologues. Germany was, as one of them complained, a land that had no sociology but only sociologists, and since each wanted to be an original they all became outsiders – a real *salon des refusés*, as Max Weber once mockingly described his own circle.

Among the many techniques evolved to eliminate rivals whom one disliked, mimicry became fashionable: anti-Marxists revealed the class attitude of their opponents, and adherents of the formal school looked down contemptuously on the sociology of knowledge, pointing out that Mannheim's ideas could be hatched only in the Romantic atmosphere of Heidelberg, which was favourable to obscurity of argumentation, dialectical over-acuteness and notions high-flown and remote. The meetings of the *Deutsche Gesellschaft für Soziologie* provided a perfect confirmation of the so-called Herring's Law, which asserts that the members of a particular profession are always especially poorly equipped in that which constitutes the specific competence of their profession: historians forget the past, psychologists cannot control their emotions, economists overspend their budget and sociologists are incapable of organizing their social life.

These defects did not prevent the sociologists from making exaggerated claims to knowledge. As early as 1910, Hermann Kantorowicz had warned his colleagues at the first meeting of the German Sociological Association against posing too often the question 'What is sociology?' since it was unanswerable; German sociologists none the less continued right up until their last meeting in 1934 to brood on the problem of deciding what profession they were actually pursuing. Entangled in painful self-consciousness, they talked more of themselves than of the German society of their time and the truly dramatic transformations which it was undergoing. And yet some of these sociologists, who could as yet not even agree on a definition of their profession, asserted that they were standing on a higher platform of knowledge and that if the politicians of the Weimar Republic would only follow their advice they would at once overcome the one-sidedness that characterized the distorted, class-conditioned perception they had of reality.

This want of unanimity among German sociologists was in many respects a reflection of the want of unity that infected the Weimar Republic and the conflicts that divided its political parties. Many writers have bewailed this state of things as the principal cause of the destruction of a political system and the suppression of an academic discipline, but, so far as sociology is concerned, we must take care not to exaggerate. Strong institutions can of course yield an abundant intellectual harvest – but they constitute no guarantee of one. Nor is the neatness of the label a reliable guide to the quality of the product: until the end of his life Max Weber, who became a professor of sociology only in his later years, regarded the designation 'sociology' as being no more than a useful convention; and whenever he spoke of 'our science', what he meant was economics. Georg Simmel became annoyed if anyone called him a sociologist – he considered himself a philosopher. German sociology was created by men who were not sociologists in the strict sense of the word, yet it is as sociologists that Max Weber, Georg Simmel and Ferdinand Tönnies will always be remembered. Who outside the narrow boundaries of the profession, however, has as much as heard of those who were 'pure' sociologists and occupied chairs of sociology and nothing but sociology – Georg Jahn of Dresden, for instance, or Andreas Walther of Hamburg?

Nor should it be forgotten that during the Weimar Republic sociology enjoyed political protection, above all through Carl Heinrich Becker. Against the heated objections of conservative historians Becker encouraged the institution of chairs of sociology, not least in the hope that this still youthful discipline would help to establish the even more youthful German democracy. Only in the French Third Republic had sociology, in the shape of Durkheim and his school, been intended to play so important a political role; yet no German sociologist was ever able to achieve a degree of influence comparable with that achieved by Durkheim – for, in spite of its unmistakable academic successes and the political encouragement it plainly if controversially received, sociology suffered, both before and during the Weimar Republic, from a lack of cultural recognition.

Sociology's hour

In October 1933 there appeared in the *Tat* – the organ of an earlier national movement in which, according to Ernst Robert Curtius, there reigned 'in contrast to the Hugenberg and Hitler press . . . a pronounced intellectualism of an academic sociological stamp' – an article justifying the book-burning that had taken place earlier in the year. This nocturnal *auto-da-fé* was described as a necessary ritual through which the new Germany had definitively renounced the heritage of the Weimar Republic and its intellectuals. The author of the article named only two of these intellectuals: Albert Einstein and Karl Mannheim. The Hungarian Jew, as the Nazis called him, was attacked not as a sociologist but as a philosopher, despite the fact that *Ideology and Utopia*, the Bible of the Weimar intellectuals, had been an assault on philosophy by a sociologist and had provoked Curtius not least for that very reason.

Only six months later the *Tat* published an article whose tone was that of an official communiqué: 'Sociology's Hour'. In this article Ernst Wilhelm Eschmann distinguished between two different species of science. The first was allied with life, a 'science of direct apprehension and intervention'[3] that wanted to know and act; the second had as its object science itself, it was merely a 'secondary science of relationships', and wherever it predominated it was a symptom of the profound sickness of an entire culture. The best example of this latter species of science was offered by sociology: it had become more and more an unending process of reflection on itself and with its demand for value-freedom had finally abandoned itself altogether. The familiar German peril lay in too strong a tendency to reduce everything to science – only a sociology that had liberated itself from this peril could hope for a renaissance. Eschmann had in mind a 'theory of how a community should be constructed'[4] and a decision-making 'ancillary welfare science'[5] when he prophesied: 'The German revolution presents sociology with a task so great, so comprehensive, that it is only with this task that the life of this science truly begins.'

Every historical epoch had had its leading discipline: the twentieth century would be the era of sociology. Hitherto sociology had shamefully neglected the analysis of the phenomena of community, and political science had in a downright perverse fashion brought to the foreground the role of the individual and his claims in relation to the state. Both disciplines had concentrated on social anomalies and pathological conditions – from now on they would devote an appropriate amount of attention to the normalities of communal and political life. Sociology had been something of a pseudo-

---

[3] E. W. Eschmann, 'Die Stunde der Soziologie', *Die Tat* 25 (1934), p. 955.
[4] *Ibid.*, p. 959.   [5] *Ibid.*, p. 958.

discipline; henceforth it had to become a profession and fulfil an eminently practical task: that of sustaining the reorientation of Germany and its reconstitution as a nation. Value-free diagnosis had to be replaced by value-orientated political therapy. That Eschmann should commend Hans Freyer, Carl Schmitt and Ernst Krieck as precursors of such a new social science is hardly surprising – but he also appealed to Alfred Weber, whose assistant he had been. At the conclusion of the article there is a discussion of various attempts to replace sociology – which was after all infected with Marxist and liberal thinking – with other disciplines such as political science or folklore. All are rejected: only sociology appeared to be in a position to fulfil the grandiose tasks the future held for Germany.

Other expressions of opinion, too, less spectacular in intention but, on the contrary, almost parenthetic and for that reason perhaps all the more surprising, make it clear that sociology was by no means regarded as a *disciplina non grata* in the *Tat* circle – as, for instance, when Giselher Wirsing investigates the views of a kind of French fascism of the left with a degree of sympathy and with suitable analytical skill, and the politician who could have become the successful leader of such a movement is described, again not without sympathy, as a 'younger professor of sociology at the Sorbonne',[6] namely Marcel Déat, a former socialist whose origins placed him within the wider Durkheim circle.

Among those whom Eschmann named as precursors of a new sociology pride of place goes to Hans Freyer. Emerging out of the environment of the youth movement, and full of sympathy for an amateur and outsider such as W. H. Riehl, in his early writings Freyer conformed to the familiar German fashion and chose life in all its vagueness as his point of orientation – 'One has first to love life before one can love any purpose of life'[7] – only to make such existential vagueness the basis of the firmest political options. To Freyer the consummation of the spirit is the state, and it is so most purely when it is at war. As 'the enclosed arena of destiny of its nation',[8] the state is a fortress; its borders, the outworks of the fortress, are constructed by the engineer – remote from culture and therefore a guarantee and safeguard of every culture. The representative of the 'innermost region of the realm', however, is the *poet*: 'His work is

---

[6] Giselher Wirsing, 'Systemkrise in Frankreich? 1789–1933', *Die Tat* 25 (1934), p. 762.
[7] Hans Freyer, *Antäus. Grundlegung einer Ethik des bewussten Lebens* (Jena: Diederichs, 1918), p. 89.   [8] Freyer, *Der Staat* (Leipzig: Wiegandt, 1925), p. 178.

essentially free of all law, because everything the law desires, namely the unity of the state and its representation as an objective structure, constitutes from the very first the autonomous meaning of the poetic work. The entire theme of spirit and state, freedom and law, is stretched between these two poles: engineer and poet.'[9] Freyer resumed this theme in his inaugural lecture at Leipzig in 1926, 'Sociology as Humanistic Science': whereas in the natural system of positivism sociology appeared as the latest natural science, to the idealist system of the German movement it was the latest humanistic science and the state was its noblest object.

In the ominous year 1932, which saw a great accumulation of declarations for and against sociology, Freyer participated in a series of lectures on the founders of sociology and dealt with the Romantics. The basic characteristic of Romantic sociology, he said, was its retreat from all social philosophy inspired by the Enlightenment, its decisive resistance 'to all rational social ideals, to all over-estimation of equality, of what was common to all men, of the abstractly egalitarian and formally democratic'.[10]

The need was to preserve this anti-Enlightenment attitude of the Romantics without being subject to the historically-conditioned limitations of their perspectives. Among these, and explicable through their being historically situated between absolutism and industrial society, was their fixation on the state governed by social rank, a fixation that attained its idealized height in such works as *Wilhelm Meister*. Thinking in terms of social rank was a logical consequence of the idea of the organic to which the Romantics adhered as to an *idée directrice*; this idea was subverted from within by a conception of the nation which in the end permitted one to view it less as an organism than as the subject of historical change.

The greatest achievement of Romantic thought, however, was the historicization of such concepts as the nation, the state, and society: it was here that the Germans were in accord with such Englishmen as Burke and such Frenchmen as de Maistre and de Bonald. It was in this spirit of restoration that a line of a tradition of conservative thinking about state and society could be drawn which, instead of dividing Germany and the West, uniquely united them.

Romantic reverence for the past and for history brought with it a predisposition for conservatism. Freyer appealed to Carl Schmitt and his *Politische Romantik* as his chief witness, but he could equally

[9] *Ibid.*, p. 179.
[10] Freyer, 'Die Romantiker', in *Gründer der Soziologie: Eine Vortragsreihe*, ed. Fritz Karl Mann (Jena: Gustav Fischer, 1932), p. 83.

well have appealed to Karl Mannheim – ought to have done so, indeed – when he spoke of the impartial intelligentsia of political Romanticism: he in fact contented himself with saying almost apologetically that he was here 'employing a modern expression'.[11]

His employment of it was not accidental, for the concept of the impartial intelligentsia allowed him to distinguish the champions of political Romanticism in Germany from the French and English opponents of the Enlightenment in respect of their social situation. Burke, for example, was not a private individual but a political publicist and a parliamentarian as well – in Germany, however, the Romantic was a 'poetizing philosopher or philosophizing poet'.[12] This union of thinker and poet without any unequivocal anchor in a definite social stratum was the distinguishing mark of the leaders of the German movement, and it was embodied by no one more clearly than by Adam Müller, whom Carl Schmitt too had described as the typical champion of political Romanticism. This was a combination that followed directly from the nature of conservative thinking itself – a mode of thinking which, compared with the liberal thinking of the Enlightenment, was almost speechless and, as Thomas Mann had remarked in the *Betrachtungen eines Unpolitischen*, rather a mood than a principle. As a necessary compensation for this speechlessness conservatism was directed not to a mere theory but to what was more than that, to a poetized theory such as writers like Novalis and Adam Müller provided. In providing it, Müller evaluated *Wilhelm Meister* quite differently from Novalis, who had lamented the preponderance of economics in the novel: to the ancestors of a German sociology Goethe's novel was great because in it 'the gospels of poetry and economics'[13] were reconciled.

What was positive in Romantic sociology was its confrontation of the thinking of the Enlightenment; what was negative in it was its adherence to a philosophy of social rank that excluded any adequate analysis of industrial civilization or of the society founded on class that was acquiring ever clearer contours. The task was to project a sociology soberly comprehending the social structure of industrial society and conceived in a spirit opposed to the Enlightenment; Freyer's sociology intended as a science of reality served this end.

That Hans Freyer, whose early writings such as *Antäus* and *Prometheus* preserved in their argument and cadence the rhythm of

[11] *Ibid.*, p. 91.   [12] *Ibid.*, p. 90.
[13] Adam Müller to Karl Gustav Baron von Brinkmann, 18 April 1803; *Adam Müllers Lebenszeugnisse*, Vol. 1, ed. Jakob Baxa (München, Paderborn and Wien: Schöningh, 1966), p. 103.

the youth movement, should have become the constructor of a sociology he called a science of reality need not surprise us. In the *state* he had set the engineer against the poet, but at bottom Freyer himself wanted to be both at once, and sociology offered him the possibility of uniting the ideological stock of Romanticism with an illusion-free view of actuality. In 1935 there appeared two publications by Freyer which offered an impressive demonstration of how these two perspectives could be combined: *Pallas Athene*, an 'ethics of the political *Volk*', and the essay, printed in the *Zeitschrift für die gesamte Staatswissenschaft*, on the 'Tasks of German Sociology at the Present Time'.

As Freyer would have it, the specifically German tradition of social science was born out of the spirit of anti-sociology, so that its predecessors included not only Lorenz von Stein, Robert von Mohl and Wilhelm Heinrich Riehl but also, and quite definitely, Heinrich von Treitschke. The content of German sociology – and here it was not possible to avoid pathos – was 'the destiny of Germany in the age of bourgeois society'.[14] While the English and French were subject to the illusion that bourgeois society was a terminal and ideal condition of human social organization, the severe and superior realism of the Germans consisted in refusing to accept this bourgeois society as being in any way a natural system but perceiving instead its historicity and changeability and the necessity of changing it.

Both French and English had their bourgeois revolutions behind them, they had come to rest both politically and theoretically and regarded bourgeois society as the most unrevolutionary of all epochs; the Germans, however, who were idealists, were hostile to ideology from the very beginning; bourgeois society constituted only the surface of a revolutionary epoch and the need was not to preserve it but to overturn it.

It was of course the conservatives to whom Freyer appealed in 1935; yet his text also calls to mind the young Karl Marx, who included in his calculations the revolutionary energies present in bourgeois society, and Heinrich Heine, who had prophesied exactly a hundred years previously that in Germany the revolution would come late but for that reason with all the greater violence:

The idea precedes the deed as the lightning the thunder. The German thunder is also a German, to be sure, and is not very nimble and comes rolling up somewhat slowly; but it will come, and when one day you hear a thunderclap

---

[14] Freyer, 'Gegenwartsaufgaben der deutschen Soziologie', *Zeitschrift für die gesamte Staatswissenschaft* 95 (1935), pp. 118–19.

such as there has never been before in the history of the world, then know: the German thunder has finally reached its goal. At this sound the eagles will fall dead from the air and in the remotest deserts of Africa the lions will bite their tails and creep into their royal caves. A piece will be played in Germany compared with which the French Revolution may seem merely a harmless idyll. [15]

Written two years after the National Socialist seizure of power, Freyer's essay declared sociology to be a product of the bourgeois epoch which might come to an end with the end of this epoch. As yet, however, things had not reached this stage: National Socialism did not mark the end of bourgeois society. Freyer cited E. W. Eschmann's article in the *Tat*: sociology's hour had struck – the hour of German sociology.

Freyer's book *Pallas Athene* was fundamentally a treatment of the same theme, though written in a different key: the essay and the book showed what varying means of expression Freyer had at his command. In prose composed of short, staccato sentences of a murmuring vagueness that rose to a poetry of commonplaces – 'Deep-breathed the rivers flow through their plains. The storm eats at the stone. Through summers and winters of millennia waxes and wanes the green of earth' [16] – Freyer brought forth great truths, 'not step by step but suddenly like visions, not proved and tested but heaped gloriously tower-high without method or demonstration'. [17] He spoke of the flame of the will, of the chaos of the deed, of flat decision and the salt of the soul; and even if these metaphors were trivialized to the language of labour corps and peasantry, they recalled to mind that one of the forms in which Romanticism was able to adjust itself to the machine and factory age was Expressionism. When Freyer spoke of '*Aufbruch und Gestalt*', [18] did the reader not involuntarily think of Karl Otten's celebrated Expressionist anthology '*Ahnung und Aufbruch*'? In early German sociology – and one can think of more examples than merely Tönnies' *Gemeinschaft und Gesellschaft* – an Expressionist tone is unmistakable: it has, in fact, been detected by one of Freyer's biographers, Elfriede Üner; and as Georg Simmel was accounted the Impressionist of German sociology, so Hans Freyer can be seen as its Expressionist.

But all his constitutional Expressionism notwithstanding, Freyer wanted to be a scientist – just as Breysig, Gundolf and Curtius

[15] Heinrich Heine, *Zur Geschichte der Religion und Philosophie in Deutschland* [1835], *Sämtliche Werke*, Vol. 9, ed. Hans Kaufmann (München: Kindler, 1964), p. 284.
[16] Freyer, *Pallas Athene: Ethik des politischen Volkes* (Jena: Diederichs, 1935), p. 37.
[17] *Ibid.*, pp. 14–15. [18] *Ibid.*, p. 95.

wanted to be Georgeans until George himself prevented it. That is why we find in Freyer the precept that to despise itself is the stupidest thing reason can do, and why his fundamental problem was his desire to be strongly expressive while at the same time rich in analytical insight. The outcome is a kind of heroic epistemology: reality is anything but reason, it is on the contrary ecstasy, contention, 'nothing but quick and distinct event. . . and nothing but readiness for the next blow'.[19] To wrest knowledge from this reality, this 'opposing passion',[20] involves precisely the opposite of leisure and contemplation: it involves struggle and exertion, asceticism and renunciation. This is why Freyer calls scientists monks of knowledge: men whose bearing always has something aristocratic and soldierly about it; a discipline of a desire for knowledge that is no longer mere curiosity but nothing but a total mobilization: 'Even he who has become out-and-out a useful member of bourgeois society preserves at the bottom of his soul a desire for banners to wave and a readiness to buckle on his sword when the drums resound.'[21]

As is so often the case, the feeling behind such an attitude had already been analysed by Nietzsche:

In *scientific men* there live the virtues of soldiers and their kind of cheerfulness – they lack ultimate responsibility. They are severe towards themselves and towards one another, and do not expect to be praised for what they do. They are more manly and have a predilection for danger, they have to make themselves *fit* to stake life for the sake of knowledge: they hate grand words and are harmless and somewhat foppish.[22]

By 1935 they could hardly be called harmless, yet the attitude described by Nietzsche in 1880 none the less characterized not only Freyer but also Ernst Jünger, the front-line soldier and author of *Der Arbeiter*, and Gottfried Benn, who, filled with a growing revulsion, in this same year (1935) chose the aristocratic form of emigration and joined the army. Even Heidegger's talk of 'knowledge service' was consciously intended to recall army service: it was a flexible and universally applicable formula that justified anything – enthusiastic collaboration, fellow travelling or inner emigration.

The name of Hans Freyer is inseparably associated with the discontinuance of the German Sociological Society (DGS) in 1934. According to the political standpoint of the observer, it amounted either to a refined rescue operation or an especially perfidious form

[19] *Ibid.*, p. 17.   [20] *Ibid.*, p. 97.   [21] *Ibid.*, p. 56.
[22] Friedrich Nietzsche, *Nachgelassene Fragmente (Sommer 1880), Kritische Studienausgabe*, Vol. 9, p. 179.

of disciplining the 'School' on political and ideological lines. Hans Freyer, with such writings as the *Revolution of the Right* (1932), was among those who created a climate in which National Socialism could flourish; yet, while publicly demanding a strong, authoritarian state, Freyer himself remained apprehensive of organization, concerned rather with style than with efficiency, and sufficiently imbued with the youth movement to think in terms of communities not parties – not even the NSDAP, to which he never belonged. Increasingly disenchanted by the Nazis, Freyer may, like many others, have laboured under the delusion he could never have contributed to the creation of a regime he found increasingly repulsive; yet it is of at least symbolic significance that it was the Expressionist among German sociologists who rendered inoperative their own professional organization – the DGS, in whose foundation Max Weber too had participated and which had never ceased to warn against the perils Germany was threatened with from political Expressionism.

Tacit agreement between literature and sociology

In his endeavour to found a specifically German tradition of sociology Hans Freyer had – only at first glance paradoxically – taken for his starting-point Heinrich von Treitschke's treatise against the social sciences. In Freyer's pupil Helmut Schelsky this development reaches its conclusion and its reversal – a fact already made clear by the title of Schelsky's 1981 publication *Recollections of an 'Anti-Sociologist'*.

As Eschmann had said before him in 1934, sociology stood, according to Schelsky, before the 'dilemma involved in having to be on one hand an empirical practical science and on the other a social–philosophical interpretative science'.[23] Schelsky warned of the threatening danger of a sociology of sociology: the more the discipline reflected on itself the weaker its awareness of its real achievements would become. Schelsky thus shared an affinity with those of his colleagues able to maintain a distance from their own discipline and with such books as David Riesman's *The Lonely Crowd*, whose motto was taken from Fielding's *Tom Jones* and which American critics recommended to novelists of the 1950s as a model to copy. Originating in the claim to being the most important instrument for

---

[23] Helmut Schelsky, *Ortsbestimmung der deutschen Soziologie* (Düsseldorf and Köln: Diederichs, 1959), p. 18.

interpreting modern industrial society, sociology had in the end to content itself with the modest role of serving mankind as an 'indirect moral theory';[24] but since, and not least under the influence of the student movement, the discipline was becoming increasingly political and turning reflection on its own foundations into a full-time occupation, Schelsky also drew conclusions personal to himself: he deserted the professional guild, went over to law school and styled himself an anti-sociologist.

This position made of Schelsky a natural protagonist in the contention that flared up over the question as to how the history of sociology during the Nazi era was to be evaluated. He accused the historiographers of the discipline of producing an account poor in practical knowledge and remote from actual experience of an epoch whose intellectual content must remain incomprehensible to anyone who had followed the evolution of Germany only from without or had reconstructed it long after the war merely from documents. He singled out one fact above all as a sign of the forgetfulness consequent on a difference in generations.

Since the total commitment to an ideology promulgated by the Nazis, and the total commitment to a profession that has evolved since 1945/48 in science, literature and journalism, what is no longer understood is that in thinkers such as Hans Freyer, Ernst and Georg Jünger, Wilhelm Eschmann, and even in 'leftists' such as Ernst Bloch . . . there arose a *synthesis of poetical and philosophic, scientific and literary, political and polemical 'worlds of expression' (Benn)* that constituted the 'signature of the age' – and this independently of whether one was a 'democrat' or what kind of democrat one was.[25]

How concerned Schelsky was, not only to describe such a community of literature and science as the characteristic form of association of the immediate German past, but also to conjure it up as a utopia, is shown in the postscript he composed to his rebuke to the intellectuals, *The Others Do the Work*. All his critics, whether lay or professional, are given a merciless dressing-down, with one exception: Heinrich Böll. To him Schelsky directs a plea for co-operation commencing with a lament over the schism between literature and science reigning in the Federal Republic:

[Böll succumbs] to an error of which many of the critical reviewers of my book believed they could convict me: that I had, in the German tradition,

---

[24] Schelsky, 'Einführung', in David Riesman, *Die einsame Masse: Eine Untersuchung der Wandlungen des amerikanischen Charakters* (Reinbek b. Hamburg: Rowohlt, 1958), p. 19.
[25] Schelsky, *Die verschiedenen Weisen, wie man Demokrat sein kann. Erinnerungen an Hans Freyer, Helmuth Plessner und andere; Rückblicke eines 'Anti-Sociologen'* (Opladen: Westdeutscher Verlag, 1981), pp. 135–6.

merely repeated again the ancient antithesis of 'spirit and power'. I would like to say clearly: what I lament is precisely the identity of 'spirit' and power in the contemporary situation of the Federal Republic, because this leads the 'spirit' ('it stands to the left') into party political power blocs which it then regards as its own and strives to make prevail. The conflict between 'formers of opinion' that has broken out in the Federal Republic is grounded in the *relations between literature and science*. Why does Herr Böll conduct controversial dialogue with the CDU, that is with such people as Kohl, Biedenkopf, etc., though naturally not with Strauss or Carstens? Because in his 'public' actions he places himself upon this plane. Why, as regards 'the other side', will he not converse with such philosophers as Gehlen or Lübbe, such political scientists as Hennis or Kaltenbrunner, or with such sociologists as Albert or Luhmann? 'Public opinion' is not in danger; the danger that threatens today is that its spiritually productive origins in literature and science, beyond party politicial or 'power-related' identifications, will become mutually incomprehensible. It is here that there lies one of the roots of 'polarization'.[26]

Schelsky had pilloried the social scientists' claim to be the 'formers of opinion' for modern society. Yet he himself in fact advanced this claim, as is made clear by the names he cites: scientist means social scientist; not a single natural scientist ever enters his mind. And the spontaneously conceived, fantastic but concretely intended proposal he placed before Heinrich Böll amounted to the idea of founding a debating society for writers and social scientists: 'Let him advocate, or even set in motion, a process by which, over a period of perhaps two years, twelve to at most twenty writers (or journalists) and scientists shall for once meet for discussions and work out together what the possibilities are for a "public opinion" sustained by "both sides"'. Although Böll did not reject this suggestion the circle was in fact never formed.

Even though Schelsky expressly emphasized that he wanted to promote such a 'tacit agreement between literature and science' within the Federal Republic not through the formal founding of an academy but rather through a kind of conversation circle, his proposal unmistakably recalled earlier endeavours in this direction: one thinks naturally of Hans Freyer, who had wanted to unite the engineer and the poet, the smith and the singer, within his national community; of Hofmannsthal, who had urged the concentration of the impartial intelligentsia in the form of a German academy; of Adam Müller, finally, the political Romantic and forefather of anti-

---

[26] Schelsky, 'Erfahrungen mit einem "Bestseller". Antwort an die Kritiker', Sonderdruck aus der 2., erweiterten Auflage von *Die Arbeit tun die anderen* (Opladen: Westdeutscher Verlag, 1975), p. 439.

sociology, who as poet and scientist had striven for the creation of a confederation of the German intelligentsia.

The problem Schelsky addressed was an old one in Germany– as it was in France or England. But the political situation had sustained a decisive transformation. In Germany it had always been the conservative poets and critics who had refused to a sociology regarded as leftist and equated with socialism its share in what Heidegger called the public exegesis of being; in the Federal Republic during the Adenauer era the literary intelligentsia had to a large extent formed itself into a movement of political opposition which acquired an increasing influence over the public with the creation of the Social Democrat–Liberal coalition; sociology at the same time politicized itself and acquired a mass following in the universities. Now a sociologist who stood in opposition was a conservative. This was what constituted the new situation: in order to assert their claim to be 'formers of opinion' conservative social scientists sought the co-operation of the men of letters of the left.

BIBLIOGRAPHY

France

Agathon 1911 *L'Esprit de la Nouvelle Sorbonne* (Paris: Mercure de France)
  1913 *Les jeunes gens d'aujourd'hui* (Paris: Plon-Nourrit)
Andler, Charles 1932 *Vie de Lucien Herr (1864–1926)* (Paris: Rieder)
Apollinaire, Guillaume 1916 *Le Poète assassiné* (Paris: L'Edition Bibliothèque des curieux)
Aron, Raymond 1934 Review of Henri Gouhier, *La Jeunesse d'Auguste Comte* [1933], in *Zeitschrift für Sozialforschung* 3, pp. 274–5
Auspitz, Katherine 1982 *The Radical Bourgeoisie: The Ligue de l'enseignement and the Origins of the Third Republic 1866–1885* (Cambridge: Cambridge University Press)
Bainville, Jacques 1948 *Journal 1901–1918* (Paris: Plon)
Barrès, Maurice 1902 *Scènes et doctrines du nationalisme* (Paris: Emile-Paul Frères)
  1922 *Taine et Renan*, Pages perdues, recueillies et complétées par Victor Giraud (Paris: Bossard)
  1929–49 *Mes Cahiers*, 12 vols (Paris: Plon)
Barrès, Maurice, and Charles Maurras 1970 *La République ou le Roi*, correspondance inédite (1888–1923) (Paris: Plon)
Benda, Julien 1945 *La France byzantine ou le triomphe de la littérature pure* (Paris: Gallimard)
  1975 *La Trahison des clercs* [1927] (Paris: Grasset)
Bonald, Louis de 1852 *Oeuvres, mélanges littéraires, politiques et philosophiques* (Paris: Librairie d'Adrien Le Clerc)
Bouglé, Célestin 1896 *Notes d'un étudiant français en Allemagne* [under the pseudonym Jacques Breton] (Paris: Calmann-Lévy)
  1905 *La Société sous la terre (Une utopie de G. Tarde)*, in *Revue Bleue* 3, pp. 333–6
  1918 *Chez les prophètes socialistes* (Paris: Alcan)
  1935 *Bilan de la sociologie française contemporaine* (Paris: Alcan)
  1938 *The French Conception of 'Culture Générale' and its Influences upon Instruction* (New York: Columbia University Teachers College)
Bourget, Paul 1902 'Notes sur Balzac: Le Sociologue', in *Minerva: Revue des lettres et des arts* 1, pp. 161–84
  1906 *Sociologie et Littérature* [Etudes et Portraits, No. 3] (Paris: Plon)
Bourgin, Hubert 1938 *De Jaurès à Léon Blum: L'Ecole Normale et la politique* (Paris: Fayard)

Bridges, J. H. 1866 *The Unity of Comte's Life and Doctrine: A Reply to Strictures on Comte's Later Writings, addressed to J. S. Mill* (London: Trübner)

Byrnes, Robert F. 1951 'The French Publishing Industry and its Crisis in the 1890's', in *The Journal of Modern History* 23, pp. 232–42

Capitan Peter, Colette 1972 *Charles Maurras et l'idéologie d'Action Française: Etude sociologique d'une pensée de droite* (Paris: Editions du Seuil)

Carré, Jean-Marie 1947 *Les Ecrivains français et le mirage allemand 1800–1940* (Paris: Boivin)

Comte, Auguste 1851 *Système de politique positive, ou traité de sociologie, instituant la religion de l'humanité* (Paris: L. Matthias)

1884 *Testament d'Auguste Comte* (Paris: 10 Rue Monsieur-le-Prince)

1966 *Catéchisme positiviste* [1852], Chronologie, introduction et notes par Pierre Arnaud (Paris: Garnier-Flammarion)

1973 *Correspondance générale et confessions*, textes établis et présentés par Paulo E. de Berrêdo Carneiro et Pierre Arnaud, Vol. 1 (1814–40) (Paris: Mouton)

1976 *Correspondance générale et confessions*, ... Vol. 2 (1841–5) (Paris: Mouton)

1977 *Correspondance générale et confessions*, ... Vol. 3 (1845–6) (Paris: Mouton)

1981 *Correspondance générale et confessions*, ... Vol. 4 (1846–8) (Paris: Mouton)

Coudekerque-Lambrecht, M. 1925 *Léon de Montesquiou: Sa vie politique. L'Action Française* (Paris: Nouvelle Librairie Nationale)

Curtis, Michael 1959 *Three against the Third Republic: Sorel, Barrès and Maurras* (Princeton: Princeton University Press)

Curtius, Ernst Robert 1921 *Maurice Barrès und die geistigen Grundlagen des französischen Nationalismus* (Bonn: Cohen)

1925 *Französischer Geist im neuen Europa* (Stuttgart: Deutsche Verlagsanstalt)

Daudet, Léon 1915a *Devant la Douleur (Souvenirs des milieux littéraires, politiques, artistiques et médicaux de 1880 à 1905*, Vol. 2) (Paris: Nouvelle Librairie Nationale)

1915b *L'Entre-deux-guerres (Souvenirs*, Vol. 3) (Paris: Nouvelle Librairie Nationale)

1922 *Les Oeuvres dans les hommes* (Paris: Nouvelle Librairie Nationale)

1929 *Ecrivains et artistes*, Vol. 6 (Paris: Editions du Capitole)

1932 *Salons et journaux* (Paris: Grasset)

1938 *Du Roman à l'histoire: Essai* (Paris: Fernand Sorlot)

1974 *Souvenirs politiques* (Paris: Editions d'Histoire et d'Art)

Delaporte, Jean 1959 *Connaissance de Péguy*. Edition revue et augmentée. 2 vols (Paris: Plon)

Deploige, Simon 1912 *Le Conflit de la morale et de la sociologie* (Louvain: Institut supérieur de philosophie; Paris: Alcan)

Digeon, Claude 1959 *La Crise allemande de la pensée française (1870–1914)* (Paris: Presses Universitaires de France)

Dimier, Louis 1917 *Les Maîtres de la contre-révolution au dix-neuvième siècle*, nouvelle édition revue et corrigée (Paris: Nouvelle Librairie Nationale)

1919   *Buffon* (Paris: Nouvelle Librairie Nationale)

1926   *Vingt ans d'Action Française et autres souvenirs* (Paris: Nouvelle Librairie Nationale)

Dreyfus, Robert 1939   *De Monsieur Thiers à Marcel Proust: Histoire et souvenirs* (Paris: Plon)

Dumas, Georges 1905   *Psychologie de deux messies positivistes: Saint-Simon et Auguste Comte* (Paris: Alcan)

Durkheim, Emile 1915   *'Germany above all': German Mentality and War* [Studies and Documents on the War, No. 5] (Paris: Armand Colin) einem Nachwort von René König (Neuwied and Berlin: Luchterhand)

1975   *Textes. I: Eléments d'une théorie sociale*, présentation de Victor Karady (Paris: Les Editions de Minuit)

1933   *On the Division of Labor in Society*, trans. George Simpson (New York: MacMillan)

Eros, John 1955   'The Positivist Generation of French Republicanism', in *The Sociological Review 3*, pp. 255–77

Faguet, Emile 1904   'Auguste Comte et Stuart Mill' [1899], in *Propos littéraires*, deuxième série, pp. 149–62 (Paris: Société française d'imprimerie et de librairie)

Friedrich, Hugo 1935   *Das antiromantische Denken im modernen Frankreich: Sein System und seine Herkunft* (München: Hueber)

Gilson, Etienne 1951   *L'Ecole des muses* (Paris: Librairie philosophique J. Vrin)

Goncourt, Edmond and Jules de 1904   *Idées et sensations*, nouvelle édition (Paris: Charpentier)

Gouhier, Henri 1931   *La Vie d'Auguste Comte* (Paris: Gallimard)

Greenberg, Louis M. 1976   'Bergson and Durkheim as Sons and Assimilators: The Early Years', in *French Historical Studies 9*, pp. 619–34

Halévy, Daniel 1941   *Péguy et les Cahiers de la Quinzaine* (Paris: Grasset)

Herr, Lucien 1932   *Choix d'écrits*, 2 vols (Paris: Rieder)

König, René 1931   *Die naturalistische Ästhetik in Frankreich und ihre Auflösung: Ein Beitrag zur systemwissenschaftlichen Betrachtung der Künstlerästhetik* (Borna and Leipzig: Robert Noske)

Lanson, Gustave 1892   'La Littérature et la science', in *Revue Bleue 50*, pp. 385–91; 433–40

1904   'L'Histoire littéraire et la sociologie', in *Revue de Métaphysique et de Morale 12*, pp. 621–42

Lasserre, Pierre 1913   *La Doctrine officielle de l'Université: Critique du haut enseignement de l'état. Défense et théorie des humanités classiques* (Paris: Garnier)

1914   *Portraits et discussions* (Paris: Mercure de France)

1920   *Les Chapelles littéraires* (Paris: Garnier)

1922   *Cinquante ans de pensée française: Le Germanisme et l'esprit humain* (Paris: Plon-Nourrit)

1924   *Mes routes* (Paris: Plon)

Lindenberg, Daniel, and Pierre-André Meyer 1977   *Lucien Herr: Le Socialisme et son destin* (Paris: Calmann-Lévy)

Littré, Emile 1864   *Auguste Comte et la philosophie positive* (Paris: Hachette)

Lukes, Steven 1972   *Emile Durkheim: His Life and Work. A Historical and Critical Study* (New York: Harper and Row)

Massis, Henri 1906   *Comment Emile Zola composait ses romans. D'après ses notes personnelles et inédites* (Paris: Fasquelle)

1923–40 *Jugements*, 2 vols (Paris: Plon)

1931   *Evocations: Souvenirs 1905–1911* (Paris: Plon)

1941   *Les Idées restent* (Lyon: Lardanchet)

1961   *Maurras et notre temps: Entretiens et souvenirs*, édition définitive augmentée de documents inédits (Paris: Plon)

1962   *Barrès et Nous*, suivi d'une correspondance inédite (1906–23) (Paris: Plon)

1967   *Au long d'une vie* (Paris: Plon)

Maurras, Charles 1916   *Quand les Français ne s'aimaient pas: Chronique d'une renaissance, 1845–1905* (Paris: Nouvelle Librairie Nationale)

1922a   *Romantisme et révolution* (Paris: Nouvelle Librairie Nationale)

1922b   *Pages littéraires choisies* (Paris: Librairie ancienne Honoré Champion)

1923   *L'Allée des philosophes* (Paris: Société littéraire de France)

1925   *Vers un art intellectuel. I: Barbarie et Poesie* (Paris: Nouvelle Librairie Nationale)

1931   *Au Signe de Flore: Souvenirs de vie politique* (Paris: Les Oeuvres Représentatives)

1948   *Maurice Barrès* (Paris: A la Girouette)

Mill, John Stuart 1961   *Auguste Comte and Positivism* [1865] (Ann Arbor: The University of Michigan Press)

Nietzsche, Friedrich 1980   *Sämtliche Werke*. Kritische Studienausgabe in 15 Bänden, ed. Giorgio Colli and Mazzino Montinari (München: Deutscher Taschenbuch Verlag)

Nizan, Paul 1931   *Aden Arabie* (Paris: Rieder)

Nolte, Ernst 1984   *Der Faschismus in seiner Epoche: Action Française, Italienischer Faschismus, Nationalsozialismus* [1963] (München: Piper)

Parodi, Dominique 1925   *La Philosophie contemporaine en France: Essai de classification des doctrines* (Paris: Alcan)

Pasteur, Louis 1939   'Discours de Réception à l'Académie Française' [1882], in *Oeuvres de Pasteur. Réunies par Pasteur Valléry-Radot*, Vol. 7, pp. 326–39 (Paris: Masson)

Péguy, Charles 1959   *Oeuvres en prose 1898–1908*, introduction et notes de Marcel Péguy (Paris: Bibliothèque de la Pléiade)

1961   *Oeuvres en prose 1909–1914*, avant-propos et notes par Marcel Péguy (Paris: Bibliothèque de la Pléiade)

Péguy, Charles, and André Suarès 1961   *Correspondance*, présentée par Alfred Saffrey (Paris: Cahiers de l'amitié Charles Péguy)

Proust, Marcel 1941   *Cities of the Plain* (London: Chatto and Windus), Vol. 2, p. 20.

1954   'Sodome et Gomorrhe', in *A la Recherche du temps perdu* (Paris: Bibliothèque de la Pléiade), Vol. 2

Rohden, Peter Richard 1941   *Die französische Politik und ihre Träger. Advokat,*

Schriftsteller, Professor (München: Bruckmann)

Rolland, Romain 1908 *Jean-Christophe à Paris. La Foire sur la place* (Paris: Ollendorf)

Romains, Jules 1933 *Problèmes européens* (Paris: Flammarion)

Rouvre, Charles de 1917 *L'Amoureuse histoire d'Auguste Comte et de Clotilde de Vaux* (Paris: Calmann-Lévy)

Sainte-Beuve, Charles-Augustin de 1855 *Portraits contemporains et divers*, nouvelle édition revue et corrigée, Vol. 1 (Paris: Didier)

Sorel, Georges 1911a 'Lyripipii Sorbonici Moralisationes', in *L'Indépendance* 1: 4, pp. 111–25

   1911b 'Un critique des sociologues', in *L'Indépendance* 2:16, pp. 73–84

   1912 'Aux temps dreyfusiens', in *L'Indépendance* 4:36, pp. 29–56

Suarès, André 1915 *Péguy* (Paris: Emile-Paul Frères)

Taine, Hippolyte 1904 *Essais de critique et d'histoire* (Paris: Librairie Hachette)

Tarde, Gabriel n.d. *Introduction et pages choisies par ses fils, suivies des poésies inédites de Tarde*, préface de H. Bergson (Paris: Louis-Michaud)

   1879 *Contes et poèmes* (Paris: Calmann-Lévy)

   1896 'Fragment d'histoire future', in *Revue Internationale de Sociologie* 4, pp. 603–54

   1974 *Underground Man* [1905], with a preface by H. G. Wells (Westport, Conn: Hyperion Press [Reprint])

   1980 *Fragment d'histoire future*, présentation de Raymond Trousson (Paris and Geneva: Slatkine Reprints)

Tharaud, Jérome and Jean 1926 *Notre cher Péguy*, 2 vols (Paris: Plon)

   1949 *Pour les fidèles de Péguy* (Paris and St Etienne: Dumas)

Thérive, André 1957 *Clotilde de Vaux ou la déesse morte* (Paris: Albin Michel)

Valéry, Paul 1957 'Une conquête méthodique' [1897], in *Oeuvres*, Vol. 1, pp. 971–87 (Paris: Bibliothèque de la Pléiade)

Vaux, Clotilde de, and Auguste Comte 1918 *Le Positivisme. Esquisse d'un tableau de la fondation de la religion de l'humanité*, Vol 3: *L'Année sans pareille* (Rio de Janeiro: Au siège central de l'église positiviste du Brésil)

England

Abrams, Philip 1968 *The Origins of British Sociology: 1834–1914: An Essay with Selected Papers* (Chicago: The University of Chicago Press)

Amberley 1937 *The Amberley Papers: The Letters and Diaries of Lord and Lady Amberley*, ed. Bertrand and Patricia Russell, Vol. 2 (London: The Hogarth Press)

Anderson, Perry 1968 'Components of the National Culture', in *Student Power*, ed. A. Cockburn and R. Blackburn, pp. 214–84 (Harmondsworth: Pelican Books)

Arnold, Matthew 1895 *Letters 1848–1888*, collected and arranged by George W. E. Russell, Vol. 2 (New York: MacMillan and Co.)

   1903 'Culture and Anarchy: An Essay in Political and Social Criticism and Friendship's Garland' (*The Works of Matthew Arnold in Fifteen Volumes*,

Vol. 6) (London: MacMillan and Co.)

1962 *Lectures and Essays in Criticism* (*The Complete Prose Works of Matthew Arnold*, Vol. 3), ed. R. H. Super, with the assistance of Sister Thomas Marion Hoctor (Ann Arbor: The University of Michigan Press)

1968 *Dissent and Dogma* (*The Complete Prose Works of Matthew Arnold*, Vol. 6), ed. R. H. Super (Ann Arbor: The University of Michigan Press)

1973 *English Literature and Irish Politics* (*The Complete Prose Works of Matthew Arnold*, Vol. 9), ed. R. H. Super (Ann Arbor: The University of Michigan Press)

1974 *Philistinism in England and America* (*The Complete Prose Works of Matthew Arnold*, Vol. 10), ed. R. H. Super (Ann Arbor: The University of Michigan Press)

1977 *The Last Word* (*The Complete Prose Works of Matthew Arnold*, Vol. 11), ed. R. H. Super (Ann Arbor: The University of Michigan Press)

Baldick, Chris 1983 *The Social Mission of English Criticism, 1848–1932* (Oxford: Clarendon Press)

Bantock, G. H. 1947 'The Cultural Implications of Planning and Popularization', in *Scrutiny* 14, pp. 171–84

Bennett, Arnold 1933 *The Journal of Arnold Bennett* (New York: The Literary Guild)

1960 *Arnold Bennett and H. G. Wells: A Record of a Personal and a Literary Friendship*, edited with an introduction by Harris Wilson (London: Rupert Hart-Davis)

Beveridge, Lord 1960 *The London School of Economics and its Problems 1919–1937* (London: George Allen and Unwin)

Bradbury, Malcolm 1970 'Literature and Sociology', in *Essays and Studies* 23, pp. 87–100

Britain, Ian 1982 *Fabianism and Culture: A Study in British Socialism and the Arts* (Cambridge: Cambridge University Press)

Buckley, Vincent 1959 *Poetry and Morality: Studies on the Criticism of Matthew Arnold, T. S. Eliot and F. R. Leavis* (London: Chatto and Windus)

Caine, Sidney 1963 *The History of the Foundation of the London School of Economics and Political Science* (London: G. Bell and Sons)

Carlyle, Thomas 1901 *On Heroes, Hero-Worship, and the Heroic in History* [1841], ed. Archibald MacMechan (Boston: Ginn and Co.)

1923 *Letters of Thomas Carlyle to John Stuart Mill, John Sterling and Robert Browning*, ed. Alexander Carlyle (New York: Frederick A. Stokes)

Clark, Jon, Ed. 1979 *Culture and Crisis in Britain in the Thirties* (London: Lawrence and Wishart)

Cole, Margaret 1946 *Beatrice Webb* (London: Longmans, Green and Co.)

1961 'The Webbs and Social Theory', in *The British Journal of Sociology* 12: 2, pp. 93–105

Cole, Margaret, ed. 1949 *The Webbs and their Work* (London: Frederick Muller)

Coleridge, Samuel Taylor 1860 *On the Constitution of the Church and State. According to the Idea of Each* (*The Complete Works of Samuel Taylor Coleridge*, ed. Professor Shedd, Vol. 6) (New York: Harper and Brothers)

Comte, Auguste 1976 *Correspondance générale et confessions*, textes établis et présentés par Paulo E. de Berrêdo Carneiro et Pierre Arnaud, Vol. 2 (1841–1845) (Paris: Mouton)

Curtius, Ernst Robert 1932 *Deutscher Geist in Gefahr* (Stuttgart and Berlin: Deutsche Verlagsanstalt)

Defries, Amelie Dorothy 1970 *Pioneers of Science: Seven Pictures of Struggle and Victory* [1928] (Freeport: Books for Library Press Reprint)

Dickens, Charles 1980 Hard Times [1854] (New York: A Signet Classic)

Dudley, Fred A. 1942 *Matthew Arnold and Science*, Publications of the Modern Language Association of America No. 57, pp. 275–94

Eliot, T. S. 1933 *The Use of Poetry and the Use of Criticism: Studies in the Relation of Criticism to Poetry in England. The Charles Eliot Norton Lectures for 1932–1933* (Cambridge, Mass.: Harvard University Press)

1939 *The Idea of a Christian Society* (London: Faber and Faber)

1948 *Collected Poems, 1909–1935* (New York: Harcourt, Brace Jovanovich)

1949 *Notes Towards the Definition of Culture* (New York: Harcourt, Brace Jovanovich)

1969 *The Sacred Wood: Essays on Poetry and Criticism* [1920] (London: Methuen)

Farrar, F. W., ed. 1867 *Essays on a Liberal Education* (London: MacMillan and Co.)

Filmer, Paul 1969 'The Literary Imagination and the Explanation of Socio-Cultural Change in Modern Britain', in *Archives Européennes de Sociologie* 10, pp. 271–91

Fox, Caroline 1882 *Memories of Old Friends. Being Extracts from the Journals and Letters of Caroline Fox . . . from 1835 to 1871*, ed. Horace N. Pym (London: Smith, Elder and Co.)

Gissing, George 1961 *George Gissing and H. G. Wells: Their Friendship and Correspondence*, ed. Royal A. Gettman (Urbana: University of Illinois Press)

Gossman, Lionel 1981–2 'Literature and Education', in *New Literary History* 13, pp. 341–71

Gross, John 1969 *The Rise and Fall of the Man of Letters: A Study of the Idiosyncratic and the Humane in Modern Literature* (New York: MacMillan)

Hainds, J. R. 1950 'J. S. Mill's "Examiner" Articles on Art' in *Journal of the History of Ideas* 2, pp. 215–34

Haldane, Richard Burdon 1929 *An Autobiography* (London: Hodder and Stoughton)

Halévy, Elie 1901–4 *La Formation du radicalisme philosophique*, 3 vols (Paris: Alcan)

Hamilton, Mary Agnes 1933 *Sidney and Beatrice Webb: A Study in Contemporary Biography* (Boston and New York: Houghton Mifflin)

Harrison, Austin 1927 *Frederic Harrison: Thoughts and Memories* (New York: G. P. Putnam's Sons)

Harrison, Frederic 1886 *The Choice of Books and Other Literary Pieces* (London: MacMillan and Co.)

1900 *Tennyson, Ruskin, Mill and Other Literary Estimates* (New York: MacMillan)

1911 *Autobiographic Memoirs*, 2 vols (London: MacMillan and Co.)

Hawthorn, Geoffrey 1976 *Enlightenment and Despair: A History of Sociology* (Cambridge: Cambridge University Press)

Hayek, Friedrich A. 1951 *John Stuart Mill and Harriet Taylor: Their Correspondence and Subsequent Marriage* (London: Routledge and Kegan Paul)

Himmelfarb, Gertrude 1971 'The Intellectual in Politics: The Case of the Webbs', in *The Journal of Contemporary History* 6: 3, pp. 3–11

Hoggart, Richard 1957 *The Uses of Literacy: Aspects of Working-Class Life with Special Reference to Publications and Entertainments* (London: Chatto and Windus)

Honan, Park 1981 *Matthew Arnold: A Life* (London: Weidenfeld and Nicolson)

Huxley, Thomas Henry 1893 *Science and Education: Essays* (New York: D. Appleton)

Hynes, Samuel 1968 *The Edwardian Turn of Mind* (Princeton: Princeton University Press)

Inglis, Fred 1982 *Radical Earnestness: English Social Theory, 1880–1980* (Oxford: Martin Robertson)

James Henry 1958 *Henry James and H. G. Wells: A Record of their Friendship, their Debate on the Art of Fiction, and their Quarrel*, ed. with an introduction by Leon Edel and Gordon N. Ray (Urbana: University of Illinois Press)

Johnson, Samuel 1977 *Selected Poetry and Prose*, ed. with an introduction and notes by Frank Brady and W. K. Wimsatt (Berkeley: University of California Press)

Kirk, Russell 1971 *Eliot and His Age: T. S. Eliot's Moral Imagination in the Twentieth Century* (New York: Random House)

Kitchin, Donald K. 1933 'The Significance of Economics Thus Conceived', in *Scrutiny* 2, pp. 258–65

Knights, Ben 1978 *The Idea of the Clerisy in the Nineteenth Century* (Cambridge: Cambridge University Press)

Knights, L. C., and Donald Culver 1932 'A Manifesto, by the Editors', in *Scrutiny* 1, pp. 2–7

Kojecky, Roger 1971 *T. S. Eliot's Social Criticism* (London: Faber and Faber)

Leavis, F. R. 1933 *For Continuity* (Cambridge: The Minority Press)

1936 *Revaluation: Tradition and Development in English Poetry* (London: Chatto and Windus)

1938 'Arnold as Critic', in *Scrutiny* 7, pp. 319–32

1943 *Education and the University: A Sketch for an 'English School'* (London: Chatto and Windus)

1948 *The Great Tradition: George Eliot, Henry James, Joseph Conrad* (London: Chatto and Windus)

1949a 'Mill, Beatrice Webb and the "English School": Preface to an Unprinted Volume', in *Scrutiny* 16, pp. 104–26

1949b 'Beatrice Webb in Partnership' (Review of Beatrice Webb, *Our Partnership*), in *Scrutiny* 16, pp. 173–6

1950 *New Bearings in English Poetry: A Study of the Contemporary Situation*

[1932], new edition (London: Chatto and Windus)

1953a 'The Responsible Critic: Or the Function of Criticism at Any Time', in *Scrutiny* 19, pp. 162–83

1963b 'A Retrospect', in *Scrutiny* [Reprint] 20, pp. 1–24

1963a *Two Cultures? The Significance of C. P. Snow. Being the Richmond Lecture 1962*, With a new Preface for the American Reader (New York: Pantheon Books)

1963b 'A Retrospect', in *Scrutiny* [Reprint] 20, pp. 1–24

1968 *A Selection from Scrutiny*, compiled by F. R. Leavis, 2 vols (Cambridge: Cambridge University Press)

1972 *Nor Shall My Sword: Discourses on Pluralism, Compassion and Social Hope* (London: Chatto and Windus)

1974 *Letters in Criticism*, ed. with an introduction by John Tasker (London: Chatto and Windus)

1975 *The Living Principle: 'English' as a Discipline of Thought* (London: Chatto and Windus)

1978 *The Common Pursuit* [1962] (Harmondsworth: Penguin Books)

Leavis, F. R., and Q. D. Leavis 1969 *Lectures in America* (London: Chatto and Windus)

1970 *Dickens the Novelist* (London: Chatto and Windus)

Leavis, F. R., and Denys Thompson 1933 *Culture and Environment: The Training of Critical Awareness* (London: Chatto and Windus)

Leavis, Q. D. 1932 *Fiction and the Reading Public* (London: Chatto and Windus)

Letwin, Shirley Robin 1965 *The Pursuit of Certainty: David Hume, Jeremy Bentham, John Stuart Mill, Beatrice Webb* (Cambridge: Cambridge University Press)

Lynd, Robert S. 1939 *Knowledge for What? The Place of Social Science in American Culture* (Princeton: Princeton University Press)

Lynd, Robert S., and Helen Merrell Lynd 1929 *Middletown: A Study in Contemporary American Culture* (New York: Harcourt, Brace and Co.)

Mackenzie, Jeanne 1979 *A Victorian Courtship: The Story of Beatrice Potter and Sidney Webb* (New York: Oxford University Press)

Mackenzie, Norman, and Jeanne Mackenzie 1973 *H. G. Wells: A Biography* (New York: Simon and Schuster)

Mairet, Philip 1957 *Pioneer of Sociology: The Life and Letters of Patrick Geddes* (London: Lund Humphries)

Marmontel, Jean François 1972 *Mémoires* [1804], édition critique établie par John Renwick, 2 vols (Clermond-Ferrand: G. de Bussac, Collection Ecrivains d'Auvergne)

Martineau, Harriet 1983 *Autobiography* [1877], with a new introduction by Gaby Weiner, 2 vols (London: Virago Press)

Marwick, Arthur 1964 'Middle Opinion in the Thirties: Planning, Progress and Political "Agreement" ', in *The English Historical Review* 74, pp. 285–98

Mazlish, Bruce 1975 *James and John Stuart Mill: Father and Son in the Nineteenth Century* (New York: Basic Books)

Mill, Anna J. 1949 'John Stuart Mill's Visit to Wordsworth, 1831', in

Modern Language Review 44, pp. 341–50

Mill, John Stuart 1859–75   *Dissertations and Discussions . . .*, 4 vols (London: Longmans and others)

  1960   *John Mill's Boyhood Visit to France. Being a Journal and Notebook Written by John Stuart Mill in France, 1820–1821*, ed. with an introduction by Anna Jean Mill (Toronto: University of Toronto Press)

  1961   *Auguste Comte and Positivism* [1865] (Ann Arbor: The University of Michigan Press)

  1963   *The Earlier Letters of John Stuart Mill 1812–1848*, ed. Francis E. Mineka, with an introduction by F. A. Hayek (Toronto: University of Toronto Press)

  1965   *Mill's Essays on Literature and Society*, ed., with an introduction by J. B. Schneewind (New York: Collier Books)

  1969   *Essays on Ethics, Religion and Society*, ed. J. M. Robson (*Collected Works of John Stuart Mill*, Vol. 10) (Toronto: University of Toronto Press)

  1972   *The Later Letters of John Stuart Mill 1849–1873*, ed. Francis E. Mineka and Dwight N. Lindley (Toronto: University of Toronto Press)

  1973–4   *A System of Logic* [1843], ed. J. M. Robson and R. F. McRae, 2 vols (*Collected Works of John Stuart Mill*, Vols. 7 and 8) (Toronto: University of Toronto Press)

  1981   *Autobiography* [1873] *and Literary Essays*, ed. J. M. Robson and Jack Stillinger (*Collected Works of John Stuart Mill*, Vol. 1) (Toronto: The University of Toronto Press)

Mulhern, Francis 1979   *The Moment of 'Scrutiny'* (London: Verso Editions)

Nietzsche, Friedrich 1980   *Sämtliche Werke. Kritische Studienausgabe in 15 Bänden*, ed. Giorgio Colli and Mazzino Montinari (München: Deutscher Taschenbuch Verlag)

Nisbet, Robert 1976   *Sociology as an Art Form* (London: Heinemann)

Packe, Michael St John 1954   *The Life of John Stuart Mill* (London: Secker and Warburg)

Palmer, D. J. 1965   *The Rise of English Studies: An Account of the Study of English Language and Literature from its Origins to the Making of the Oxford English School* (London: Oxford University Press)

Pappe, H. O. 1960   *John Stuart Mill and the Harriet Taylor Myth* (London and New York: Cambridge University Press)

Parrinder, Patrick 1976   'H. G. Wells and Beatrice Webb: Reflections on a Quarrel', in *The Wellsian: The Journal of the H. G. Wells Society* 1, pp. 11–17

Peacock, Thomas Love 1896   *Gryll Grange* [1861] (London: MacMillan)

Pease, Edward R. 1916   *The History of the Fabian Society* (New York: E. P. Dutton)

Plumb, J. H., ed. 1955   *Studies in Social History: A Tribute to G. M. Trevelyan* (London: Longmans, Green and Co.)

Ratcliffe, S. K. 1910   'Sociology in the English Novel', in *The Sociological Review* 3, pp. 126–36

Richards, I. A. 1926   *Science and Poetry* (New York: W. W. Norton and Co.)

1928   *Principles of Literary Criticism* (New York: Harcourt, Brace and Co.)

1976   *Complementarities*, Uncollected Essays ed. John Paul Russo (Cambridge, Mass.: Harvard University Press)

Robson, John M. 1966   'Harriet Taylor and John Stuart Mill: Artist and Scientist', in *Queens Quarterly* 73, pp. 167–86

Schneewind, J. B., ed. 1968   *Mill* (New York: Anchor Books)

Sharpless, F. Parvin 1967   *The Literary Criticism of John Stuart Mill* (The Hague and Paris: Mouton)

Shaw, George Bernard 1969–70   *An Autobiography 1856–1950*, selected from his writings by Stanley Weintraub, 2 vols (New York: Weybright and Talley)

Shaw, George Bernard, ed. 1911   *Fabian Essays in Socialism* [1889] (Boston: The Ball Publishing Co.)

Simart, Maurice 1917   'Herbert-George Wells Sociologue', in *Mercure de France* 120, pp. 193–221

Simey, T. S. 1961   'The Contribution of Sidney and Beatrice Webb to Sociology', in *The British Journal of Sociology* 12: 2, pp. 106–23

Simon, W. M. 1964   'Auguste Comte's English Disciples' in *Victorian Studies* 8, pp. 161–72

Snow, C. P. 1959   *The Two Cultures and the Scientific Revolution*, The Rede Lecture 1959 (New York: Cambridge University Press)

Soffer, Reba N. 1982   'Why Do Disciplines Fail? The Strange Case of British Sociology', in *The English Historical Review* 97, pp. 767–802

Spencer, Herbert 1860   *Education. Intellectual, Moral and Physical* (New York and London: D. Appleton and Co.)

1904   *An Autobiography*, 2 vols (London: Williams and Norgate)

Stephen, Leslie 1907   *Studies of a Biographer*, 4 vols (London: Smith, Elder and Co.)

Strachey, Lytton 1918   *Eminent Victorians* (New York: Harcourt, Brace and Co.)

Taine, Hippolyte 1864   *Le Positivisme anglais: Etude sur Stuart Mill* (Paris: Germer Baillière)

1897   *Histoire de la littérature anglaise*, dixième édition, revue et augmentée … tome cinquième et complémentaire: *Les Contemporains* (Paris: Hachette)

1899   *Notes sur l'Angleterre* (Paris: Hachette)

Tarde, Gabriel 1974   *Underground Man* [1905; translation of *Fragment d'Histoire future*], with a preface by H. G. Wells (Westport: Hyperion Press)

Thompson, Denys 1933   'A Cure for Amnesia', in *Scrutiny* 2, pp. 2–11

Thompson, Denys, ed. 1984   *The Leavises: Recollections and Impressions* (Cambridge: Cambridge University Press)

Tillyard, E. M. W. 1958   *The Muse Unchained: An Intimate Account of the Revolution in English Studies at Cambridge* (London: Bowes and Bowes)

Trilling, Lionel 1939   *Matthew Arnold* (New York: W. W. Norton and Co.)

Véran, Jules 1937   'Le Souvenir de Stuart Mill à Avignon', in *Revue des Deux Mondes* 107, pp. 211–22

Vogeler, Martha Salmon 1962 'Matthew Arnold and Frederic Harrison: the Prophet of Culture and the Prophet of Positivism', in *Studies in English Literature 1500–1900* 2, pp. 441–62

Webb, Beatrice 1952 *Diaries 1912–1924*, ed. Margaret Cole, with an introduction by Lord Beveridge (London: Longmans, Green and Co.)

1956 *Diaries 1924–1932*, ed. with an introduction by Margaret Cole (London: Longmans, Green and Co.)

1975 *Our Partnership* [1948], ed. Barbara Drake and Margaret Cole, with an introduction by George Feaver (Cambridge: Cambridge University Press)

1978 *Diary 1873–1943*, typescript on microfiche (Cambridge: Chadwyck-Healey)

1979 *My Apprenticeship* [1926], with an introduction by Norman MacKenzie (Cambridge: Cambridge University Press)

1982 *Diary I 1873–1892: Glitter Around and Darkness Within*, ed. Norman and Jeanne MacKenzie (Cambridge, Mass.: The Belknap Press of Harvard University Press)

1983 *Diary II 1892–1905: All the Good Things of Life*, ed. Norman and Jeanne MacKenzie (Cambridge, Mass.: The Belknap Press of Harvard University Press)

1984 *Diary III 1905–1924: The Power to Alter Things*, ed. Norman and Jeanne MacKenzie (London: Virago Press in association with the London School of Economics and Political Science)

Webb, Sidney, and Beatrice Webb 1932 *Methods of Social Study* (London: Longmans, Green and Co.)

1978 *Letters 1873–1947*, ed. Norman MacKenzie, 3 vols (Cambridge: Cambridge University Press)

Wells, H. G. 1905 *A Modern Utopia* (London: Chapman and Hall)

1907 'The So-Called Science of Sociology', in *Sociological Papers* 3, pp. 357–77

1910 *The New Machiavelli* (New York: Duffield and Company)

1914 *An Englishman Looks at the World. Being a Series of Unrestrained Remarks upon Contemporary Matters* (Leipzig: Tauchnitz)

1934 *Experiment in Autobiography. Discoveries and Conclusions of a Very Ordinary Brain (since 1866)* (New York: MacMillan)

1968 'The Faults of the Fabian' [1906], in Samuel Hynes, *The Edwardian Turn of Mind*, pp. 390–409 (Princeton: Princeton University Press)

1972 *H. G. Wells: The Critical Heritage*, ed. Patrick Parrinder (London: Routledge and Kegan Paul)

Willey, Basil 1970 *Cambridge and Other Memories 1920–1953* (London: Chatto and Windus)

Williams, Raymond 1958 *Culture and Society, 1780–1950* (New York: Columbia University Press; London: Chatto and Windus)

1983 *Writing in Society* (London: Verso Editions)

Woods, Thomas 1961 *Poetry and Philosophy: A Study in the Thought of John Stuart Mill* (London: Hutchinson)

Woolf, Leonard 1972 *Beginning Again: An Autobiography of the Years 1911 to*

1918 (New York, Harcourt Brace Jovanovich)

1975   *Sowing: An Autobiography of the Years 1880 to 1904* (New York, Harcourt Brace Jovanovich)

Woolf, Virginia 1976–8   *Letters II–IV: 1912–1931*, ed. Nigel Nicolson and Joanne Trautmann, 3 vols (New York: Harcourt Brace Jovanovich)

1978   *The Captain's Deathbed and other Essays* (New York: Harcourt Brace Jovanovich)

1980   *Diary III: 1925–1930*, ed. Anne Olivier Bell, assisted by Andrew McNeillie (New York: Harcourt Brace Jovanovich)

1982   *Diary IV: 1931–1935*, ed. Anne Olivier Bell, assisted by Andrew McNeillie (New York: Harcourt Brace Jovanovich)

Wordsworth, William 1883   *The Poetical Works*, ed. William Knight, 4 vols (Edinburgh: William Paterson)

Germany

Adamy, Bernhard 1980   *Hans Pfitzner: Literatur, Philosophie und Zeitgeschehen in seinem Weltbild und Werk* [Veröffentlichungen der Hans Pfitzner-Gesellschaft, Vol. 1] (Tutzing: Hans Schneider)

Baier, Horst 1981–2   'Die Gesellschaft-Ein langer Schatten des toten Gottes: Friedrich Nietzsche und die Entstehung der Soziologie aus dem Geist der Décadence', in *Nietzsche-Studien* 10/11, pp. 6–33

Bantock, G. H. 1947   'The Cultural Implications of Planning and Popularization', in *Scrutiny* 14, pp. 171–84

Becker, Carl Heinrich 1919   *Gedanken zur Hochschulreform* (Leipzig: Quelle und Meyer)

1925   *Vom Wesen der deutschen Universität* (Leipzig: Quelle und Meyer)

1930   *Das Problem der Bildung in der Kulturkrise der Gegenwart* (Leipzig: Quelle und Meyer)

Below, Georg von 1920   *Soziologie als Lehrfach: Ein kritischer Beitrag zur Hochschulreform* (München and Leipzig: Duncker und Humblot)

1921   'Zur Geschichte der deutschen Geschichtswissenschaft II', in *Historische Blätter* 1: 2, pp. 173–217

1928   *Die Entstehung der Soziologie*. Aus dem Nachlasse herausgegeben von Othmar Spann (Jena: Gustav Fischer)

Benjamin, Walter 1934   'Zum gegenwärtigen gesellschaftlichen Standort des französischen Schriftstellers', in *Zeitschrift für Sozialforschung* 3, pp. 54–78

Benn, Gottfried 1968   *Gesammelte Werke in acht Bänden*, ed. Dieter Wellershoff (Wiesbaden: Limes)

Bertram, Ernst 1920 *Nietzsche. Versuch einer Mythologie* [1918] 4, unveränderte Aufl. (Berlin: Georg Bondi)

1967   *Dichtung als Zeugnis. Frühe Bonner Studien zur Literatur*, mit einem Nachwort herausgegeben von Ralph-Rainer Wuthenow (Bonn: Bouvier)

Blätter für die Kunst 1964   Einleitungen und Merksprüche der Blätter für die Kunst (Düsseldorf and München: Küpper)

Boehringer, Robert 1968   Mein Bild von Stefan George [1951], 2., ergänzte Aufl. (Düsseldorf and München: Küpper)

Borchardt, Rudolf 1918   *Rede über Hofmannsthal* [1902], 2. Aufl. (Berlin: Hyperion)

   1920   *Stefan Georges Siebenter Ring* [1909]; Borchardt, *Prosa 1*, pp. 119–162 (Berlin: Ernst Rowohlt)

   1928   *Handlungen und Abhandlungen* (Berlin-Grunewald: Horen-Verlag)

   1973   *Prosa IV* (Stuttgart: Klett)

Brackmann, Albert 1929   'Kaiser Friedrich II. in "Mythischer Schau" ', in *Historische Zeitschrift* 140, pp. 534–49

Breysig, Kurt 1944   *Das Recht auf Persönlichkeit und seine Grenzen* (Berlin: De Gruyter)

   1962   *Aus meinen Tagen und Träumen. Memoiren, Aufzeichnungen, Briefe, Gespräche*, aus dem Nachlass herausgegeben von Gertrud Breysig und Michael Landmann (Berlin: De Gruyter)

   1964   *Gedankenblätter*, ed. Gertrud Breysig (Berlin: De Gruyter)

Breysig, Kurt, and Stefan George 1960   *Gespräche, Dokumente* (Amsterdam: Castrum Peregrini Presse)

Brodersen, Arvid 1970   'Stefan George und sein Kreis. Eine Deutung aus der Sicht Max Webers', in *Castrum Peregrini* 91, pp. 5–24

Brose, Karl 1974   'Nietzsches Verhältnis zu John Stuart Mill', in *Nietzsche-Studien* 3, 152–74

Curtius, Ernst Robert 1919   *Die literarischen Wegbereiter des neuen Frankreich* (Potsdam: Kiepenheuer)

   1921   *Der Syndikalismus der Geistesarbeiter in Frankreich* (Bonn: Cohen)

   1929   'Hofmannsthal und die Romanität', in *Die Neue Rundschau* 40, p. 654–9

   1930   *Die französische Kultur: Eine Einführung* (Berlin and Leipzig: Deutsche Verlagsanstalt)

   1932   *Deutscher Geist in Gefahr* (Stuttgart and Berlin: Deutsche Verlagsanstalt)

   1948   *Europäische Literatur und Lateinisches Mittelalter* (Bern: Francke)

   1954   *Kritische Essays zur europäischen Literatur* [1950], 2., erweiterte Aufl. (Bern: Francke)

   1982   'Soziologie – und ihre Grenzen' [1929], in *Der Streit um die Wissenssoziologie, 2: Rezeption und Kritik der Wissenssoziologie*, ed. Volker Meja and Nico Stehr, pp. 417–26 (Frankfurt am Main: Suhrkamp)

Dahme, Heinz-Jürgen, and Otthein Rammstedt, ed. 1984   *Georg Simmel und die Moderne: Neue Interpretationen und Materialien* (Frankfurt am Main: Suhrkamp)

Dahmen, Hans 1926   *Lehren über Kunst und Weltanschauung im Kreise um Stefan George* (Marburg: Elwert)

David, Claude 1952   *Stefan George: Son oeuvre poétique* (Lyon and Paris: IAC [Bibliothèque de la Société des Etudes Germaniques])

Dilthey, Wilhelm 1922   *Einleitung in die Geisteswissenschaften* [1883] (Dilthey, *Gesammelte Schriften*, 1) (Leipzig and Berlin: Teubner)

   1923   *Briefwechsel zwischen Wilhelm Dilthey und dem Grafen Paul Yorck von Wartenburg 1877–1897* (Halle: Niemeyer)

   1933   *Von deutscher Dichtung und Musik. Aus den Studien zur Geschichte des deutschen Geistes* (Leipzig and Berlin: Teubner)

1954 *Die grosse Phantasiedichtung und andere Studien zur vergleichenden Literaturgeschichte* (Göttingen: Vandenhoeck und Ruprecht)

1961 *Die Geistige Welt. Einleitung in die Philosophie des Lebens, Erste Hälfte, Abhandlungen zur Grundlegung der Geisteswissenschaften* [1923] (Dilthey, *Gesammelte Schriften*, 3., unveränderte Aufl.) (Stuttgart: Teubner; Göttingen: Vandenhoeck und Ruprecht)

1962a *Einleitung in die Geisteswissenschaften* [1883] (Dilthey, *Gesammelte Schriften* 1, 5., unveränderte Aufl. (Stuttgart: Teubner; Göttingen: Vandenhoeck und Ruprecht)

1962b 'Die Einbildungskraft des Dichters', *Bausteine für eine Poetik* [1887] (Dilthey, *Gesammelte Schriften* 6, 4. Aufl., pp. 103–241) (Stuttgart: Teubner; Göttingen: Vandenhoeck und Ruprecht)

1962c 'Die drei Epochen der modernen Ästhetik und ihre heutige Aufgabe [1892]; Dilthey, *ibid.*, pp. 242–87

Du Bois-Reymond, Emil 1886 *Reden*, erste folge: *Litteratur, Philosophie, Zeitgeschichte* (Leipzig: Veit und Co.)

Durkheim, Emile 1969 *Journal Sociologique*, introduction et notes de Jean Duvignaud (Paris: Presses Universitaires de France)

Düwell, Kurt 1971 'Staat und Wissenschaft in der Weimarer Epoche. Zur Kulturpolitik des Ministers C. H. Becker', in *Historische Zeitschrift*, Beiheft I [*Beiträge zue Geschichte der Weimarer Republik*, ed. Theodor Schieder], pp. 31–74

Eliot, George 1963 'The Natural History of German Life' [*Westminster Review* 66 (1856), pp. 51–79], in *Essays of George Eliot*, ed. Thomas Pinney, pp. 266–99 (London: Routledge and Kegan Paul)

Eliot, T. S. 1932a 'A Commentary' (to *Fiction and the Reading Public* by Q. D. Leavis), in *The Criterion* 11, p. 676–83

1932b 'A Commentary' (to *Deutscher Geist in Gefahr* by E. R. Curtius), in *The Criterion* 12, pp. 73–9

1933 'A Commentary' (to editions of the *American Review* and *The Symposium*), in *The Criterion* 12, pp. 642–7

1947 Letter to *The Times*, 25 January 1947, p. 7.

Enright D. J. 1944 'Stefan George and the New Empire', in *Scrutiny* 12, pp. 162–71

1948 'The Case of Stefan George', in *Scrutiny* 15, pp. 242–54

Eschmann, Ernst Wilhelm 1932 'Soziologie der Wirklichkeit!' [Rezension von Hans Freyers *Soziologie als Wirklichkeitswissenschaft*], in *Die Tat* 24, pp. 813–14

1933 'Spengler und die Wirklichkeit', in *Die Tat* 25, pp. 673–8

1934 'Die Stunde der Soziologie', in *Die Tat* 25, pp. 953–66

Evans, Arthur R., Jr., ed. 1970 *On Four Modern Humanists: Hofmannsthal, Gundolf, Curtius, Kantorowicz* (Princeton: Princeton University Press)

Fleischmann, Eugène 1964 'De Weber à Nietzsche', in *Archives Européennes de Sociologie* 5, pp. 190–238

Freyer, Hans 1918 *Antäus. Grundlegung einer Ethik des bewussten Lebens* (Jena: Eugen Diederichs)

1925 *Der Staat* (Leipzig: Wiegandt)

1926 'Soziologie als Geisteswissenschaft' [Antrittsvorlesung an der Universität Leipzig], in *Archiv für Kulturgeschichte* 16, pp. 113–26

1930   *Soziologie als Wirklichkeitswissenschaft. Logische Grundlegung des Systems der Soziologie* (Leipzig and Berlin: Teubner)

1932   'Die Romantiker', in *Gründer der Soziologie: Eine Vortragsreihe*, ed. Fritz Karl Mann (Jena: Gustav Fischer)

1935a   *Pallas Athene. Ethik des politischen Volkes* (Jena: Eugen Diederichs)

1935b   'Gegenwartsaufgaben der deutschen Soziologie', in *Zeitschrift für die gesamte Staatswissenschaft* 95, pp. 116–44

Gábor, Eva 1983   'Mannheim in Hungary and in Weimar Germany', in *Newsletter, International Society for the Sociology of Knowledge* 9: 1/2, pp. 7–14

Gay, Peter 1968   *Weimar Culture: The Outsider as Insider* (New York: Harper and Row)

George, Stefan 1953   *Briefwechsel zwischen George und Hofmannsthal* [1938], 2, ergänzte Aufl. (München and Düsseldorf: Küpper)

1967   *Tage und Taten: Aufzeichnungen und Skizzen* [1933] (Düsseldorf and München: Küpper)

1968   *Stefan George 1868–1968: Der Dichter und sein Kreis*, Eine Ausstellung des Deutschen Literaturarchivs im Schiller-Nationalmuseum Marbach am Neckar (Stuttgart: Turmhaus Verlag)

1971   *Stefan George Kolloquium*, ed. Eckhard Heftrich, Paul Gerhard Klussmann and Hans Joachim Schrimpf (Köln: Wienand)

1974   *Stefan George. Dokumente seiner Wirkung.* Aus dem Friedrich Gundolf Archiv der Universität London herausgegeben von Lothar Helbing und Claus Victor Bock, mit Karlhans Kluncker (Amsterdam, Castrum Peregrini Presse) [Publications of the Institute of Germanic Studies, University of London, 18]

1983   *Werke.* Ausgabe in vier Bänden (München: Deutscher Taschenbuch Verlag)

Glöckner, Ernst 1972   *Begegnung mit Stefan George*, Auszüge aus Briefen und Tagebüchern 1913–1934, ed. Friedrich Adam (Heidelberg: Stiehm)

Glockner, Hermann 1969   *Heidelberger Bilderbuch*, Erinnerungen (Bonn: Bouvier)

Gothein, Eberhard 1924   *Die Renaissance in Süditalien* [1886], mit einer biographischen Einleitung herausgegeben von Edgar Salin, 2. Aufl. (München and Leipzig: Duncker und Humblot)

Gothein, Percy 1955   *Das Seelenfest.* Aus einem Erinnerungsbuch [1923] (Den Haag: Castrum Peregrini 21)

1956   'Letzte Universitätsjahre. Der Rod des Vaters', in *Castrum Peregrini* 26, pp. 7–32

Graver, Suzanne 1984   *George Eliot and Community: A Study in Social Theory and Fictional Form* (Berkeley: University of California Press)

Grimm, Jacob, and Wilhelm Grimm 1984   *Deutsches Wörterbuch* (München: Deutscher Taschenbuch Verlag)

Grünewald, Eckhart 1982   *Ernst Kantorowicz und Stefan George. Beiträge zur Biographie des Historikers bis zum Jahre 1938 und zu seinem Jugendwerk 'Kaiser Friedrich der Zweite'* (Wiesbaden: Franz Steiner)

Gundolf, Friedrich 1911   *Shakespeare und der deutsche Geist* (Berlin: Georg Bondi)

1914   *Stefan George in unserer Zeit* [1913], 2. Aufl. (Heidelberg: Weiss)

1921   *George* [1920], 2., unveränderte Aufl. (Berlin: Georg Bondi)

1930   *Gedichte* (Berlin: Georg Bondi)

1962–3   *Briefwechsel mit Herbert Steiner und Ernst Robert Curtius*, eingeleitet und herausgegeben von Lothar Helbing und Claus Victor Bock [*Castrum Peregrini* 54, 55, 56] (Amsterdam: Castrum Peregrini Presse)

1965   *Briefe*, neue Folge, ed. Lothar Helbing and Claus Victor Bock [*Castrum Peregrini* 66, 67, 68] (Amsterdam: Castrum Peregrini Presse)

1980   *Beiträge zur Literatur- und Geistesgeschichte*, ed. Victor A. Schmitz and Fritz Martini (Heidelberg: Lambert Schneider)

Heidegger, Martin 1983   *Die Selbstbehauptung der deutschen Universität*, Rede, gehalten bei der feierlichen Übernahme des Rektorats der Universität Freiburg i. Br. am 27.5.1933. / Das Rektorat 1933–34, Tatsachen und Gedanken, ed. Hermann Heidegger (Frankfurt am Main: Klostermann)

Heine, Heinrich 1964   *Sämtliche Werke*, ed. Hans Kaufmann (München: Kindler)

Hildebrandt, Kurt 1965   *Erinnerungen an Stefan George und seinen Kreis* (Bonn: Bouvier)

Hofmannsthal, Hugo von 1957   *Natur und Erkenntnis: Essays* (Berlin and Darmstadt: Deutsche Buch-Gemeinschaft)

1977   *Gesammelte Werke in Einzelausgaben*, ed. Herbert Steiner, *Prosa III* (Frankfurt am Main: S. Fischer)

1979a   *Reden und Aufsätze I (1891–1913)* (Frankfurt am Main: S. Fischer)

1979b   *Reden und Aufsätze II (1914–1924)* (Frankfurt am Main: S. Fischer)

1980   *Reden und Aufsätze III (1925–1929)* (Frankfurt am Main: S. Fischer)

Hofmannsthal, Hugo von, and Rudolf Borchardt 1954   *Briefwechsel*, ed. Marie Borchardt and Herbert Steiner (Frankfurt am Main: S. Fischer)

Hofmannsthal, Hugo von and Josef Redlich 1971   *Briefwechsel*, ed. Helga Ebner-Fussgänger (Frankfurt am Main: S. Fischer)

Honigsheim, Paul 1926   'Der Max Weber-Kreis in Heidelberg', in *Kölner Vierteljahrshefte für Soziologie* 5, pp. 270–87

Jaensch, E. R. 1932   'Deutscher Geist in Gefahr? Zur Auseinandersetzung mit dem Buche von E. R. Curtius', in *Westdeutsche Akademische Rundschau* 2: 13

1933   *Die Lage und die Aufgaben der Psychologie: Ihre Sendung in der Deutschen Bewegung und an der Kulturwende* (Leipzig: Barth)

1934   *Der Kampf der deutschen Psychologie* (Langensalza, Berlin and Leipzig: Julius Beltz)

Jahrbuch für die geistige Bewegung 1910–12   Jahrbuch für die geistige Bewegung, ed. Friedrich Gundolf and Friedrich Wolters, 3 Jahrgänge (Berlin: Georg Bondi)

Jaspers, Karl 1932   *Max Weber. Deutsches Wesen im politischen Denken, im Forschen und Philosophieren* (Oldenburg: Stalling)

Jens, Inge 1979   *Dichter zwischen rechts und links. Die Geschichte der Sektion für Dichtkunst der Preussischen Akademie der Künste dargestellt nach Dokumenten* [1971] (München: Deutscher Taschenbuch Verlag)

Jolles, Frank 1967   'Die Entwicklung der wissenschaftlichen Grundsätze des George-Kreises', in *Etudes Germaniques* 22, pp. 346–58

Kahler, Erich von 1920 *Der Beruf der Wissenschaft* (Berlin: Georg Bondi)

Kantorowicz, Ernst 1930a 'Über Grenzen, Möglichkeiten und Aufgaben der Darstellung mittelalterlicher Geschichte', in *Der Ring*, 18, pp. 333–5

1930b ' "Mythenschau": Eine Erwiderung', in *Historische Zeitschrift* 141, pp. 457–71

Käsler, Dirk, Ed. 1976–8 *Klassiker des soziologischen Denkens*, 2 vols (München: Beck)

Kaufmann, Walter 1978 'Nietzsche als der erste grosse Psychologe', in *Nietzsche-Studien* 7, pp. 261–87

Kehr, Eckart 1965 *Der Primat der Innenpolitik. Gesammelte Aufsätze zur preussisch-deutschen Sozialgeschichte im 19. und 20. Jahrhundert*, herausgegeben und eingeleitet von Hans-Ulrich Wehler (Berlin: De Gruyter)

Kerényi, Karl, and Thomas Mann 1945 *Romandichtung und Mythologie: Ein Briefwechsel* (Zürich: Rhein-Verlag)

Kessler, Harry Graf 1928 *Walther Rathenau: Sein Leben und sein Werk* (Berlin-Grunewald: Klemm)

Kirk, Russell 1971 *Eliot and His Age: T. S. Eliot's Moral Imagination in the Twentieth Century* (New York: Random House)

Kjellén, Rudolf 1915 *Die Ideen von 1914: Eine weltgeschichtliche Perspektive* (Leipzig: Hirzel)

Klages, Ludwig 1902 *Stefan George* (Berlin: Georg Bondi)

Kojecky, Roger 1971 *T. S. Eliot's Social Criticism* (New York: Farrar, Straus and Giroux)

Kommerell, Max 1928 *Der Dichter als Führer in der Deutschen Klassik: Klopstock–Herder–Goethe–Schiller–Jean Paul–Hölderlin* (Berlin: Georg Bondi)

1967 *Brief und Aufzeichnungen 1919–1944*. Aus dem Nachlass heraus-gegeben von Inge Jens (Olten and Freiburg: Walter)

König, René 1984 'Über das vermeintliche Ende der deutschen Soziologie vor der Machtergreifung des Nationalsozialismus', in *Kölner Zeitschrift für Soziologie und Sozialpsychologie* 36, pp. 1–42

König, René, and Johannes Winckelmann, eds. 1963 *Max Weber zum Gedächtnis. Materialien und Dokumente zur Bewertung von Werk und Persön-lichkeit* [*Kölner Zeitschrift für Soziologie und Sozialpsychologie*, Sonderheft 7] (Köln and Opladen: Westdeutscher Verlag)

Kraft, Werner 1956 'Rudolf Borchardt und Stefan George', in *Die Neue Rundschau* 67, pp. 473–90

Landfried, Klaus 1975 *Stefan George – Politik des Unpolitischen*, mit einem Geleitwort von Dolf Sternberger (Heidelberg: Stiehm)

Landmann, Edith 1920 *Georgika. Das Wesen des Dichters. Stefan George: Umriss seines Werkes, Stefan George: Umriss seiner Wirkung* (Heidelberg: Weiss)

1930 'Wissen und Werten', in *Schmollers Jahrbuch* 54, pp. 287–303

1963 *Gespräche mit Stefan George* (Düsseldorf and München: Küpper)

Landmann, Michael 1980 *Erinnerungen an Stefan George. Seine Freundschaft mit Julius und Edith Landmann* [*Castrum Peregrini* 141–2] (Amsterdam: Castrum Peregrini Presse)

Langbehn, Julius 1890 *Rembrandt als Erzieher. Von einem Deutschen* (Leipzig: Hirschfeld)

Lange-Kirchheim, Astrid 1977 'Franz Kafka: "In der Strafkolonie" und

Alfred Weber: "Der Beamte'", in *Germanisch-Romanische Monatsschrift* (Neue Folge) 27, pp. 202–21

Lenk, Kurt 1964 'Das tragische Bewusstsein in der deutschen Soziologie', in *Kölner Zeitschrift für Soziologie und Sozialpsychologie* 16, pp. 257–87

Lepsius, M. Rainer, ed. 1981 *Soziologie in Deutschland und Österreich 1918–1945* [*Kölner Zeitschrif für Soziologie und Sozialpsychologie*, Sonderheft 23] (Opladen: Westdeutscher Verlag)

Lepsius, Sabine 1935 *Stefan George. Geschichte einer Freundschaft* (Berlin: Verlag Die Runde)

Lieber, Hans-Joachim 1974 *Kulturkritik und Lebensphilosophie. Studien zur deutschen Philosophie der Jahrhundertwende* (Darmstadt: Wissenschaftliche Buchgesellschaft)

Loose, Gerhard 1968 'Ludovico Settembrini und "Soziologie der Leiden" '; 'Notes on Thomas Mann's *Zauberberg*', in *Modern Language Notes* 83, pp. 420–9

Lübbe, Hermann 1974 *Politische Philosophie in Deutschland. Studien zu ihrer Geschichte* [1963] (München: Deutscher Taschenbuch Verlag)

Lukács, Georg (von) 1911 *Die Seele und die Formen* (Berlin: Egon Fleischel)
1953 *Thomas Mann* [1949], 3. Aufl. (Berlin [DDR]: Aufbau-Verlag)
1962 *Die Zerstörung der Vernunft* [1954], in Lukács, *Werke*, Vol. 9 (Neuwied and Berlin: Luchterhand)

Mann, Heinrich 1960 *Essays* (Hamburg: Claassen)

Mann, Thomas 1957 'Huit Lettres inédites à Pierre-Paul Sagave', in *Cahiers du Sud* 44, pp. 373–86
1960 *Thomas Mann an Ernst Bertram. Briefe aus den Jahren 1910–1955*, ed. Inge Jens (Pfullingen: Neske)
1968 *Das essayistische Werk*, Taschenbuchausgabe in acht Bänden, ed. Hans Bürgin (Frankfurt am Main: S. Fischer)
1974a *Nachträge* [*Gesammelte Werke in dreizehn Bänden*, 13. Band] (Frankfurt am Main: S. Fischer)
1974b 'Ein Brief zur Situation des deutschen Schriftstellers um 1910', in *Thomas-Mann-Studien* 3, pp. 9–12
1979 *Tagebücher 1918–1921*, ed. Peter de Mendelssohn (Frankfurt am Main: S. Fischer)
1981a *Buddenbrooks. Verfall einer Familie* [1901], in Thomas Mann, *Gesammelte Werke in Einzelbänden*, Frankfurter Ausgabe, ed. Peter de Mendelssohn (Frankfurt am Main: S. Fischer)
1981b *Frühe Erzählungen* [Frankfurter Ausgabe] (Frankfurt am Main: S. Fischer)
1982 *Leiden und Grösse der Meister* [Frankfurter Ausgabe] (Frankfurt am Main: S. Fischer)
1983a *Betrachtungen eines Unpolitischen* [1918], Nachwort von Hanno Helbling [Frankfurter Ausgabe] (Frankfurt am Main: S. Fischer)
1983b *Über mich selbst: Autobiographische Schriften*, Nachwort von Martin Gregor-Dellin [Frankfurter Ausgabe] (Frankfurt am Main: S. Fischer)
1984 *Rede und Antwort. Uber eigene Werke, Huldigungen und Kränze. Über Freunde, Weggefährten und Zeitgenossen* [Frankfurter Ausgabe] (Frankfurt am Main: S. Fischer)

Mann, Thomas, and Heinrich Mann 1984   *Briefwechsel 1900–1949*, erweiterte Neuausgabe (Frankfurt am Main: S. Fischer)

Mannheim, Karl 1921   'Heidelbergi Levél' ['Heidelberger Brief'], in *Tüz* (Bratislava), 15. November–1. Dezember, pp. 46–50

1922   'Heidelbergi Levelek' ['Heidelberger Briefe'] II, in *Tüz*, 15. April–1. Mai, pp. 91–5

1929   *Ideologie und Utopie* (Bonn: Cohen)

1932   *Die Gegenwartsaufgaben der Soziologie. Ihre Lehrgestalt* (Tübingen: Mohr/Siebeck)

1934   'German Sociology', in *Politica* 1, pp. 12–33

1937   'Zur Diagnose unserer Zeit', in *Mass und Wert* 1:1, pp. 100–21

1958   *Mensch und Gesellschaft im Zeitalter des Umbaus* [1935–1940] (Darmstadt: Wissenschaftliche Buchgesellschaft)

1982   'Zur Problematik der Soziologie in Deutschland' [1929], in *Der Streit um die Wissenssoziologie, 2. Band: Rezeption und Kritik der Wissenssoziologie*, ed. Volker Meja and Nico Stehr, pp. 427–437 (Frankfurt am Main: Suhrkamp)

1984   *Konservatismus. Ein Beitrag zur Soziologie des Wissens* [1925], ed. David Kettler, Volker Meja and Nico Stehr (Frankfurt am Main: Suhrkamp)

Meinecke, Friedrich 1921   'Drei Generationen deutscher Gelehrtenpolitik', in *Historische Zeitschrift* 125, pp. 248–83

Meja, Volker, and Nico Stehr, eds. 1982   *Der Streit um die Wissenssoziologie*, 2 vols (Frankfurt am Main: Suhrkamp)

Mendelssohn, Peter de 1975   *Der Zauberer. Das Leben des deutschen Schriftstellers Thomas Mann*, Erster Teil, 1875–1918 (Frankfurt am Main: S. Fischer)

Mohler, Armin 1972   *Die konservative Revolution in Deutschland 1918–1932: Ein Handbuch* [1950], 2., völlig neu bearbeitete und erweiterte Fassung (Darmstadt: Wissenschaftliche Buchgesellschaft)

Mommsen, Wolfgang J. 1959   *Max Weber und die deutsche Politik 1890–1920* (Tübingen: Mohr/Siebeck)

Moot-Materialien & Ergänzungen 1939–49 Kopie des Sozialwissenschaftlichen Archivs der Universität Konstanz

Müller, Adam 1966   *Adam Müllers Lebenszeugnisse*, 2 vols, ed. Jakob Baxa (München, Paderborn and Wien: Schöningh)

Muller, Jerry Zucker 1984   'Radical Convervatism and Social Theory: Hans Freyer and The Other God That Failed' (unpublished Ph.D. dissertation, Columbia University, Ms., 673 pp.)

Nietzsche, Friedrich 1980   *Sämtliche Werke*, Kritische Studienausgabe in 15 Bänden, ed. Giorgio Colli and Mazzino Montinari (München: Deutscher Taschenbuch Verlag)

1982   *Briefe* (Januar 1885–Dezember 1886) [*Briefwechsel. Kritische Gesamtausgabe*, ed. Giorgio Colli and Mazzino Montinari, 3. Abteilung 3. Band] (Berlin and New York: De Gruyter)

Nohl, Herman 1911–12   'Die Deutsche Bewegung und die idealistischen Systeme', in *Logos* 2, (1911/12) pp. 350–9

Nolte, Ernst 1984   *Der Faschismus in seiner Epoche: Action Française, Italienischer Faschismus, Nationalsozialismus* [1963], 6. Aufl. (München: Piper)

Plessner, Helmuth 1982   *Gesammelte Schriften VI. Die verspätete Nation* [1935–

1959] (Frankfurt am Main: Suhrkamp)
Rathenau, Walther 1926 *Briefe*, 2. Band (Dresden: Reissner)
  1929a 'Zur Mechanik des Geistes oder vom Reich der Seele' [1913; Rathenau, *Gesammelte Schriften*, 2] (Berlin: S. Fischer)
  1929b 'Von kommenden Dingen' [1917; Rathenau, *Gesammelte Schriften*, 3] (Berlin: S. Fischer)
Renan, Ernest 1923 *L'Avenir de la science: Pensées de 1848* [1890], 20th edition (Paris: Calmann-Lévy)
  1960 *Oeuvres complètes*, tome 9, édition définitive établie par Henriette Psichari (Paris: Calmann-Lévy)
  1968 *Correspondance 1845–92* [*Oeuvres complètes*, tome 10] (Paris: Calmann-Lévy)
Riehl, Wilhelm Heinrich 1854 *Die Naturgeschichte des Volkes als Grundlage einer deutschen Social-Politik*, 2. Band: *Die bürgerliche Gesellschaft* [1851], 2., neu überarbeitete Aufl. (Stuttgart and Tübingen: Cotta)
  1855 *Die Naturgeschichte des Volkes als Grundlage einer deutschen Social-Politik*, 1. Band: *Land und Leute* [1854], 2. vermehrte Aufl. (Stuttgart and Augsburg: Cotta)
  1873 *Freie Vorträge*, erste Sammlung (Stuttgart: Cotta)
  1885 *Freie Vorträge*, zweite Sammlung (Stuttgart: Cotta)
  1925 *Wanderbuch als zweiter Teil zu 'Land und Leute'* [*Die Naturgeschichte des Volkes als Grundlage einer deutschen Socialpolitik*, 4. Band: *Wanderbuch*, 1869] (Stuttgart and Berlin: Cotta)
  1935 *Die Volkskunde als Wissenschaft* [1858], der Vortrag von Wilhelm Heinrich Riehl mit einer Einleitung von Max Hildebert Boehm (Tübingen: Laupp'sche Buchhandlung)
Rolland, Romain n.d. *Jean-Christophe à Paris. La Foire sur la place*, 36th edition (Paris: Ollendorff)
  n.d. *Jean-Christophe à Paris. Dans la maison*, 26th edition (Paris: Ollendorff)
Rosenbaum, Eduard 1956 'Uber eine Vorform soziologischen Denkens', in *Freundesgabe für Ernst Robert Curtius zum 14. April 1956*, pp. 167–81 (Bern: Francke)
Rothacker, Erich 1933 'Nationale Soziologie', in *Westdeutsche Akademische Rundschau* 3: 1
Rychner, Max 1932 'German Chronicle', in *The Criterion* 11, pp. 705–10
Sagave, Pierre-Paul 1960 *Recherches sur le roman social en Allemagne* (Aix-en-Provence: Editions Ophrys)
Salin, Edgar 1954 *Um Stefan George. Erinnerung und Zeugnis* [1948], 2. Aufl. (Düsseldorf: Küpper)
  1963 *Lynkeus: Gestalten und Probleme aus Wirtschaft und Politik* (Tübingen: Mohr/Siebeck)
Salz, Arthur 1921 *Für die Wissenschaft. Gegen die Gebildeten unter ihren Verächtern* (München: Drei Masken Verlag)
Schelsky, Helmut 1958 *Einführung zu:* David Riesman, *Die einsame Masse* [1950], pp. 7–19 (Reinbek b. Hamburg: Rowohlt)
  1959 *Ortsbestimmung der deutschen Soziologie* (Düsseldorf and Köln: Diederichs)
  1975a *Die Arbeit tun die anderen. Klassenkampf und Priesterherrschaft der*

Intellektuellen (Opladen: Westdeutscher Verlag)

1975b *Erfahrungen mit einem "Bestseller". Antwort an die Kritiker*, Sonder-druck aus der 2., erweiterten Aufl. von *Die Arbeit tun die anderen* (Opladen: Westdeutscher Verlag)

1981 *Rückblicke eines 'Anti-Soziologen'* (Opladen: Westdeutscher Verlag)

1982 *Jugend und Alter. Gedichte oder so etwas Ähnliches* (Privatdruck)

Schiller, Friedrich 1983 *Gedichte*, 3. Buch-Votivtafeln [*Werke, Nationalausgabe*, ed. Norbert Oellers, 2. Band, Teil I] (Weimar: Hermann Böhlaus Nachl.)

Schmalenbach, Herman 1922 'Die soziologische Kategorie des Bundes', in *Die Dioskuren: Jahrbuch für Geisteswissenschaften* 1, pp. 35–105

Seekamp, H. J., R. C. Ockenden and M. Keilson 1972 *Stefan George/Leben und Werk. Eine Zeittafel* (Amsterdam: Castrum Peregrini Presse)

Seidel, Alfred 1927 *Bewusstsein als Verhängnis*, aus dem Nachlasse herausgegeben von Hans Prinzhorn (Bonn: Cohen)

Simmel, Georg 1913 *Goethe* (Leipzig: Klinkhardt & Biermann)

1917 'Das Goethebuch', in *Die Neue Rundschau* 28, pp. 254–64

1920 *Grundfragen der Soziologie* (Individuum und Gesellschaft) [1917]. 2. Aufl. (Berlin and Leipzig: De Gruyter)

1921 *Der Konflikt der modernen Kultur* [1918], 2. Aufl. (München and Leipzig: Duncker & Humblot)

1922 *Zur Philosophie der Kunst. Philosophische und kunstphilosophische Aufsätze*, ed. Gertrud Simmel (Potsdam: Gustav Kiepenheuer)

1957 *Brücke und Tür: Essays des Philosophen zur Geschichte, Religion, Kunst und Gesellschaft*, im Verein mit Margarete Susman herausgegeben von Michael Landmann (Stuttgart: K. F. Koehler)

1958 *Buch des Dankes an Georg Simmel. Briefe, Erinnerungen, Bibliographie.* Zu seinem 100. Geburtstag am 1. März 1958, herausgegeben von Kurt Gassen & Michael Landmann (Berlin: Duncker und Humblot)

1968 *Soziologie. Untersuchungen über die Formen der Vergesellschaftung* [1908], 5. Aufl. (Berlin: Duncker & Humblot)

1977 *Philosophie des Geldes* [1900], 7. Aufl. (Berlin: Duncker & Humblot)

1982 *Verlorene und gefundene Briefe Georg Simmels an Célestin Bouglé, Eugen Diederichs, Gabriel Tarde*, zusammengestellt von Werner Gephart Ms., 38 pp.

1984 *Das Individuum und die Freiheit: Essais* (Berlin: Wagenbach)

Singer, Kurt 1955 'Erinnerung an die Georgika', in *Castrum Peregrini* 25, pp. 50–7

Sokel, Walter H. 1959 *The Writer in Extremis: Expressionism in Twentieth Century Literature* (Stanford, Ca.: Stanford University Press)

Sorel, Georges 1927 *Les Illusions du progrès* [1908] (Paris: Marcel Rivière)

Soziologentage 1911 Verhandlungen des Ersten Deutschen Soziologentages vom 19.–22. Oktober 1910 in Frankfurt am Main (Tübingen: Mohr/ Siebeck)

Spaemann, Robert 1959 *Der Ursprung der Soziologie aus dem Geist der Restauration: Studien über L. G. A. de Bonald* (München: Kösel)

Spengler, Oswald 1924 *Der Untergang des Abendlandes. Umrisse einer Morphologie der Weltgeschichte* [1918], 2 vols (München: C. H. Beck)

Staël, Mme de 1926 *De l'Allemagne* [1810] (Paris: Flammarion)

Steinmetz, Rudolf 1931 'Poezie als oorsprong van sociale normen (Stefan George en zijn kring)', in *Mens en Maatschapij* 7, pp. 335–59

Stern, Fritz 1963 *Kulturpessimismus als politische Gefahr: Eine Analyse nationaler Ideologie in Deutschland* (Bern, Stuttgart and Wien: Scherz)

Susman, Margarete 1959 *Die geistige Gestalt Georg Simmels* (Tübingen: Mohr/Siebeck)

　1964 *Ich habe viele Leben gelebt. Erinnerungen* (Stuttgart: Deutsche Verlagsanstalt)

Thormaehlen, Ludwig 1962 *Erinnerungen an Stefan George*, aus dem Nachlass herausgegeben von W. Greischel (Hamburg: Hauswedell)

Tönnies, Ferdinand 1917 'Kommende Dinge?' [Rezension von Walther Rathenau: *Von kommenden Dingen*], in *Die Neue Rundschau* 28, pp. 829–38

　1887 *Gemeinschaft und Gesellschaft. Abhandlung des Communismus und des Socialismus als empirischer Culturformen* (Leipzig: Fues's Verlag [R. Reisland])

Treitschke, Heinrich von 1859 *Die Gesellschaftswissenschaft: Ein kritischer Versuch* (Leipzig: Hirzel)

　1929a 'Der Sozialismus und seine Gönner' [1874], in *Aufsätze, Reden und Briefe*, ed. Karl Martin Schiller, 4. Band, pp. 122–211 (Meersburg: Hendel)

　1929b *Gedichte und Briefe* [*Aufsätze, Reden und Briefe*, 5. Band] (Meersburg: Hendel)

Troeltsch, Ernst 1922 *Der Historismus und seine Probleme*, Erstes Buch: *Das logische Problem der Geschichtsphilosophie* (Tübingen: Mohr/Siebeck)

　1925a *Deutscher Geist und Westeuropa. Gesammelte kulturphilosophische Aufsätze und Reden*, ed. Hans Baron (Tübingen, Mohr/Siebeck)

　1925b *Die Revolution in der Wissenschaft* [1921]; Troeltsch, *Gesammelte Schriften*, 4 [*Aufsätze zur Geistesgeschichte und Religionssoziologie*], pp. 653–77 (Tübingen: Mohr/Siebeck)

Üner, Elfriede 1980 *Hans Freyer in der deutschen Soziologie bis 1933: Ein Beitrag zur wissenschaftssoziologischen Einordnung seines Werkes und seiner Wissenschaftsgemeinschaft* (Soziologische Diplomarbeit, Universität München)

Vallentin, Berthold 1960 *Gespräche mit Stefan George 1902–1931* [*Castrum Peregrini* 44–45] (Amsterdam: Castrum Peregrini Presse)

Verwey, Albert 1936 *Mein Verhältnis zu Stefan George. Erinnerungen aus den Jahren 1898–1925* [Dutch edition, 1934] (Leipzig: Heitz)

Viénot, Pierre 1931 *Incertitudes allemandes: La crise de la civilisation bourgeoise en Allemagne* (Paris: Librairie Valois)

Wach, Joachim 1925 *Meister und Jünger: Zwei religionssoziologische Betrachtungen* (Leipzig: Eduard Pfeiffer)

Weber, Alfred 1927 *Ideen zur Staats- und Kultursoziologie* (Karlsruhe: G. Braun)

Weber, Marianne 1926 *Max Weber: Ein Lebensbild* (Tübingen: Mohr/Siebeck)

Weber, Max 1921 *Gesammelte politische Schriften* (München: Drei Masken Verlag)

　1923 *Gesammelte Aufsätze zur Religionssoziologie. III. Das antike Judentum*, 2., photomechanisch gedruckte Aufl. (Tübingen: Mohr/Siebeck)

1924   *Gesammelte Aufsätze zur Soziologie und Sozialpolitik* (Tübingen: Mohr/ Siebeck)

1934   *Die protestantische Ethik und der Geist des Kapitalismus* [1905] (Tübingen: Mohr/Siebeck)

1956   *Wirtschaft und Gesellschaft. Grundriss der verstehenden Soziologie* [1921], 4., neu herausgegebene Aufl., besorgt von Johannes Winckelmann (Tübingen: Mohr/Siebeck)

1958   *Gesammelte politische Schriften* [1921], 2., erweiterte Aufl., mit einem Geleitwort von Theodor Heuss, neu herausgegeben von Johannes Winckelmann (Tübingen: Mohr/Siebeck)

1964   *Max Weber: Werk und Person*. Dokumente ausgewählt und kommentiert von Eduard Baumgarten (Tübingen: Mohr/Siebeck)

1968   *Gesammelte Aufsätze zur Wissenschaftslehre* [1922], 3., erweiterte und verbesserte Aufl., ed. Johannes Winckelmann (Tübingen: Mohr/ Siebeck)

Weinrich, Harald 1978 'Thirty Years After Ernst Robert Curtius' Book "Europäische Literatur und Lateinisches Mittelalter" (1948)', in *Romanic Review* 69, pp. 261–78

Wirsing, Giselher 1933 'Volk und Geist', in *Die Tat* 25, pp. 513–20

1934 'Systemkrise in Frankreich? 1789–1933', in *Die Tat* 25, pp. 753–68

Wolfskehl, Karl 1910 'Die Blätter für die Kunst und die Neuste Literatur', in *Jahrbuch für die geistige Bewegung* 1, pp. 1–18

Wolters, Friedrich 1930 *Stefan George und die Blätter für die Kunst. Deutsche Geistesgeschichte seit 1890* (Berlin: Georg Bondi)

Worringer, Wilhelm 1921 *Künstlerische Zeitfragen* (München: Bruckmann)

Wuthenow, Ralph-Rainer, ed. 1980 *Stefan George in seiner Zeit. Dokumente zur Wirkungsgeschichte*, 1. Band (Stuttgart: Klett/Cotta)

1981 *Stefan George und die Nachwelt. Dokumente zur Wirkungsgeschichte*, 2. Band (Stuttgart: Klett/Cotta)

Wysling Hans 1967 ' "Geist und Kunst": Thomas Manns Notizen zu einem "Literatur-Essay" ', in *Thomas-Mann-Studien* 1, pp. 123–233

INDEX